The Development of
Neo-Confucian Thought

The Development of
Neo-Confucian Thought

by

Carsun Chang

COLLEGE AND UNIVERSITY PRESS

NEW HAVEN, CONN.

Paperbound Edition, 1963
Published by COLLEGE AND UNIVERSITY PRESS
by arrangement with BOOKMAN ASSOCIATES

MANUFACTURED IN THE UNITED STATES OF AMERICA BY
UNITED PRINTING SERVICES, INC.
NEW HAVEN, CONN.

Preface

There are three cultures which have exercised a preponderant influence on the thought of the world in the past twenty-five centuries: that of China, that of India, and that of the Eastern Mediterranean area. Developing in different geographical settings and tracing their beginnings to a remote past, each of them came in time to stress a basic need of the human race which the others also stressed, but not to the same degree. Now that our world, through science and engineering, has become geographically one, each of these cultures has its own contribution to make toward rounding out the whole. To the unmatched understanding of Nature that the West has achieved, we can now advantageously add the perceptions won by a long line of Chinese thinkers in the ethics and the art of human relationships, and by Indian seers in their unremitting search for reality beyond the temporal world.

Though all three of these quests are equally valid, and can claim special insights in their own spheres, not one of them can justly maintain that it alone can realize all the possibilities of man. Only as these and other cultures fertilize each other can the human race rise to the new level of consciousness that our unified world requires.

It is in the hope of promoting a better comprehension of one of China's great philosophies — Confucianism — that Dr. Chang has written this book. But, wishing to present the subject in its broadest perspective, he views it through the eyes of a long line of thinkers known as Neo-Confucianists. They began their reappraisal in the eighth century, flourished vigorously in the eleventh and twelfth centuries, and produced notable interpreters and critics down to recent times. This movement was far more than a revival of the ancient Confucian heritage; it was a reassessment and revaluation of that heritage in a new climate of opinion, a climate powerfully modified by two rival philosophies: Taoism which was native to China, and Buddhism which had been introduced from India after the first century of our era. These rival systems effec-

5

tively stimulated the Neo-Confucianists to fresh thinking, mainly by providing them with a richer psychological vocabulary and a metaphysics that first captivated, and ultimately baffled them. Thereupon they returned to a more intensive study of the great classical texts of their own Confucian tradition, reinterpreting them, however, in this new and broader setting.

This ferment of ideas spread beyond the boundaries of China to Korea and Japan where, thanks to the use of the same written symbols, the writings of the Neo-Confucianists were many years later read and discussed. Parallel schools of thought and individual expositors arose, exercising by their teachings and their writings an immense influence on ethical ideals, on education, on theories of government, and on patterns of life. In fact, apart from some knowledge of this movement, the intellectual life of Korea and Japan in the past three centuries cannot be adequately understood. All this is part of the long struggle of the human mind to gain a firmer foothold on life. As we approach the dawn of a new era in human relations, no people can be so sure of their foundations that they can ignore, without loss, the sincere efforts of Chinese thinkers to define man's duties in society and make his moral quest both reasonable and attractive.

By putting into English for the first time many excerpts from the conversations and writings of these Neo-Confucian thinkers, and by standardizing key terms that had been variously rendered, Dr. Chang has performed an important service. The great influence that Indian thought — in its Buddhist form — came in time to exercise on the Chinese mind is clearly brought out, though the elements in it which the Chinese could not accept are not overlooked. The parallels drawn with the thought of Aristotle and Plato not only make the reasoning clearer, but give the reader a fresh perception of the essential unity of mankind. Even more telling perhaps are the comparisons with the thought of Kant; for it is Kant's stress on the priority of the moral will over the theoretical understanding that brings him close to Chinese thought. For to the Chinese, philosophy did not mean the formulation of a theory, however useful that may be, but the discovery of how virtue could best be exemplified in life.

ARTHUR W. HUMMEL

Foreword

There are, it seems to me, at least two reasons why a book on Neo-Confucianism should be written at the present moment.

The first is that, in the light of what is happening in the world, the subject of Chinese studies by Western scholars should be re-examined from a fresh point of view. I think it is a fair statement that the approach to the study of China has been that of an extinct civilization, similar to that of ancient Greece and Rome or of ancient Egypt. The very existence of that strange word "Sinology" seems to imply the post-mortem examination of a culture which for all practical purposes, so the Western scholars believe, has no longer any vitality today. There is no need for me to say that this approach is both erroneous and dangerous. China happens to be animated by a living consciousness of the most impressive historical continuity. It is an organism and not a museum.

In this museum approach which has prevailed since the inception of Chinese studies it is inevitable that some landmarks are considered as being more interesting than others. For years therefore the effort of the Western scholar has been directed to a continuous and often hackneyed exposition of the basic thought of Confucius, Laotse and their contemporaries and immediate successors. No systematic study of Chinese ideas, covering the last fifteen hundred years or so, has, so far as I know, been undertaken.

The time has arrived, I believe, to make a new approach, to regard the vast realm of China's cultural heritage as a landscape of infinite variety, in which the mountain peaks, the plateaus and luxuriant valleys contribute equally to its total effect, or as a stream in which its whirlpools and moss-laden banks account quite as much for its beauty as its cataracts and waterfalls.

The term "Neo-Confucianism" means the new philosophy of the Confucian school since the Tang Dynasty. What I have

7

attempted to do in this book, in a modest and imperfect way, is to describe the main trend of Chinese thought covering a period which, dating from the Tang Dynasty, stems mainly from the Sung Dynasty down to the end of the Ching Dynasty. It is a period of well over a thousand years, equivalent, in English history, to the period from the time of the Danish invasions to the end of Victoria's reign. My task as a guide will have been accomplished if I succeed, even in a limited way, in directing the attention of Western readers away from the lofty mountain peaks and in arousing some interest in the other parts of the intellectual landscape.

The second reason is that I have been constantly asked the question whether communism has come to stay in China — whether, in other words, it has superseded China's traditional thought and way of life. It seems to me that so important a query involving, as it does, the whole of the spiritual and intellectual life of an ancient culture, cannot be resolved by a simple affirmative or negative answer. It is true, however, that in the study of Chinese thought of the period which the present work seeks to examine, there is a parallel from which possibly significant lessons may be drawn. If communism is an alien thought which today plays so important a role in the life of the Chinese people, so was Buddhism, which was indeed the first non-Chinese system of thinking to take root in the Chinese consciousness.

I do not believe, however, that the similarity goes much farther. I submit that the impact of communism on the life of the Chinese people is strong and even decisive. But I am firmly convinced that it is essentially a political and economic or social arrangement. It is at best an instrument for the attainment of certain international objectives. As such it may introduce substantial changes in the institutional life of the Chinese people, though I seriously doubt that it will make much difference in the structure or the content of Chinese thought.

The influence of Buddhism was clearly of a different order. It went straight to the marrow of Chinese thinking. If any comparison is to be made, it must be made to the impact of Aristotelianism on the structure of scholastic thought in the Middle Ages in Europe or to that of Hellenism on Western thinking

during the Renaissance. In all of these cases I believe the transformation was central rather than peripheral: the result was a
new intellectual and spiritual entity. It is scarcely possible to
affirm that Chinese thought, after the rich speculative method
of Buddhist enquiry had had a chance to play freely on the
Chinese mind, could remain the same. Even so, after hundreds
of years, some of the basic values of the earlier Chinese thought
were either not impaired or Buddhism itself accquired a Chinese
flavor. It is obvious that China remains China, and India, India.
The chapters in this book, dealing as they all do with the influence of Buddhism on mature Chinese thinkers from Han Yü
of the Tang Dynasty down, should be a very clear indication
that they held tenaciously to their own heritage, even though
their approach and method of enquiry had been drastically transformed. I do not share in the belief of many observers that
communism could make any substantial inroad into the Chinese
consciousness. That it will be or that it is already being transmuted into something different from the land of its origin, is
a certainty which it will do well for us to hold to.

After all is said and done, it is important for us to remember
that communism has won followers in China only because the
orthodox Western thought has not made the success that it should.
The chapter "Chinese Thought under the Impact of the West"
tries to show just how the maladjustment has come about. If
only the momentous advances in science and technology as well
as the evolution of democratic government and administration
of the West were made familiar to Chinese thinkers without the
bitterness and even the hatred which unfortunately accompanied
them in the form of aggression or imperialism, the Chinese situation would have been quite different. If China came to know
the West as she came to know Buddhism, there would have been
a receptivity of mind, a friendly response, which could have been
productive of the highest good. There would then have been no
room for the invasion of so heterodox a view as communism. As
it was, throughout the nineteenth century, the impact of the West,
in the political and social no less than in the cultural and spiritual
sphere, was one of attempted annihilation. It demanded the sus-
pension of China's traditional values or even of its identity. That

was why, in the study of China's history, scholars readily acquired the museum method of approach, as if the wish was father to the thought. The result was antagonism, frustration and resistance when there should have been friendly co-operation and a willingness to absorb.

The present book, by showing the relationship of Buddhism to Chinese thought will I hope, bring home the conviction that a friendly response, on the part of China, to the richness of Western thought, in its orthodox form, as it expresses itself in the systematic exploration and understanding of nature, in its devotion to the ideals of liberty, of equality, of the integrity and dignity of the individual, and to the sense of democratic partnership, is not only necessary but must be made possible by a totally new approach. The initiative must be taken by the West. And when it is properly taken, we should not be surprised to see how rapidly communism in China will disintegrate. If there is one thing that I am sure of about my people, it is that they are essentially sane and rational. They value the things that are central. They are at heart an orthodox people, because orthodoxy usually stands for what is basic and permanent. They are not by nature or discipline heterodox, but they can become so when they are desperately driven to it.

It is always a pleasure to record the many debts of gratitude which I owe in the course of the preparation of this work. None of the friends who gave so unstintingly of their time and energy are responsible for any of the views which I have expressed. These must remain exclusively my own. The book was written during long hours of quiet and pleasant study in the Library of Congress. My deep thanks are due to the librarian, to the staff of the Oriental Division and to Dr. K. T. Wu and his colleagues for the many kindnesses which they extended to me. Dr. A. W. Hummel read through the entire manuscript and gave me valuable suggestions, especially in the matter of language. He has placed me under further obligation by writing the Preface. Mr. Edwin Beal very kindly read the chapters on Ku Yen-wu and Chu Chih-yu. Dr. Horace I. Poleman's assistance in the rendering of Sanskrit terms is deeply appreciated. Dr. Rufus Suter gave me constant encouragement for which I feel grateful. His knowledge of Western philosophy and his interest in Chinese culture have proved to be of great value

And now, lastly, I must express my profound thanks to my friend Dr. Chang Hsin-hai, research professor at Long Island University. He gave me long and arduous hours at every stage in the preparation and writing of this book. He placed his extensive knowledge of both Eastern and Western thought at my disposal. Without his assistance all I can say is that it would have been hardly possible for the work to see the light of day. More than this it is unnecessary for me to say.

San Francisco   CARSUN CHANG
March 15, 1957

Table of Contents

CHAPTER ONE

Introduction:
Confucianism in
Chinese History, and a
Comparison with Western Philosophy

China is the land of Confucianism. The Chinese view of life has, to a very large extent, been molded by Confucius; or perhaps it would be more correct to say that the Confucian view is based on the ancient Chinese tradition, so that the view of Confucius and that of the Chinese stem from the same root.

This Chinese view affirms life in the world of men and affairs. Human relations are its center of interest. It is an assertion of human existence and effort, and it considers living a harmonious life with one's neighbor as man's first duty.

The Confucian way of thinking is related to what is embodied in actual existence or the concrete facts of life. It does not go in for abstract discussion. This does not mean there is no interest in universal principles in so far as these principles have a bearing upon life. For instance, Confucius was fond of acquiring knowledge of the world around him. He advised his pupils to learn the names of birds, animals, and plants.[1] He described himself as a man of wide knowledge who had never won renown in any specialized field.[2]

He assembled a vast throng of pupils — some three thousand of them — and so was a great educator or teacher. He went from one feudal lord to another in the hope of finding an opportunity to put his ideas of reform into practice. Not until he was an old man did he discover that this opportunity would not occur. No feudal government ever made use of his services. Accordingly, he returned to his native state and devoted himself to editing ancient books which were a heritage from earlier periods. These books, called the *Classics*, became the Bible of China.

The question arises whether Confucianism is a religion. The Chinese themselves look upon Confucius as a sage, a teacher, an example of personal cultivation. Even after the introduction of Buddhism from India, the two systems of Confucianism and Buddhism stood on equal footing. There was much argumentation between the proponents of these two systems of thought but the question was never raised as to whether Confucianism is a religion. It was not until China entered into contact with the West that the problem arose. The missionaries from Europe — first the Catholics of the seventeenth century, and then the Protestants of the nineteenth century — somehow felt the need to settle the issue. The Jesuits and Dominicans, however, only went as far as the matter of ancestor worship. It was the Protestant missionaries who focused their attention on the religious aspect of Confucianism.

W. E. Soothill, for example, wrote in his *The Three Religions of China*: "There are three recognized religions in China. Of these Confucianism is generally counted as the State religion, but Taoism and Buddhism are also recognized. Buddhism was imported from India, but Confucianism and Taoism are native religions which have grown out of a common stock. The primitive religion originated in a prehistoric Animism, but, before the separation of Confucianism and Taoism, it had already reached a higher stage, while still retaining its animistic and magical elements."[3]

Soothill's celebrated predecessor at Oxford, J. Legge, the translator of the *Classics,* attempted to answer in his book *The Religions of China* the question: "But is Confucianism really a religion?" in the following manner: "I use the term Confucianism as covering first of all, the ancient religion of China."[4]

I should like to emphasize that this way of interpreting Confucianism is of purely Western origin. To the Chinese scholar it must always appear strange.

Confucius was never regarded as a prophet by his people, nor as a Messiah. He never called himself The Lord or The Light. He said: "I am not one who was born in possession of knowledge. I am one who is fond of antiquity and earnest in seeking knowledge."[5] Again he said: "While you are not able to serve man, how can you serve the spirits? While you do not know life, how can you know death?"[6] In other words, Confucius had no intention of talking about a supermundane world or of founding a religion.

The interpretation of Confucianism both by Soothill and by Legge as including a concept of the origin of Chinese religion is unjustified, because it was something which occurred many thousands of years previously, in an age for which Confucius cannot be held accountable. Confucius merely continued the observance of customs which antedated him by many generations, but this was not equivalent to establishing a form of worship.

Confucius's own words about religion were as follows: "I sacrifice to the dead as if they were present. I sacrifice to the spirits as if they were present."[7] In other words, Confucius took the attitude of "as if", just as he did in regard to life after death.

Thus, no Chinese scholar in the last two thousand years has considered Confucius as the founder of a religion. There are such founders in India, Arabia, or Palestine — but not in China. This then is the background for my treatment of Confucianism as an ethical or philosophical system, rather than a religion.

Not only was Confucianism not a religion, but, even as an ethical or philosophical system, it underwent many changes in the course of history. A comprehensive picture of Confucianism through the ages may be derived from its four periods: (1) Confucianism as one of many rivals in the age of the "Hundred Schools"; (2) Confucianism in the Former Han Dynasty as the most privileged and authoritative of all the "schools"; (3) Confucianism as eclipsed by Buddhism and Taoism; (4) Confucianism reborn, or the Renaissance of Confucianism, known as Neo-Confucianism, which is the special subject of the present study.

(1) CONFUCIANISM AS ONE OF MANY RIVALS IN THE AGE OF THE "HUNDRED SCHOOLS."

This period marks the beginning of the history of Chinese thought. It was also the period of Spring and Autumn (B.C. 722-481), when Confucius left us with the *Lun-yu* (Analects), containing his views about ethics and philosophy. He stood for the theory of the "rectification of names", by which he meant that if each person fulfills his duties as father, son, king, minister, husband, wife, elder brother, friend, in accordance with the definition of these respective terms, the community will be well-ordered. Confucius is also known for his advocacy of *Jen* as the fundamental virtue or the starting point for the cultivation of all other virtues. He discussed ethical problems in a scattered way, though he declared that a pervading unity runs through the whole system. He compared his thoughts to a river which "flows unceasingly day and night."[8]

Confucius was once advised by some hermits not to trouble himself about trying to ameliorate the lot of mankind. From the tone of these hermits we may assume that they were Taoists, and were therefore opposed to him.

Another group who attacked the Confucian school was the school of Mo Ti, who championed the doctrine of universal love. This theory was contrary to the principle of graded love as advocated by Confucius. The Moists recommended frugal funeral services, and scorned music as something useless. Mo Ti worked hard to spread his teachings, and doubtless his reputation as a strategist and defender of the capital of the land of Sung was an aid to his success.

In the period of the "Warring States" (480-222 B.C.) Mencius continued the tradition of the Confucianists. He expounded Confucian doctrines in greater detail than the master himself. Mencius succeeded in evoking a system. He elaborately set forth the theory of the goodness of human nature, and the doctrine of intuitive knowledge. He emphasized the importance of the role of the rational mind, and he advocated government under *Jen,* to follow the example of Yao and Shun which is the Chinese version of Plato's philosopher-kings.

Though Mencius theoretically gave a helping hand to the cause of Confucianism, he was no more successful than Confucius himself in enlisting actual support from the feudal governments. In Mencius' day the men who were popular were the itinerant scholar-diplomats, men like Su Ch'in and Chang I, who advocated, respectively, a horizontal or east-west policy favoring the Kingdom of Ch'in, which lay in the western part of China; and a vertical or north-south policy, favoring a coalition against Ch'in by the six kingdoms, lying north and south, and in the part of China east of Ch'in. These wandering scholar-diplomats, who resembled in some measure the Sophists of ancient Greece, were popular because they championed the cause of the specific kingdoms — such as Ch'in, or the other six kingdoms.

Another group who won popular acclaim in Mencius' day was the Legalist school. Shang Yang, Shen Pu-hai, Han Fei and Li Ssu championed regimentation, abolition of the privileges of aristocratic families, universal military service for the adult male population, and increased food production. "If in a country," wrote the Legalists, "there are the following ten things: odes and history, rites and music, virtue and personal cultivation, benevolence and integrity, sophistry and intelligence — then the ruler will have nobody to employ for defense and warfare. If a country is governed by means of these ten things, it will be dismembered as soon as an enemy approaches. And even if no enemy approaches, it will be poor."[9] The attack on Confucianism is obvious.

There is no doubt that Mencius had nothing better to offer the rulers of the feudal states than the Legalists. Moreover, it was the Legalists who knew how to fit in with the issues of the times. So it was they rather than Mencius who gained the upper hand in the politics of the day.

Besides Mencius there was another scholar, Hsun-tzu, who developed Confucianism, though in a different direction. Hsun-tzu took human nature for what it is. Thus, he is known in the history of Chinese thought as the advocate of the doctrine that human nature is evil. Some of his pupils went over to the Legalist school.

The breakdown of the regime of the "Warring States Period" and the establishment of the universal empire in China under

Ch'in Shih Huang-ti was the result of the combined efforts of the itinerant scholar-diplomats and the Legalists. The role of the Confucianists with reference to these political events was that of spectators. They had nothing to offer. They were theorists, not exponents of *realpolitik*.

During the life-time of Confucius (551-479 B.C.) and Mencius (371?-289?), and even later in the Ch'in dynasty, Confucianism had no privileged position as the orthodox teaching in China. Confucianism was merely one school among others, and did its best to hold its own in argument with the others, only for the sake of survival.

(2) CONFUCIANISM IN THE FORMER HAN DYNASTY AS THE MOST PRIVILEGED AND AUTHORITATIVE SCHOOL

The canonization of Confucian teaching took place in 136 B.C. when Tung Chung-shu, an expert on the *Ch'un-ch'iu* (*Spring and Autumn Annals*), submitted a memorial to Emperor Wu-ti suggesting that all books not within the field of *Lu-i* (*Six Classics*) be prohibited from circulation. Wu-ti approved this suggestion, and formally proclaimed Confucianism, in which the Six Classics formed an integral part, as the official teaching of the land.

This canonization appears to be the first act to elevate the Confucian Classics to the status of orthodoxy. It should not be supposed, however, that the imperial authorization by Emperor Wu-ti of the Han Dynasty made the Six Classics known for the first time, or even that it gave them the first privileged position they ever held. The Classics had existed for ages before the Han Dynasty, and had been known even to the ancients. In *Chuang-tzu* it is said: "How enlightened was the policy of past ages is evidenced in the records which historians have preserved for us. The presence of this enlightenment in the canons of poetry, history, rites and music has been made clear by many scholars of Chou and Lu *i.e.*, Confucianists. The aim of the *Book of Poetry* is to teach what aspiration is; the *Book of History*, how events actually happened; the *Book of Rites*, what proper conduct is; the *Book of Music*, what harmony is; the *Book of Change*, what the mysterious principles of the world are; and the *Spring and Autumn Annals*, what the duties of all members of society should be. Spread all over the world, this enlightment is focused in the Middle Kingdom, and the learning of all schools renders homage to its power."[10] These words of the last chapter of *Chuang-tzu*, show that the Six Classics were recognized long before Han Wu-ti, whose contribution was merely to make frank acknowledgement of a condition which already existed. Though the authenticity of this last chapter, as a genuine product of the authorship of Chuang-tzu, is sometimes doubted, its allusion to the Six Classics gives evidence that they held a high position before the time of Emperor Wu-ti, and also explains why they were revered as authoritative. ⌐

The prestige of the Confucian canon did not begin with Wu-ti, but his action was merely a formal acknowledgement of its already existing authority. ⌐In other words, the books edited by Confucius, and deeply rooted in the Chinese mind, had already gained wide circulation and approval. Another aspect of this process may be seen in the Confucian school's making use of a canon to which the Chinese mind was already accustomed so that it did not have to sponsor a new line of thought as in the case of Lao-tzu or Mo-ti. ⌐

⌐After the official sanctioning of the Confucian canon, it was studied in the government academy, and chairs were founded for professors to expound it. But even after the achievement of this degree of orthodoxy, the Classics did not become so all-pervasive that the other schools were forced out of existence. The canonization of the Classics meant only that candidates for the civil service examinations were required to write their essays on the basis of the Six Classics, and that the texts of other schools could not be used for this purpose. Ssu-ma T'an's essay, *The Fundamental Principles of the Six Schools* is proof that these systems of belief were equally recommended, though the emphasis was clearly on Confucianism.

The canonization of the Confucian Classics was in fact partially a result of the establishment of a unified empire under Ch'in Shih Huang-ti and its continuation under the Han Dynasty. Wu-ti's action may even be regarded as a continuation of the Ch'in emperor's policy of book-burning or thought-control though it was of course not as drastic or as violent.

From the time of the sanctioning of the Confucian Canon the philosophy of Confucianism became more and more scholastic and lost vitality. Within this school developed two branches: one following the so-called modern script, the other adhering to the old script texts. When professorial chairs were founded for the exposition of the Classics, it seems that the text-books used were written in the former of these two scripts; but later, texts composed in a more old-fashioned character were found, among which was the *Tso-chuan*, a commentary on the *Ch'un-ch'iu*. Many scholars did not approve of the discovered old script books, because it meant the abandonment of their own texts. Hence, the two branches under Confucianism arose, which had a long conflict with one another. In the government academy the professors championed the use of the modern texts, while Lü Hsin at the end of the Former or Western Han Dynasty advocated the inclusion of the old script texts as the authentic Confucian Classics. In the middle of the Later or Eastern Han Dynasty, the two kinds of texts underwent a process of amalgamation in the hands of Cheng K'ang-ch'eng and others.

But this work of textual commentation did not satisfy the people! It was then that Taoism and Buddhism began to make inroads into the popular mind.

(3) CONFUCIANISM AS ECLIPSED BY BUDDHISM AND TAOISM

Political unity of the empire was achieved under the Ch'in and Han Dynasties. The canonization of the Confucian Classics, which accompanied this political achievement, was actually a part of the process of cultural unification.

I may say that the two Han Dynasties (the Former or Western and the Later or Eastern) were about the most religious periods in Chinese history. Magic, superstition, astrology and theosophy flourished. Any religious founder in China at that time could have made use of this psychology to start a cult. In fact, Taoism, as a religion in the Later Han Dynasty, and Buddhism were introduced in the same period.

Tung Chung-shu who was the first man to suggest to the Han Emperor Wu-ti that the Confucian Classics be canonized, in his memorial said: "My historical researches in the 'Spring and Autumn' period show a correlation between heaven and man which is so close that a number of lessons are suggested. When there was misgovernment in the country, heaven brought calamities like flood and drought as a warning. When, in spite of these, the government did not reform, anomalies or irregularities such as eclipses of the sun and moon occurred. When the government still persisted in not bettering itself, rebellion took place and its collapse followed. Thus the heart of heaven was full of love for the ruler, and every effort was made to warn him to desist from misrule."[11]

These words of Tung Chung-shu mean that mis-government leads to the displeasure and anger of heaven. This, in turn, suggests that heaven can show pleasure and displeasure, joy and anger. It would not be appropriate to say that for Tung Chung-shu heaven meant God, but at any rate he believed that heaven knew what was going on in the world, and understood how to punish those who are responsible for misrule. Tung Chung-shu's belief in the correlation between human affairs and astronomical phenomena was a result of his faith in the theory of *Yin* and *Yang* and the five elements.

But the best proof that the age of the two Hans was characterized by a religious mentality is to be drawn from the remarkable fact that in that period Confucius was not considered as a teacher or as a human being: he was regarded as a god. In one of the books of prophecy, *Ch'un-ch'iu-wei-han-han-tzu* it is written: "Confucius said: 'I have read historical records, have drawn up ancient charts, and have investigated the anomalies of heaven in order to guide legislative measures for the emperors of the Han Dynasty.' "[12] If it is true that the institutions of the Han Dynasty were conceived in the work of Confucius, then was not Confucius a prophet?

In another book of prophecy of the *Ch'un-ch'iu-wei-yen-kung-t'u* (*The Expository Chart of Confucius*) it is written: "The mother of Confucius, Cheng-tsai, making a trip to the slope of Ta-meng, dreamt that she was invited by the Black Emperor to have intercourse with him. The emperor told her: 'You will give birth to a child in a place where mulberry trees grow. The child's head will appear like a mountain, so he will be called *Ch'iu* [mountain]. He will be the first of the Sages. On the bosom of Confucius will be written the characters: HE IS A SUPREME LEGISLATOR.' "[13]

The story of the conception of the First Sage by his mother, Cheng-tsai, is akin to that of the Virgin Mother so familiar to Christians. Confucius as "the supreme legislator" was regarded in every sense as a prophet and a seer.

The story is typically Han. The prophetic books of the Han Dynasty could only have been written in that period. Other prophetic remarks attributed to Confucius may be found in inscriptions on stone monuments from the same period. These sayings are traceable to the *Yin-Yang* theory of the time of the "Warring States", and were composed in the Han Dynasty in a most vivid style.

With the kind of mentality thus prevailing, two religions — Taoism, which was of native Chinese origin and Buddhism, which was an importation from India — began to make progress in the Later Han Dynasty. The nature of this early Taoism is well expressed in the following passage from the *History of the Later Han Dynasty*. "Chang Chio, living in Chu-lu, considered himself a great and wise man. He believed in the doctrines of the Yellow Emperor and Lao-tzu, and when Yu Chi's book, the *T'ai-p'ing-ching* [probably the first book of the Taoist school, though it contains later accretions] came into his hands, he made use of it, as well as of charms, holy water and prayer, to cure disease. Many were the sick men who recovered their health thereby. Multitudes followed Chang Chio. He sent out eight disciples to proselytize. After a decade the number of his converts rose to hundreds of thousands, who were scattered in the different provinces. . . . . Chang Chio called himself the General of Heaven; his younger brother, the General of Earth; and another brother, the General of Man."[14]

Eventually Chang's movement came to the attention of the government, which looked upon the faithful as rebels, and took measures to suppress them.

Another personage connected with the founding of the Taoist religion was Chang Tao-ling. In the biographical sketch of Chang

Lu in the *History of the Three Kingdoms* it is said: " His [Chang Lu's] father, Chang Tao-ling, lived in Szechwan, in the Ko-ming Mountain, and became interested in *Tao*. He wrote a book about *Tao* to convert the people. Those who believed in him were supposed to give him five bushels of rice."[15] The rules of the Taoist religion are to be found in Yu Chi's *T'ai-p'ing-ching*. This work contains the following commandments:

    I.   Drink no wine.

   II.   Live according to the Four Seasons, which means that there shall be no killing in spring and summer.

 III.   Establish inns for travelers, free of charge.

 VI.   Give mutual aid. It is sinful for one who is rich not to give money to the needy, it is sinful for one who is strong not to give a helping hand to the weak.

   V.   When one is sick one may recover one's self by confessing one's mistakes and taking holy water.

These rules were later revised. Though Chang Chio and Chang Tao-ling were the actual founders of the cult, the faithful always considered Lao-tzu its founder. He played the same role for Taoism which Christ played for Christianity. The bibles of the Taoist religion are the book by Lao-tzu and the *Chuang-tzu*.

The Taoist religion went through a long process of development. It was not a pure religion in the sense of promoting an other-worldly existence. Indeed it tried to prolong human life in this world, and to perform miracles for that end. Taoism as a religion should not be confused with Taoism as a philosophy. The latter was far more speculative and purer than the former.

The popes of the Taoist religion dwelt in the Dragon-Tiger Mountain of Kiangsi Province. The first of these popes was authorized in A.D. 1016 by Emperor Chen-tsung of the Sung Dynasty, but the faithful liked to trace their line back to Chang Tao-ling of the Later Han Dynasty. Until the beginning of the Ming there were forty-two of these Teachers of Heaven. The most recent Taoist pope escaped from the Dragon-Tiger Mountain in Kiangsi, and fled to Shanghai when the Communists conquered China.

So much for the indigenous Chinese religion Taoism. Let us now turn to the Buddist importation from India. Buddhism is traditionally alleged to have been introduced into the Middle Kingdom after a dream by Emperor Ming-ti of the Later Han Dynasty, that is in A.D. 64. His Majesty dreamt that he saw a golden man about ten and a half feet tall, with a halo round his head, who flew through the hall of the palace. The next day the emperor asked his ministers to explain the dream. One of them, Fu Ni, said, "It is the Buddha of India." Then Ming-ti sent two emissaries to India to bring back the sacred books of Buddhism.

The attribution of the coming of Buddhism to a dream is extremely doubtful. The phantasy of an emperor furnishes no key to our understanding why this religion was brought into China.

My own explanation is as follows. The explorer Chang Ch'ien, who was sent out to the Western Territory in B.C. 138, reached Yueh-chih (Bactria) in about B.C. 123. His arrival there must have been headline news not only to Emperor Wu-ti but also to the Indian Buddhists, who were awaiting the opening of a route to China. After B.C. 123 many Indian and Central Asian monks probably learned Chinese as preparation for a China mission. The long period between B.C. 123 and A.D. 64 leaves us in the dark about the relationship between India and China, although it is on record that in A.D. 64 Emperor Ming-ti sent emissaries to India to seek the Buddhist *Sutras*. It is interesting, however, to note in a biography of Prince Ying of Chu, the brother of Ming-ti, that an imperial decree of A.D. 65 was quoted as saying that silk sent by the Prince to His Majesty should be forwarded as a gift to the *Upasaks* (novices) and *Sramnas* (monks). One cannot help but wonder how such translated terms as *Upasaka* and *Sramnas* could have come into use if Buddhism had been introduced only one year previously. Emperor Ming-ti reigned from A.D. 58 to 75, and was thus a contemporary of Kaniska, the Indo-Scythian King of Northern India in the first century of the Christian era. Crowned probably in A.D. 78 or at an even earlier date and with the dynastic title of Kushan, Kaniska was the conqueror of Bactria, and no doubt he played an important role in the spread of Buddhism from India into Tibet and China. But my point is that

the coming of Buddhism into China must have occurred many
years before the age of Ming-ti and Kaniska or, in other words,
that it must have antedated A.D. 64, the year of Ming-ti's dream.
This dream was perhaps a formal announcement by the Buddhists to commemorate the birthday of their religion in China.

Taking the usage of the translated terms *Upasaka and Sramnas*
as a barometer, we have to assume that they must have been
preceded by a period when the Indian and Central Asia monks
learned the Chinese language and were in the habit of translating
Buddhist terms into Chinese equivalents. It would have probably
taken from fifty to a hundred years for the various steps to be
completed, and for these terms to be adopted in an imperial decree. So my guess is that the penetration of Buddhism into the
Middle Kingdom can only have occurred between the end of the
Former Han Dynasty and the beginning of the Later Han Dynasty.
According to a chapter on Buddhism and Lao-tzu in the *History
of the Wei Dynasty,* there was, during the reign of Emperor Ai-ti,
"in the first year of Yuan-shou [i.e. 6 B.C.] a scholar named Ch'in
Ching who learned the Buddhist *Sutras* from an emissary of
the king of Yueh-chih. The Chinese heard about them, but
they could not understand or believe them." This emissary could
have been sent by Kaniska. This was the forging of the first
ideological link between China and India.

Before and after A.D. 64 there was much preparatory work
to do in translating Sanskrit *Sutras* into Chinese. Such questions
as what terms to use in rendering Buddhist concepts, and what
literary style to follow in writing "Buddhist Chinese," were difficult to solve. Fortunately, in the Chin (or Tsin) Dynasty Taoism
had been revived, so that Taoist terms were at hand to express
the thought of the Buddhist *Sutras.* This was the first step in
the development of a Buddhist terminology.

Later, when Chinese Buddhism had become mature and independent, the faithful disciples abandoned the Taoist expressions and created new words of their own. But this is a long
history, a sketch of which will be given chronologically in the
chapter on Han Yü. What I want to say here is that during
the period of introduction of Buddhism into China many first-

rate scholars put away the Confucian Classics, although they still
had to remember them for purposes of the state examination.
The appreciation of Buddhism in China was widespread and
profound. Between the devotees of the new religion and the
followers of Confucius there arose in time a number of controversies about such topics as the abandonment of family life by
monks, freedom from taxation and military service for monks, and
the theoretical emptiness of the Buddhist dogma, which was in
opposition to the Confucian affirmation of living. This opposition
went underground for a while but at length arose in Han Yü's
(768-824) time in the middle of the T'ang Dynasty.

(4) CONFUCIANISM REBORN, OR THE RENAISSANCE OF
CONFUCIANISM KNOWN AS NEO-CONFUCIANISM.

The period of Neo-Confucianism marks the awakening of
the Chinese to their own cultural tradition. It was impossible
for them to give up Buddhism, since it had exerted so strong
an influence on them for so long. Nevertheless, the Chinese tried
to return to Confucianism — by way of Buddhism. In order to
counteract the law of impermanence, the doctrine of *Anataman,*
and the theory of emptiness, they had to construct a new philosophy which should be based on the ideas and terms of Confucianism. The twin motives of a return to Confucianism and the
struggle against Buddhism, spurred the founders of Neo-Confucianism to build a philosophical system which was, in a sense
a counter-argument against the Buddhist doctrines of impermanence, *Anataman,* and world as illusion.
The sponsors of this new philosophy had to build a system
which would contain a cosmology to account for the creation of
the universe, an ethics treating mankind as a unity and affirming
the value of human effort, and an epistemology to determine the
basis of knowledge of what *is* and what *ought* to be. Without
such a comprehensive philosophy, the leaders of the new movement would have been unable to present an adequate counter-
argument against Buddhism. This new philosophy became known
as "the science of reason" or the science of "human nature as
reason," because "reason is the common basis of knowledge, and

the universals of natural or ethical knowledge are found only by reason in human nature."

From this basic study of reason and human nature, the devotees of the new philosophy went further to create a fresh educational method, a revived sense of social obligation, "the rural contract" (a form of local self-government), and an improved kind of government in general. The seeds of this new movement were sown by Han Yu in the T'ang period; it developed more fully in the Sung and Yuan Dynasties and reached its climax in the philosophy of Wang Shou-jen in the Ming period. It declined and fell at the end of the Ming period but its inertia kept it going, as the school of Chu Hsi, until the opening of China to the West. It may be said that the dominant factor in Chinese thought for the last thousand years has been this Neo-Confucianist movement, which, like the Renaissance in Europe, began with the revival of old books, but ended by creating a new world-view. While the European Renaissance produced science, industry, technology, democracy, and a fresh economic life in the modern world, Chinese Neo-Confucianism failed to achieve any of these things. Nevertheless the basic principles of its philosophy are worth our careful study.

It is interesting however to inquire, before we begin our task, whether Confucian and Neo-Confucian philosophy, on the one hand, and Western philosophy, on the other hand, are different in kind, or whether they are merely different species of the same genus. One very important difference is obvious at the outset, and that is, the Confucianists and their spirited offspring take the realm of human relations and ethics as their principal *data*, whereas for most Western thinkers in the modern period the world of nature and the quest for knowledge have been the center of their chief interest.

The Chinese Confucianists seldom occupied themselves with the problems of knowledge and methodology, while the European philosophers, before they dealt with the substance, first prepared the ground by elaborating critically the technique of clear and connected thinking. In recent times, with the stress on the importance of scientific method and the development of the new physics of relativity and atomic energy, the difference between Oriental and Occidental thought has become even more obvious.

However, though the gap between Eastern and Western philosophy seems to be a very wide one, there are certain features common to both. Philosophy is after all an effort to understand life and the universe around us. There is thus an identity of aims, though there may be frequently differences of approach. Here is an example of a parallel thought between Confucius and Socrates:

Confucius' Rectification of Names.

In the *Lun-yu* (*Confucian Analects*) "Tzu-lu said: 'The ruler of Wei has been waiting for you, in order that you administer the government with him. What do you consider to be the first important task?' The Master replied: 'To rectify names.' Tzu-lu said: 'So, indeed! But you are wide of the mark! Why must there be such rectification?' The Master said: 'How uncultivated you are, Yu! A man of noble character in regard to what he does not know, should show a cautious reserve. If names be not correct, language is not in accordance with the truth of things. If language be not in accord with the truth of things, affairs cannot be carried on to success.' . . . When Duke Ching of the Kingdom of Ch'i asked Confucius about government, Confucius replied: 'The prince should be prince, the minister should be minister, the father should be father, and the son should be son.' "[17]

Socrates' Definition.

In the *Theaetetus* "Socrates said: 'When therefore any one forms the true opinion of anything without definition you may say that his mind is truly exercized, but has no knowledge; for he who cannot give and receive a definition of a thing, has no knowledge of that thing; but when he adds the definition, he may be all that I have been denying of him, and is perfected in knowledge.' Theaetetus asked: 'Can you give me an example of such a definition?' Socrates said: 'As for example, in the case of the sun, I think that you need only know that the sun is the brightest of the heavenly bodies which revolves about the earth.' Theatetus: 'Certainly.' Socrates: 'Understand why I say this: the reason is, as I was saying, that if you get at the difference and distinguishing characteristic of each thing, then as many persons say, you will get at the definition or explanation of it; but while you lay hold only of the common and not of the characteristic notion, you will only have the definition of those things to which this common quality belongs.' "[18]

Confucius' last comment clearly reveals the meaning of the "rectification of names." To the Westerner his remark may at first sound like tautology. But such is not the case. Confucius stresses that every member of a community ought to carry out his duty in accordance with what is essential and necessary,

or in consonance with the meaning of the term which stands
for his position in society. On the surface, it may seem that while
Socrates searches for the definition of a word in terms of the
characteristic nature of the thing to which the word refers, Confucius talks about the duties of the members of a community.
But let us abstract from the content of the subject, and confine
our attention to the terms themselves: prince, minister, father or
son. Does Confucius fail to mention what is the essential and
constitutive function implied in each of these words representing
various members of the community? I must say: "No!" Like
Socrates, Confucius tries to discover the characteristic of each of
them. It is then that he can rightly define the name. It is not
accurate to say that while Socrates seeks the definitions of terms
and thus talk logic, Confucius talks of only ethics. Neither can
avoid exploring the essential features of the terms in which he
is interested. Confucius' "rectification of names" and Socrates'
"definition" really amount to the same thing though each expresses himself in a different form and speaks a different language.
But to return to our parallel columns:

The Lun-yü

Confucius said: "A scholar whose
mind is set on the *Tao* and who is
ashamed of bad clothes and bad food
is not fit to be discussed with."

Confucius said: "He who aims to
be a man of noble character, in his
food does not seek to gratify his ap-
petite, nor in his dwelling place does
he seek ease and comfort."[19]

The Phaedo

"Socrates asked: 'Do you think that
the philosopher ought to care about
the pleasures — if they are to be called
pleasures — of eating and drinking?'
'Certainly not', answered Semmias.
'And what about the pleasures of
love — should he care for them?'
'By no means.'
'And will he think much of the
other ways of indulging the body, for
example, the acquisition of costly rai-
ment, or sandals, or other adornments
of body? Instead of caring about them,
does he not rather despise anything
more than nature needs? What do
you say?
'I should say that a true philosopher would despise them.' "

The Chinese sage and the Greek philosopher both agree that
knowledge is limited. Confucius emphasizes learning; Socrates
does the same thing except that he demands definitions and clear

thinking. But an example of this Socratic insistence is also found in Confucius. "I do not," he says, "open the truth to one who is not eager to get knowledge, nor help out anyone who is not anxious to explain himself. When I present one corner of a subject to anyone and he cannot learn the other three, I do not repeat my lesson."[21]

Socrates' art of midwifery, by which he enticed the idea of his collocutors into the light of day, and then examined them, would certainly have been appreciated by Confucius.

Both the Chinese sage and the teacher of Plato held the conviction that one should die for the cause in which one believes.

Confucius: "If a man in the morning knows what *Tao* is, he may die in the evening without regret."[22] In another place Confucius said: "The determined scholar and the man of virtue should prefer to be killed for a virtuous cause, rather than cling to life at the cost of the virtuous cause."[23]

Socrates: "And the true philosophers, Simmias, are always occupied in the practice of dying, wherefore also to them least of all men is death terrible." "Will he who is a true lover of wisdom . . . still repine at death? Will he not depart with joy? Surely he will, O my friend, if he be a true philosopher. For he will have a firm conviction that there, and there only, he can find wisdom in her purity."[24]

So much for the comparisons of Confucius with the Socrates of the Platonic Dialogues. Here are some points of similarity between Mencius and Socrates.

The *Meng-tzu*

Mencius: "The disciple of Kung-tu said: 'All are equally men, but some are great men, and some are little men; how is this?' Mencius replied: 'Those who follow that part of themselves which is great are great men; those who follow that part which is little are little men.' Kung-tu pursued: 'All are equally men, but some follow that part of themselves which is great, and some follow that part which is little — how is this? Mencius answered: 'The senses of hearing and seeing have nothing to do with thinking, and are obscured by external things. . . . To mind belongs the office

The *Phaedo*, (Phaedo)

Socrates: " 'Then when does the soul attain truth? For in attempting to consider anything in company with the body she is obviously deceived.' Yes, that is true. 'Then must not true existence be revealed to her in thought if at all?' 'Yes.' And thought is best when the mind is gathered to herself and none of these things trouble her — neither sound nor sights nor pain nor any pleasure — when she has as little as possible to do with the body, when she has no bodily sense or feeling, but is aspiring after being?' And all experience shows that if we would have pure knowledge of anything we must

The *Meng-tzu*

of thinking. By thinking, it gets the right view of things; by neglecting to think, it fails to do this . . . let man first stand in the supremacy of the nobler part of his constitution, and the inferior part will not be able to take it from him. It is simply this which makes the great man.' "[25]

The *Phaedo*, (Phaedo)

quit the body and the soul in herself must behold things in themselves: and then I suppose that we shall attain that which we desire, and of which we say that we are the lover, and that is wisdom."[26]

It is no exaggeration to say that these parallel quotations, not only in verbal form but also in spirit, show a remarkable kinship. But why should there be such similarity? The answer is that the objective of Western and Eastern philosophy is the same. Both seek eternal truth, whether in ethics or in theoretical knowledge — a truth which is impossible to find in the senses, but which lies in the forms of thought or of mind. This similarity is not accidental as a study of the methodology of Eastern thought will amply prove.

In the study of methodology it is important to understand how conclusions are reached and whether they are reliable. The question of concepts is fundamental, because concepts are the instrument by which knowledge of things becomes possible. The following passage from Mencius shows how, according to Eastern philosophy, a concept is formed. "Thus", he says, "all things which are the same in kind are like one another. Why should we be in doubt in regard to man, as if he were the solitary exception to this rule? The sage and we are the same in kind. Therefore, I say: Men's mouths agree in having the same relishes; their ears agree in enjoying the same sounds; their eyes agree in recognizing the same beauty. Shall their mind alone be without that which they similarly approve? What is it, then, of which they similarly approve? It is, I say, the principles of reason and the determination of righteousness."[27]

Mencius discussess here the universality of concepts. What we conceive, in other words, is the common nature in accordance with which the particulars or individual things are fashioned and rendered intelligible. The nature of the concept as a class-name for things of the same genus is what Mencius is talking about. Class-

names, such as "animal" or "man", are known only as conceived by
the mind, whereas the innumerable instances under each class-name
are perceived by the senses. When the common nature or the universal of a group of particulars is discovered, a class-name is conferred
upon them. This is the work of the mind, and with this work
of the mind that which is approved by mankind at large finds
expression. Mencius concludes by explaining that the common
approval of which he is speaking is of two kinds: (1) approval by
the principles of reason, *i.e.*, in Western terminology by the principles of theoretical knowledge (logic, epistemology, principles
of sciences, etc.);   (2) approval by the principles of righteousness,
i.e. in the Western sense by the principles of ethics. In Chinese
thought these two areas of inquiry are brought so close together
that the principles of knowledge are often obscured.

Closely allied to this topic is another discussion by Mencius
on the problems of abstract nouns. "Mencius asked Kao-tzu: 'Do
you say that by nature you mean life, just as you say that white
is white?' 'Yes, I do,' was the reply. Mencius added: Is whiteness
of a white feather like that of white snow, and the white of white
snow like that of white jade?' Kao-tzu said: 'Yes!' " After affirming the predicability of whiteness as a property of different white
things, Kao-tzu fell into a trap prepared by Mencius. The discussion continued with a conversation about *essentia* and *differentia*,
which lies at the bottom of the division between species. "Mencius
inquired: 'Is the nature of a dog like the nature of an ox, and
the nature of an ox like the nature of a man?' "[22] Asked about
these questions, Kao-tzu was speechless for he knew that he was
outwitted.

In these extracts from the *Meng-tzu (The Book of Mencius)*
the reader will have observed that the rudiments of logic were
already known to the Chinese in the days of the Second Sage.
If we combine Mencius' treatment of the concept with Confucius'
"rectification of names," and with Mo-ti's and Hsun-tzu's discussions of logical principles, we may say that although the Chinese
produced no text-book similar to Aristotle's *Organon*, yet the principles of logic were implicit in their discussions. They could not
be other than logical.

Thus far we have been concerned with the comparative study of philosophy in China and Greece. If we come down to the Sung Dynasty, that is to Neo-Confucianism, we shall find that the similarities already noticeable in the ancient period became more pronounced. Let me illustrate this by a few examples. For instance, there were the Ch'eng brothers who, after Chou Tun-i, Shao Yung and Chang Tsai, had tried to construct a new cosmology, and set out to establish a fresh starting point for philosophy. The attempt is suggestive of Descartes, who, for the same purpose, enunciated his celebrated *"Cogito, ergo sum!"* The elder Ch'eng brother, Ch'eng Hao, also suggests Kant, because of his stress on "reason". "The expression *t'ien-ri* [heavenly reason]", says Ch'eng Hao (and he means natural law in the general sense) "was the product of my own contemplation."[29]

The "reason" to which he alludes has an affinity with the "reason" of Kant's *Critique of Pure Reason* and *Critique of Practical Reason*. Later, Ch'eng Hao's younger brother, Ch'eng I, developed the theory to a point where it became a truly fresh starting point for philosophy, for Ch'eng I held that "human nature is reason."[30]

This statement, "Human nature is reason", appears and sounds strange to the European philosopher. But when it is clearly analyzed and explained he will surely say the Western and Eastern thought is basically similar. In Occidental philosophy there are the two schools of rationalism and empiricism. The empiricist holds that knowledge comes from sensations or impressions, while the rationalist argues that the idea of causal law does not appear in the data which are findable by the senses. There are forms of thought, in other words, among which is the idea of causal law, underlying our judgments. Ch'eng I's statement "Human nature is reason" means no other than the rationalist doctrine that forms of thought exist *a priori* in the mind.

Fundamental to all reason, according to Ch'eng Hao, is the dialectical alternation between opposites. *"Yin has Yang"*, he says, "as its counterpart. Good has evil as its counterpart. When *Yang* grows, *Yin* declines. When good increases, evil decreases. This theory of opposites is applicable to all types of phenomena. Human beings must keep this in mind."[33] These words remind us of a passage in *Phaedo*, where Socrates says: "Are not all things which have opposites generated out of their opposites? I mean such things as good and evil, just and unjust — and there are innumerable other opposites which are generated out of opposites. And I want to show that in all opposites there is of necessity a similar alternation."[34]

So much for the Ch'eng brothers, whom I shall treat at greater length later. We come to Chu Hsi for another example. It was Chu Hsi who continued the development of the theory of Ch'eng Hao and Ch'eng I in the Southern Sung Dynasty. He is separated from Aristotle by an interval of fifteen centuries. Yet the series of coincidences in their thought is extraordinary. Chu Hsi and Aristotle both agree that the One does not exist apart from the Many. They concur in denying independent existence to the universal as separate from the individual. There is further agreement between the Stagirite and the Chinese philosopher that matter cannot exist independently of form. In the words of Chu Hsi, no *ch'i* [matter] exists without *ri* [reason or form]. Aristotle holds that an immaterial form-principle exists, while the Chinese thinker asserts that *ri* is prior to *ch'i* in principle.

We come, lastly, to Wang Shou-jen of the Ming Dynasty. While Chu Hsi was close to dualism, or rather *Advaita*, in the Indian way of labeling, Wang Shou-jen developed Neo-Confucianism into monistic idealism. He rebelled against the Sung philosopher's bifurcation of nature and mind, and carried the Confucian tradition in a direction of his own. In his *Chuan-hsi-lu, Record of Instruction and Practice,* where his theory is set forth, he quotes the following conversation: "The master asked: 'What, according to you, is the mind of the universe?' The disciple answered: 'I have often heard that man is the mind of the universe.'" Here the position arrived at would seem to be anthropocentric, but Wang Shou-jen pursues the subject further. "What is it in a man", he asks, "that is called his mind? It is simply his spirituality or consciousness. From this we know that in the universe the only reality is spirituality or consciousness. Man, because of his bodily form, is separated from the whole. One's own spirituality or consciousness is the ruler of heaven, earth, spirits and things . . . If heaven, earth, spirits and things are sepa-

rated from one's own spirituality or consciousness, they cease to
be. And if my spirituality or consciousness is separated from them,
it ceases to be also. Thus, all these constitute a unity, and are
mutually inseparable."[31]

Other aspects of Wang Shou-jen's thought bear affinities to
William James' voluntarism and Rudolph Eucken's activism.
The wealth of his ideas will be explored more fully in a later
chapter.

This comparative study of the philosophies in the Occident
and Orient is no outgrowth of any personal whim. It is based
upon objective fact. But though some remarkable similarities
have come to light, it nevertheless remains true that Chinese philosophy possesses its own peculiar features, making it quite unlike
any other philosophy in the world. As I see it, there are four
unique characteristics which we shall now proceed to study point
by point.

(1)   The philosophical interest of the Chinese is focussed
on moral values. The Chinese take the view that the center of
the world is man. The ordering of human relations ought to be
the philosopher's first consideration. How, for instance, should
the members of a community — prince and subject, father and son,
et al. — live together? Confucius' answer is familiar: "A youth
when at home should be filial and when abroad he should respect
his elders. He should be earnest and truthful. He should overflow
in love to all. He should cultivate the friendship of the good.
When he has time and opportunity he should, after the performance of these things, devote himself to literary studies."[32] These
sentiments are also frequently found to apply to other members
of society: to the king and his ministers, to fathers, husbands and
wives. For the various members of society there are different virtues, some of which are common to all, and others peculiar to
each. The teleological view of the universe, which is basic in
Chinese thought, has led to this interest in moral value, which,
for the Chinese, has a more important function than logic, epistemology, or anything else pertaining to pure abstract intellectual
knowledge.

(2)   This Chinese concern with ethical problems has often
given Western philosophers the impression that Chinese thought

is too practical and too worldly. But this impression is false. The Chinese have attempted to find explanations for all phenomena. Thus, they sought a solution to the problem of world-creation, which was a challenge to their imagination. They conceived of heaven as the source of *Tao,* and went to pains to explain this relationship in terms of *Yin* and *Yang,* the forces of nature, or in terms of change. Their metaphysics has always been rationalistic, without supernaturalism. A brilliant example of this appeal to reason is the well-known metaphysical study, the *Tao-te-ching.* Also the *Meng-tzu* is a system of rationalism. The cosmology of Chou Tun-i and the discussion of *ri* and *ch'i* by Chang Tsai and Chu Hsi show that abstract theoretical analyses were a vital part of Chinese thought in the Sung Dynasty.

The Buddha himself once declared to his followers that their belief in him should be based upon reason. The Chinese mind is even more profoundly rationalistic. For the Chinese thinker there is no fundamental gap between God and nature. If there is any difference between the metaphysical and the physical it is a difference of degree only, and not of kind. What is physical is traceable to the metaphysical; what is metaphysical is to be explained in terms of the manifestation of the phenomena of this world.

(3) The philosophical interest of the Chinese is most concerned with mind-control. This emphasis may be compared to the Western enthusiasm for methodology. The Chinese believe that because mind is often obscured by desire, bias and narrow-mindedness, mental purification is a prerequisite for the attainment of truth. Once selfish motives have been eliminated, the mind can become impartial, clear and farsighted. Desirelessness, according to Chou Tun-i; realization of Knowledge and mental concentration according to Chu Hsi; and unity of knowledge and action, according to Wang Shou-jen — these were three ways in which to attempt the search for a criterion of truth.

(4) A fourth characteristic of Chinese philosophy, distinguishing it from Western thought, is the stress on the practical realization of one's philosophy, even to the point of martyrdom. When a man is interested in *Tao* and wishes to devote himself to it, the first thing for him to do is to put the principles of which he is convinced into practice — to exemplify them in his person, in his

family life, and in his pulbic duties for his country. Greed for money, indulgence in sexual life, and eagerness for advancement in civil service, to give a few examples are, needless to say, not conducive to the realization of the *Tao*. Anger, violence, boasting, talkativeness are likewise obstacles and should be avoided. When Hsieh Liang-tso, a pupil of Ch'eng Hao, made his first call upon his master, he bragged about his good memory which he showed by reciting passages from the histories. Ch'eng Hao asked: "Why should you memorize so much? Storing up so much in your mind does not mean that you have any great aspiration for *Tao*."[35] Hsieh felt ashamed on hearing these words and broke out in perspiration. He then abandoned his habit of memorizing and devoted himself more attentively to thought and contemplation. The Chinese philosopher is not satisfied with mere knowledge or the intellectual formulation of philosophical principles, but must devote himself to putting into practice the principles which form his conviction.

If, for instance, a Neo-Confucianist scholar was the incumbent of a high offical position, he would be considered as unworthy of his name unless he remonstrated with his emperor against his wrong-doings. Chu Hsi's memorials to Emperor Ning-tsung, condemning persons of evil repute surrounding him, caused the philosopher to be dismissed from the government. Wang Shou-jen's impeachment of the eunuch Liu Chin landed him as an exile in Kweichow Province. The frankness of these men in their petitions to their emperor has always been widely appreciated in China, and both Chu Hsi and Wang Shou-jen were regarded as examples worthy of being followed. At about the end of the Ming Dynasty, many philosophers who were members of the Tung-lin party sacrificed their lives for talking frankly and honestly to their emperor. This means that a Confucianist or Neo-Confucianist was expected to die for his convictions. Wen T'ien-hsiang's death at the end of the Sung Dynasty, and Liu Tsung-chou's death at the end of the Ming Dynasty, were such examples of martyrdom. Confucius said: "A man of noble character should prefer to be killed in a virtuous cause rather than to seek his life at the cost of his virtue."[37]

Be this as it may, Western scholars, like Alfred Forke and Heinrich Hackmann, have complained that Chinese philosophy lacks the structure of a system, and that the Chinese language, since it does not possess the grammatical forms of the Indo-Germanic languages, is ambiguous. The first so-called defect of the lack of system is because of the peculiar mode of presentation: the early thinkers expressed their ideas in aphoristic forms, without caring for complete discussion in every aspect. This does not mean however that Chinese philosophy is intrinsically without system. Confucius said: "There is a pervading unity in my *Tao*." For certainly no one can say that the *Tao-te-ching* is unsystematic, though it is true that it is not any mere verbal or linguistic system. If one studies the *Meng-tzu* carefully one will also find a system of rationalism; so also there is a system of empiricism in Hsü-tzu. The same can be said of Chu Hsi and Wang Shou-jen.

As for the second defect, linguistic ambiguity, there is some truth in the criticism. Chinese philosophical terms are to a certain extent ambiguous. The Chinese language is radically different from the languages of Europe, so that dissatisfaction, on the part of Europeans, with Chinese philosophical expressions is natural. But the important thing is to understand the basic positions of these thinkers, and there should be no difficulty in expressing them in the language which the Westerner can understand.

All in all, Chinese philosophy does contain some aspects which are bound to appear unfamiliar in Western eyes. The greater part of Chinese philosophical literature seems to the Westerner to be written in a manner not in accordance with Occidental standards. But our interest should surely be in its essential thought, and it is my aim to present that thought as clearly and as completely as possible. This should help to dispel the feeling of strangeness which many a Westerner experiences when studying Chinese philosophy, and should help to create real mutual understanding between the West and East.

I have meticulously avoided making any distortion which would seem to bring Chinese philosophy closer to Western thought than it actually is, because without intellectual honesty a fair and objective study is impossible. To see similarity in dissimilarity, and dissimilarity in similarity is the truest guide to a sound understanding. I can not do better than quote a few lines from Plato's *Philebus* to conclude the present introductory chapter: "In the first place as to whether these unities have a real existence, and then how each individual unity, being always the same, and incapable either of generation or of destruction, but retaining a permanent individuality, can be conceived either as dispersed and multiplied in the infinity of the world of generation, or as still entire and yet contained in others, which latter would seem to be the greatest impossibility of all, for how can one and the same thing be at the same time in one and in many things? These, Protarchus, are the real difficulties, and this is the one and many to which they relate; they are the source of great perplexity if ill decided, and if rightly determined are very helpful."[37]

Jowett, in his introduction to the *Philebus*, gives the following comment: "The world of knowledge is always dividing more and more; every truth is at first the enemy of every truth. Yet without this division there can be no truth; nor any complete truth without the reunion of the parts into a whole."[38] Intellectually, the east and the west have been divided for more than two thousand years. It is time for a synthesis into the unity of an Idea.

References

1. *Lun-yü*, Book 17, Chapter 9.
2. *Ibid.*, Book 9, Chapter 1.
3. Soothill, *The Three Religions of China*, Oxford University Press, London, 1923, p. 24.
4. J. Legge, *The Religions of China*, Charles Scribner's Sons, New York, 1881, p. 4.
5. *Lun-yü*, Book 7, Chapter 19.
6. *Ibid.*, Book 11, Chapter 11.
7. *Ibid.*, Book 3, Chapter 12.
8. *Ibid.*, Book 9, Chapter 16.
9. *Shang-tzu*, (Book of Lord Shang), Chapter 1, Paragraph 4.
10. *Chuang-tzu*, Chapter 33, "T'ien-hsia p'ien" (The World).
11. *Han-shu* (History of the Former Han Dynasty), Book 56 (Biography of Tung Chung-shu).
12. *Ch'un-ch'iu-wei-Han-han-tzu* (Books of Prophecy of Ch'un-ch'iu).
13. *Ibid.*, Yen-K'ung-T'u (Expository Chart of Confucius.)
14. *Hou Han-shu* (History of the Later Han Dynasty), Book 101, Biography 61 (Biography of Huang-fu Sung).
15. *San-kuo chih* (History of the Three Kingdoms), Book 8, (Biography of Chang Lu).

16. *T'ai-p'ing ching* (Supposed the earliest work on the Taoist religion. In its original form it consisted of 170 books. Now only 67 books are extant, the others having been lost.), 85th series.

17. *Lun-yü*, Book 13, Chapter 3.

18. *The Dialogues of Plato*, translated into English by B. Jowett, in 4 vols., Charles Scribner's Sons, New York, 1890, Vol. 3. Theaetetus, pp. 409, 417.

19. *Lun-yü*, Book 1, Chapter 14.

20. *The Dialogues of Plato*, Volume 1, Phaedo, p. 390.

21. *Lun-yü*, Book 7, Chapter 8.

22. *Ibid.*, Book 4, Chapter 8.

23. *Ibid.*, Book 15, Chapter 8.

24. *The Dialogues of Plato*, Volume 1, Phaedo, p. 394.

25. *Meng-tzu*, Book 6, Part 1, Chapter 15.

26. *The Dialogues of Plato*, Volume 1, Phaedo, pp. 391-393.

27. *Meng-tzu*, Book 6, Part 1, Chapter 7.

28. *Ibid.*, Book 6, Part 1, Chapter 4.

29. *Sung-Yüan hsüeh-an* (Philosophical Records of the Sung and Yuan Dynasties, Book 13, Ch'eng Hao. Hereafter cited as *P.R.S.Y.*

30. *Ibid.*, Book 15, Ch'eng I.

31. Wang Shou-jen, *Collected Works of Wang Yang-ming, Ch'uan-hsi lu* (Book of Instruction and Practice), Vol. 3.

32. *Lun-yü*, Book 1, Chapter 6.

33. *P.R.S.Y.*, Book 13, Ch'eng Hao.

34. *The Dialogues of Plato*, Volume 1, Phaedo, p. 397.

35. *P.R.S.Y.*, Book 14, Ch'eng Hao.

36. *Lun-yü*, Book 15, Chapter 9.

37. *The Dialogues of Plato*, Volume 3, Philebus, p. 149.

38. *Ibid.*, Volume 3, Jowett's Introduction to the Philebus, p. 127.

CHAPTER TWO

Fundamental Principles
of the Philosophy of Reason

This book on Neo-Confucianism is an exposition of the development of Chinese thought from the Sung Dynasty and earlier. The prefix "Neo" suggests that although the roots of this philosophy were in Confucian soil, it grew up in an entirely new climate.

Neo-Confucianism was one of the results of the introduction to China of Buddhism from India. Neo-Confucianism was no product of the cross-breeding of Buddhism and the Chinese tradition, but rather a declaration of independence from Buddhism after China had been under the influence of Indian thought for a long period. This, however, did not leave the Chinese mind entirely free from some of the more valuable elements in the Buddhist way of thinking.

Without the introduction of Buddhism into China there would have been no Neo-Confucianism, and this despite the fact that according to Chinese practice Confucian scholars were exceedingly reluctant to admit the influence of Buddhism, and were anxious to make clear that they would have no traffic whatever with that school of thought.

But whether Buddhism influenced the Chinese mind is one question, and whether the Neo-Confucianist thought system contained the elements of Buddhism is quite another. No doubt, Chinese thought received a tremendous impact after Buddhism reached China, because Buddhism was more speculative, more metaphysical, and had a complete system of its own. When the cogitations of the Chinese scholars eventually found their way back home, there developed a self-conscious reflection, and a new Chinese thought structure was built up. This is what is known as Neo-Confucianism.

This new philosophy was known under a variety of names in the literature contemporaneous with it. For instance, in the *History of the Sung Dynasty* it was called *Tao-hsüeh*, and in the title *Ri-hsüeh tsung-ch'uan* it was known under the first two words *Ri-hsüeh*. It was also known as *Hsin-ri-hsüeh* meaning "philosophy of human nature qua reason", or simply as *Hsüeh*, as in the titles *Sung Yüan hsüeh-an* (*Philosophical Records of the Sung and Yüan Dynasties*) and *Ming-ju hsüeh-an* (*Philosophical Records of the Ming Scholars*).

The reason why there was no definite name in the Chinese language for Neo-Confucianism was that the field which the new philosophy covered was so wide that nobody could consider it as a single entity under one name. Each thinker took down his own notes, or wrote his own articles, without giving any thought to the idea that he was contributing to a unified intellectual and social movement, which should have a name of its own. An analogous situation occurred in Europe just after the awakening of modern western philosophy. Locke and Hume in the titles of their books referred to "Human Understanding," Spinoza's great work was entitled *Ethics,* Kant wrote critiques of "Pure" and "Practical Reason," Hegel was the author of a *System of Logic,* etc. They all discussed the same subjects, but there was no common name. The scope was too vast to admit of any names more inclusive than the separate names of the various special fields studied.

Similarly the Chinese philosophers of the Sung period devoted their efforts to the search for the essential and the fundamental. Ultimately, they believed they found *Ri** as an overall concept. At this point it should be explained that *Ri* means the principle which underlies the entire universe, that is the realm of value and of knowledge. It has the meaning of natural law. But this term in

---

* Throughout this book the usual Romanization· for this word, pronounced *Li,* is not used in order not to confuse it with *Li* meaning propriety or decency. Instead it will be referred to as *Ri.*

Chinese covers a wider field than the term natural law. It is close to the term law in a general sense, not in a legal sense. Since the time of the Sung philosophers, *Ri* has become the fundamental concept of Chinese philosophy, just as the term *Tao* was fundamental to Confucius and Laotse.

Thus Ch'eng Hao said: "When I found that in every thing and every event there is reason, I was so glad of this discovery that I could not help but swing my hands and dance with my feet."

Ch'eng Hao's joy arose from his appreciation that his discovery, *Ri*, was the most essential and fundamental of all the subjects his brother philosophers were studying. He found that there are four basic principles of human nature: *Jen, I, Li,* and *Chih.*

The four words *Jen, I, Li,* and *Chih* are common and ever-recurring terms in Chinese philosophy.

In ancient times they were explained as the virtues of human nature. In terms of Western philosophy they should be considered the fundamental categories of valuation judgments and knowledge.

The first three terms, *Jen, I,* and *Li* clearly belong in the realm of valuation judgments, while the fourth, *Chih,* is an intellectual process, and comes near the Western term intellect or knowledge. The four terms cover two different kinds of judgment, which point should be made clear at the outset of this work.

Dealing with each term individually, I should like to make the following explanation:

1. *Jen* is usually translated as benevolence, good-will, or humaneness. There are those who consider *Jen* identical with love. Undoubtedly *Jen* cannot be separated from love, but in the Neo-Confucian sense, *Jen* is a standard of love, which varies in different cases: the love an individual has for his parents, wife, brother, sister, child, friends and country. *Jen* means love on a rational basis, which is to be measured and suited to each case. Though the nature of *Jen* is love, it should be expressed in a measured and proportionate way. Thus, *Jen* has a rational basis, and is a category for the judgment of love.

2. *I* is normally translated as right, righteousness or justice. In the Neo-Confucian sense *I* means the right way of dealing with persons or problems. In other words *I* means the right way of dealing with matters.

3. *Li* is generally translated as propriety, decency, ritual, ceremony and by numerous other terms. Its use is so widespread that it has become ambiguous. Other meanings for it are good manners, modesty and consideration.

4. *Chih* means knowing or knowledge. By knowing one differentiates this from that, black from white, etc. This term comes closest to the Western equivalent for intellect or knowedge. *Chih* deals with the objects of the physical world, although it also is a part of a valuation judgment.

If these four principles determine human action then human nature may be said to contain the fundamental principle called *Ri*. Ch'eng Hao's brother, Ch'eng I, coined a phrase which afterwards prevailed, namely: "Hsing is *Ri*," or "Human nature is reason."

When the word *Hsing* is omitted from this phrase, the philosophy it denominates is called simply *Ri-hsüeh*, "Philosophy of reason," which suggests analogy to the Kantian concepts of pure and practical reason. *Ri-hsüeh* and *Hsing-ri-hsüeh* were the most prevalent terms under which this type of philosophy was described, and these terms express the basic data which the Sung school studied.

But now let us leave the terms *Ri* (reason) and *Hsing* (nature), and betake ourselves to some fundamental questions. In China and the West the same problems have interested people since the beginning of thought — such problems as: What is the origin of the universe? What is the reality behind phenomena? What is the meaning of human life? Where lies the validity of our knowledge? These questions and their answers were the focal points, as they still are, of philosophical enquiry.

After thousands of years of separate development the philosophies of the East and West have evinced certain peculiarities. In Greece the philosophers were busy with wisdom and unchangeable truths. In Europe of the Middle Ages they were interested in universals and beings. Recently, the main questions with which European and American philosophers have been concerned are the world of nature and the validity of knowledge. In the East on the other hand, the centers of philosophical interest have been the meaning of human life and deliverance from suffering. This difference of emphasis and of outlook in philosophical thought can be accounted for by the complexity of spiritual and material conditions of life. But there are also, as I have said in the first chapter, certain fundamentals common of both.

More specifically, there are the three principles of the Sung philosophy which can be traced back to Confucius and Mencius. (1) *Tao as reality*. *Tao* in its original meaning signifies way or course of nature. In the *Chung-yung* it is said: "*Tao* is that from which one cannot for a single instant depart. That from which one may depart is not *Tao*."[2] *Tao* is what Plato calls the region of purity and eternity and immortality and unchangeableness. But with the development of philosophical thought, the term underwent changes in significance. In the *Chung-yung* and *Tao-te-ching*, for instance, it means the highest concept, while in the *Lun-yü* and *Meng-tzu* it means sometimes the same thing, but sometimes it is also used fragmentarily in the sense of proper way.

An apt quotation from the *Lun-yü* illustrating this fragmentary but normal sense is: "Wealth and high position are what man desires. One prefers not to stay with them if they are not acquired according to *Tao*. Poverty and humble position are what man dislikes. One prefers not to leave them if one cannot do so without running counter to *Tao*."[3] Here, of course, *Tao* means the moral or right way. When Confucius said "One should be inspired by *Tao*",[4] he was alluding to the noblest truth. He discussed the rules of conduct with his disciples, but was unwilling to tell them about the supreme principles of the universe. It seems furthermore that his disciples complained of his reticence in speaking of nature and the *Tao* of heaven. This expression: "*Tao* of heaven", indicates that in Confucian thought the term *Tao* had begun to be understood as the highest concept.

In the *Meng-tzu*, *Tao* is, as has already been said, sometimes used in the same sense as in the *Chung-yung*, that is, as the noblest truth or highest good. Thus it is said: "Tao is like a great road."[5] But in general, in the *Meng-tzu*, the term refers to a subjective conviction or theory. Following are a few examples of Mencius' usage of this word: "I do not dare to set forth before the King any but the *Tao* of Yao and Shun."[6]

"Now Mo [Mo ti] considers that in the regulation of funeral services a spare simplicity should be the *Tao*."[7]

"The *Tao* of Yao and Shun, without a benevolent government, could not secure the tranquil order of the kingdom."[8]

"The *Tao* lies in what is near, but men seek for it in what is far. The work lies in what is easy, but men seek for it in what is difficult. If each man would love his parents and show due respect to his elders, the whole land would enjoy tranquility."[9]

"It is said in the Book of *Poetry*:

'Heaven in producing mankind
Created a world of things
In which there are the invariable rules of nature.
It is the endowment of the people
That they observe the invariable rules
And that they are fond of this admirable virtue.'

'The author of this ode', said Confucius, 'was one who knew *Tao*.' "[10]

From these examples we may see that although Mencius used *Tao* in the sense of a great road, he fluctuated by understanding it sometimes as the name of the highest concept of being or of ultimate reality, and at other times as the proper way in daily life.

Traditionally, the *Chung-yung* is attributed to Tzu-ssu (492-431 B.C.), the grandson of Confucius, but in the light of modern research the book seems rather to have been written under the influence of the school of Lao-tzu, because many terms are used there in a more highly speculative sense than was usual in the Confucian tradition.

Be this as it may, the *Chung-yung* begins as follows: "What is Heaven-given is what we call nature. To be in conformity with nature is what we call *Tao*. The cultivation of *Tao* is what we call culture or education. The *Tao* is that from which one cannot for an instant depart. That from which one may depart is not *Tao*. Wherefore it is that the superior man watches over what his eyes cannot see, and is in fear and awe of what his ears cannot hear."[11]

These sayings certainly allude not only to rules of human life, but also to something which goes beyond the senses, that is, to something metaphysical.

Later, in the same book is the comment: "The *Tao* according to the superior man is to be found everywhere, and yet it is a secret. The simple intelligence of ordinary men and women may understand something of the *Tao;* but in its utmost reaches there is something which even the wisest and holiest of men cannot understand."[12] Then elsewhere in the *Chung-yung* is a remark reminding one of Aristotle's Unmoved Mover: "The truth is what completes itself. The *Tao* is what goes of itself."[13]

My translation of these last two sentences may appear strange to the reader accustomed to the renditions of Ku Hun-ming or Legge; but it is completely true to the Chinese text. This becomes evident when the reader compares it with the following passage:

"The absolute truth is unceasing. Being unceasing, it is everlasting. Being everlasting, it is self-evident. Being self-evident, it is eternal. Being eternal, it is vast and deep. Being vast and deep, it is transcendental and intelligent. Because it is vast and deep it can become the ground for all existence. Because it is transcendental and intelligent it can embrace all existence. Because it is eternal, it perfects all existence. In vastness and depth it is like the earth. In transcendental intelligence it is like heaven. Eternal, it is the infinite itself.

"Such being the absolute truth, it manifests itself without being seen; it produces changes without motion; it accomplishes its ends without action."

"Thus the *Tao* of heaven and earth may be summed up in one brief characterization — it obeys only its own immutable law, and the way in which it produces the variety of things is unfathomable."[14]

Obviously, as the preceding passage shows, the *Chung-yung* did not confine itself to the rules of practical life, but speculated on the nature and work of heaven. Speculation of this sort was very near Lao-tzu's idea that *Tao* is the sponsor of all creation. It also approaches the Western idea of the Absolute. Interestingly enough, when the Sung philosophers reached the conclusion that Chinese philosophy must be recast on a more speculative basis it was to the *Chung-yung* that they turned, as containing the very concepts which

they believed should be clarified. Thus it was that the Ch'eng brothers took out the chapter *Chung-yung,* from the *Book of Rites* and
set it up as an independent treatise. They also extracted the chapter
Ta-hsüeh. The idea of recasting Chinese philosophy was not derived
from the *Chung-yung,* rather the *Chung-yung,* because it contained
similar ideas, was adapted by the Ch'eng brothers for their own
purpose.

When, in the Sung dynasty, the teaching of the Confucian
school was revived, the philosophers who revived it — the exponents
of Neo-Confucianism — made *Tao* or *Ri* (*reason*) the highest concept of their philosophical speculation.

In Chu Hsi's *Reflective Thoughts,* a collection of the remarks
of the Sung philosophers, the first chapter, entitled: *The Reality
of Tao or Tao Itself,* is devoted to first principles. For instance,
the first principle of reality is the foundation for the ethical life,
theory of knowledge, and government. This arrangement represents a reform in methodology, and in fact it effected a complete
change in the structure of philosophy. Whereas, Confucius and
Mencius had always begun their lessons by a discussion of the
rules of practical life, the Sung philosophers began their lessons
with a discourse on the reality of *Tao* — something which Confucius and Mencius had never done, as we know from the complaints
of their disciples. Why did the Sung philosophers alter this tradition? The answer is that since the Buddhists taught that the world
is an illusion, the thinkers of the Sung Dynasty had to have a counterproposal.

Following this first chapter of *Reflective Thoughts* about the
Reality of Tao, Chu Hsi continued with a chapter entitled: *Way
of Approach or Way of Learning,* which dealt with the supremacy of
virtue, inspiration for the attainment of Sagehood, and *largesse de
coeur.* Part of this section is the *Western Inscription* of Chang Tsai.
Here let it be emphasized again that Chu Hsi's approach to philosophy was radically different from that of Confucius because the
former took his departure from the fundamental principle of the
universe.

More interesting still is the inclusion of Chou Tun-i's *Diagram
of the Supreme Ultimate* in the early part of Chu Hsi's *Reflective
Thoughts.* "The great expanse of heaven," he said, "is soundless and

without smell, but in the ante-manifestation stage lies the seed of all existences and all transformations. It is traceless and inexpressible, yet it is the absolute to which nothing can be added."[15] As we know, this great philosopher regarded the Supreme Ultimate as the highest reason, which is incorporeal or metaphysical. In short, I believe, *Tao* is the equivalent of the Greek *Logos*, because *Tao* means truth, reality, the cosmic process, the life-principle. *Tao* is the same as that which, in the West, is repeatedly described in the words: "There is one *Logos*, the same throughout the world, which is itself homogeneous and one. This wisdom we may win by searching within ourselves; it is open to all men to know themselves and be wise."

As has already been mentioned, Ch'eng Hao achieved the discovery of *Ri* (reason) which for him consisted in the juxtaposition of opposites, such as motion and rest, *Yin* and *Yang*, the One and the Many; and since the Sung Dynasty, the terms *Tao* and *Ri* have been interchangeable. *Tao* is the general concept; *Ri* the more specific. Chu Hsi in his explanation of the Supreme Ultimate called it the highest reason. Thus *Ri* becomes the highest general concept, and there is clear evidence that *Tao* and *Ri* are mutually interchangeable. Indeed, I may say without exaggeration that *Tao* or *Ri* as mentioned earlier in this chapter is both the uniformity of nature and the divine will of heaven, or God. *Tao* or *Ri* suggests the universal reason of the Stoics.

Affirmation of the Phenomenal World. So much for the first point, *Tao* as reality. We come now to the second point, a contribution by the Neo-Confucianists which resulted from their reaction to the Buddhist idea that the world is an illusion. The question was: Is the world real or unreal?

The theory of world-illusion is based upon the Buddhist doctrine of *Svabhavasunyata* or *Nissvabhavah* that a thing has no self-essence. Instead each thing is made of five *Skandas* (aggregates). In Chinese this teaching is called *Wu-tzu-hsing* (no self-essence or no self-substance), the last word *(hsing)* also meaning nature. Chinese scholars misunderstood the question as having to do with nature. In reality, the original Sanskrit meant "no self-substance", "no self-essence". But the Chinese scholars erroneously turned the discussion towards nature, and then carried it even farther into human nature. This Chinese precedure was no doubt anomalous, but the result was a discussion which involved the whole universe; whether the universe is Being and Reality, or Non-being and Non-reality. In the end, for the Chinese the problem became: Should the world be affirmed or negated?

Chang Tsai in his theory of the Great Harmony said that the world is made of ether. It is being, not emptiness. He tried to show that even in a void there is matter, so that nothing in the universe can be called a void. However, neither Chu Hsi nor the Ch'eng brothers agreed with Chang Tsai that creation was based upon a material element. On the contrary, Chu Hsi greatly appreciated Chou Tun-i's *Diagram of the Supreme Ultimate,* because it presupposed a stage of nothingness, which turned out to be the fountain of manifoldness. In other words, this *Diagram* presented a picture in which the Divine Will of God created the world of being. The idea is the same as the first step of the dialectical development in Hegel's Logic, where Being and Nothing are intermediated by Becoming — a conception implied in Chou Tun-i's Diagram.

Now the *Diagram of the Supreme Ultimate* was nothing more than a counterproposal to the Buddhist doctrine of the world as illusion, or of the five *Skandas* as imagination. In this counterproposal, furthermore, was embedded the *Tao* as Divine Reason immanent in the cosmic process and directed towards a rational and moral end in the realm of human existence. So it becomes clear, at last, how in Chinese thought the question of no self-essence became the problem of reality, and thence spread into the field of human nature.

The Chinese philosophers made the observation that men are endowed with knowing, willing and loving, so that they must apply these gifts to life and to human relations in general. Knowing, willing and loving are in their very essence affirmative, so that they must belong to the natural order of men who dwell in a world of reality — not in a dream-world of illusion. The early exponents of Sung philosophy clung to the theory of the four virtues as the fundamental forms of thought behind the world and human life.

But they also had to account for the existence of evil in human nature. In the old days there had been a dispute between Mencius who held that human nature is good, and Hsün-tzu who maintained that it is bad. Chang Tsai made a distinction between two kinds of human nature — the kind that belonged to the physical side only and the kind that had to do with essence. This latter kind was reason, which is the gift of heaven, whereas the former was tied up to flesh and desire. Chang Tsai's theory implied that evil is not rooted in the spirit, but is associated with matter. This doctrine resolved the question once for all into whether man is by nature good or evil, and Chang Tsai in this respect, was highly regarded, by Chu Hsi, who said of him: "The controversy is settled by him forever."[16]

Besides making this counter-proposal to the Buddhist doctrine of world-illusion, the Sung philosophers tackled the problem of *hsing* (human nature) and emphasised the role of *hsin* (mind), which is close to *hsing*. Because of their proclivity for saying "Yea" to life and the universe they postulated that reason or the Categorical Imperative is born with man. The existence of the four cardinal virtues: *Jen, I, Li,* and *Chih,* was the best proof of this. But they considered reason to exist on a higher level. For example, the virtue *Jen,* according to the Chu Hsi school, is the reason for love, which is intrinsically good. Love, on the other hand, remains at a natural or lower level, tied up with human sense. This means that the sensory function of mind and consciousness is to contact the natural world, *i.e.,* to operate at a level lower than that where reason holds sway. This dualistic theory of human nature and mind was an open attack on Buddhism. It showed one, that Buddhism does not recognize the existence of cosmic reason which appears in a form of categorical imperative — a failure of recognition which resulted from the Buddhistic disbelief in the reality of the world. The Neo-Confucianist theory of two natures showed secondly that the Buddhist conception of mind was inadequate, because it took into consideration only the function of mind at the natural level, and was wholly ignorant of the higher level of reason.

However, in spite of the importance attached to *hsing* by the Chinese scholars, and less stress on mind, scholars have understood since the days of Confucius and Mencius that mind plays a vital role. Confucius and Mencius both knew that the work of the mind is to think.

Mencius especially knew well the function of the mind. But in spite of this, the Chinese mind went into a state of stagnation at the beginning of the Former Han Dynasty, and did not begin to work actively until the introduction of Buddhism into China. But the first period produced nothing original because it was absorbed in the work of translation and learning. It was the thinkers of the Ch'an school who first emphasized the mind. "You are the Buddha," they said. "You and the Buddha are one. The Buddha is living in you."[17] It was the Ch'an thinkers who succeeded in again making the Chinese scholars conscious of the great importance of mind.

In a special chapter of the *T'ung-shu* (*Comprehensive Understanding*) Chou Tun-i said that thinking is the foundation of sagehood. In the Chinese sense, thinking is not limited to the logical process, but is extended to include concern with right or wrong in the moral sense. The author of the *Philosophical Records of the Sung and Yüan Dynasties* was of the opinion that this chapter on thinking in the *T'ung-shu* is like the eye of the picture of a dragon, which means that it is the most vital part of the whole picture. Later, Ch'eng I came to compare knowing with a light beckoning a traveler. Just as without light one could not go far, so without knowing one cannot start doing anything. Chu Hsi, following Ch'eng I, placed maximum importance on the role of knowledge, proving that he was fully appreciative of how much is involved in the cognitive functions of the mind. This appreciation proved the greatest stimulus the Sung philosophers received from the Ch'an thinkers.

When the development of this new philosophy came into the hands of Lu Chiu-yüan and Wang-Shou-jen, they abandoned the two-level theory. Theirs was a new formula: "Mind is reason", which was a way of saying that reason is not confined to a higher level, but that in one and the same mind it works both ways, that is, transcendentally and naturally. These two philosophers attributed both logical awareness and awareness of the morally right and wrong to mind — a standpoint which would have been impossible had the way not been paved by the Ch'an school. It goes without saying, of course, that Liu and Wang applied the Ch'an theory of mind only on methodology, and did not follow the Ch'an doctrine of the world as illusion. Here we reach a stage where the Sung philosophy was hardly distinguishable from the Ch'an theory of mind *minus* the theory of emptiness. The Chinese scholars were eminently successful in extracting the best part of Ch'an thought without compromising their own tradition.

As a reaction against Wang Shou-jen there was at the end of the Ming Dynasty and during the Ch'ing Dynasty a counter-movement: "Back to the Classics!" and "Back to Chu Hsi!" which demanded a more positive foundation for philosophy. This "Back to Chu Hsi!" movement was only an aftermath and not the first crop of Neo-Confucianism. It is interesting to note that while Wang Shou-jen's philosophy was on the decline in China, it was transplanted to Japan during the seventeenth century by Nakae Toji, and continued until the middle of the nineteenth century when some of its adherents took an active part in the Meiji Reformation.

In this whole period, from Han Yü (A.D. 781-824) down to Tseng Kuo-fan (1811-1872), which lasted about one thousand years, Chinese philosophical thinking centered around Neo-Confucianism. It is an intellectual heritage which is not only worth studying in and of itself, and a knowledge of its contents and their implications may well prove useful in creating an understanding between the East and the West as well as the spiritual integration of the world.

References

1. *P.R.S.Y.*, Book 13, Ch'eng Hao.
2. *Chung-yung*, Chapter 1.
3. *Lun-yü*, Book 4, Chapter 5.
4. *Ibid.*, Book 7, Chapter 6.
5. *Meng-tzu*, Book 6, Part 2, Chapter 2.
6. *Ibid.*, Book 2, Part 2, Chapter 2.
7. *Ibid.*, Book 3, Part 1, Chapter 5.
8. *Ibid.*, Book 4, Part 1, Chapter 1.
9. *Ibid.*, Book 4, Part 1, Chapter 11.
10. *Ibid.*, Book 6, Part 1, Chapter 6.
11. *Chung-yung*, Chapter 1.
12. *Ibid.*, Chapter 12.
13. *Ibid.*, Chapter 25.
14. *Ibid.*, Chapter 26.
15. Chu Hsi (ed.), *Chin-ssu-lu* (Reflective thoughts), T'ai-chi t'u-chieh (Commentary on the Diagram of the Supreme Ultimate).
16. *P.R.S.Y.*, Book 17, Chang Tsai. Chu Hsi's valuation of the two kinds of nature is to be found here.
17. Words of this kind are common to all Ch'anists in the first period. *Cf.* the Lu-tsu t'an-ching (T'an-ching of the Sixth Patriarch).

CHAPTER THREE

Institutions
according to the School
of the Philosophy of Reason

The present chapter will describe the institutions which grew out of or were supported by the Sung school of philosophy. Institutions, it may be said, do not necessarily have any connection with philosophy, but in this case many institutions were suggested by the school, and had their roots in the basic ideas of Neo-Confucianism. For example, the principle that good government is dependent upon rectification of mind and realization of true will, took many practical forms.

Neo-Confucianism covered many subjects: cosmology, metaphysics, epistemology, ethics, psychology. These constituted its theorectical side. But Neo-Confucianism also had a practical side, by which it laid down a pattern of life which dominated China from the Sung Dynasty until her contact with the West. What was this pattern? It may be summarized under five headings: (1) *Tao-t'ung* (Line of Succession of the *Tao*); (2) A science of sagehood, which reflected the influence of the bodhisattva; (3) Canonical books; (4) A new kind of academy, which came into existence in every district; (5) A program of governmental and public administration. These five headings stand for five types of institutions, by means of which Neo-Confucianism was able to exert profound practical influence on Chinese society for many centuries.

(1) *Tao-t'ung*.

This line of succession bears a certain analogy to the idea of Apostolic Succession of certain Christian denominations. Or to explain it in another way: In Europe, if a philosopher builds a system, another philosopher is free to develop it in whatever direction his thought may lead him. Thus, Kant founded a system, but Fichte, Schelling and Hegel went beyond Kant. In China, however, a system is more rigid. Take the case of Neo-Confucianism, for instance, which we may regard as the end-product of a line of succession which can be traced back to Mencius. Mencius initiated two criteria, defining the thought to be transmitted thereafter in the orthodox line of succession. These criteria were: (1) Yao and Shun are the symbols of ideal rulers, much like the Philosopher-Kings in the Platonic sense. (2) Human nature must be judged to be good. If a philosopher in later ages deviated from either of these criteria, he was not admitted into the Temple of Confucius, which meant that he did not belong in the orthodox line of succession. An example of one who deviated from the second criterion was the celebrated philosopher Hsün-tzu, who taught that human nature is evil. An example of one who ran counter to the first criterion was Ch'en Liang (1143-1194) who admired emperors of the Han and T'ang Dynasties, as well as Yao and Shun. Chu Hsi dismissed him as unworthy of being called a Confucianist.

The *Tao-t'ung* theory was first formulated by the scholar Han Yü of the T'ang Dynasty, whom I shall present later in more detail as a precursor of Neo-Confucianism. "Yao," said Han Yü, "handed this line of succession down to Shun. Shun handed it down to Yü. Yü handed it down to T'ang. T'ang handed it down to King Wen and King Wu and to the Duke of Chou who in turn handed it down to Confucius. Confucius transmitted it to Mencius. After the death of Mencius, this line of succession was cut off. Hsun-tzu and Yang Hsiung knew how to choose, but they were not painstaking enough. They could talk, but they were not thoroughgoing."[1]

Chu Hsi also had some interesting comments to make about *Tao-t'ung*. "After the death of Mencius," he said, "the *Tao* of the

Sages was not handed down. Scholars occupied themselves with writing in fine literary style, and in mixing their knowledge with the theories of Lao-tzu and the Buddha. Moreover, their way of personal cultivation and governmental administration was motivated by their own selfish interests. There was thus a great departure from the orthodox path. Therefore, the virtue of the emperors never reached the height of the period of the Three Dynasties, nor could the conduct and quality of the people reach the standards of those dynasties. This continued for more than a thousand years.

"After an interval of many generations, Chou Lien-hsi (Chou Tun-i) suddenly came on the scene. He sought the mysteries of the sages and wise men, and studied the origin of creation. He discovered something original, which he expressed in his books, even though he could only describe in outline the mysteries over which he pondered. Nonetheless, the abstruse topics of the destiny and nature of human life and of self-cultivation and public administration, were complete in his outline. Then came the two Ch'eng brothers, who knew Chou Tun-i personally, and who received what he handed down. Chou's theory prevailed. Now the scholars could free themselves from the vulgarity of ordinary essay writing, and the enticements of the heretics. Henceforth, personal cultivation and public administration went beyond the mere acquisition of selfish ends and aspired towards the ideal kingship of Yao and Shun. Such was the contribution of these three masters."[2]

Immediately after Chou Tun-i and the Ch'eng brothers came Chu Hsi in the line of succession. There were also many others whose tablets were placed in the Temple of Confucius by decrees of the emperors of the various dynasties.

The Chinese conception of *Tao* is based upon a system of ethical values which in addition to being discussed in the writings of philosophers was supposed also to be actualized in the good government of Yao and Shun, and in the exemplary lives of Confucius, Mencius and Chu-Hsi. Every sage, whether he was an emperor like Yao or Shun, or a scholar like Confucius, illuminated the *Tao* in his own way: the one in public administration, the other in his writings. The *Tao* itself is always considered as self-existent like the sun and the moon, but whether it shines or remains hidden depends upon the human beings who illuminate it.

(2) The Science of Sagehood.

After the main principles of the Sung school of philosophy were established, the school came to be known as the philosophy of sagehood, or of the quality of being wise. Its devotees emphasized that unless one rectified one's mind and realized the true will one would be unqualified to devote one's life to philosophy. This kind of life required unremitting devotion and determination to become a sage or a wise man. One must strive indefatigably to conform to the ideal of Confucius and Mencius.

Among the near disciples of Confucius was Yen Hui of whom it was said: "Yen Hui was nearly perfect, yet he was often empty,"[3] meaning that he had given up all his worldly goods. Ch'eng I, a founder of the Sung philosophy, when he went to take the state examination, was assigned the question: "What is the philosophy to which Yen Hui devoted himself?" In his answer, Ch'eng I elaborated on that worthy's self-abnegation and devotion to *Tao*, implying that anyone who wished to live according to the standards of Neo-Confucianism must relinquish all desire for high office or profit, and must look with contempt upon the pursuit of power and wealth.

Another qualification for admission to the school of the Sung philosophers was abandonment of the heresies of Lao-tzu and the Buddha. The Neo-Confucianists, though they had learned from the Ch'an thinkers, felt that in the Buddhist doctrines there was too much talk about calmness and emptiness; in other words, they believed that the Buddhists were over-zealous in their efforts to minimize the normal activities of life. Lao-tzu and the Buddha sought ideals too sublime and too remote from the scene of man's responsibilities.

The Sung philosophers were untiring in their explanations of how to attain sagehood. Chou Tun-i in his *T'ung shu* said: "A sage should aspire after the *Tao* of heaven. A wise man should aspire after sagehood. A scholar should aspire to be wise. I Yin and Yen Hui were two great wise men. I Yin felt it a personal disgrace if he could not make of his emperor a Yao or a Shun. Moreover he felt as if people had publicly slapped him whenever he found a common man to be destitute. This is the ideal pattern for one in public

office. Yen Hui was capable of such self-control that he never
visited his anger on another from whom he had received injury.
Also he never repeated a fault. His behavior was such that he would
not deviate from the principle of *Jen* for a period of three months.
In aspiration one should emulate I Yin; in scholarship and philosophy, one should emulate the self-control of Yen Hui. If one can go
beyond these two, one will be a sage; if one can only equal them,
one will be a wise man; and if one lags behind them, one will at
least have a good name."⁴

This enthusiasm for seeking after sagehood and wisdom was
kept alive among the Neo-Confucianists from Chou Tun-i to the
last of his followers.

Chou Tun-i's pupil, Ch'eng I, also made some interesting comments on how to achieve sagacity and wisdom. "It will be all in vain
if learning leads to no awakening," said Ch'eng I; "when one begins to study and learns how to think, one will be on the road to
sagehood."⁵ He added: "In ancient times there was only one kind
of study. At present there are three, even if we omit the heretical
schools: namely, literature, philosophy, and Confucianism. If one
wishes to attain to *Tao* one will find the study of the Confucianists
the right course to follow."⁶

Yin Shun, a disciple of Chu Hsi, makes twenty-one suggestions
about how to achieve sagehood. "Is sagehood learnable?" he asked,
"Yes," was the answer. "Is there something essential?" "Yes. There
is one thing essential; desirelessness. When one is desireless, one
is calm and empty; and then when one acts one will follow a
straight way. Calmness and emptiness produce enlightenment.
With enlightenment comes a largeness of view. When one takes the
right course of action one will be objective and fair. When one is
enlightened and has breadth of view and when one is objective
and fair, one is near sagehood."⁷

Among the suggestions Yin Shun also wrote: "When will has
not come forth from your heart, when words have not come forth
from your mouth, even the spirits cannot find you out; and no person can blame you. Nevertheless, you should still be watchful over
yourself. You should observe the proper rules. When you are alone
in the privacy of your room, you should do nothing to cause shame
even in the presence of rain-drops falling from the roof."

The Neo-Confucianists emphasized the importance and indispensability of learning in the effort to achieve sagehood. Thus, they pointed out that Confucius and Mencius were not born sages; they acquired sagacity by devotion to study — or, as we should say today, by "book learning." Sagehood has nothing to do with supernatural knowledge; it is attainable by reading and reflection.

The innumerable homilies of the Sung philosophers on sagehood reminds one of the faith of the Bodhisattva:

> "Perceiving all in one,
> And one in all,
> The Bodhisattva diligent in his work
> Is never given to indolence.
> Pain he shuns not, to pleasure he clings not,
> For he is ever bent on the deliverance of all beings;
> To him all Buddhas will themselves reveal,
> And of their presence he is never weary.
> He is in the profoundest depth of the Dharma
> Where is found the inexhaustible ocean of merit.
> All sentient beings in the fivefold path of existence
> He loves as he does his own child,
> Removing things unclean and filthy."[8]

For the Sung philosophers the two highest examples of personality were: Yen Hui who was full of wisdom, and I Yin who saved the people from misery. They exemplified the virtues of *Jen* and *I*, which are the counterparts or the Indian Buddhist virtues of *Karuna* (mercy) and *Prajna* (intelligence).

(3) Canonical books.

At first the philosophers of the Sung school spent their energy in groping for different aspects of the *Tao* or Ultimate Reality, the world we actually experience in our daily lives. They wrote much on these subjects. But it was soon discovered that their writings, being new, lacked sufficient cogency to hold the minds of the people. Hence the leaders of the school went back to the *Five Classics*, edited by Confucius and to the *Four Books*, in order to provide sanction for their teachings.

These *Five Classics* are the *Shu-ching* (*Book of History*), the *Shih-ching* (*Book of Poetry*), the *I-ching* (*Book of Changes*), the *Li-chi* (*Book of Rites*), and the *Ch'un-ch'iu* (*Spring and Autumn Annals*). Upon re-studying these works, the Sung philosophers felt that the time-honored classics did not provide a philosophical system. So eventually they had recourse to the *Four Books*. These became the canon of the school.

The Four Books are the *Lun-yu*, the *Meng-tzu*, the *Ta-hsueh* and the *Chung-yung*. The first two of these works were naturally included in the canon because they were by Confucius and Mencius. The last two were extracted by the Neo-Confucianists from the afore-mentioned *Li-chi* (*Book of Rites*). It is these last two which actually furnished the foundation for the complete philosophical system that the Neo-Confucianists hoped to build.

The canon of the Sung school included, in addition to the *Five Classics* and the *Four Books*, the commentaries of Chu Hsi, the Ch'eng brothers and others. It was necessary that these commentaries should not deviate too far from the original thought of Confucius, or from the other older scholars. But at the same time the commentaries had to support the principles of the new school. In other words, through the commentaries, the *Five Classics* and the *Four Books* became a reflection of the philosophical system of the Neo-Confucianists. The emperors who ruled in the first year of the Ming Dynasty went to the extent even of issuing decrees that only the commentaries of Chu Hsi and his school were authoritative, which meant that thereafter candidates at the state examinations had to base their essays on the interpretations of the Neo-Confucianists. This enhanced the prestige of Chu Hsi to the point where he became second only to Confucius himself. Whereas formerly there had been K'ung Fu-tzu (or Confucius) and Meng Fu-tzu (or Mencius), there was now also Chu Fu-tzu — "Fu-tzu" being an honorific term meaning Master or Teacher.

In the Sung Dynasty there originated the saying that "The *Four Books* are the stepping-stones to the *Five Classics*, and the *Chin-ssu-lu* (by Chu Hsi) is the stepping-stone to the *Four Books*." This reflects the position Chu Hsi had attained. Starting out to be merely a collection of the utterances of the founders of the Sung philosophy, the *Chin-ssu-lu* was raised to the level of the *Four Books* and the *Five Classics*. The title means "Record of Reflective Thoughts", and was incorrectly translated by J. P. Bruce as "Modern Thought".[9] Bruce must have been unaware that the two words "chin-ssu" are from *Lun-yu*: "When one studies wisely, is serious in will, questions to the point and reflects on what is near [i.e. nearest to one's personal life], herein lies the quality of *Jen*."[10] This "reflects on what is near" is the literary translation of "chin-ssu", and it means "reflection on one's self," or "reflective thoughts". The word "chin" has nothing to do with being modern.

But, to return from this brief digression, the *Chin-ssu-lu*, a collection of the sayings of the Sung philosophers, gives a comprehensive view of the subject matter and the systematic character of the Neo-Confucian philosophy. The table of contents of this work may interest the reader:

Book I.   Reality of *Tao*
   II.   The Way of Approach.
   III.   Realization of Knowledge.
   IV.   Nourishment of Mind.
   V.   Self-control.
   VI.   Principles of Family Life.
   VII.   Coming out (into public life).
         Remaining at Home (doing one's private business).
   VIII.   Essence of Government.
   IX.   Public Administration.
   X.   Principles of Civil Service.
   XI.   Education.
   XII.   Admonitions.
   XIII.   Ways of Discerning Heretical Schools.
   XIV.   Devotion to Sagehood and the Quality of being a Wise Man.

A characteristic of the *Chin-ssu-lu* is that it begins with the reality of *Tao*, which sets the work quite apart from the *Lun-yu* or the *Meng-tzu*. The latter two are discursive dialogues and discussions of various aspects of life. In other words, they do not present a philosophical system, whereas Chu Hsi's *Chin-ssu-lu* starts with ultimate reality and proceeds to self-cultivation, family life, public administration, etc. It is a systematic presentation, taking its departure from first principles and reaching conclusions on practical life.

The *Chin-ssu-lu* became in time one of the most prominent books of the Neo-Confucianist school. Anyone wishing to be a philosopher in the orthodox tradition had to study it and act according to it. Chu Hsi himself once remarked that this work must be the first book to be read. It remained so until comparatively recent times, for I vividly remember, in my own boyhood, seeing lovers of the *Chin-ssu-lu* reading it attentively with incense burning on their desks.

(4) Academies.

To be sure, schools existed in China long before the Sung Dynasty. But the academies founded by the Neo-Confucianists had peculiarities of their own, which distinguished them from all earlier institutions of learning. They were created in most cases by individual philosophers. Wherever a philosopher had assembled a group of students there grew up an academy. At first, there were not many; they could be seen on hill-tops, on the shores of a lake, in a forest or by a water-fall. They are said to have been originally patterned after the ashrams of the Indian Buddhist monks, who devoted their lives to study and dwelt in remote places. They also bear some slight resemblance to the monasteries of mediaeval Europe.

The aims and curricula of the Sung academies took form gradually, and often differed according to the original concepts of their founders. As long as the influence of the founder was still vividly fresh, his institution would be vigorous, often marked by hot discussions between champions of varying opinions. Later, the academies became governmental institutions: in each district there would be one or two of them, established for the benefit of the local scholars. It was then that the academies lost much of the earlier vigor. Their ultimate decline began about the time when China came in contact with the West.

Let us, however, return to the early days when the aims and policies of the new academies were first formulated by Chu Hsi and the other great philosophers of the period. Chu Hsi was appointed governor of Nan-k'ang (Kiangsi Province), and went to Lu-shan (Kuling), where he found a beautiful place called Pai-lu-tung (White Deer Grotto). A hermit had lived there in the T'ang Dynasty. He had been in the habit of sending a white deer to market to bring back his daily necessities — hence the name White Deer Grotto. Deeply impressed by the atmosphere of this grotto, Chu Hsi memorialized the Emperor for permission to establish an academy there and thus it acquired the name *Pai-lu-tung-Shu-yuan* (White Deer Grotto Academy). The emperor sent a gift of books and Chu Hsi obtained additional lands in the neighborhood, the rental from which he used to defray the cost of running the academy. A history of the *Pai-lu-tung-Shu-yuan* recorded the size of the estate, the properties rented as well as its income and expenditures. That academy was the prototype of the Neo-Confucianist academy.

Before proceeding to a consideration of the rules of the White Deer Grotto Academy, the reader should be reminded that the period we are now considering is the Eleventh Century of the Christian Era, when knowledge had not been placed in water-tight compartments. The instruction given was about one's personal life, one's family life, one's obligation to the government — in short, about moral values. If the reader keeps in mind this difference between the curriculum of the White Deer Grotto Academy and that of the modern university, he will understand the meaning of the rules which Chu Hsi drew up for his Academy. The rules were as follows:

SECTION I.

A. Between parents and children there should be love.

B. Between the emperor and his subjects there should be a proper sense of duties.

C. Between husband and wife there should be a certain separation in regard to work.

D. Between elder and younger persons there should be order and harmony.

E. Between friends there should be mutual confidence.

These were the injunctions of Yao and Shun to their prime ministers and were known as the Five Teachings. The methods of learning them were:

SECTION II.

- A. Study extensively.
- B. Inquire accurately.
- C. Think carefully.
- D. Analyse clearly.
- E. Put into practice earnestly.

The first four instructions aim at the investigation of principles. The last covers a wide field, beginning with personal cultivation and extending to one's relations with others and to one's duties as a public servant.

SECTION III.

- A. One's commitments to others should be characterized by loyalty and honesty.
- B. One's conduct should be characterized by seriousness and watchfulness.
- C. A man should control his indignation and diminish his desires.
- D. He should correct his mistakes and pay attention to do the good.

These are the principles of personal cultivation.

Then come the basic rules for participation in public affairs, namely:

SECTION IV.

- A. Ascertain what is right without any consideration of personal profit.
- B. Be enlightened by *Tao* without calculating the merits to be rewarded.

Finally, there are the principles governing relationships with others:

SECTION V.
A.   What you do not like for yourself do not do to others.
B.   When things go wrong, come back to yourself and reflect.

Such was the program of Chu Hsi's Academy. As already stated, this academy became the model for other academies, even though the philosophical opinions of the founders might differ from those of Chu Hsi. Thus, for instance, Lu-Chiu-yüan and Wang Shou-jen, as a result of their emphasis on the importance of the role of mind, modified their educational program to stress the theory that mind is reason. The Lu-Wang school opposing Chu Hsi's way for an elaborate list of readings made a direct appeal to mind. But in spite of such differences, the academy as an educational institution was greatly valued and warmly advocated by all Neo-Confucianist philosophers.

These thinkers, indeed, were at one in believing that education is the most important activity of public administration, for they knew that only through education could the people be enlightened. Accordingly, their curricula stressed moral education, and intellectual education in so far as it stimulated reading, arguing and theorizing, for moral education itself involves intellectual agility. Occasionally physical education in the form of archery, horsemanship and dancing was included. By moral education was meant rectification of the mind, realization of a true will, cultivation of the person, regulation of the family, government of the country, and peace of the world.

The purpose of education, according to the Neo-Confucianists, was to create a good moral climate among the people. But what had been and what still was required by the civil service examination was only the ability to write essays in the elegant literary style, and that, in the opinion of the Sung philosophers, was no education in the true sense of the word. Thus, the kind of education typified by Chu Hsi's White Deer Grotto Academy was a genuine innovation introduced for the purpose of arousing new convictions in the students and building up their character. Initiated in the Sung Dynasty, this novel kind of education persisted through the Yüan and Ming Dynasties, but unfortunately fell into disuse when China came into increasing contact with the West during the Ching Dynasty.

(5) Government.

The Neo-Confucianist school had an adequate *Weltanschauung,* comprising cosmology, theory of knowledge, and a view of human life. Just as it deduced its program of education from its world-view, so also it deduced its theories of government. It always talked in the name of Yao and Shun and the emperors of the Three Dynasties as affording the ideal pattern of government rule. Its program of government was so revolutionary that it had to represent these emperors as being trained like the Guardians of Plato's *Republic.* The ancient Chinese philosopher-kings were supposed to have cultivated their persons by rectifying their minds and realizing their true will, so that they understood the needs of the people. Whether these emperors really existed is not an important question, but in the *Shu-ching* one finds their maxims and their advice about how to purify the heart, and how to unify the mind with the highest good. In actual administration, the Sung philosphers of course knew that they could not confine themselves to experiences recorded in the ancient *Classics,* but that they must pay attention to the needs and circumstances of the moment.

A memorial by Ch'eng Hao on a proposed government program designed to benefit the people is as good an example as any to illustrate the Neo-Confucianist theory of government.

(I). *Imperial tutor.* Although an emperor has absolute power, still he should give heed to the ideas of others. This will enable him to avoid blindness and bias.

(II). *Six ministries.* Governmental organization in China may be traced to ancient times when there were six departments, viz.: (1) the prime-ministership, the function of which was to co-ordinate all the organs of government; (2) the department of military defense; (3) of justice; (4) of ceremonies; (5) of food; and (6) of education. In Ch'eng Hao's view the governmental organization of his own day had to be reformed, so as to bring it in line with this ancient pattern. It had become so confused and inefficient that the people suffered.

(III). *Land survey and food distribution.* Our philosopher pointed out that the people can live only when they have enough land to cultivate. Hence a clear cadastral survey to show property rights, and a fair distribution of land were necessary. He regretted that the ancient institution of parceling land and allotting it to each man as his private property had been discontinued after the T'ang Dynasty. In his own time, Ch'eng Hao added, the rich owned large estates, covering vast areas, whereas the poor did not have enough property even to bore a hole in the ground.

(IV). *Local government.* In agreement with the Chinese proverb that good rule begins in the rural area, Ch'eng Hao believed that government should emanate from the villages. These small settlements were based upon various kinds of groupings, according to family name, profession, or neighborhood. Our philosopher was especially impressed with the idea that such groupings make possible mutual concern in ethical matters, sickness, famine, flood, etc. It is precisely because of the healthy moral climate which such reciprocal interests generate that the village should serve as the foundation for government.

(V). *Elective system.* Voting and polls did not, of course, exist in the Sung period, but at one time in China there was something approaching an election. Anyone regarded as a good and capable man could be recommended by the people of his district to be sent to the capital to participate in political affairs. This plan of popular recommendation of officials for some reason later disappeared, suspended perhaps by the development of formal examinations. "Now-a-days," said Ch'eng Hao, "the selection of men is not based upon popular recommendation, and those who attend the examinations are not well prepared for this kind of service. There is consequently a decline in the number of capable men in the government."

(VI). *Military service.* In ancient times military service consisted of occasional employment of peasants or farmers, who after their period of service returned to their labors. No separate or independent military class existed. Ch'eng Hao observed, however, that in his time the soldiers had become separated from the farmers and assumed a tyrannical, overbearing attitude, and did nothing productive — a situation which he deplored. He advocated merging the soldiers with the farmers.

(VII). *Food.* Ch'eng Hao favored a policy of storing food. In ancient times, the practice had been to lay aside every three years enough for one year, thus at the end of thirty years accumulating enough for nine years. A government without three years' storage was bound to fail. Our philosopher, describing the contrast between his own day and that of ancient times, said: "At present robbers thrive in agricultural areas, and the weak suffer and die. When a wide-spread famine continues year after year, and there is no storage, what are the people to do? What can they live on?" He advocated a return to the ancient system of grain storage. In matters of such vital importance, it was wrong to leave anything to chance, he felt.

(VIII). *The Four Professions.* According to Ch'eng Hao there should be in any country four classes of people, or, in other words, four occupations: scholars, farmers, craftsmen or artisans, and tradesmen. If this were so, every man should have a way of successfully earning his living. Farmers should comprise 80 or 90 percent of the total population, for then food and clothing would be well supplied, and there would be no suffering among the people. "But," said Ch'eng Hao, again comparing his time with antiquity, "in the capital nowadays are more than one million unemployed persons, who owing to their poverty may become rogues." Ch'eng recommended that the urban population be reduced by sending large numbers of people back to the rural communities.

(IX). *Natural resources.* By natural resources Ch'eng meant what we mean today: forests, wild animals, fish, etc. He advocated a conservation program whereby the various resources would be exploited only at the proper seasons. Otherwise, natural wealth would be prematurely exhausted. Like our modern conservationists, he lamented the wasteful destruction of the forests by fire and cutting, and the useless slaughter of game.

(X). *Expenditures to accord with status in life.* Our philosopher believed that confirmations, weddings, funerals, sacrificial offerings, clothing, carriages, furniture and other utensils should be in harmony with one's position in life. If all men were moderate in these respects, more resources would be left for society at large. He declared that in his own day etiquette and ceremonies were not properly observed, and that people vied with one another in extravagance. Wealthy tradesmen spent more money than high officials — an intemperate show that was certain to cause disorder.[12]

From these ten items of a proposed program for government, one may see how much Ch'eng Hao stressed the welfare of the people. The public interest was, for him, the starting-point of administration. He attached especial importance to fair distribution of land and ample supply of food among his fellow-countrymen.

It is interesting to note that when Chu Hsi was appointed governor of Nan-k'ang [Kiangsi] he tried to put part of Ch'eng Hao's program into practice. What he wished to do first of all was to set right the distribution of land by a cadastral survey, and to prepare for possible famine by putting food storage into effect. Then he wanted to take in surplus grain, while the price was cheap, in order to adjust it at a certain parity. This phase of Chu Hsi's policy, however, was less in accord with Ch'eng Hao's ten points than with the theories of Wang An-shih, a reformer-statesman of the Sung Dynasty who had sponsored many economic novelties, such as farm credit, grain storage, and the ever-normal granary. Wang An-shih's theories implied too much regimentation to be popular in China, and they aroused the opposition of both the government and the scholars, including the Neo-Confucianists. Nevertheless, Chu Hsi in Nan-k'ang tried out some of the ideas of Wang An-shih, and even commented that though the reformer-statesman might be wrong in other respects, at least his farm credit and ever-normal granary schemes were sound, and should not be contested. Chu Hsi wrote an essay about this last proposal, explaining why it should be instituted for the good of the people.

Thus far my discussion of the Neo-Confucianist theory of political administration has been on the functions of the central government. The Sung school also drew a blue-print of local government called the *Rural Contract,* which bore to Chinese local government an analogous relation to that which Rousseau's *Social Contract* bears to democratic government in the West.

The first man to promote the idea of *Rural Contract,* and to put it into practical effect with good moral results, was a friend of Chu Hsi named Lu Ta-chün. The reader will have a clearer idea of this conception if he remembers that local government in China was different from local government in the West, which concerns itself with the regulation of legal, political and economic matters, such as road building, police, tax rate, etc. Local government in China was concerned (1) with exchange of advice about moral conduct, (2) mutual admonition in case of mistake, (3) observance of etiquette in social intercourse, *e.g.,* courtesy calls and attendance at weddings, and funerals, (4) mutual help in emergencies, *e.g.* fires, flood, robbery, sickness, destitution. The *Rural Contract* involved the idea that everybody should help everybody else.

This conception of Lu Ta-chün had vitality, and it lasted, with revisions to meet changing circumstances, down until the time of the Ming Dynasty, when Wang Shou-jen as governor of Kiangsi Province, modified it in order to make it applicable to the southern part of the province. Even then it remained the same in principle.

Wang Shou-jen set forth his version of the *Rural Contract* in a foreword in which he emphasized the importance of the influence of community-environment on the conduct of people. If a man deserts his family and becomes a bandit, the fault should not be laid entirely to him. Chiefly the blame should go to the officials who failed to provide adequate education for the evil-doer, to the village-elders who did not give him timely warning, and to his neighbors and companions who fell short of inducing him to do good. The *Rural Contract* which Wang Shou-jen envisaged was an arrangement by which country people could be brought together under a moral obligation to be friendly towards each other, to give mutual aid in emergencies, to avoid law-suits — in short, to behave themselves and to avoid evil.

Wang Shou-jen's draft describing the organization of the *Rural Contract* called for: (1) a president, (2) two vice-presidents, (3) four judges of the moral conduct of the members of the *Contract,* (4) four secretaries, (5) four executive secretaries, (6) two men in charge of protocol. The draft recommended the keeping of three books: (1) a book listing the members of the *Contract* with annotations concerning their conduct, kept by the executive secretaries. (2) and (3) books recording the good and bad deeds respectively of the members of the *Contract,* kept by the president. The former of these last two books, the one recording the virtuous acts, should be explicit and definite. The latter should be moderate and subtle in its terminology.

Any person joining the *Contract* had the privilege of submitting difficult questions to the community. The president would then bring the questions up at a conference, for the purpose of working out a practical settlement in accordance with the principles of rectitude. Wang Shou-jen's draft emphasized that the president and judges of the *Contract* should never shun their responsibilities in determining such questions, because otherwise they would lead the members into error.

Tardiness in paying taxes; stealing oxen, horses, etc.; and seeking revenge should be prohibited. Members of the same *Contract* should see to it that when their sons and daughters reach marriageable age they marry, and that parents should not demand excessive dowries. Too much money should not be spent on one's parent's funeral.

Wang Shou-jen's draft went into considerable detail as to procedure at meetings of the *Contract.* At such convocations, the president should read aloud the articles of the *Contract,* and advise the members to observe them seriously and sincerely. Insincerity in these matters might well bring punishment down upon one's head from the gods. After the reading, the members should stand and express their approval. Then, the four secretaries should go to a place convenient for recording good deeds, for publicly informing wrong-doers of their mistakes, and for giving the latter the opportunity of self-defense. Following these serious functions there should be a feast. At the conclusion of the feast, the president should rise and say: "If one has done a good deed, and if one's name is thereby recommended at this gathering, the occasion is no doubt very happy. Nevertheless, if one as a result becomes too self-righteous, this attitude is likely to lead to mistakes. If, on the other hand, one has committed a misdeed, and one is thereby admonished at the meeting. Nevertheless, if one repents and reforms, this attitude can lead to virtuous conduct. Therefore, those who have done good should not be overly elated, and those who have done ill should not think of themselves as irrevocably wicked."[13]

In modern times, the *Rural Contract* of Lu Ta-chün and Wang Shou-jen became a means for advising people about how to become good citizens.

* * * *

When Neo-Confucianism began to evolve its system it soon showed signs of crystalizing into peculiar modes of behavior, into definite political attitudes, and into codes for evaluating character and institutions. This phase of its development resulted in a certain exclusiveness, and in a sense of uneasiness at mixing with outside personalities and schools. Thus, for example, one of the great founders of Neo-Confucianism, Ch'eng I, was regarded as an arch-enemy by the school of Wang An-shih, which was in political power during Ch'eng I's day. Also the followers of Su Ch'e [Su Tung-p'o] were suspicious of the Sung philosophers.

This antagonism between the Neo-Confucianists and the authorities was well illustrated at a later date in the relationship between the great Neo-Confucianist synthizer, Chu Hsi, and two officials, Ch'ing Kuei and Ts'ai Chin, of the Southern Sung Dynasty. These officials favored a peace-policy towards the Tartars of Northern China, while the philosopher insisted upon a firmer attitude. As a result, Ts'ai Chin persecuted the followers of Chu Hsi as championing a false philosophy.

During the Sung Dynasty, there were two more or less systematic persecutions of the Neo-Confucianist school, the chief targets of which were its heads, namely, Ch'eng I of the Northern Sung and Chu Hsi of the Southern Sung. But others also suffered, including prime ministers and ministers who were not actually followers of the school. Two blacklists were drawn up by the authorities; one called the *Yüan-yu Black List* (A.D. 1087) and the other the *Ch'ing-yüan Black List* (1195).

The followers of the Sung philosophy, however, had a calmness of mind which enabled them to face persecutions with equanimity. Ch'eng I, before his death, advised his disciples not to attend his funeral services. "Follow my doctrine", he said, "and put it into practice. That is enough for me." He knew, in other words, that a great attendance at his funeral would be only a show, and would do no good to the cause. A similar story of fortitude is told of Chu Hsi. After his name had become well-known he was granted an audience by the emperor, and would have been elevated to a very high post if the minister in power at the time, Han T'o Chou, had not been jealous of him, and had not accused the philosophers of the *Tao-hsüeh* of being guilty of false teaching. Consequently, Chu Hsi had to beg permission to withdraw from the court. Han T'o Chou, not content with the damage he had already done, issued an order prohibiting all assemblage for philosophical discussion, and Chu Hsi with fifty-eight others was blacklisted three years later (1198).

In spite of persecution, the Sung school fufilled its mission of completing the revival of Confucianism. Members were prepared to suffer, and thus, Wen T'ien-hsiang died when the Mongols imprisoned him, and in the last days of the Ming Dynasty, many Neo-Confucianists were sacrificed in the cause of the dynasty. Others who were not of sufficient importance to die, did their best to preserve the spirit of loyalty. Such a man was Huang Chung-hsi, author of the *Sung Yüan hsüeh-an* and the *Ming-ju hsüeh-an,* who made many attempts to save the Ming from the Manchus, and who swore an oath never to serve under a foreign dynasty. He never did! Other Neo-Confucianists, for instance, Wang Shou-jen and Tseng Kuo-fan, were sufficiently fortunate to live in better times. The former, though he was once exiled for opposing a eunuch named Liu Chin lived to become governor of Kiangsi province, and to wage a victorious struggle against a rebel prince. Wang was the most successful statesman of all the Neo-Confucianists. Tseng Kuo-fan, who lived towards the close of the Ch'ing Dynasty carried out a campaign against the T'ai-Ping rebels as successful as his predecessor's military exploit in the service of the Ming.

In success or failure, the Neo-Confucianist philosophers abided faithfully by their convictions. In private study, in government service, during national disaster, when the regime was toppling, they remained courageous. They also met philosophical opposition. For example, towards the end of the Ming, Ku Yen-wu attacked Wang Shou-jen's system as too full of empty talk about *hsing* (human nature) and *hsin* (mind). Ku, in fact, blamed the fall of the Ming on the metaphysical vaporizings of the Neo-Confucianists. Also, Yen Yüan in the Ming Dynasty condemned the Sung school for being too much preoccupied with meditation, and for not paying enough attention to the practical arts like archery, and horsemanship which would have been useful in fighting the Manchus. But in spite of all antagonism, whether political or doctrinal, the Sung philosophers succeeded in reviving Confucianism, and in laying the foundations of Chinese spiritual life for the period from Han Yü down to Tseng Kuo-fan — a period of a thousand years. Not the least of the achievements of Neo-Confucianism was that it gave its followers the strength to face bravely the calamities at the end of the Sung and Ming Dynasties.

References

1. Han Yü *Collected Works,* Book 11, *Vid.*: the essay Yuan Tao (Inquiry into Tao). Hereafter this work will be referred to as *Han Yü*).

2. *Cheng-i t'ang ch'uan-shu* (Cheng-i t'ang Collectanea), *Chu-tzu wen-chi* (Collected Essays of Chu Hsi), Book 9, Dedication to the Temple of Three Teachers in Yuan-chou District Academy.

3. *Lun-yü*, Book 11, Chapter 18.

4. *P.R.S.Y.*, Book 11, Chou Tun-i.

5. *Cheng-i t'ang Collectanea, Erh-ch'eng yu-lu* (Dialogues of the Ch'eng Brothers).

6. *Loc. cit.*

7. *Ibid.*, Collected Essays of Yin Shun.

8. D. T. Suzuki, *Outlines of Mahayana Buddhism,* Luzac and Company, London, 1907, p. 401.

9. J. P. Bruce, *Chu Hsi and His Masters,* Probsthain and Co., London, 1923, pp. (xiii), 74.

10. *Lun-yu,* Book 19, Chapter 6.

11. *P.R.S.Y.,* Book 9, Chu Hsi.

12. *Ibid.,* Book 14, Ch'eng Hao.

13. Wang Shou-jen, *Collected Works of Wang Yang-ming,* Book 17.

CHAPTER FOUR

Han Yü: The Pioneer

Before discussing Han Yü and his disciples Li Ao and Chang Chi, who were the pioneers of the Neo-Confucianist movement, it is necessary to say something about the history of Buddhism in China from its introduction during the Han Dynasty to the time of Han Yü.

The development of Chinese culture has been independent and isolated from the outside world, although many things such as musical instruments, plants, and the calendar were contributions from other countries. Buddhism from India is the one great exception. The stupendous work of the translation of the Buddhist *sutras* in the early days and making them understood in China was extremely difficult. Its success was largely due to the Indian and Central Asian monks who disregarded the hardships of journeying to China and remained there until their task was completed. They were indefatigable in their efforts not only in translating the *sutras*, but also in helping to develop a new terminology and a new style for this vast Buddhist literature. That prepared the ground for the Chinese monks who later, in their anxiety to acquire a knowledge of the *sutras* in the original language, went to India. Fa Hsien in the Chin (Tsin) Dynasty and Hsüan Tsang in the T'ang Dynasty were two notable examples.

During the early period of the introduction of Buddhism into China, there was no more than an effort to understand the *sutras,* without paying attention to the different schools or sects into which Buddhism, like other religions, was divided. The first reference to the inclusion of Buddhist books in Chinese literature was in

Wei Shui's *History of the Wei Dynasty* (A.D. 336-534), which included a chapter on Buddhism and the teachings of Lao Tse. This chapter was quite extraordinary in the sense that its appearance among the official dynastic histories was a recognition that Buddhism had become part of the Chinese heritage — something which had never previously taken place. Wei Shui did not give an elaborate account of the new religion, but that it should find a place in his history is indicative of the fact it had become so widespread it could no longer be ignored. The *History of the Wei Dynasty* was followed by the *History of the Sui Dynasty* in which Buddhist literature was referred to in a *Miscellany*. A few Buddhist works were listed, but there was no mention of any *sutra*. Then came the *New History of the T'ang Dynasty*, in which the author, Ou-yang Hsiu, a statesman and scholar, named only Buddhist texts and commentaries written by the Chinese. He included no translations. Aside from these dynastic histories, a few catalogues of Buddhist writings compiled by the contemporaries of Wei Shui were published.

To show the wide interest in the propagation of Buddhism in China it may be interesting to give a list of some of the monks who came to China:

INDIAN AND CENTRAL ASIAN MONKS WHO CAME TO CHINA
AND TRANSLATED BUDDHIST SCRIPTURES

Name of Monk   Date of arrival in China and/or Period of sojourn

Name of Monk	Date
Matanga	A.D. 67?
Dharmaratna	67?
An-shih-ko or Lokottama (from the land of the royal family Arsaces)	147-170
Dharmakala	222-250
Dharmasatya	254
Kalaruci	281
Dharmaraksha	284-313
Moksala	291
Dharmaratna	381-395
Sanghadeva	383-398
Dharmanandi	384-391

Name of Monk   Date of arrival in China and/or Period of sojourn

Buddhabhadra	398-421
Punyatara	399-415
Kumarajiva	401-412
Vimalakshas	406-418
Dharmayasas	407-415
Buddhayasas	410-413
Dharmaraksha	414-452
Nandi	419
Buddhajiva	423
Dharmamitra	424-442
Kalayasas	424-444
Buddhavarman	433-439
Sanghavarman	433-442
Gunabhadra	435-468
Dharmagatayasas	481
Sanghabhadra	488
Dharmaruki	502-507
Sanghapala	506-520
Ratnamati	508
Bodhirucci	508-536
Buddhasanti	520-539
Gautma Dharmajina	538-582
Paramartha	548-569
Narendrayasas	556-589
Jainagupta	559-600
Dharmagupta	590-619
Prabhakaramitra	627-633
Atigupta	652-654
Buddhapala	676
Divakara	676-688
Bodhirucci	684-727
Devaprajna	689-691
Sikshananda	695-710

Name of Monk	*Date of arrival in China and/or Period of sojourn*
Subhakarasimha	716-740
Vajrabodhi	710-732
Amoghavajra	724-774
Dharmadeva	973-1001
Danapala	980

This table is not a complete list of the monks who came to China to translate the Buddhist Scriptures. The names of many were preserved in Chinese characters only, so that it has been impossible to recover the original Sanskrit. For this and other reasons, many names have been omitted.

TABLE SHOWING THE NUMBER OF INDIAN AND CENTRAL ASIAN TRANSLATORS, THE NUMBER OF BUDDHIST SCRIPTURES, AND THE NUMBER OF FASCICLES OF THE SCRIPTURES.

Dynasty	*No. of Translators*	*No. of Books*	*No. of Fascicles*
Later Han (A.D. 25-220)	12	192	395
Wei (A.D. 220-264)	5	12	18
Wu (A.D. 222-280)	5	189	417
West Chin (Tsin) (A.D. 265-316)	12	333	590
East Chin (Tsin) (A.D. 317-419)	16	168	468
Fu-ch'in (A.D. 351-394)	6	15	197
Yao-ch'in (A.D. 384-417)	5	94	624
Ch'i-fu-ch'in (A.D. 385-431)	1	56	100
Former Liang (A.D. 502-556)	1	4	6
North Liang (A.D. 555-587)	9	82	311
Liu-sung (A.D. 420-477)	22	465	717
Hsiao-ch'i (551-577)	7	12	33
Hsiao-liang (A.D. 555-587)	8	46	201
Toba Wei (A.D. 386-534)	12	83	274
Kao-ch'i (A.D. 550-577)	2	8	52
Yü-wen-chou (A.D. 561-581)	4	14	29
Ch'en (A.D. 557-589)	3	40	133
Sui (A.D. 589-618)	9	64	301
T'ang (Hsuan-tsung) (A.D. 712-741)	37	301	2170
Totals	176	2278	7046

TABLE SHOWING NUMBER OF CHINESE MONKS WHO WENT TO
INDIA, BY CENTURIES (IN THE CHRISTIAN ERA).

Period	No. of Monks
Latter part of Third Century, A.D.	2
Fourth Century, A.D.	5
Fifth Century, A.D.	61
Sixth Century	14
Seventh Century	56
First half of Eighth Century	31
Total	169

In the third and fourth centuries most of the Chinese pilgrims who wanted to reach India never did so. They arrived as far as the so-called "Western Territories", of Sinkiang or New Territory of China.

TABLE OF TRANSLATED BUDDHIST SCRIPTURES CLASSIFIED
ACCORDING TO THEIR NATURE

(*Data* taken from the K'ai-yüan Catalogue, A.D. 730)

Classification	No. of Scriptures	No. of Fascicles
I. Mahayana		
(1) Sutra	515 (or 563)	2173
(2) Vinaya	26	54
(3) Abhidharma	97	518
II. Hinayana		
(1) Sutra	240	618
(2) Vinaya	54	446
(3) Abhidharma	36	698
III. Works of Sages and Wise Men		
(1) Indian	68	173
(2) Chinese	40	368
Totals	1076 (or 1124)	5048

These tables show the depth and breadth of Buddhist penetration into China. It is worth noting that in the earlier centuries books were translated by Indian and Central Asian monks along with Chinese monks, but later the Chinese monks went to India themselves, in order to learn Sanskrit on the spot and translate the works independently. Millions of Chinese were ordained and thousands of pagodas were built.

The most celebrated of the Chinese monks who traveled and studied in India was Hsüan Tsang. He stayed there from 633 to 644. He was welcomed by Emperor T'ai-tsung upon his return to his homeland and then commissioned to spend the next twelve years in translating the Indian *sutras*. During this period he rendered into Chinese 74 books in 1330 fascicles. That marked the climax of Indian thought and Buddhism in the Middle Kingdom.

The Chinese scholars however, never felt really at home with Buddhism. Discussion and controversy between the Neo-Confucianist philosophers and the Buddhist believers were frequent. Antagonism was even more bitter between the Buddhists and the Taoists because both were religious enthusiasts and jealous of each other. Not uncommonly Buddhist monasteries were burned down, and the Buddhists suffered persecution. During the reign of Emperor Hsien-tsung (A.D. 805-820), Han Yü took the initiative to address a memorial to His Majesty protesting against Buddhism. This incident occured in 819, three years before Han Yü's death.

This memorial presents an interesting contrast to the pious devotion of the translators of the Buddhist Scriptures as shown in the tables above. The protest arose on the occasion of a plan to bring a piece of Buddha relic to the capital for exhibition — a proceeding to which Han Yü strenuously objected. His memorial began in this way: "Buddhism is a doctrine which originated among barbarians. It came to China in the Later Han Dynasty, and the ancients never heard it." Then the author listed the Chinese emperors who reigned before Buddhism, some for fifty, others for seventy-five or even a hundred years. These he compared with Ming-ti, the emperor of the Han Dynasty under whom Buddhism came to China, but whose reign lasted only eighteen years. Han Yü pointed out that during those dynasties when Buddha was devotedly worshipped reigns had in most cases been short. "What then is the use of worshipping the Buddha?" "I have heard", he continued "that Your Majesty sent out a number of monks as emissaries to welcome the Sri in Fen-hsiang and that there will be an investiture and parade for the benefit of Your Majesty; that the Buddha-bone will be put on exhibition in the palace and also in various monasteries. . . . I know well that Your Majesty cannot be induced by Buddhism to believe that blessings can come from this sort of glorification. Perhaps Your Majesty thinks that because of the good harvest this year the people can afford to pay for a splendid show."

He continued: "When the ordinary people see that an emperor as great as Your Majesty worships the Buddha piously, it is natural for them to sacrifice all that they have for the Buddha. They may burn their heads and fingers and give up their money for the Buddha. When one person begins, thousands will follow his example. If this is not stopped, I fear that cases of cutting elbows and bodies as sacrifices will occur. A decline of good manners will naturally follow. It is not a matter of small importance.

"The Buddha was born in a barbarian country. His language was different from that of the Chinese, his clothes were different, he could not speak about the merits of our ancient emperors. If he were living today and asked for an audience, Your Majesty would probably receive him and order the officials of the protocol to give him a dinner party. Then he might be presented with new clothes, and sent away, in order to prevent his corrupting our people.

"Furthermore," continued the author, "this dried bone from the dead body of the Buddha is filthy. How can it be allowed to go on exhibition in the palace?" Han Yü then asked the emperor Hsien-tsung to hand the bone to the authorities to be thrown into the water or fire. "When it has disappeared completely the doubts of the world will be cleared away, and some of the unnatural seductive power of Buddhism will be destroyed."[1]

When the emperor read this memorial he was greatly displeased, and exiled Han Yü to Kwangtung Province. The emperor's indignation was aroused not so much by the critic's opposition to Buddhism as by the fact that he mentioned the brevity of the reigns of the emperors who worshipped Buddha. Might not Han Yü have meant to hint that His Majesty's own reign would be short? His attack on Buddhism was in fact typical of the Chinese mentality, which finds little to interest itself in religion. It is full of common sense and is interested only in the concrete things of life. It did not find any need for a deep spiritual faith. So the worship of the relics of the Buddha was meaningless to Han Yü and to the kind of mentality which he represented. This is why after being absorbed in Buddhism for as long as six centuries, Chinese scholars found it more comfortable to return to Confucianism, even though they appropriated a good deal of Buddhist methodology.

With this account of the introduction of Buddhism into China, and some familiarity with Han Yü's attitude towards this foreign religious importation, we are now in a position to consider the life and character of this great pioneer of the Neo-Confucianist movement.

Han Yü was born in Honan Province in A.D. 768, and died in 824. He learned all the *Classics* and other rare books between his fourteenth and twentieth year. It was also during this period that he first arrived in Ch'ang-an, capital of the T'ang Dynasty, and became acquainted with two of the leading literary figures of the day: Tu Ku-chi and Liang Su. These men were opposed to the highly florid style of writing, usually in symmetrical form, which was then prevalent. They won Han Yü's sympathy and he decided to create a new literary style. In this he succeeded so well that the style has dominated China for the last one thousand years.

At twenty-five Han Yü received the degree of *chin-shih*, and was on the road to a civil service career. For the next decade he remained in Ch'ang-an profusely writing essays and sending them to influential men. In 796 he received an appointment from Tung Chin, governor of his home province, Honan, to be the inspector of magistrates of various districts. But unfortunately the governor died two years afterwards, and a rebellion broke out in K'ai-feng, capital of the province so that Han Yü had to flee to Hsu-chou in the northern part of Kiangsu Province. The following year he obtained the local magistracy, but did not stay long, because soon he was appointed to a professorship in the Junior Academy, which required his return to Ch'ang-an. He was later promoted to a censorship, but shortly afterwards, because he memorialized the throne on the prevalency of starvation among the people, and on the scandals of the palace-market, he was dismissed and exiled to Yang-shan as magistrate. This was the first of a series of demotions which he suffered because of his frankness. This first exile, however, lasted only a year, and he devoted his time to writing essays, one of which was the famous *Inquiry into Tao*.

In 806 Han Yü was appointed professor at the Senior Academy by Emperor Hsien-tsung. Subsequently he was elevated to the post of senior clerk in the department of justice, only to be asked, later on, to resume his duties as academy professor. In the meantime, he lodged a protest with the emperor favoring a local magistrate against a prefect, and as a result was exiled again — this time to Feng-chi as sub-magistrate. But in 814 he was recalled and appointed senior clerk in the ministry of civil service and at the same time became editor of the board of historiography. Three years later he became an army-inspector under prime minister P'ai Tu, who at the time was commander-in-chief at the battlefield of Huai-hsi. When the fighting was ended Han Yü returned to Ch'ang-an as under-secretary of the department of punishment — a post which because of its relative importance demanded more loyalty than usual from him to his emperor. But in 819, on the occasion already alluded to, the son of Heaven issued an order welcoming a Buddhist relic, and Han Yü allowed his loyalty to get the better of him by writing a strongly worded remonstrance to the emperor. As a result, he was for the third time demoted, and exiled to Chao-chou, in Kwangtung Province, as prefect. Emperor Hsien-tsung died shortly afterwards, and Han Yü was restored to favor, as under-secretary in the ministry of defense. The remaining four years of his life were spent in this position. He died in 824, at the age of fifty-seven.

It is clear from this brief biological sketch that Han Yü did not succeed in doing much for his country in an official capacity. But at least his personality was revealed in three respects: as a government worker he was honest and frank in addressing memorials to the emperor; in spite of demotion and exile he was fearless; and he typified the faithful minister. His courage and fortitude set the example for Chu Hsi and Wang Shou-jen, who followed in his footsteps in a later period.

As a reformer Han Yü's supreme achievement was the creation of a new literary style. His writings were appreciated by great essayists like Ou-yang Hsiu, Su Tung-po, and many others through the centuries. But how did Han Yü's reform affect the Chinese literary style? During the Wei and Chin Dynasties and during six other dynasties which ruled in southern China, it was fashionable to write in the ornate or "symmetrical" style. Each sentence consisted of four or six words, and was decorated by beautiful couplets such as "wind" and "moon"; "cloud" and "dew"; "flower" and "grass". But this way of writing came to be regarded as a deterioration of Chinese literature, because of the abnormal emphasis on form at the expense of substances or content.

Han Yü's literary friends, Tu Ku-chi and Liang Su took strong objection to this way of writing, but it was Han Yü himself who proved to be the effective reformer. From boyhood he buried himself in the *Classics,* and studied how the ancients spoke and wrote. The so-called "symmetrical style", he concluded, was unworthy of survival. It was merely decorative and was incapable of conveying the meaning or ideas which people really wished to express. Han Yü discarded all conventional ways of writing, coining new terms and evolving a style of his own. His school came to be known as that of the classical language, even though, in point of fact, his writing was in no way merely an imitation of the classical period. The four or six word construction was abandoned. In its place he created a style which was spontaneous and flexible. It was the *pai-hua* movement of an earlier age. Han Yü wanted a style completely shorn of decorative verbiage. He wanted to have in its place a style that was rigorous, full of vitality, and adequate to express the writer's thoughts, and he created it.

But he was more than a literary champion of the *Classics.* Remarkable for his wide reading and intellectual curiosity, he revived two philosophers: Mo Ti and Hsün-tzu, both of whom had been condemned by Mencius. The work attributed to the former of these thinkers had been completely forgotten after the Chin (Tsin) Dynasty, and except for Han Yü's appreciative essay was not brought back to life until Liang Ch'i-ch'ao and Hu Shih, at the end of the Ch'ing Dynasty, became interested in its logical theories. Hsün-tzu had been sharply criticized by Mencius for his teaching that human nature is evil. Our literary reformer insisted that although Hsün-tzu's theory was not always in consonance with that of Confucius, both philosophers sought the same goal. He proposed however to edit Hsün-tzu's book so that all the objectionable parts might be taken out.

Like Dr. Samuel Johnson who resembled Han Yü in more than one sense, the pioneer of Neo-Confucianism was large and heavy. Whether he ate as heartily as the Englishmen we have no way of knowing, but he loved to sleep, and he perspired so abundantly that he was in the habit of lying on a bamboo mat on his bed. Han Yü was also fond of gambling, and was skillful at it. An interesting story is told about him as a gambler. It seems that at one time he won a painting through gambling and he wrote a famous essay about it, enumerating all the persons, horses, oxen, camels, and the other animals and birds in that work of art. He described them one by one and the result was an essay of a very original kind. He liked also to display this painting to others, and on one occasion a censor to whom he showed the painting said that it belonged to him. "I lost it twenty years ago!"[2] Han Yü was so deeply touched that he gave him the painting.

Han Yü had a wonderful sense of humor as many of his essays show, like *Goodbye to the Ghosts of Poverty, Career for a Scholar,* and *Biography of Mao Yin.* "Mao Yin" of this last named essay is not the name of a man, but means "Hair" and "Tip". The essay deals with the life of the brush which Chinese use for writing. An example of Han Yü's power as a satirist can be seen in the following essay:

GOOD-BY TO THE GHOSTS OF POVERTY!

On the last day of the first month of the sixth year of Yüan-ho (A.D. 811) I asked my boy to make a cart from a willow tree and a boat from grass, to equip them with grain, to let an ox lead the cart, and to fit the boat with a sail. Then I bowed three times before the Ghosts of Poverty and, bidding them goodbye, addressed them thus: "I have heard that you are going away soon. I do not ask you for the destination of your trip. I give you a cart and a boat, both equipped with grain, as food for you on your journey, with the hope that wherever you go you will live under favorable conditions. You have rice to eat and wine to drink, on your way, and you have companions to accompany you from one place to another. Since you can fly like the wind and compete with light-ning, you will suffer no delay, and I, on my side, shall do what lies within my power. I suppose that you have made your decision to leave here!"

Then I remained silent, and I seemed to hear a sound, sometimes laughing, sometimes weeping, or coughing or singing. The sound frightened me. My hair stood on end and my body trembled. I was not certain whether anybody was present or not, for I had not time to investigate. Finally a voice spoke as follows: "I have lived with you for more than forty years. During your boyhood I did not find that you were dull. When you were learning and ploughing, you were eager for fame and an official career. I cared for you with unvarying mind. I saw the Ghosts of Doors and Windows chasing you, and I scolded them. I spied for you, and did other things for you. When you were exiled to the south, to a sultry and humid place, I was insulted by the other ghosts because I was not a native. When you worked in the government academy I furnished you with cabbages and salt. I was the only one who protected you, while others were rather disgusted with you. From first to last I was faithful to you, and had no evil intentions toward you. Why have you insinuated that I should leave? Perhaps you have heard some slander against me. Since I am a ghost, I have no use for a cart or a boat. Since I can smell what is good or bad, I have no need of food. I am by myself, I have no need of companions. Since you know much about me, can you tell me the number of persons I have with me? You are blunt, and hence, no doubt, wise. I have already divulged something to you, so I had better tell you all."

I answered: "Do you think that I really know nothing about you? The number of your companions is neither six nor four. It is ten less five, or two subtracted from seven. Each of these has his way and has put me in a dreadful position by moving his hand or turning his tongue. It is their doings which have made me ugly in appearance and improper in talk. *First*, they made me suffer from poverty in wisdom. Since I am honest and straightforward I could not help but be rough and unpolished, for I was ashamed to say deceitful and calumnious things against others. *Second*, they made me suffer from poverty in scholarship. I enjoy profundity and subtleness, and boast about numbers and vocabulary. I like to do research in the *Classics*. *Third,* they made me suffer from poverty in writing. I am not a specialist in any one field. I am fond of the rare. I amuse myself by learning what is impractical for everyday life. *Fourth,* they made me suffer from poverty in fortune. My shadow is different from my body. My appearance is ugly, but my heart is good. I prefer to remain behind in gaining profit, but I am the first one to shoulder responsibility. *Fifth,* they made me suffer from poverty in friends. I undergo hardships for my friends, and show my heart to everybody, but after a moment they all treat me as if I were their enemy. These five ghosts have given me five kinds of suffering. They have made me starve and go without clothing. They have slandered me with evil words. They have caused me so many perplexities that no explanation could straighten me out. What they have done in the morning, they have repeated in the evening. They have come swarming like flies, and have run after each other like dogs. After having been chased away, they returned a second time. Their talk unfinished, they have gazed with turning tongues. They have danced and laid themselves down. Sometimes they have clapped their hands and stamped their feet and smiled among themselves."

Then they told me: "You know our names. Because of our doings you have asked us to leave. Among us, some may be smart; others may be mad. Who knows how long one is to live? Yet we have made your name immortal. There is a great difference between a petty and a noble man. When one is in disfavor in one's life-time, one is inspired by heaven. When one has been the owner of jewels, one prefers to give them up in exchange for a goat-skin. When one has been stuffed with delicate foods, one is fond of rye and oats. Now you are so well-known in the world that nobody can equal you. After you were exiled you were called back. If you do not believe us, you may refer to the books of poetry and history."

After hearing these words, I felt depressed. Yet I thanked them. I burned the cart and the boat, and welcomed *them back as honored guests.*[3]

For an appreciation of Han Yü as literary critic and man of letters, no better statement can be found than Ou-yang Hsien's *Biography of Han Yü* in his *New History of the T'ang Dynasty.* "Han Yü was of the opinion that the best authors after the Han

Dynasty were Ssu-ma Hsiang-ju, Ssu-ma Ch'ien, Liu Hsiang and Yang Hsiung. It is hard to find later writers who are equal to these. Han Yü penetrated deeply into the fundamentals of literature and was very original in his own writing. His essays: *Inquiry into Tao, Inquiry into Human Nature, What is the Nature of a Teacher?* and many others are comprehensive and profound. He may be classed as next to Mencius and Yang Hsiung. His essays have the value of being supplementary to the *Six Classics*."[4] This appreciation indicates that Ou-yang Hsien considered him not only as a literary man but also an advocate of Confucianism. His Confucianist views will be shown more clearly in my summary of his essay, *Inquiry into Tao,* which presents him as a thinker opposed to foreign importations. He wished to see the Chinese people regain confidence in their own culture.

Let us then turn now to this immortal essay, the *Inquiry into Tao,* where Han Yü made the most vigorous and brilliant defense of Confucianism.

"To love extensively", says Han Yü, "is *Jen.* To do what is appropriate is *I* (righteousness). The way by which one can reach them is *Tao.* What is self-sufficient and independent of the outside is *te* (virtue). *Jen* and *I* are terms with definite unchangeable meanings. *Tao* and *te* are positions which one may leave vacant. (i.e., while the meanings of *Jen* and *I* are precise and fixed, the meanings of *Tao* and *te* are speculative.) As far as the possession of *Tao* is concerned, the possessor may be a nobleman or a common person. As for *te,* it may be a blessing or a disaster. The belittling of *jen* and *i* by Lao-tzu cannot destroy these two ideas; it shows instead the narrowness of Lao-tzu's vision. If one sits in a well and looks at heaven one will say that heaven is small. But in reality this smallness is conditioned by one's position: it is not the actual smallness of heaven. *Jen* and *I* in the mind of Lao-tzu are merely caressing and particularizing. From his point of view, therefore, *Jen* and *I* have little value. What he calls *Tao* is his view of *Tao,* not *Tao* in our sense. What he calls *te* is his view of *te,* not *te* in our sense. In our sense *Tao* and *te* are closely related to *Jen* and *I* — a truth recognized by everybody. But in the meaning of Lao-tzu, *Tao* and *te* are stripped of the nature of *Jen* and *I,* and are reduced to a mere prejudice."

Han Yü's point is that Lao-tzu's interpretation of *Tao* (the way) and *te* (virtue) is too speculative and metaphysical. Better to hold fast to the view of the Confucian school that *jen* and *i*, imbedded in our human nature, are on a more solid foundation.

Han Yü proceeds to narrate, in his terse style, the historical development of Chinese thought. "After the decline of the Chou Dynasty", he says, "Confucius died. In the Ch'in Dynasty there was the Burning of the Books. In the Han Dynasty the teachings of the Yellow Emperor and Lao-tzu were practiced. Buddhism was introduced in the dynasties of Chin [Tsin], Wei, Liang and Sui. In those days people who discussed *Tao, te, jen* and *i*, if they were not followers of Yang Chu or Mo Ti, were followers of Lao-tzu or the Buddha. When they joined the one school they attacked the other. The school they joined was their master, the school they attacked was their slave. In joining they praised, in separating they condemned. Under such circumstances how could people find the real nature of *jen, i, Tao* and *te*? The followers of Lao-tzu considered Confucius to be their master's disciple. The followers of the Buddha considered Confucius to be *their* master's disciple. After the adherents to the school of Confucius had become accustomed to such talk they took pleasure in its falseness and demeaned themselves to the extent of declaring that this talk might be right and might even derive from their own sect. They not only spoke such words but wrote them down in their books. Alas! Those who sincerely wished to know the truth about *jen, i, Tao* and *te* — where could they find it? What a pity that people are interested in miracles and wonders! They never go to the beginning to see what ensues. Instead they clamor after marvels."

It is true that after the introduction of Buddhism philosophical discussion in China became an impure mixture of the three schools. The book *Hung-ming-chi*, which is a collection of arguments, and counter-arguments of the Buddhists and Confucianists is an example of how the boundary line between these two schools became blurred.

"In ancient times", Han Yü continues, "there were four classes of people, but now their number has grown to six. In ancient times there was one kind of teaching, but now there are three. There are six people asking for food to every farmer. There are six people asking for utensils to every artisan. There are six persons doing business to every tradesman. This is why many people become poor and stoop to stealing and robbing. In the old days most suffering came as a result of shortages. Whereupon the sages came forth, and taught the people how to produce, and how to feed and protect themselves in their communities. The institutions of kingship and of learning were established. The sages cleaned away insects and wild animals and enabled the people to settle down on land. Clothes were made when the people felt cold. Food was made available when they were hungry. Houses were built for those who lived too close to the woods and for those who dwelt too near to the earth. Craftsmanship came into existence for the purpose of making utensils; trade for the purpose of exchanging what one had for what one had not; medical science and drugs to cure disease; burials, funerals and sacrifices to teach filial love and gratitude; ceremonies to impart knowledge of order and social distinctions; music to enable one to give expression to one's passions and repressions. Besides all these humane contributions made possible by the Sages, government was introduced for the purpose of ruling the people in such a way that incompetence and negligence could be brought to light; administration of justice was established to punish those who acted contrary to the law. Contracts, seals, bushels, scales, and weights were invented as standards to prevent deception. Cities, castles, shields and arms were invented as protection to prevent disorder. These measures were all instituted to enable people to cope with injury and calamity.

"From Lao-tzu, however, we heard only that as long as there are sages robbers will persist, and that not until bushels and scales are abolished strife will cease among the people. These words of Lao-tzu are simply nonsense. Without the sages the human race would have been destroyed long ago. And why? Because men having no feathers, fur, scales or shells to cover their nakedness would have been unable to survive excessive heat and cold, and because men unarmed by teeth or claws could not have fought for food.

"The king is he who issues orders. His subordinate ministers are they who receive orders from him and execute them for him in behalf of the people. The people are they who produce wheat, rice, hemp, and silk, make utensils, trade in goods and money, and serve the government. A king who fails to issue orders does not fulfill his duty as a king. A minister who does not execute his royal masters's orders for the welfare of the people should be cashiered. People who do not produce food, silk and hemp, make utensils and carry on trade in order to serve the government, should be killed.

"Lao-tzu's advice, on the other hand, was that the institutions of king, minister, parents and child should be abolished, and that the ways and means for production and protection should be disregarded. Only then could men seek for purity, calmness, emptiness and annihilation. The followers of Lao-tzu were fortunate that they were born after the period of the Three Dynasties so that they avoided the condemnation of Yü, T'ang, Wen, Wu, the Duke of Chou and Confucius. In spite of Lao-tzu's teaching, the fact is that one may be a Sage regardless of one's title — even if, for example, one is called king or emperor. Summer clothes should be greencloth, winter clothes should be fur. When thirsty one should drink, when hungry one should eat. The means may be different, but all alike issue from the same knowledge. Now the followers of Lao-tzu preferred the state of nature, where no artificiality exists. In other words, they wanted to ask people in winter, 'Why do you not wear light clothes?', or people who were hungry, 'Why do you not drink?' "

It is clear from the rather lengthy argument translated above how deftly Han Yü appeals to the visible and concrete details of life in order to condemn the subtle and other-worldly doctrines of the Buddha and Lao-tzu. He is like those Western philosophers who, standing on solid ground, argue against the schools of rationalism. In this respect the Chinese and British resemble each other.

But to return to Han Yü's *Inquiry into Tao*. He next quotes from the *Ta-hsüeh* (Great Learning) to defend firmness and positiveness in questions involving human life. "In the old days", he says, "those who intended to illuminate bright virtue in the world first governed their country well. Those who intended to govern their country well first kept their family in order. Those who intended to keep their family in order first cultivated their person. In order to cultivate their person they first rectified their mind. In order to rectify their mind they first realized a true will. It was their purpose, after rectifying their mind and realizing a true will, to accomplish something constructive for the good of the people.

"But now the followers of Lao-tzu and the Buddha who talk about rectification of the mind ignore this world and their native land and reduce the normal duties ordered by heaven to nothingness. Following the ideas of Lao-tzu, a son does not have to consider his father as a father, nor does a man have to regard the king as a king. He does not have even to discharge his duties as a subject."

In these last two paragraphs our pioneer of Neo-Confucianism means to fight against the world-negating views of the Buddhist monks who pay no taxes, render no military service, and who even discard family life. Since the Chin [Tsin] Dynasty (265 A.D.), many Chinese scholars had attempted to defend the monastic life by the argument that the monk is under no obligation to render services to the temporal power. Han Yü did not take this attitude and that was why he attacked the monks so vehemently.

Then Han Yü stigmatized Lao-tzu and Buddha as "barbarians", though he knows perfectly well that the former was born in China. "When Confucius wrote the *Ch'un-ch'iu*", he says in his frontal attack, "the feudal lords who adopted barbarian rites were considered barbarians. Those who were converted to the Chinese way of life were considered Chinese. In the *Classics* it is said: 'The barbarians even *with* a king were not to be compared to the Chinese even *without* a king.' In the *Shih-ching* it is said: 'The *Jung* and *Ti* [minority groups] should be disciplined. The *Chin* and *Shu* [other minority groups] should be corrected. Alas! At the present time the laws of the barbarians are considered superior to the doctrines of the former emperors. This will lead to the barbarization of the whole Chinese world.' "

Eventually Han Yü returns to his starting point. "To love extensively is *jen*. To do what is appropriate is *i*. The way by which one can reach them is *Tao*. What is self-sufficient and independent of the outside is *te*. The books one ought to read are the *Shih-ching*, the *Shu-ching*, the *I-ching* and the *Ch'un-ch'iu*. A community should be governed by ceremonies, music, discipline and administration. The professions by which all men should be occupied are those of the scholar, the farmer, the artisan and the tradesman. The social positions are king and minister, parent and child, teacher and friend, husband and wife. The people's clothing is hemp and silk. Their dwellings are houses and palaces. Their food is wheat, rice, fruit, vegetables, fish and meat. This is the *Tao*, which is easily understood. This is the doctrine which is readily put into practice. If one takes this as the basis and applies it one will live happily and harmoniously. In dealing with others, one should be friendly and fair. As for one's own mind, let it be calm and peaceful. As for the world and the community, let one find a sound administrative policy, satisfactory to everybody. During life one should fulfill the normal duties. Then when one offers sacrifices heaven will accept them. When oblations are made in the temples the spirits will enjoy them. What mode of *Tao* is this? It is *Tao* in our sense, not in the sense of Lao-tzu and Buddha."

Han Yü's exposition of the theory of the Line of Succession for *Tao* is precise. "Yao", he says, "transmitted this line of succession to Shun. Shun transmitted it to Yü. Yü transmitted it to T'ang. T'ang transmitted it to Wen, Wu and the Duke of Chou. The last three personages transmitted it to Confucius. Confucius transmitted it to Mencius. After Mencius' death the line of succession was cut off. Hsün-tzu and Yang Hsiung could make distinctions but they were not sufficiently fine; they could discuss but not thoroughly."

Finally, there is in *Inquiry into Tao* a rather blunt method for disposing of Buddhism — a method which may strike the modern reader as medieval. "Before the time of the Duke of Chou", remarks Han Yü, "those in high position were the rulers who had power to execute their policies. Since the Duke of Chou, subordinates have done all the discussing. They stretch out their arguments interminably. If you ask me, 'What is to be done?' I shall answer, 'When there is water, stop it. When there is fire, extinguish it.' Let a man be a man. Buddhistic books should be burned. Monasteries should be used as dwelling-places. The *Tao* of the former emperors should be made clear to everybody. The bachelors, the widows, those who are childless and they who are crippled will be protected. This is what must be done."[5]

One may be impressed by the small amount of philosophizing in these passages translated from Han Yü's most philosophical work. His comments seem to be mere commonplaces about Chinese life. But it is precisely this rejection of the subtle and metaphysical way of thinking characteristic of Buddhism and the cult of Lao-tzu that brought Chinese philosophers back to their own tradition.

In this *Inquiry into Tao* there is one point which cannot be overemphasized if Han Yü's doctrine is to be rightly understood, and if indeed the Neo-Confucianism for which he acted as a pioneer is to be adequately appreciated. The point is that Han Yü clings firmly to the theory that *Jen* and *i* are the foundation of all moral values. The recognition of this principle is, for Han Yü, the categorical imperative. Once there is this recognition, denial of the validity of the moral law becomes impossible. *Jen* and *i* are forms of thought with reference to the judgment of moral values, so that the basis of morality cannot be twisted by Lao-tzu's speculation on *Tao* and *te*.

Two other points in the essay are also worthy of emphasis. (1) Han Yü was the first to formulate the theory of the line of succession of *Tao*. (2) He gave a priority to Mencius, assigning him a conspicuous place in the pantheon of Confucianism.

It is interesting to note the attitude towards the Four Books of this great precursor of Neo-Confucianism. He often quotes from the *Ta-hsüeh*. On his death-bed he told his disciple Chang Chieh that he had planned to write a commentary on the *Lun yü*. His disciple Li Ao stressed the importance of the *Chung-yung*. Indeed, Han Yü's school may be regarded as the forerunner of the movement which accepted the Four Books as the necessary introduction to the study of the Five Classics.

Now let us take leave of the *Inquiry into Tao,* and consider more briefly two other literary contributions of Han Yü. Oddly enough, in spite of his avowed antagonism to Buddhism, he presented essays to the Buddhist monks. These essays may be found in his *Collected Works.* During his lifetime he was adversely criticized for writing these essays, and it was even insinuated that he had become converted to Buddhism. His defense was the elegantly simple remark: "When I was in Chao-chou I met a monk named Ta-tien. He is very clever and knows the nature of *Tao* and *ri*. He can transcend the visible and physical; he enjoys himself in the world of *ri*, and he never worries about human affairs."[6] These words suggest that Han Yü understood the strength of Buddhism and Taoism. But for an orderly guide to human life he preferred Confucianism.

In conclusion another quotation from Ou-yang Hsiu will be appropriate. In his *New History of the T'ang Dynasty*, from which I have already extracted an appreciation of Han Yü, there is a general evaluation of the group around him, that is, of such men as Li Ao and Chang Chieh as well as of the master himself. Ou-yang Hsiu was sufficiently far-sighted to assign to Han Yü a position in the history of Chinese thought long before Sung philosophy had started.

This general evaluation is converged in the following passage: "Beginning with the period of Chen-yüan (A.D. 784) and ending with the period of Yüan-ho (A.D. 820), Han Yü was the sponsor of a new style based on the language of the *Six Classics*. He fought against the low ebb literature had fallen to. He recovered the robust from the worn out, and the true from the false. He demanded that he should be considered as equal to Ssu-ma Ch'ien and Yang Hsiung. Even Pan Ku, author of the *History of the Han Dynasty*, was looked down upon by Han Yü. His essays were perfect examples of his new point of veiw. He rejected worn out phrases and coined new terms. He was original in that he was able to discover novel modes of expression. Ideas poured forth like water from the ocean, yet he never contraviewed the spirit of the former sages. Han Yü's *Tao* may be compared to that of Mencius, and he criticized Hsün-tzu and Yang Hsiung as being inadequate.

"His suggestions and remonstrances to the emperor, and his lending a helping hand to others in time of need, were typical of his honesty and frankness. He was not cowardly but showed great courage, and he was always defending *Jen* and *I*. There can be no doubt that he was a man seriously interested in *Tao*.

"From the Chin [Tsin] Dynasty down to the Sui Dynasty, Buddhism and Lao-tzu's ideas dominated, and the *Tao* of the sages was on the decline. Scholars leaned towards what was prevalent and gave support to both of these heterodox schools. Han

Yü alone remained faithful to the sages. He suffered much, but always stood up again after he had been knocked down. At first he had no followers, but as time went on his stature began to grow.

"When Mencius fought against Yang Chu and Mo Ti about two centuries after the death of Confucius, Han Yü attacked Buddhism and the ideas of Lao-tzu after these cults had dominated China for a millenium. The effort Han Yü used to recover the prestige of orthodox truth was tremendous, and the result was a service equal to that of Mencius. Accordingly, Han Yü's work was superior to that of Hsün-tzu or Yang Hsiung. After his death he was glorified as T'ai Shan [a mountain] and the Polar Star."[7]

References

1. *Han Yu,* Book 39.
2. *Ibid.,* Book 13.
3. *Ibid.,* Book 36.
4. *Hsin T'ang Shu* (New history of T'ang Dynasty), Book 176.
5. *Han Yu,* Book 11.
6. *Ibid.,* Book 18, Cf. letter to Meng Chien.
7. *Hsin T'ang Shu,* Book 176.

CHAPTER FIVE

Disciples of Han Yü:
Chang Chieh and Li Ao

Han Yü had a group of pupils with whom he carried on a lively philosophical discussion. Two of them, Chang Chieh and Li Ao, were particularly worthy. The question of human nature was much argued among his students, possibly as a reaction to the Buddhist belief that the world is an illusion. Chang Chieh was dissatisfied with his master's failure to make a complete and systematic study of all the problems connected with Confucianism. "The moral climate of to-day", wrote this pupil, "is deteriorating and is inferior to that of ancient times. This is because of the decline and fall of the doctrine of the sages. After the death of Mencius, Yang Chu and Mo Ti indulged themselves in subtle and extraordinary theories in order to be attractive. Mencius tried to correct them, thus reviving the doctrine of the sages. But in the Ch'in Dynasty China went through a book burning period. And in the Han Dynasties the practices of the Yellow Emperor and Lao-tzu prevailed and were popular among the people. Then Yang Hsiung published his *Fa-yen* as a counter-argument. When the Han Dynasties declined, the doctrine of the Buddha came into China from the western regions. For generation after generation the books of the Buddha were translated and spread by the Chinese. Along with the theories of the Yellow Emperor and Lao-tzu, Buddha was considered to have expressed the deepest philosophical thought."

The drift of the thinking in this quotation from Chang Chieh is similiar to Han Yü's *Inquiry into Tao.*

Here is another quotation on how the sages contributed to the physical and intellectual life of mankind. "When the sages found that human beings suffered from the want of a power of self-preservation, they discovered metal, water, fire, earth, grain, and medicine, in order to give mankind comfort. Building on the foundation of the knowledge of goodness, they taught men the virtues of *Jen* and *I,* in order to create orderly life for the community. Therefore, human life continued to be lived in harmony. Thus, in material life men became well supplied with what was furnished by the sages, but in spiritual life they departed from the teachings of the sages, and were attracted by the theories of the heretical schools. They forgot the doctrines concerning the proper relations between king and minister, between parents and children, between husband and wife, and between friends, and so there was disorder everywhere. This was much deplored by good men. After the *Fa-yen* written by Yang Hsiung, there was a period of a thousand years in which nobody was interested in the *Tao* of the sages. You, Han Yü are the only man today who discusses it. The misguided people, although they seem to listen to you, will not believe in you, but rather contradict you. This is not the way to raise the educational standard of the people. You are a man of high intellectual attainments, and your writings are equal to those of Mencius and Yang Hsiung. So I propose that you should be the author of a book in order to revive the *Tao* of the sages. The people of this generation and of later generations will appreciate the work you have done in combatting heresy. It is far better for you to engage in these important labors than to live among the vulgar people and carry on their idle talk."

Chang Chieh believed that the life of a sage should be dignified and ascetic, a type of life which was actually practiced by the Sung philosophers. His advice to Han Yü was: "Those who decide to practice the *Tao* of the sages should live an exemplary life. But you seem to find pleasure in stories which have no substance. This shows a deficiency of moral excellence. In carrying on a controversy you do not weigh the arguments of your opponents. You take pride in yourself and derive satisfaction from mere verbal victories. This is another defect from which you suffer."

And Chang Chieh of course took strong exception to Han Yü's fondness for gambling. "Those who observe the teachings of the *Six Classics*," he says, "should follow a normal way of life. How can we find pleasure in gambling and in thus making money from others? This is something a gentleman should not do. What you write is not contrary to what was taught by the ancients, but your manner of living is not normal and rational. I hope that you will give up gambling and all idle talk. You should communicate with the scholars of the world. You should do your best to be the successor of Mencius and Yang Hsiung, and to correct the mistakes of Yang Chu, Mo Ti, Lao-tzu, and the Buddha. Then the *Tao* of the sages can, perhaps, be revived in this period of T'ang. That will be your greatest achievement."[1]

This hope of continuing the work of Confucius and Mencius, so fondly cherished by Chang Chieh, was only fulfilled later by the Sung Philosophers. They made a complete study of *Tao*, in comparison with which Han Yü's few articles appeared scattered and unsystematic.

Han Yü wrote two replies to the complaints by Chang Chieh. In the first he said that he would wait until his fiftieth or sixtieth year before writing a book. In the second, he said that he felt rather reticent about writing a more elaborate attack on the Buddhists and Lao-tzu because he would offend too many people. "The Buddha and Lao-tzu have a history of six hundred years to back them up. Their teachings are wide-spread. It is not easy to get rid of them in the evening when one only has received the order in the morning."[2]

So much for Chang Chieh. Now let me turn to the second of the two pupils. Li Ao received the *chin-shih* degree in A.D. 789, and then was appointed as an editor on the Board of History. Afterwards, he was sent out as prefect to various provinces. While in Lang-chou in Hunan Province, he called on the Ch'an monk, Yao-shan-wei-yen, to learn the Buddhist method of meditation. Li Ao died somewhere between 841 and 846.

The biographical sketch of this philosopher in the *Old History of the T'ang Dynasty,* and in the *New History of the T'ang Dynasty,* makes Li Ao a complete Confucianist. His memorials to the emperor were only on matters pertaining to government and historiography. Also, from his *Collected Works*, one learns that he was opposed to building Buddhist monasteries and Buddhist prayers for the dead.

Buddhist sources, however, create a different impression of the man. In these there is evidence that Li Ao was interested in Buddhism, especially in the Ch'an sect. On the matter of his visit to the monk Yao-shan-wei-yen, these sources say that upon his arrival, the monk continued to study his *sutras* without paying the least attention to the guest. When a servant announced: "The prefect is here!" Li Ao said loudly: "It is better to hear your name than to talk with you personally," and angrily turned to leave. The monk then spoke up: "Why do you believe your ears but not your eyes?" Li Ao then asked politely: "What is *Tao?*" The monk made a gesture with his fingers pointing above and below, but the prefect did not understand. Then Yao-shan-wei-yen recited a verse: "Like the cloud in heaven and water in a bottle," to which Li Ao replied with the following poem:

"You are doing exercises to make your body like a stork;
You have two boxes of *sutras* under thousands of pine trees.
An answer to my question about *Tao* is no more than the
    words:
Like the cloud in heaven and water in a bottle."[3]

Not only was Li Ao's call on Yao-shan-wei-yen evidence of his interest in Buddhism, but so also was his intimate friendship with Liang Su, author of a book entitled *General Principles of Samdhi*, published between A.D. 780 and 783, which discussed the T'ien-t'ai sect of the Buddhist religion.

These two sources have unfortunately produced two diametrically opposite views of Li Ao. My own view is that he was neither opposed to Buddhism nor was he converted to Buddhism. It is possible that the truth lies, perhaps, somewhere in the middle.

Li Ao studied the *Book of Rites* and was much under the influence of Han Yü. His daily life was that of a Confucianist; but in matters of mental discipline, he was much attracted to the

Ch'an sect of Buddhist thought. In one of his letters (to a Mr. Yang, a departmental minister), he requested that the collection of taxes for building Buddhist monasteries be stopped, and he strongly denounced the expenditure of these funds. But in the very same letter he wrote of the "people who know how to purify the mind by the doctrine of Buddhism".[4] Such was his attitude towards the religion from India. It was not part of his daily life, but its technique of mind control had a strong appeal for him.

Li Ao was more of an introspective thinker than his master, Han Yü. He pondered over philosophical problems of the *Tao*, and his speculations reached a height approaching that of the Sung philosophers. His ideas are found mostly in his three essays entitled *Return to Human Nature*. Though his efforts took the form of discussion in Confucianist terms, the driving influence of Buddhism behind him is quite clear. This will become clearer as we proceed. In the first of these essays, he says:

"Why is it that a man can become a Sage?" asks Li Ao. His answer is: "Because a man possesses human nature. How can a man's nature be corrupted? By the emotions. There are seven such emotions: joy, anger, grief, fear, love, disgust, and desire. When the emotions are out of control human nature lives in obscurity. It is not that human nature should be blamed. Rather it is the coming and going, by turn, of the seven emotions, which prevents human nature from being fully developed. For example, when water is troubled at its source, its stream will be impure; when fire is smoking, its light will not be bright. One cannot say that the water itself is impure, or that the fire is not bright. When there is no sand, the stream will be clear; when there is no flame, the fire will be bright. When emotions are not aroused, human nature will be fully developed. Yet human nature and emotions cannot be separated from each other. Without human nature, there would be no expression of emotions. The emotions are derived from human nature. The emotions are not self-constituted. They depend upon human nature. Human nature cannot constitute itself: it expresses itself through emotions. Human nature is what is ordered by Heaven. When a sage is endowed with it, he will reach the stage of not doubting. The emotions are what is expressed when human nature is in action. When the people indulge themselves in the emotions, they are blind to what is fundamental. A sage is not a man who is without emotions. A sage is a man who is a master of his emotions and keeps calmness of mind. He comes without going, he acts without speaking, he has light without shining. In his work he cooperates with heaven and earth. His changes are in accordance with the Yin and the Yang. Though he has emotions, he does not seem to have them. Ordinary people have their human nature too. It is not different from that of the sage. But they can be blinded by their emotion and then they do not know what human nature is."

Li Ao's theory about the relation between human nature and emotion was, no doubt, influenced by the Buddhist idea of putting out the flame of Tanha or craving, and by the Sunyata conception of the Buddha-nature. The functions of human nature and emotion were known to the Chinese for ages. But the relation as it is described by Li Ao is new. It was afterwards expounded by the Sung philosophers who changed the term "emotion" into "desire".

Li Ao undertook to explain how the perfect enlightenment of the sage can be reached. This emphasis again is something which the Chinese learned from Buddhism, because the Buddhists stressed that one can attain perfect wisdom through "Prajnaparamita". It is interesting to note that Li Ao called a Sage the *awakened,* or *enlightened one,* which is equivalent to the Buddhist term *Bodhi.*

Let us read Li Ao's own words: "Fire, when it is hidden in the mountain-rock or forest-trees may not be said to be no fire. Water, when it remains in the valley as a source and does not flow out may not be said to be no water. When stone is not struck and when wood is not rubbed, there will be no fire to burn or to make things dry. When the source of water is not opened, it cannot flow out to form the Yangtze, the Yellow River, the Huai or the Tsi. When the emotions are not checked, one cannot return to one's nature and look at the world with a sense of detachment. A sage, therefore, is one who is first awakened. When one is awakened, one is enlightened. Otherwise one is in confusion. When one is in confusion, one is obscured. Light and obscurity are opposites, but they are not inherent in human nature. There is no use talking about how they are in opposition to each other. Since light is opposed to obscurity, once the obscurity disappears there will be no need to seek light. Truth, therefore, is the nature of the Sage. It is calm and immovable. It is wide, vast, clear and bright. It shines all over the world. By his nature he knows why truth is such, and he knows whether he should remain quiet or move, whether he should speak or remain silent, and how every thing must live up to its standard. The expression 'return to nature' means that the Sage should seek nature unceasingly, and that he is capable of returning to the source whence he came. In the *I-ching* is the passage: 'The Sage who cooperates with heaven and earth in regard to his moral excellence equals the sun and moon in respect to light, resembles the four seasons for his order, and may show blessings and calamities brought upon him by the gods. When he precedes heaven he observes, of course, the times imposed by heaven. As compared with Sages, men and even gods are relatively powerless.' This is a quality which depends upon nothing outside, but issues from nature."

Li Ao, in these words, was attempting to describe perfect wisdom. Being a Confucianist he expressed his ideas in Confucianist terminology, using such terms as "truth", "enlightenment", "heaven" and "earth". What he actually meant was the Buddhist conception of *Prajnaparamita*.

Quoting from the *Chung-yung*, our philosopher wrote: "Only the absolute truth can fulfill its nature. When one's own nature can be fulfilled then one can also fulfill the nature of others. When one can fulfill the nature of things one can cooperate in the creative work of heaven and earth. When one can cooperate in the creative work of heaven and earth one is a member of the trio of heaven, earth, and mankind. Next to him one able to fulfill his nature to such an extent is capable of developing his nature only partially. By partial development one may also possess truth and have shape. To have shape means to manifest. To become manifest means to be distinct, full of light. Whosoever is full of light activates. Whosoever activates changes. Whosoever changes creates. Only those who realize truth can be creative."

The ideas expressed here are purely Chinese, and are quoted from a Chinese book. Yet they approach remarkably near the Buddhist conception of Perfect Wisdom. Their philosophical sense was fully grasped after the Buddhist idea of Perfect Wisdom was introduced into China.

Then Li Ao proceeded to discuss the relation of sagehood to rites and music. He said: "The sages know that a man whose nature is necessarily good can exert himself to the extent of becoming a sage, and so can conduct rituals to establish order and music to create harmony. To live in harmony is the foundation of music. To move in agreement with order is the foundation of the rites. When one is in a chariot one hears the harmonious sound of the bells. When one takes a walk one hears the sound of the jade hanging on one's body. So music never stops when there is no reason to stop it. Seeing, listening, speaking, and acting should all be done according to the rites. This is the way to make men forget their desires and return to nature and the heavenly order. *Tao* is no other than perfect truth. When one realizes the Truth unceasingly one can be empty. When emptiness remains forever, one is enlightened. When enlightenment is limitless, one can shine everywhere without losing anything. This is the utmost realization of nature and the heavenly order. It is a pity that people do not seek to achieve this state, especially when others never try to obstruct the effort. This shows how ignorant the human is."

The reader will have observed that all the quotations Li Ao has given are from Confucian books. But it must have been obvious that the interpretations he offers are Buddhist. This is clear, for instance, in his remark: "When emptiness remains forever, one is enlightened." It will also be explicit in an assertion to be discussed later that "right thinking means no thinking and no deliberating", to which Li Ao gave a far more speculative meaning than Confucius ever did. The conception is derived from the Buddhist idea: "The thoughtless is our objective. The thoughtless is the right thought."

Li Ao's *Return to Human Nature* consists, as I have said, of three essays. The foregoing translation forms the greater part of the first essay. The middle part I shall omit. But I should like to present to the reader the last part of the first essay which deals with Li Ao's determination to carry on the work of the realization of *Tao*.

"Since the Ch'in Dynasty," he writes, "the theory of the *Tao* has been obscured. What has been taught is sentences, phrases, ceremonies, and the practice of swordmanship. The question of nature and of the heavenly order has not been discussed. Hence, this is a period of abeyance. After abeyance, however, comes a period of revival. Perhaps I am the man to do this work of resuscitation. In my sixth year I began to study, but at first I was only interested in literature. Now I have devoted myself already for four years to the study of *Tao.* Many people to whom I have talked have not appreciated my efforts. Lu Ch'ien, however, commented: 'What you have said is from the mind of Confucius. In the East a sage cannot be other than as you have described him. I hope that you will continue successfully in your work.' Alas! Though books about nature and the heavenly order are still extant, nobody is interested in them. Everybody has joined the schools of Lao-tzu, the Buddha, Chuang-tzu and Lieh-tzu. They all believe that the Confucianist scholars were not learned enough to know about nature and the heavenly order, but that they themselves are. Before those who raise this hue and cry I do my best to demonstrate the opposite. I write down all I know in order to expound truth and light. I hope that *Tao,* which has been obscured and neglected, may be revived and transmitted again. Thus, I give my book the title: *Return to Human Nature.* If Confucius should come to life to-day he would not consider my talk worthless."[5]

There can be no doubt about Li Ao's conviction that in writing these essays he was fulfilling a great mission. It was nothing less than the revival of Confucianism. Thus, we must consider him among the forerunners of the Neo-Confucianist movement of the Sung Dynasty.

The second essay in *Return to Human Nature* gives Li Ao's prescription of the way to his objective. Again he speaks the language of Confucius, but again the influence of Buddhism is implicit. This essay is written in the form of questions and answers, and may be summarized as follows:

"Question: Mankind has been blinded for a long time. How can one return to nature? You must lead us to it. What is the way?

"Answer: As long as there is no deliberating and no thinking, one's emotions are not in action. When emotions are checked one has the right way of thinking. Right thinking means no deliberating and thinking. In the *I-ching* it is said: 'Where evil thoughts are cleared, truth will be kept!' In the *Shih-chung* it is said: 'Think of no evil things.' These maxims tell us the way of the fasting mind. As long as there is calmness there is also agitation. As calmness and agitation work unceasingly, this is emotion. In the *I-ching* it is said: 'Blessings, unhappiness, repentence, and misery — all derive themselves from movements.' Then how can one return to nature? My answer is that when in calmness one knows that the mind is not thinking, that is, that there is a fasting of the mind. When one knows that the mind itself does not lie in thinking, one can give up both inactivity and activity. The mind is in a state of absolute calmness. This is the Utmost Truth. It is said in *I-ching*: 'The movement of the Universe is towards oneness.'

"Question: When there is no deliberation and no thinking, things will yet attract one from the outside, and responses will come from the inside. How can you stop this?

"Answer: Emotions are the corrupted forms of nature. If one knows that they are corrupted, corruption will disappear. When the mind is calm and not in action, the corrupted thoughts will stop naturally. As long as one's nature is enlightened, no corruption can be produced. To stop emotion by emotion requires a great emotion. Can emotion really be stopped by emotion? In the *I-ching* it is said: 'Yen Hui, when he commits something wrong, always knows it. When he knows it, he never repeats the same thing again.' Also in the *I-ching* it is said: 'Return from a distance when you do not go far. Then there will be no repentance. It will do you good.'

"Question: If in the mind itself there is no thinking, then one cannot hear when there is sound, and one cannot see when a thing comes to one.

"Answer: It is not human that one does not hear and see. It will be enough if one knows that one sees clearly and hears clearly, but not merely sees and hears. One knows all and acts in every way. One's mind is calm and shines all over the world. This is the enlightenment of Truth. In the *I-ching* it is said: 'Change is thoughtless and actionless. It is calm and without action. When anything appears to the senses, the reason why it is so will be understood."

The way of interpreting the mind is Confucian, but at the same time it shows clearly the influence of the Buddhist theory of *Sila* (conduct), *Samadhi* (meditation), and *Panna* (intuitive knowledge). The meaning is the same as that expressed in the dictum: "No *Panna* without *Samadhi*; no *Samadhi* without *Panna*." Yet Li Ao, though he is influenced by Buddhism, aims at personal cultivation for the purpose of putting human relationships of family and government in order.

"Question: What is the meaning of the sentence, 'Realization of knowledge is the examination of things?'

"Answer: Things are the expression of the manifoldness of the world. Examination means reaching things. When one reaches things, one is clear and can distinguish between them without being attached to them. This is the realization of knowledge, which means reaching things. When knowledge is realized, there is true will. When there is true will, the mind is rectified. When the mind is rectified, there is personal cultivation. When there is personal cultivation, the family life is in order. When family life is in order, the country will be well governed. When countries are well governed, there will be peace in the world. This means that a man's work consists in cooperation with heaven and earth."[6]

If one reads these three essays of Li Ao carefully, one may see that all the fundamental concepts of the Neo-Confucianism philosophy of the Sung Dynasty are there — such concepts as *Tao*, Truth, Enlightenment, Emptiness, Calmness, the idea of the sage, watchfulness in time of solitude. They are all there, in Li Ao's essays, although he does not elaborate on them as the Sung philosophers did afterwards. In the last essay of *Return to Human Nature* he expressed his determination to devote himself to *Tao* in a manner which suggests the vow of a believer in a faith.

The influence of Buddhism over Li Ao's way of thinking was the effect of Liang Su and Yao-shan-wei-yen, his teachers. Regardless of all these accretions to the interpretation of the *I-ching,* the *Chung-yung,* and the *Ta-hsüeh,* Li Ao's work was in the interest of the revival of Confucianism.

References

1. *Han Yü*, Book 14, Chang Chieh's letter to Han Yü.
2. *Ibid.*, Book 14.
3. *Fo-fa-chin-t'ang-pien* (The Stronghold of Buddhist Dharma), Book 9.
4. Li Ao, *Collected Works*, Book 10.
5. *Ibid.*, Book 2.
6. *Ibid.*, Book 2.

CHAPTER SIX

Buddhism as Stimulus to Neo-Confucianism

The basic thoughts of Confucianism, whether orthodox Confucianism or Neo-Confucianism, is concerned mainly with human relations, moral values, and concrete life, which places it in great contrast to Buddhist thought. The latter, is highly speculative, full of imagination, and other-worldly. Chinese thought *affirms* life and the world; Indian thought negates them.

Buddhism was introduced at the time of the decline of orthodox Confucianism, and was something quite foreign to the Chinese people. It was a religion, a faith, the ultimate aim of which was deliverance from a world of suffering. It was also equipped with a great number of rational arguments at its base. Buddhism as a religion and an institution was in conflict with the Confucian pattern of life. Consequently, at first there was much opposition to it.

But in spite of official Confucian antagonism, Buddhism's theoretical system proved attractive to Chinese scholars. Moreover, when it was introduced, China was in disorder and in the grip of civil war. Confucianism had lost its validity, and the people were ready to devote themselves to a doctrine which emphasized the other-worldly.

During the Chin [Tsin] Dynasty (A.D. 265-419), when the school of Lao-tzu and Chuang-tzu prevailed, the terminology of these two philosophers was used to translate Buddhist texts. In the early period of the introduction of Buddhism many terms of Taoist origin were applied to Buddhism, such as *Tao, wu-wei* (inaction), emptiness, naturalness, "To do nothing and to leave nothing undone." This method of translation facilitated understanding by the Chinese of Buddhism, because it presented strange ideas in familiar dress. With the progress of translation, however, such novel Buddhist concepts as *Prajnaparamita*, (transcendental wisdom) Impermanence, Five *Skandas* (aggregates) and *Dyana* (meditation) required the coining of new Chinese terms which eventually meant independence from Taoism.

At first the work of translation was difficult because the Central Asian and Indian monks knew no Chinese, and the Chinese, who knew no Sanskrit, were unfamiliar with Buddhist ideas. Mutual understanding of texts and their expression in readable Chinese were practically impossible. Luckily, a few Central Asian monks had studied some Chinese before they came to China, and gradually a few Chinese mastered a little bit of Buddhism, thanks to the gradually accumulating Chinese texts.

This chapter cannot deal in detail with the Central Asian and Indian monks who actually did the translating, but mention is made of a few Chinese and Indians who contributed to the building of the Buddhist library. For instance, there was Tao-an, a Chinese monk who lived from 312 to 385, in the Chin [Tsin] Dynasty. He was so enthusiastic about Buddhism that he read every translated Buddhist tract he could find, and he was also the first to compile a catalogue of Chinese Buddhist works. Another was Kumarajiva, born in 343 or 344 in Kucha. He translated the basic texts of the Mahayana, and contributed most to Chinese Buddhism, although he himself was a Brahmin of India. While living in Ch'an-an from 401 to 413 he rendered into Chinese 35 books in 294 fascicles. Following are the titles of some of these:

1. *Sukhavatyamritavyuha-sutra.*   NANJIO. NO. 200
2. *Viseshakmita-Brahma-paripricca.*   NANJIO. NO. 190
3. *Sata-sastra.*   NANJIO. NO. 1188
4. *Sarvastivada-pratimoksha.*   NANJIO. NO. 1160
5. *Mahaprajnaparamita Sastra.*   NANJIO. NO. 1169
6. *Madhyamika-sastra*   NANJIO. NO. 1179

7. *Dasabhumi-vibhasha-sastra*	NANJIO. NO. 1180
8. *Dvadasanikaya-sastra.*	NANJIO. NO. 1186
9. *Satyasiddhi-sastra*	NANJIO. NO. 1274
10. *Samyuktavadana-sutra*	NANJIO. NO. 1366
11. *Vajracchedika-Prajnaparamita-sutra*	
	NANJIO. NO. 10
12. *Dasabhumika-sutra.*	NANJIO. NO. 105
13. *Sutralankara-sastra.*	NANJIO. NO. 1182
14. *Saddharmapundarika-sutra.*	NANJIO. NO. 134
15. *Bodhi hridaya-vyuha-sutra.*	NANJIO. NO. 99

From this list it is clear that the Madyamika school of Buddhism was introduced into China by Kumarajiva, because the basic texts of this school (numbers three, six and eight above) were translated into Chinese by him; and it is equally clear that he was responsible for the introduction of the sect of the *Satyasiddhi-sastra* into China, because he also translated that work. Indeed, Kumarajiva is regarded as one who laid the foundations of Buddhism in China, and his contributions are often compared with those of two other men: Hsuan-tsang and Paramartha.

Translation began from the latter Han Dynasty (A.D. 25-219), and continued through the T'ang and Sung Dynasties. Meanwhile the way in which the project was carried on changed in some degree. Before and during the Kumarajiva period those books were translated which were given the translators. Later, the Chinese monks tried to find out for themselves what they wanted, as was the case with Hsüan-tsang who rendered into Chinese the texts of the Yogacarya school which he had been unable to find in his homeland, and who re-translated the text of the *Mahaprajnaparamita-sutra* because in the old form it seemed unsatisfactory to him. In short, in time the Chinese pilgrims who journeyed to India began to formulate something more or less definite in their own minds about what they wanted to get. Such was the case with Fa-hsien, who went to India deliberately to fetch the texts of the *Vinaya-tripitaka.* A similar tendency was exhibited by the Indian monks subsequent to Kumarajiva. They translated works which had hitherto not existed in China. Through the cooperation of the Chinese and Indian monks gradually the whole of the *Tripitaka* was accumulated in the Chinese language.

Even more interesting is how Buddhism influenced Chinese thought. Prior to the age of the formation of Neo-Confucianism there was in China an era of Buddhist fermentation. With the growth of the work of translation of Buddhist texts, and contemporaneously with the period from the split of China into north and south (371 A.D.) to the commencement of the Sui Dynasty (589), there developed in China a number of Buddhist schools or sects. These were:

1. The School of the *Satyasiddhi-sastra.*
2. The School of the Three Sastri (*Madhyamika-sastra, Sata-sastra, Dvadasanikaya-sastra*).
3. The School of the *Nirvana-sutra.*
4. The School of the *Dasabhumika-sutra-sastra.*
5. The School of Pure Land.
6. The School of Ch'an beginning with Bodhidharma.
7. The School of the *Mahayanasamparigraha-sastri-vyakhya* (first translated by Paramartha in 593 A.D.)
8. The School of Abhidharma.
9. The School of T'ien-t'ai (a purely Chinese sect.)

Then in the T'ang Dynasty (618 to 906 A.D.) there developed four more Buddhist sects or schools in China: the Schools of Vinaya, Yogacarya, Avatamsaka, and Mantra respectively. Thus, the total number of Buddhist sects in China was thirteen, though eventually two disappeared (numbers four and seven), leaving only eleven.

Buddhism was a powerful stimulus to Chinese thought if for no other reason than that it provided the concepts of *Sunyata* (void), *Non-atman* (no-self), Impermanence, Twelve *Nidanas* (causes of dependence), Five *Skandas* (aggregates), *Bhutatathata* (suchness), *Bodhi* (awakening), etc., which gave the Chinese mind a great deal of material for reflection. Then, when the various schools arose, the Chinese mind was given further opportunity to explore the nuances of meaning among them.

One sect would teach the objective or subjective reality of the phenomenal world, another would say that the phenomenal world is an illusion; one would teach that the devout should learn Buddhism by studying books handed down from generation to generation, another would insist that the only way to learn Buddhism was to apply one's own mind and not resort to books; one would find conflicts among the sects, another would try to reconcile them. These different ways of thinking among the Buddhists occupied the Chinese mind, and consequently aroused it to action.

Among the thirteen (or eleven) schools there were three which were pure Chinese products, grown on the native soil of China. These were (1) the Ch'an sect, (2) the T'ien-t'ai sect, and (3) the Avatamsaka sect. Ch'an is the Chinese equivalent of the Sanskrit *Dyana* and the Japanese Zen. Every Buddhist school has to do with *Dyana*, which means meditation, but the devotees of Ch'an, besides being concerned with this work of *Dyana* in general, had their own peculiarities. Thus their doctrines may be examined separately as constituting a special sect.

The Ch'an school was founded by the first Indian patriarch, Bodhidharma. The date of his arrival and stay in China is controversial, because his life was colored by innumerable legends and reports very often contradicting each other. In Tao Hsüan's *Biographies of Eminent Monks,* Bodhidharma is described as one who lived in the Ch'i Dynasty. In the same source it is said also that he came to Kwangtung province during the Southern Sung period — which preceded the Ch'i Dynasty. This book, which was written during the age of T'ang, gives the earliest report of Bodhidharma's arrival in China and is more reliable than later records.

On the basis of Tao Hsüan's testimony I can agree with a recent statement by Dr. Hu Shih that Bodhidharma's arrival must be dated about A.D. 470-475. Tao Hsüan also mentions that the place of Bodhidharma's death is unknown. According to traditional records he was buried in A.D. 536. Thus the stories of his return to India, and of his meeting with Sung Yün at Ts'ung-ling, are disposed of. What Bodhidharma taught the Chinese may be summed up in the following lines:

"This is a special transmission which goes beyond the
    Scriptures,
There is no use in setting it down in writing,

> Better to appeal directly to the mind of man.
> When one sees one's own nature, Buddhahood will be
> attained."[1]

Later, the Ch'an school became the most influential in China and
swept away all the other Buddhist sects. It possesses a great wealth
of records treating of its line of succession. Thus we know that
after Bodhidharma the second patriarch was Hui-k'o (486-598),
the third was Seng-ts'an (606), the fourth Tao-hsin (580-651), the
fifth Hung-jen (605-675), and the sixth Hui-neng (638-713), whose
body I myself have seen, still preserved in a monastery in Kwangtung province.

The fundamental tenets of Ch'an thought are the doctrines
essential to Buddhism in general, and it puts aside such merely
incidental teachings as the *Skandas,* the *Nidanas,* and epistemological analysis. Let me present two *gathas,* one from each of the
first two patriarchs of the Ch'an school, since they go back to an
Indian origin. First, a *gatha* of Mahakasyapa:

> "Pure and immaculate is the nature of all sentient things;
> From the very beginning there is no birth, no death;
> This body, this mind — a phantom creation it is;
> And in phantom transformation there are neither sins
>   nor merits."

Then a *gatha* uttered by the Buddha in the presence of Mahakasyapa when the latter became the transmitter of the Good Law:

> "The Dharma is ultimately a Dharma, which is no
>   Dharma;
> A Dharma which is no-Dharma, is also a Dharma:
> As I now hand this no-Dharma over to thee,
> What we call the Dharma, the Dharma — where after all
>   is the Dharma?"

The Ch'an sect emphasizes emptiness. The work of mind is to
grasp the idea of emptiness. This word "emptiness" was expressed
by Bodhidharma in the following conversation with Emperor Wu
of the Liang Dynasty (A.D. 502-556): Emperor Wu asked: "What

is the first principle of the Holy Doctrine?" Bodhidharma's answer was: "Vast emptiness, and there is nothing in it to be called Holy." The emperor again asked: "Who is it then that is now confronting me?" The reply he received was: "I know not."[3] Emptiness, therefore, is the basic idea of the Ch'an school.

How this idea of emptiness was elaborated is very interesting, and may be comprehended with some degree of clarity by a study of the conversations, or *Koans*, of the Ch'an believers. For instance,

A layman worried about a disease went to the second patriarch, Hui-k'o, and begged: "Pray cleanse me of my sins." Hui-k'o said: "Bring your sins here and I will cleanse you for them." This means that sins are neither within, without, nor in the middle. Only mind counts.

Again: Tao-hsin begged of the second patriarch: "Pray show me the way to deliverance." Hui-k'o said: "Who has ever put you in bondage?" Tao-Hsin said: "Nobody." Then the Master said: "If so, why should you ask for deliverance!"[4]

The Japanese scholar D.T. Suzuki has described the national character of the Chinese and has told us how it happened that the Chinese could feel at home with Ch'an thinking. Says Suzuki: "The Confucian verdict that the superior man never talks about miracles, wonders and supernaturalism is a true expression of Chinese psychology. The Chinese are thoroughly practical. They must have their own way of interpreting the doctrine of Enlightenment as applied to their daily life, and they could not help creating Zen as an expression of their most spiritual experience."[5]

Elsewhere Suzuki asks: "Did they [i.e., the Chinese] adopt the intellectual method of the Sunyata school?" And he answers: "No, this too was not after their taste, nor was it quite within the reach of their mental caliber."[6]

The very fact that the Chinese translated the works of the Sunyata school is in itself evidence that the method of that school *was* within their "mental caliber;" but there is no point in arguing with Suzuki.

Suzuki also writes: "The Prajna-Paramita was an Indian creation and not Chinese. They [the Chinese] could have produced a Chuang-tzu or those Taoist dreamers of the Six Dynasties, but not a Nagarjuna or a Shankara. The Chinese genius was to demon-

strate itself in some other way. When they began inwardly to
assimilate Buddhism as the doctrine of Enlightenment, the only
course that opened to their practical minds was to produce Zen."[7]

Dr. Suzuki says further: "Chinese minds, ever since the coming
of Bodhi-Dharma, worked on the problem of how best to present
the doctrine of Enlightenment in their native garment cut to
suit their modes of feeling and thinking; it was not until after
Hiu-neng that they satisfactorily solved the problem, and the great
task of building up a school to be known thenceforward as Zen
was accomplished."[8]

Suzuki is right in saying that Ch'an is a product of Chinese
thought. But there is more to be said about the relation of Ch'an
to Neo-Confucianism. (1) This sect believes in the goodness of
human nature — just as was taught by Mencius. Here is a fundamental kinship between Ch'an and Confucianism. (2) According
to Ch'an, every sentient being possesses Buddhahood. Mencius
taught the doctrine that every man can be a Yao or Shun. (3) The
Ch'an insists that anyone can understand Buddhism who makes a
direct appeal to mind. This approach was adopted by the Sung
Neo-Confucianists Lu Chiu-yüan and Yang Chien. From it comes
some idea of the intimate connection between Ch'an and Neo-
Confucianism.

We come now to the second Buddhist sect indigenous to Chinese soil, namely, T'ien-t'ai. The very name of this school shows
its Chinese origin, although there have been attempts to trace it
back to the Indian Nagarjuna as its first patriarch. A group of
students after digesting the contents of the following books:

> Saddharmapundarika-sutra
> Mahaprajnaparamita-sastra
> Nirvana-sutra
> Mahaprajnaparamita-sutra

then proceeded to set up their own system. The real founder of the
T'ien-t'ai school or sect was Chih-i (531-597), who lived in the
T'ien-t'ai Mountains and ordained more than four thousand
priests. Hence the name of the school. Its distinguishing characteristic is interest in finding a key to the heterogeneous mass of

Mahayana literature, and for this purpose it proposed the principle known as "Assignment of the Buddha's Teachings to the Five Periods." If a student keeps this key in mind he will learn that the various aspects of Buddhist thought are not in conflict, but that they complement each other.

The Five Periods are, according to the T'ien-t'ai School, as follows:

(1) The first three weeks of the Buddha's life after he had attained enlightenment. In this interval he preached before a gathering of Bodhisattvas and heavenly beings the *Buddhavatam-sakamahavaipulya-sutra*.

(2) The twelve years following these first three weeks, when he preached the Four *Agmas*. Turning to the *Wheel of the Law* he explained the Four Truths about suffering, salvation from suffering, and the Eightfold Way

(3) The eight years following the twelve years just mentioned. He told his disciples that the great work of saving the whole world lay before them, that is, that they should aim at the ideal of the Bodhisattva. He preached the *Vimalakirti-nirdesa-sutra*, the *Viseshaknita-Brahma-paripriccha-sutra*, the *Lankavatara-sutra*, the *Pratyutpanna-Buddhasammukha-vastitasamadhi*, the *Surarnaprab-hasa-sutra* and the *Srimala-Devi-simhanada*.

(4) The next twenty-two years. The Buddha tried to explain that the Hinayana is only a preparatory stage and beyond it is the more advanced stage of perfect wisdom. He preached the *Mahapraj-naparamita-sutra*.

(5) The last eight years of his life. In this final period the Buddha preached that every individual may attain Nirvana. The idea of universal salvation is crystallized in the Saddharma-Pundarika-sutra, the fundamental text of the T'ien-t'ai School. On the last day of the Buddha's life he preached the *Nirvana-sutra*, which is also included among the works in this last period.

This Five-Period Theory is not a mere manipulation or *tour de force* of Chinese Buddhists, but is founded upon the various *sutras* themselves. It is an example of the Chinese way of compromise as applied to the reconciliation of conflicting texts.

The T'ien-t'ai sect has a formula for summarizing its system of thought: (a) In one mind there are three kinds of contemplation; (b) in a single thought there are 3,000 aspects of 10 *Dhatus* [worlds]. The 10 Dhatus [worlds] are (1) hell, (2) beasts, (3) hungry ghosts, (4) *asuras* [demons], (5) men, (6) heavenly beings, (7) Pratyekabuddhas, (8) Sravakas, (9) Bodhisattvas, (10) *Buddhas*. Of these *Dhatus*, or worlds, the first three are concerned with evil, and are further classified according to whether their inhabitants are engaged in evil work of high, middle, or low class. Similarly, those who live among the *asuras*, men, and heavenly beings, are engaged in doing good deeds, and are graded according to these same three classes. The *Pratyekabuddhas* practice the Four Noble Truths, the *Sravakas* are familier with the twelve Nidanas [causes of dependence], the Bodhisattvas practice the six *Paramitas*, and then there are the *Buddhas. Pratyekabuddhas, Sravakas, Bodhisattvas*, and *Buddhas*, differ in degree of perfection, but are alike in that they belong in the worlds of Dyana [meditation].

These 10 *Dhatus* [world] affect each other mutually, so that in reality 100 *Dhatus* are generated. Each *Dhatu* has 10 features, namely: essence, nature, *Dharma*, power, action, cause, condition, effect, retribution and final identity. If we multiply 100, representing the number of *Dhatus* by 10, representing the number of features of each *Dhatu*, we get 1000 characteristics. At last, if we multiply this 1000 by three, representing the three domains of *Skandas*, sentient beings, and *Bhajana Loka*, [world of inanimate things] we get 3000 aspects of the 10 *Dhatus*, or in short, 3000 *Dhatus*.

The Tien-t'ai analysis of the three kinds of contemplation presents the dialectic of the Madyamiha sect. There are three viewpoints from which contemplation may proceed. These and the dialectic by which they all culminate in the revelation of the Truth of the Middle, are more or less self-explanatory in the following table:

A.

From Viewpoint of Emptiness

1. Negation of Being	Truth of Emptiness
2. Negation of Emptiness	Falsehood
3. Negation of both Being and Emptiness	Truth of the Middle.

B.

From Viewpoint of Falsehood

1. Positing of Being   Falsehood
2. Positing of Emptiness
   Truth of Emptiness
3. Positing of both
   Being and Emptiness   Truth of the Middle

C.

From Viewpoint of Middle

1. Negation of both Being and Emptiness,
   in sense of non-duality,   Truth of Emptiness.
2. Positing of both Being and Emptiness,
   in sense of non-duality,   Falsehood.
3. Non-negating of both Being and Emptiness,
   and Non-positing of both Being and
   Emptiness   Truth of Middle.[9]

This system as briefly outlined above was created by Chih-i, who ordained more than four thousand priests. T'ien-t'ai spread throughout China, and beyond China into Korea and Japan. It exists to this day.

We now come to the third Buddhistic sect indigenous to Chinese soil. This was the school based on the *Avatamsaka-sutra*.

Dr. M. Winternitz in his *History of Indian Literature* says: "In the Buddhist Dictionary *Maha-Vyutpatti*, a work called Buddhavatamsaka is mentioned in a list of Mahayana-sutras, immediately after the *Satasahasrika, Pancavimsatisaharika* and the *Astasahasrika-Prajna-Paramitas*. Both in the Chinese Tripitaka and Tibetan Kanjur, there is a large body of writings thus entitled. It is the sacred scripture of the Avatamsaka school which arose in China between 557 and 589 A.D. and of the Japanese Kegon sect. According to Chinese sources, there are supposed to be six different Avatamsaka-sutras, the largest of which contained 100,000 *gathas* and the smallest 36,000. The latter was translated into Chinese in 418 A.D. by Buddhabhadra together with other monks. Sikshananda made a translation in 45,000 *gathas* between 659 and 699 A.D. Though no Avatamsaka or Buddhavatamsaka Sutra has come down in Sanskrit, and there is a Gandavyuha-Mahayana Sutra, which corresponds to one of the Chinese translations of the Avatamsaka. The main contents of the Gandavyuha are the wanderings of the youth Sudhana, who travels all over India on the advice of the Bodhisattva Manjusri, in order to acquire the highest knowledge essential for Enlightenment. He wanders from land to land, seeking instruction from various persons, monks and nuns, lay adherents both male and female, from a merchant, a king, a slave, a boy, also from the goddess of the night, from Gopa, the wife of Sakayamuni and from Maya, the mother of Sakayamuni, until, finally, by the favor of the Manjusri, he arrives at perfect knowledge through the instrumentality of the Bodhisattva Samantabharda."[10]

Such is the story of the *Avatamsaka-sutra*. Particular emphasis should be given to the Avatamsaka school in China. Quite naturally, any Buddhist sect in China tries to trace its lineage back to an Indian founder. Thus, the Avatamsaka sect claims Nagarjuna as its source. Actually, however, this school was started by the following Chinese monks:

First Patriarch	Tu-fa-shun, or Tu-shun	557-640 A.D.
Second Patriarch	Chih-yen	601-668
Third Patriarch	Fa-tsang (Hsien-shou)	643-712
Fourth Patriarch	Ch'ing-liang	738-806
Fifth Patriarch	Kuei-shan (Tsung-mi)	780-841

Reports on the dates of birth and death of these five patriarchs are conflicting. Though the school was based on the *Avatamsaka-sutra*, its philosophical principles were worked out by Tu-shun, Chin-yen, and especially Fa-tsang, who has often been regarded as its true founder, and after whom (in his second name) the school is sometimes called the Hsien-shou sect.

This school, like the T'ien-t'ai, also strove to find a formula by which the mass of Buddhist literature could be brought together into a single unit. In contrast to the T'ien-t'ai, which classified Buddhist literature into five periods of preaching by the Buddha, the Avatamsaka divided Buddhist literature into five catagories, as follows:

(1) The Hinayana school, whose doctrine based on the theory of being as perceived by the six senses (sight, hearing, smelling, tasting, touch, will).

(2) The first stage of Mahayana Buddhism, based on *Alaya-vijnana* (a kind of consciousness).

(3) The final stage of Mahayana Buddhism, which is presented as the theory of *Bhutatathata* (suchness).

(4) The stage of sudden conversion, based on the *Vimalakirti-nirdesa*.

(5) The stage of perfection, based on the *Avatamsaka-sutra*. By this way of thinking all sects of Buddhism are covered, and yet each is left to its own viewpoint. For the Avatamsaka sect, the *Avatamsaka-sutra* contains the all-embracing doctrine.

The school we are considering tried to build a system in which there would be no contradiction between the phenomenal world and the world of reality or of "emptiness" in the Buddhist conception, and in which all kinds of universes would be melted together into one great harmony.

The system of the Avatamsaka is based upon three basic perceptions: (1) the perception of true emptiness, (2) the perception of no barrier between fact and truth, (3) the perception of all-inclusive comprehension. These three perceptions are more elaborately set forth in the metaphysical principles:

(1) Everything is simultaneously sufficient unto itself and yet complementary to every other thing. A being (A) stands by itself. Yet its standing by itself is constituted by the existence of other beings: (B, C, D). A is inseparable from itself in the past that is, in the future, A is sufficient unto itself through the three times: past, present and future.

(2) The One and the Many, though different from each other, are compatible. The Many is reducible to a common denominator called Being. Yet each being stands by itself, and so is many.

(3) All kinds of beings may develop themselves without mutual frustration.

(4) The cosmic whole is a net of *Indra*. It is like the thousands of lamps in a room. The thousands of lamps constitute the light of the room, yet each lamp is, in itself, a light. The light of one lamp is helped by the light of the others, and so a unitary system of light is evolved.

(5) All beings, great and small, feel "at home." The principles of interpenetration and affinity are complex, yet a simple sense of security is ubiquitous.

(6) What is visible and what is invisible are mutually complementary.

(7) What is homogeneous and what is heterogeneous are mutually interpenetrant.

(8) The beings of the three times: past, present and future, constitute a unity.

(9) All beings are nothing but transformation of the mind of the *Bhutatathata* (suchness).

(10) The principles here enunciated are not merely speculative, but may be found manifested in the phenomenal world.

About Fa-tsang Dr. Suzuki says: "The Indian genius makes it [the mind] develop into a Dharmadhatu, which is so graphically depicted in the form of Vairocana Tower with all its Vyuhas and Alankaras. In the Chinese mind, the heavenly glories resplendent with supernatural lights so wonderfully described in the Gandavyuha, are reduced once more into the colors of this grey earth."[11]

What Dr. Suzuki is trying to say is that out of the *Avatamsaka-sutra* a philosophical system, interpreted by human reason, was built by the five Chinese patriarchs of the Avatamsaka school — especially by Fa-tsang.

So much for the three sects of Buddhism indigenous to Chinese soil: Ch'an, T'ien-t'ai, Avatamsaka. Their birth is remarkable evidence of the intense activity of the Chinese mind in the Middle Ages. Having learned from Indian Buddhism, the Chinese created their own systems, but always, of course, remaining close to the fundamental concepts of the parent religion.

Besides these three schools, another sign of the maturity of the Chinese mind was the Yogacarya school founded by Hsüan-tsang. This school was heavily engaged in translation, but among the translations a book entitled *Vidyamatrasiddhi-sastra* was compiled, which was an *abstract*, rather than a translation, of the Ten Commentaries. In the old days, before the time the Chinese became interested, such an *abstract* would have been impossible.

Leaving behind the story of the progress of these Buddhist schools, I shall now give a picture of how the Confucianist scholars lived with and felt towards the Buddhist monks. From the start, the Chinese literati were sympathetic towards the monks who introduced Buddhism into China. The Chinese scholars perceived that the Indian and Central Asian monks had left their own country in order to propagate the faith, and they respected them highly for their consecrated courage and devotion, and assisted them in their work. Indeed, the Confucianist literati were on better terms with the Buddhist monks than were the Taoists. From the age of Tao-an, co-operation between Chinese and Buddhist monks was intimate and uninterrupted.

By the time of the T'ang Dynasty, Buddhism was already a constituent part of Chinese cultural life. Buddhist monasteries were institutions approved by the government, translation of Sanskrit texts was sponsored by the emperors, and Buddhist monks, who generally could write Chinese prose and poetry, were intimate friends of Chinese scholars. Since the monks devoted themselves to their private tasks, were aloof and took a highly detached view of human affairs, the Confucianist literati had high regard for their friendship.

In the preceeding chapter I have shown how bitter Han Yü was towards Buddhism. But it should be remembered that this was his official attitude, his attitude in public life as a government policy-maker. In private life, he maintained pleasant relations with a monk called Ta-tien. On one occasion when a critic pointed out his inconsistency in this matter, Han Yü remarked: "Your story that I am converted to Buddhism is mere gossip. When I was in Ch'ao-chou I met an old monk called Ta-tien [a Ch'an disciple of the monk Shih-t'ou, 700-790 A.D.], who was intelligent and well-versed in philosophy. Since I was living in exile in a remote place, and could find no person with whom to discuss, I invited him to come to the city and stay about two weeks. Ta-tien is a man who looks with contempt upon the world, and who has his own convictions about truth. He is not one whit stirred by what is going on in the world. Though I did not understand his discourses, I was well aware that his mind was thoroughly intelligent and unaware of puzzles. Such a man is rare, and I was glad to consider him an acquaintance. When I went by sea to make a sacrificial offering to a deity, I called upon him. Later, I sent him some clothing as a gift. This was a way of expressing my humane sentiments, and had nothing to do with belief in Buddhism."[12]

Is this "apology" of Han Yü good enough to provide him adequate clearance? In Chu Hsi's opinion it was a death-blow to Han Yü's fight for the *Tao*. Editing Han Yü's *Collected Works*, Chu Hsi said that though the great stylist wrote the *Inquiry into Tao*, he had never undergone a thorough training in understanding *Tao*, and hence his susceptibility to Ta-tien's arguments.

In Chou Tun-i's works we find a poem which he wrote on the wall of a house where Ta-tien once dwelt. The poem goes:

> "Han Yü, a self-appointed Confucian,
> Fought against Buddhism and Lao-tzu
> In his *Inquiry into Tao*.
> Though he was unfamiliar with Ta-tien's discussions,
> He was on good terms with him and left him clothing."[13]

This case of Han Yü is proof of how Buddhism penetrated into the inner circle of Chinese scholars. The connection of Li Ao, Han Yü's disciple, with Buddhism is indicated even more clearly in his essay *Return to Human Nature*.

Another Confucianist worth mentioning for his relation to Buddhism was Liu Tsung-yüan, a contemporary of Han Yü, and second only to him in literary prestige. Liu Tsung-yüan seems not so much an antagonist of Buddhism as a converted believer. In his *Collected Works* we find an essay written by him on the occasion of his giving a posthumous name to the sixth patriarch, Hui-neng, of the Ch'an School. Said Liu:

"The doctrine of the Buddha came later [that is, after Lao-tzu and Chuang-tzu]. The Buddha in tracing back to man's origin agreed with the Chinese doctrine that human life was born in the stage of tranquillity. Emperor Liang-wu-ti was fond of doing meritorious deeds. When he pointed this out before Bodhidharma, the latter was unimpressed. Six successions later Hui-neng became patriarch. At first he worked in the kitchen of the monastery. His words were rare, but those who listened found that whenever he spoke, what he said was full of meaning. Finally he was given the accrediting symbols as successor to the patriarchate, but escaped to a remote place for sixteen years, until he had convinced himself that he was capable of representing the doctrine. Thence he moved to Ts'ao-ch'i where he ordained thousands of priests. His main theme is: (1) Non-action is reality. (2) Being is emptiness. His teaching begins with the theory of the innate goodness of human nature, and ends with the same. There is no need of artificial work, because reality is, in itself, tranquillity. Emperor Chung-tsung [705-710] twice invited him to the capital, but he refused to come. His fundamental approach is to appeal to the mind. His book is circulated throughout the world, and those who follow Ch'an thinking regard Ts'ao-ch'i as the source."[14]

It is interesting to observe that Liu Tsung-yüan was one of the very few who presented Buddhist doctrine in a fair and objective way. Even more interesting he reminds us that Hui-neng begins with the theory of the innate goodness of human nature, and ends with the same. In Hui-neng we find proof of the mutual interpenetration and cross-fertilization of Ch'an and Neo-Confucianism.

The greatest stimulus which Buddhism gave to the Chinese mind was that it induced Chinese scholars to go back to the base of Confucianism and build their own system there. When they found in Buddhism a gigantic system, they soon conceived the idea that they too must have a cosmology, a theory of human nature, an attitude towards human life, family and government. In other words, they must have metaphysics, ethics, epistemology, etc. Some problems they were able to unravel by re-interpreting texts in their own ancient books. Other mysteries could be resolved only by original inquiry.

At this point we can try to see how the concepts of Neo-Confucianism were related to Buddhism.

Without question there was a nationalistic element in the cause of the Neo-Confucianist movement. Chinese scholars considered it a disgrace that they should have lived for centuries under an Indian *Weltanschauung*.

At first, there was an attempt at reconciliation. Interpreters liked to insist that the Buddha and Confucius preached the same *Tao*. But this attitude actually was an effort to disguise the Chinese weakness of not having a philosophical background. From the time of Han Yü until the Sung founders of Neo-Confucianism, a new system began to ripen. An essay by Li Ao, for instance, says the essence of human nature is tranquillity, and that evil comes from the stirring of the emotions. This idea, clearly of Buddhist origin, is simply a Chinese expression of the Buddhist dogma that emotions and desire are defilement. But when we come to the accomplishments of Neo-Confucianism in the Sung Dynasty, such as the *Diagram of the Supreme Ultimate* by Chou Tun-i, and the discussion of the Great Harmony by Chang Tsai, we find the Chinese mind offering counter-proposals to the Buddhist idea of emptiness. Later the Ch'eng brothers came on the scene and established the Sung philosophy on a rational basis, so that Chinese philosophy could no longer be said to be without a firm theoretical foundation.

Such a vast speculative structure could not help but provide a background revivified for discussion of the moral values as envisaged by Confucius and Mencius. In this sense, Confucianism itself was put on a new foundation, because it was provided with a propaedeutic of speculative, theoretical, and systematic study — something which had never been done before.

On the whole, the Neo-Confucianist system was built up under the influence of Buddhism, but despite this it never lacked the basic Chinese attitude of world and life-affirmation. The Chinese resisted the concept of emptiness, and stood firmly on their own ground of the affirmation of moral values. They interpreted the Buddhist ideas of all-embracing love and all-knowing intelligence in the sense of *Jen* and *Chih,* which are the sources of human activity.

Under the influence of the Indian way of thinking speculatively and gigantically, what the Chinese had formerly thought of in a personal and concrete way, they now re-conceived in terms of the entire universe as background. Thus, after having learned from Buddhism that Mother-earth in her oneness creates diversities of seeds and yet knows no discrimination in her innermost being, Chang Tsai in his *Western Inscription* said: "My body reaches as far as the borderline of heaven and earth; the commandment of heaven and earth constitutes my nature; men are my brothers; animals and inanimate objects are my fellow-creatures."[15] Chang Tsai meant that love must be as wide as the universe. Again, just as for Buddhism the *Tathagata* reveals itself in the infinity of worlds and preaches the Law universally, so for Neo-Confucianism the *Tao* and the representative of the *Tao,* the Sage, are everywhere and omnipresent, and the latter is enlightened and impartial.

Following the Buddhist advice that the heart of all beings should be kept bright and calm, the Neo-Confucianist philosophers revived the saying of the *Li-chi* (Book of Rites): "Tranquillity at the time of a man's birth is his nature."[16]

The Neo-Confucianists, like the Buddhists, taught the people that one must, as far as possible, stay away from lust, desire, and stirrings of the heart. In other words, elimination of desire and observance of the dictates of reason were recommended. That is, the moral law should be the goal of life.

Besides *Jen* and *Chih,* the Neo-Confucianist equivalents to the Buddhist virtues of *Karuna* (love) and *Bodhi* (intelligence), the Neo-Confucianists added a new virtue, *Ching,* which has a close affinity to the Buddhist *Samadhi* or meditation.

In this connection three other important concepts should be discussed. These are *Hsing,* or self-essence in the Buddhist sense, *Hsin* or mind, and *Hsing* as human nature. The Buddhists believed that the world is an illusion, and that the *Atman* (the self) or substance is the product of conditions and is not intrinsically real. Now the Chinese term *Hsing* was used in this context, as the self-essence which has no reality. But the Chinese, through misunderstanding of the original Sanskrit term for self-essence or self-substance, became intensely interested in this term *Hsing,* taking it as the equivalent for the Chinese word for human nature. This is why the discussion of human nature became wide-spread among scholars like Han Yü and the founding fathers of the Sung Dynasty. The Chinese never believed that the world is an illusion. On the contrary, they were incurably convinced of its reality. Thus, in their speculations they commenced with the Supreme Ultimate, which on the one hand was nothingness, but on the other hand was *Tao* of *Ri,* They began, that is to say, with reality, not the void. When, in their speculation they came down to man, they maintained that the discussion of human nature could have no meaning unless it was concerned with concrete man as actually born. Accordingly the question of human nature was not only metaphysical, but was inseparable from universal reality.

In this connection there are the four Chinese words: *Ming-hsin-chien-hsing*, meaning "to know the mind, and to find the essence of reality", the advice of the Ch'an Buddhists. The last two words, *chien-hsing,* stand for the inquiry into whether the universe is real or empty, or rather this is what the Buddhists originally *intended* as the meaning. However, the Chinese misunderstood it, and interpreted the words as referring to man's own nature, to human nature, rather than to universal nature, or to nature as such. Thus, paradoxically, what is prominent in Chinese philosophy and the question of nature which in China is conceived as exclusively related to man, arose from a failure to comprehend the full meaning of the Sanskrit term for self-essence. Yet, because mankind is a part of the universe, this misunderstanding produced a discussion which was meaningful for the subject as a whole.

Next let us look for a moment at the concept of mind. From the time of Mencius, Chinese philosophers recognized *thinking* as the function of mind; but this function was understood in the main as limited to logical inference and to approval and disapproval of the morally right and wrong. The Chinese never were aware of the wonderful work of mind which Bodhidharma revealed to them.

Ch'an advice of this kind put the mind in a more self-reliant and responsible position than any to which Chinese philosophers had formerly assigned it. The Chinese had become accustomed to thinking of books as the basis from which knowledge is derived. But for Bodhidharma it was no use to depend on books. By this insight, Bodhidharma meant three things: (1) A man knows what is right and wrong without being able to read. (2) A man *originally* knows what is right and wrong; that is to say, he is innately good. (3) By appealing directly to the mind, without recourse to ready-made knowledge, the mind is trained to greater alertness. This discovery of the active role of mind would have been impossible without the introduction of Ch'an thinking.

It should be added that Ch'an furnished a powerful stimulus to the revival of Confucianism in China. Though the Ch'eng-Chu school fought bitterly against the Ch'an sect the fact is that few T'ang or Sung scholars were without contact with Ch'an monks or Buddhist books. After the T'ang Dynasty, Ch'an was the only sect fit for survival among all the Buddhists schools, and it became the most powerful. It had great influence over the Sung philosophers who were fond of fraternizing with its monks.

The last concept to be dealt with in this chapter is *hsing,* as human nature. From the age of Mencius, the Confucian school believed that human nature is innately endowed with the four cardinal virtues: *Jen, I, Li* and *Chih.* These are the standards of what is morally right and wrong. As long as he is equipped with them, he cannot do otherwise than know what is right and wrong. When the Sung philosophers came on the scene, they called these four virtues *Ri,* or reason or heavenly reason. They look upon the human mind as operating at two levels: the transcendental level of heavenly reason, which sets up the standard of right and wrong; and the empirical or natural level, which feels, wills and decides. This was the theory of the Ch'eng Chu school — although the reader will remember that among the Neo-Confucianists there was also the Lu-Wang school, which took the contrary point of view that mind performs both of these functions, to be sure, but at one level.

Now this ancient Chinese conviction that human nature is endowed with a kind of moral standard, has received much reinforcement from the Buddhist doctrine that the *Tathagatha* womb is the treasure in which the essence of Tathagathahood remains: or from the doctrine of the Yogacarya school that *Alayavijnana* or *Manovijnana* is the all-embracing Intelligence; or from the teaching of Ch'an that everyone possesses the nature of Buddhahood.

If in the *Tathagatha-garbha* all mental possibilities are stored, Mencius cannot have been wrong when he maintained that man is born with moral standards in his nature. Buddhist doctrines of the sort we have just been considering cannot help but serve as props to the Chinese house of thought, making it unshakeable on its foundations.

Doubtless it would be superfluous to go further into detail about the relationship between Buddhism and Neo-Confucianism. However, in conclusion, I shall offer a few examples of how *formulae* of the two traditions correspond:

A.

(1) *Bodhicitta* consists of two aspects:
      (a) The aspect of Bhutatathata (no birth, no death)
      (b) The aspect of birth and death.
(2) According to the Neo-Confucianist cosmology:
      (a) The Ultimate of Nothingness
      (b) The Supreme Ultimate.
          or
      (a) The metaphysical world of *Tao*.
      (b) The physical world of matter or utensils (instruments)

B.

(1) The Buddhist belief:
      (a) The world of forms is Emptiness.
      (b) Emptiness is the world of forms.
(2) The Neo-Confucianist says:
      (a) There are no events outside of *Tao*
      (b) There is no *Tao* outside of events.

C.

(1) Everyone possesses Buddhahood.
(2) Everyone can become a Yao or Shun

D.

(1) One is many; many are one.
(2) Reason is one; manifestations are many.

Confucianism was recast on a more speculative, systematic, and metaphysical foundation, after its contact with Buddhism. This revitalized Confucianism was the Neo-Confucianism which began in the Sung Dynasty and lasted until the end of the Ch'ing Dynasty.

References

1. The remarks attributed to Bodhidharma in this terse and concise form are not to be found in Tao Hsuan's *Kao-seng chuan*, (Biographies of Eminent Monks), written in the T'ang Dynasty, but are recorded in the *Ch'uan-fa cheng-tsung-chi*. The Definite Line of Succession in the True School of the Transmission of the Law), by monk Chi Sung (A.D. 1007-1072) of the Sung Dynasty. Such *formulae* must have been coined in a later period, rather than during the life-time of Bodhidharma.

2. Two Gathas in *Ching-te ch'uan-teng lu* (The Transmission of the Lamp during the Reign of Ching-te, A.D. 1004-1007, of the Sung Dynasty), Book 1.

3. This conversation between Emperor Liang Wu-ti and Bodhidharma is not found in Tao Hsuan's *Biography of Bodhidharma*, but in *The Transmission of the Lamp...*, Book 3.

4. *Ibid.*, Book 3.

5. D. T. Suzuki, *Essays in Zen Buddhism* (First Series), Luzac and Co., London, 1927, p. 90.

6. *Loc. cit.*

7. *Loc. cit.*

8. *Ibid.*, p. 92.

9. The meaning of four kinds of Teachings. *Taisho Tripitaka*, no. 1913, pp. 774-780, Tokyo.

10. M. Winternitz, *A History of Indian Literature*, Vol. 2, translated from the original German by Mrs. S. Ketkar and Miss H. Kohn and revised by the author, published by the University of Calcutta, 1933, pp. 324-325.

11. D. T. Suzuki, *Essays in Zen Buddhism* (Third Series), Luzac and Company, London, 1934, p. 52.

12. *Han Yü*, Book 18.

13. Chou Tun-i *Collected Works*, Book 8.

14. Liu Tsung-yuan, *Collected Works*, Book 6.

15. Chang Tsai, *Collected Works*, Book 1.

16. *Li-chi* (The Book of Rites), Chapter on music.

CHAPTER SEVEN

Cosmological Speculations of Chou Tun-i

Under pressure of the different schools of Buddhism with their thousands of volumes and their practice of meditation, Chinese scholars began to concern themselves with the problem of how to revive Confucianism. The formation of Chinese Buddhist schools in the Sui and T'ang Dynasties gives evidence that the Chinese mind had begun to ferment. The T'ien-t'ai school, the Ch'an school, and the Hua-yen school are examples of how the Chinese could think and rebuild systems according to their own pattern. Then, as the T'ang Dynasty advanced, it manifested its strength in the courage with which its soldiers fought on the battle-field, in the sense of beauty and delicacy expressed by its poets Tu Fu and Li P'o, and in the religious fervor exemplified by its monks Hsüan-chuang and I-ching, who traveled to India in order to translate Buddhist *Sutras* into Chinese.

Just as the T'ang Dynasty was characterized by vigor and emotion, so the Sung Dynasty, which succeeded it, asserted its originality in other ways. Ou-yang Hsiu (A.D. 1007-1072), for instance, in an essay *Concerning the Foundation,* argued that the best method of opposing Buddhism was to examine whether you yourself are physically and spiritually strong. Han Yü's technique of refutation, he thought, was inadequate. If you yourself are strong internally and externally no disease can harm you. Conversely, the most effective method of defending yourself is to make yourself mentally and physically powerful.

Ou-yang Hsiu's suggestion was that China must have her own convictions and philosophical beliefs. He shows us some interesting examples in history to illustrate his point. When Mencius realized that Yang Chu and Mo Ti were corrupting China he created his doctrine of *Jen* and *I* in order to combat them. Then, after his teaching gained the upper hand, the popularity of the two thinkers disappeared. Later, during the Han Dynasty, the Hundred Schools were in the ascendancy. This was when Tung Chung-shu undertook to investigate the Confucian books, and as soon as Confucius came to the top the other schools withdrew from the public stage. Thus it is plain, argued Ou-yang Hsiu, that when your own foundations are firm you can successfully resist invasions of your mind and will.

Ou-yang Hsiu's suggestion was, in fact, an anticipation of what actually happened, for his contemporaries Chou Tun-i (1017-1073), Shao Yung (1011-1077), Chang Tsai (1020-1077), and Chou's two disciples Ch'eng Hao (1032-1085) and Ch'eng I (1033-1107), a-chieved what he had proposed.

The first of these five philosophers, Chou Tun-i, we shall now consider. He was born in Tao-chou District in Honan Province. His official career commenced with the appointment, in his twenty-fifth year, as justice-of-the-peace in Fen-nien District. As councilor to the governor of Nan-an, he further distinguished himself by vigorously opposing the death-sentence which Wang K'uei, the commissioner of justice, had pronounced against a certain criminal. Our philosopher objected to the verdict so strenuously that he threatened to relinquish his hand-tablet (the insignia of his office) unless the death sentence was reversed. Wang K'uei gave in and the criminal was pardoned.

During this period of official employment in Nan-an, Chou Tun-i made the acquaintance of Ch'eng Hsiang, father of Ch'eng Hao and Ch'eng I, afterwards famous as philosophers in their own right, and was invited to be their tutor. Shortly afterwards, however, he was transferred as magistrate to Pin-chou District, then to Kuei-yang District, so he had little opportunity to teach the two brothers.

In his thirty-eighth year, Chou Tun-i became prefect of Nan-k'ang in Kiangsi province to the delight of the inhabitants, who were confident that his decisions would be just no matter what the case. A curious anecdote resulted from this period of his life. It seems that Chou became ill and fell down unconscious, when a friend, P'an Shih-hsing, expecting him to die, felt in his pockets to find out how much money he carried. All he found was a bag containing about 100 pieces of cash (10¢).

Chou Tun-i was later transferred to Ho-chou District in Szechwan Province, again as magistrate.

In his fifty-fourth year, he was appointed commissioner of justice of the Kuang-nan Route (Kwangtung province), where another incident happened which endeared him to the people. The prefect of Tuan-chou, a man named Tu Chih, knew that a certain kind of stone found there made excellent ink tablets and wanted to monopolize its sale. He forbade the people to dig for it, thus becoming known as Tu-10,000-Stones. Chou Tun-i disgusted with what the prefect did, memorialized the emperor requesting that an order be issued rendering it illegal for any official in Tuan-chou to buy more than two pieces of ink tablet.

Then Chou Tun-i was sent to Nan-k'ang as prefect. His love of natural beauty overwhelmed him for he was so impressed by the scenery around Ku Ling Mountain that he built a study there called the Lien-ch'i Studio. Here he settled down, and here he died in his fifty-seventh year.

This brief sketch of the facts of our philosopher's life, interesting as it is in a picture of the public career of a great thinker, will be incomplete without some reference to a few of his sayings which illustrate his philosophical *Weltanschauung*. For instance, Chou Tun-i never cut the grass in front of his window. When he was asked why he replied that he wanted to see how creatures in the world grow and flourish. Again Chou Tun-i, who was learned in the literature of the Taoist and Buddhist sects, was once asked about the meaning of the *Saddharmapundarika Sutra*. He answered that the meaning is the same as the meaning of one of the hexagrams in the *I-ching*, namely *ken*, which signifies "keeping still," or "ceasing to take pleasure in worldly goods."

A longer saying to illustrate Chou Tun-i's philosophical world view is to be found in his essay *Love of the Lotus* where he expresses his deep love of that plant. "Among all kinds of loveable plants," he writes, "on land or in the water, the Ch'in Dynasty poet, T'ao Yüan-ming, adored the chrysanthemum. After the T'ang Dynasty, most people turned to the peony. I myself love the lotus because it grows out of the shiny mud and yet is not defiled, and because it lives in the pure and rippling water without appearing like a too fascinating and seductive lady. It has a system of tubes inside and is straight outside. Without branches or spreading vines its scent comes from afar. And how pure is that fragrance! It is stately and unsullied. It is better to look at it from a distance than from too near — like a lady's petticoat. I consider the chrysanthemum to be a hermit among plants and the peony a flower signifying riches and power. But the lotus is a flower with a noble character. Alas! Where is a lover of the chrysanthemum like T'ao Yüang-ming? Who will love the lotus as much as I? Most people love only the peony!"[1]

This essay, besides revealing some of the philosopher's personality, also shows the affinity of Neo-Confucianist thought of the Sung Dynasty for Buddhism, which took the lotus as its symbol.

If Chou Tun-i's character and *Weltanschauung* are partially disclosed in his own sayings, further light will be shed by the testimony of someone else namely, the author of the *History of the Sung Dynasty,* who appreciated his achievements highly. In it reference was made to the poet Huang T'ing-chien who esteemed Chou Tun-i's aloofness from worldly affairs, and nobility of character. He compared him to a brisk breeze and to the moon after a rainfall. Chou was deeply engaged in reflection and had no desire for fame. He did everything possible for the people but never accepted rewards. Abstentious in his personal habits, he was generous in his assistance to widows and lonely persons. Rather than increase the social contacts with his contemporaries he preferred to make friends with the great minds of the past. His learning was vast and he applied himself incessantly. His *Diagram of the Supreme Ultimate* "traces the roots of the unity of the world, and the beginning of the manifestations of manifoldness."[2]

Curiously there is an analogy between the development of modern philosophy in Europe, and Sung philosophy. Just as Descartes, Spinoza, and Leibnitz started out with their ambitious metaphysical schemes of the unity of the world, so did the Sung philosophers attempt to explain the unity of the world, from its very origin down to the development of human life.

Descartes explained the world in the three terms of Matter, Mind, and God, with God as the ultimate reality. Spinoza substituted the term, Substance, for God, and Mind and Matter were two attributes of God. Leibnitz agreed with both of his predecessors that God is the ultimate reality, but he thought that between the other two constituent parts, Mind and Matter, there was no absolute distinction, since the one is not purely extension, nor is the other purely thought. According to Leibnitz, there exists no unalloyed mental substance, and no unalloyed material substances. In other words, the same substance may be both mental and material. He reconstructed the idea of substance by calling it Monad, a force which is equally mental and material. What is lower on the scale is called matter. What is more highly developed is called mind. But there is no absolute line of demarcation. Everything in the world — whether physical, vegetable, or mental — is a mixture of both, which is called the Monad. Each Monad lives its own life, independent of every other Monad. Each Monad is "windowless."

This brief statement on the great metaphysical schemes of the unity of the world may be of use for purposes of comparison when we come to Chou Tun-i's *Diagram of the Supreme Ultimate.*

Perhaps it is superfluous to say again that the Buddhists taught we Chinese much concerning the nature of reality, the nature of the Buddha, and the nature of human life. From this religion out of India we learned that there is no *Atman* or self substance, except as a combination of the Five *Skandhas*: form, *vedana* (sensation), *samjna* (conception), *sansakara* (deeds), and *vijnana* (consciousness). I mention this spiritual debt again, even at the risk of being repetitious, because it is important to realize that it was to this Buddhist scheme that the Chinese had to offer, as a counter-proposal, a worldview which accounts for the creation of the universe down to the time of the development of human life. This effective counter-proposal was first accomplished by Chou Tun-i in his *Diagram of the Supreme Ultimate.*

I agree with those who hold the view that his *Diagram* was drawn first by the Taoist School, and that subsequently Chou Tun-i revised it and put it in its present form. The document indeed has philosophical interest, and for those who desire to examine the different versions, tracing them back to their early Taoist origins, there is much to hold their attention. We shall here however study the *Diagram* only in so far as it is related to Sung philosophy.

CHOU TUN-I'S EXPLANATION OF THE T'AI-CHI-T'U (DIAGRAM OF THE SUPREME ULTIMATE)

"The Ultimate of Nothingness, but in turn the Supreme Ultimate! When the Supreme Ultimate moves, it produces *Yang*. When motion reaches the utmost, it comes to a standstill. When there is standstill, it produces *Yin*. After the utmost of the standstill, motion comes back again. But motion is followed by another period of rest — these alternatively constitute the primordial factor. When either *Yin* or *Yang* is diffused, the one or the other constitutes a mode — one of the modes. By the transformation of *Yang* and the copulation of *Yin*, water, fire, wood, metal, and earth are produced. These five elements are happily diffused causing the rotation of the four seasons. The five elements are thus no other than *Yin* and *Yang*, *Yin* and *Yang* are no other than the Supreme Ultimate. The Supreme Ultimate is, in itself, the Ultimate of Nothingness.

"When the five elements are produced, each has its own character. The truth of the Ultimate of Nothingness and the essence of the two modes and the five elements are wonderfully integrated and consolidated. The *Tao* (i.e., the way) of *Ch'ien* [first diagram of the *I-ching* meaning "creative"] brings out the male; the *Tao* of *K'un* [second diagram of the *I-ching* meaning "receptive"] brings out the female. Out of the mutual affection of these two vital forces grows the manifoldness of things. By the process of production and reproduction a variety of things spring up infinitely. But mankind is endowed with the best: it becomes *Homo sapiens*. Man is born with the shape of a man, and is endowed with knowledge by the gift of the spirit. He lives through the mutual workings of the five elements. As a result, good and evil, and thousands of kinds of action diversify themselves. The Sages decided the fundamental principles of *Chung* (the Golden Mean), *Cheng* (Fairness), *Jen* and *I*. The principal way of approach is Serenity, and the sages fixed the human standards. Therefore, the sages cooperated with Heaven and Earth in regard to moral excellence, just as the sun and moon cooperate in regard to light. As there is order in the four seasons, so there is harmony in human society. A man of noble character cultivates himself, and becomes blessed. A small man disobeys the laws of the universe and so incurs misfortune.

"The *Tao* of Heaven is *Yin* and *Yang*. The *Tao* of Earth is softness and hardness. The *Tao* of Man is *Jen* and *I*. When one is familiar with what is the beginning and what is the end, one knows also what is life and death. Great is the *I-ching!* It is the ultimate truth."[3]

This Diagram and its explanation are a Chinese version of the theory of the creation and evolution of the universe.

In the Chinese mind God is the Prime Mover or the Highest Good. But He is also the architect who has a plan for the whole universe. As an architect, He must have material with which to build, as the architect of a building must have timber, brick, and mortar. In the case of God's construction of the world, the material is called "matter", or "ether" or in Chinese *Ch'i*.

Behind the material there are two primordial forces or energies, one called *Yin,* the other *Yang. Yin* and *Yang* are merely symbols. They can mean many things. *Yin* stands for the inactive, female, receptive, and shadow. *Yang* stands for activity, the male, initiative and light. Neither of these is self-sufficient; each must have the cooperation of the other. When *Yin* reaches the utmost degree of standstill, it must come back to motion. When *Yang* reaches the utmost degree of motion, it must go back to rest, that is, to *Yin*. The Chinese did not have the idea that the world is built with one form of matter: water, or fire, or the atoms of Democritus. They believed in the existence of these two forces and in their interaction as the primordial power of the creation of the universe. The present day Western scientific terms of "positive" and "negative" are the closest equivalents for *Yang* and *Yin*. This does not mean that the ancient Chinese knew anything about the nuclear structure of an atom, including the positive and negative electrons. They were interested in the flux and in the unceasing change of phenomena, and they came to the conclusion that these two forces, *Yin* and *Yang*, inactivity and activity, must be at the bottom of all processes of change, such as the periodical return of the four seasons, and the reproduction of animals and plants.

The five-element-theory is an old and complicated one. It is not far-fetched to say that in some way it may be related to the four-elements-theory (fire, air, earth, and water) of India and Greece. Just as the Greek philosopher, Heraclitus, gave a meaning to fire by identifying it with the Divine Spirit, so the Chinese expanded the signification of the five elements until they embraced all the phenomena in the universe. The following table shows the wide scope of the five elements in representing the different aspects of nature:

Wood	East	Spring	*Jen*	Liver	Blue
Fire	South	Summer	*Li*	Heart	Red
Earth	Middle		*Hsin* (Honesty)	Spleen or Stomach	Yellow
Metal	West	Autumn	*I*	Lungs	Black
Water	North	Winter	*Chih*	Kidneys	White

Thus, the five element theory may be applied in the following fields: (1) moral values, (2) geography, (3) seasons, (4) physiological organs, (5) colors. The theory of the five elements was developed so elaborately that it can explain any aspect of the life of nature. It was invented by the School of *Yin* and *Yang*, and later was adopted by the Taoists and Confucianists. Chou Tun-i, basing his thought on this tradition, applied the theory in its conventional sense.

The culmination is reached when Chou Tun-i states his conclusion: "The truth of Ultimate of Nothingness, and the essence of the two modes and the five elements, are wonderfully integrated and consolidated." Here he is referring to the creation.

Finally, Chou Tun-i explains the teleological purpose of the universe, which is, of course, anthropocentric, and is exemplified in the moral values set up by the Sages.

I should like to add that in the Chinese mind the five elements are neither mind nor matter in the sense of Descartes, who separated them altogether; nor in the sense of Spinoza, who made mind and matter two attributes correlated with each other under the same God. The five elements, according to the Chinese, are rather like the Monads of Leibnitz, which are neither mind nor matter separately, but are immaterial and material at the same time. This is the reason why the five elements stand for matter and also for moral values. There can be no doubt that the Leibnitzean idea of obscure consciousness, *petites perceptions,* and unconscious mental states would have been approved by the Sung and Ming philosophers. Indeed, Wang Shou-jen expressed the idea: "The reason why drugs can cure human disease is that in the smallest particle of matter there is a world of souls." Here Wang Shou-jen agreed with Chou Tun-i, who showed in the third picture of his *Diagram* that every finite thing possesses its own Supreme Ultimate. On the other hand, the Chinese idea of God is similar to that of Spinoza, because the Chinese deny the personal God of Christianity just as Spinoza did.

In connection with the world and Heaven, I may also mention that the first Chinese presupposition for a world-scheme is the world-constructing reason. To reason we owe the existence of the world, that is, being or knowability or rationality. God is reason, but without matter there would be no existence. Existence requires matter, but whatever there is of blind necessity or evil in the world arises from the nature of this matter. The idea which Plato expressed in the *Philebus,* the World-builder, the Absolutely Good, producing all generated things and making them good, is the starting-point of the Weltanschauung of the Sung philosophers.

The Chinese believe that since the universe is built according to reason, it is the work of God. Reason manifests itself in this world, where God also is. We cannot conceive of the cosmos with God outside it. In other words, God is immanent in the universe, and everything is fashioned according to His idea. God is everywhere, and everything is His work. Thus, I may say that the Chinese conception of the Deity represents Him as immanent and pantheistic rather than personal and transcendental.

After this brief excursion into the philosophy of religion I shall retrace my steps to describe the influence of Chou Tun-i's *Diagram* on the minds of the Sung Dynasty. That influence was tremendous. He attributed the unity of the cosmos to the world-constructing reason. Every aspect of life he traced back to the Supreme Ultimate. He stressed the ideas of *Jen* and *I*. He emphasized the concept of truth as the Prime Mover. For an approach to the ideal of sagehood he recommended Serenity. All these contributions, first made by him to the Chinese philosophical heritage, were followed carefully in a later age by thinkers who were brought up in the Confucianist tradition.

Between Chu Hsi and Lu Chiu-yüan a long polemic was carried on concerning the *Diagram of the Supreme Ultimate*. A brother of Lu, named Lu Chiu-shao, wrote the letter which set off the controversy, but before we launch into this subject, it may be well to say a word emphasizing the depth of Chu Hsi's attachment to the *Diagram*. He wrote a commentary on it in 1173, when he was forty, which he did not reveal to his students until 1188. Three days before his death, in 1200, he delivered a lecture on the subject. His whole life was consecrated to the *Diagram of the Supreme Ultimate,* and once it brought him into trouble, for a censor requested that he be impeached, and Chu Hsi asked permission to resign from his official post. This polemic is merely one of the many evidences of Chu Hsi's passion for the *Diagram of the Supreme Ultimate*.

As I have already mentioned, the controversy was set off by Lu Chiu-shao, a brother of the Lu who subsequently carried it through. Lu Chiu-shao wrote to Chu Hsi asserting that Chou Tun-i's *Diagram of the Supreme Ultimate* differed from the same author's *Comprehensive Understanding* in that the expression: "ultimate of nothingness" does not occur in the latter work. Lu Chiu-shao's inference was that the former book must have been written in Chou Tun-i's immaturity, and he doubted that "ultimate of nothingness" was a valid conception.

Chu Hsi answered Lu Chiu-shao as follows: "The first phrase: 'The ultimate of nothingness, but in turn the supreme ultimate' is the phrase with which you show disagreement. In my view, if the ultimate of nothingness be not first mentioned, the term 'supreme ultimate' will mean only something finite, not the origin of the manifoldness of the universe. If the primary expression: 'ultimate of nothingness' be not followed by the term: 'supreme ultimate', the ultimate of nothingness will be just a sign of emptiness, and will not generate a world of manifoldness. The sentence structure shows how fine, thoroughgoing, and subtle was Chou's thought. What follows the initial phrase is comprehensive, systematic, orderly and understandable. It is a master-piece of art, immortal and irrefutable. If in one's reading one is unable to grasp the meaning of so clear and concise an idea, the difficulty is in one's self, not in the author of the *Diagram*."

After this introductory correspondence between Lu Chiu-shao and Chu Hsi, Lu Chiu-yüan took over. He and Chu Hsi wrote two letters each, totalling 10,000 words. I shall not translate these letters in detail because the content has to do mostly with mutual misunderstandings and with disputes about the meanings of words. But I shall confine myself to giving the main contentions on either side.

The first letter of Lu Chiu-yüan contains the following points:

(1) In Chou Tun-i's *T'ung-shu* (*Comprehensive Understanding*), the words 'ultimate of nothingness' do not occur. Lu Chiu-yüan is not sure that this expression originated from Chou Tun-i himself. But he does not mean to imply that the *T'ai-chi-t'u* was a forgery by somebody else. His meaning seems to be that this essay must have been the fruit of Chou Tun-i's immaturity. At any rate, when Chou wrote the *T'ung-shu* he avoided the words: "Ultimate of nothingness." The reason for the omission might be that he found the concept invalid.

(2) Lu Chiu-yüan criticized Chu Hsi's statement: "If the ultimate of nothingness be not first mentioned, the term 'supreme ultimate' will mean only something finite, not the origin of the manifoldness of the universe. If the primary expression: 'ultimate of nothingness' be not followed by the term: 'supreme ultimate', the ultimate of nothingness will be just a sign of emptiness, and will not generate a world of manifoldness." The term 'supreme ultimate' Lu Chiu-yüan insisted was a discovery of the sages. Its original meaning as the source of the manifoldness of things was settled long ago. This signification cannot be altered by the mere mentioning or failure to mention this or that name. In the *I-ching* is the saying: "In change there is the supreme ultimate." The presupposition of this

Classic is Being. How can Being be transmuted into non-being or nothingness? In the *I-ching*, despite the fact that the expression "ultimate of nothingness" is never used, the term "supreme ultimate" is, nonetheless, not liable to being misunderstood as a reference to something finite, rather than to the root of the manifoldness of the universe.

(3) "Your (i.e. Chu Hsi's) interpretation is that the term, 'ultimate of nothingness,' means 'immaterial' or 'above the physical world,' while the 'supreme ultimate' means 'reason.' Then Lu Chiu-yüan counter-argued: In the *I-ching* it is said: "What is above the physical word is *Tao*." In the same book it is also said: "What makes *Yin* appear at one time, and *Yang* at another time, is Tao." If *Yin* and *Yang* constitute *Tao,* then all the more may this be said of the supreme ultimate. How can one be so stupid as to misunderstand the term 'supreme ultimate' as referring to a finite thing? It is, therefore, superfluous to add the term, 'ultimate of nothingness.' If one is afraid that the term 'supreme ultimate' is liable to misinterpretation in a physical sense, all that is necessary is to qualify it by some such adjective as 'invisible', or 'inaudible.'

(4) In the last section of this letter, Lu Chiu-yüan attacked Chu Hsi by calling him one who had been contaminated by the school of Lao-tzu. Lu Chiu-yüan said: "As far as I know, this *Diagram* was handed down by Mu Po-chang and his teacher, Ch'en Hsi-i. Ch'en Hsi-i was a follower of Lao-tzu. The expression, 'ultimate of nothingness', was first coined by Lao-tzu in his chapter, *Keeping to the Female,* and is found in the books of our sages. In the first chapter of the *Tao-te-ching,* Lao-tzu said: 'Nameless is the beginning of the world; having name is the mother of the manifoldness of things.' That first phrase in Chou-Tun-i's *Diagram of the Supreme Ultimate,* 'The Ultimate of Nothingness, but in turn the supreme ultimate,' comes to the same meaning. Here lies the incorrectness and the bias of the doctrine of Lao-tzu. How could you overlook so important a point!"[6]

Finally, Lu Chiu-yüan asked why the term 'ultimate of nothingness' could not be found in Chou Tun-i's *T'ung-shu.* Even the Ch'eng brothers, who wrote many books and articles, never used this expression. "I wonder why you, (i.e., Chu Hsi) should believe in, and glorify this *Diagram* so much!"

Chu Hsi's replies were as sharp and to the point as Lu Chiu-yüan's questions. His letter began with a comment about the coinage of new terms in the *Classics*. The ancient authors, he said, of the *I-ching*, Emperor Fu-hsi and King Wen, never used the term 'supreme ultimate'. Confucius was the first to use it. After Confucius, Chou Tun-i coined the expression 'utimate of nothingness'. This indicates that the earlier and later sages worked along the same lines and stood on common ground. But it does not mean that those who used no new terms knew less, nor that those who used new terms knew more. Chu Hsi's point is that novel terms are coined in the course of thought-currents. One should not expect them prematurely. When the time is ripe, one cannot prevent their appearance, nor should one take the view that they are false. Chu Hsi went on to mention seven points in which he could not agree with Lu Chiu-yüan.

(1) He charges Lu with misinterpreting the meaning of the word *'chi'*, 'ultimate'. This word, he says, means 'the utmost'. Since this idea is so high and so far reaching it cannot be construed as other than 'supreme ultimate'. According to Lu Chiu-yüan, however, the word should mean 'Golden Mean' or 'reason'. Since, says Lu, *'chi'* signifies the ridge-pole of a roof, the highest horizontal timber of a house, and since it sometimes is equi-distant from the four sides, therefore the meaning of the word is extended to the sense of 'Golden Mean.' But, counters Chu Hsi, the original signification of the term had nothing to do with the idea 'mean.' This is the source of the first point in Lu's confusion.

(2) Chu Hsi mentions that Lu's quotation from the *T'ung-shu*: "The Golden Mean is the utmost", is irrelevant to the idea of the supreme ultimate. He says that this quotation is the last sentence of the preceding section, and does not belong to the section about the One and the Many, which treats of the ultimate. This is the source of the second point in Lu's confusion.

(3) Since Chou Tun-i perceived clearly that the reality of the *Tao* is immaterial, and that neither Being nor Nothingness can be

predicated on it he coined the term 'ultimate of nothingness'. In so doing he disregarded the critical remarks of others and also his personal advantage. He was bold enough to announce what other people were too shy to say. But he discovered a new concept. It is a pity that Lu does not see the point.

(4) As to Lu Chiu-yüan's quotation: "What makes *Yin* appear at one time and *Yang* at another, is Tao," Chu Hsi replies that this sentence does not mean that *Yin* and *Yang* are metaphysical (above the physical). *Yin* and *Yang* are physical, and the reason for their existence lies in the *Tao* itself. From the viewpoint of the utmost of predicability of the *Tao,* the *Tao* may be called the supreme ultimate. From the viewpoint of the operation of the supreme ultimate, the supreme ultimate may be called the *Tao.* They are called by two terms, but they are one and the same thing. Why has Chou Tun-i called this unity the ultimate of nothingness? It is immaterial and shapeless. Though it stood before the world was created, it remains since creation. Though it is above *Yin* and *Yang,* still it is inside of *Yin* and *Yang.* It is immaterial, yet it is the essence of the whole universe. Lu Chiu-yüan's condemnation of the term, 'ultimate of nothingness', will only lead the people to the impression that the supreme ultimate is something which is finite and material. This is the source of Lu's fourth point of confusion.

(5) Lu Chiu-yüan attacked Chu Hsi for his explanation without the term "ultimate of nothingness", the term "supreme ultimate" will degenerate into meaning only something finite, in which case it cannot refer to the origin of the manifoldness of things. Without the term "supreme ultimate", the ultimate of nothingness will fall into emptiness and annihilation, and will be unable to be the origin of the manifoldness of things. But Chu Hsi considers that he has been fair in his treatment of both sides (i.e., Being and Nothingness). He admits, however, to having said, perhaps, too much. Chu Hsi is strongly opposed to the remarks of his opponent that the idea of the supreme ultimate was settled long ago, and that its truth has nothing to do with whether one mentions it or not. This is the source of the fifth point of Lu's confusion.

(6) Chu Hsi comes to Lu Chiu-yüan's quotation from the *I-ching.* In this Classic is the assertion that there "is" the supreme

ultimate, and Lu says that nothingness should not be asserted in this connection. Chu Hsi is astonished at Lu's remark that he (Chu) as a philosopher should not mix Being and Nothingness in such a context. Chu Hsi is of the view that the word "is" here does not mean a kind of being which is material and visible. This word "is" does not signify the being of the two modes and five elements, which are physical and visible. One should not mix the word "is" with finite and material. Neither should one mix "nothingness" with emptiness and annihilation. This is the source of the sixth point of Lu's confusion.

(7) The expression "Wu-chi", ultimate of nothingness, in Lao-tzu's book means "limitless" or "infinite". This is the same as Chuang-tzu's expressions, "Door of the limitless" and "Wilderness of the limitless". One should not confuse this expression "Wu-chi" of Lao-tzu with Chou Tun-i's "ultimate of nothingness". This is the source of the seventh point of Lu's confusion.[7]

After the exchange of these two letters between Lu Chiu-yüan and Chu Hsi, both continued the debate, but their subsequent words were repetitious and I shall not deal with them.

The main point of their controversy was the question of the two concepts: "ultimate of nothingness" and "supreme ultimate". Lu Chiu-yüan held the view that the term "supreme ultimate" was clear enough to explain the origin of the manifoldness of things. Chu Hsi, who believed that the *Diagram of the Supreme Ultimate* was an attempt to explain the origin of creation, accordingly, was confident that before the creation there was a state of nothingness. But this state of nothingness was not emptiness or annihilation. Before the operation of the supreme ultimate, we may assume that there was the ultimate of nothingness. It is Hegel's conception of being, which was divided into three *momenta*: pure being, nothing, and becoming. Hegel based his logical theory on the doctrine of thesis, antithesis, and synthesis. Thus, he put "becoming" between "being" and "nothing", as a bridge. But in Chou Tun-i's sense, the ultimate of nothingness and the supreme ultimate work at the same time, and they are the two aspects of the same reality. There is no real distinction between them, but one may imagine that there are two stages. Here it will be useful to explain my translation of the first sentence of the Explanation of the *Diagram of the Supreme Ultimate*: "The ultimate of nothingness, but in turn the supreme ultimate". One may also say that the ultimate of nothingness becomes the supreme ultimate. But in Chu Hsi's understanding, the interval between the two is so close that the insertion of a stage called "becoming" is unnecessary. Therefore, I simply say: "The ultimate of nothingness but in turn the supreme ultimate", which is, in other words, the assertion that the one cannot be interpreted as standing for nothingness, nor the other as referring to Being. The linking word between these two terms is the Chinese conjunction, *erh,* meaning "but in turn", in order to come near the Chinese sense.

This *Diagram* and its explanation caused a great deal of discussion among the Sung philosophers — just as in European metaphysics the problem of God, Freedom, and Immortality were the source of conflicts between the Rationalists and the Empiricists. Those who stood on solid ground denied any knowledge of such entities as God, Freedom and Immortality, while others tried to prove the existence of God by human reason. In China those who stood on solid Confucian ground were interested in the moral life of humanity. Hence, for them, the assumption was enough that there is heaven, or that there is the supreme ultimate. On the other hand, those who were more speculative went farther and inquired about the origin of the creation. Hence, they came to the idea of nothingness.

During the Ming Dynasty the debate on the *Diagram* still went on. Huang Tsung-yen, brother of Huang Tsung-hsi, author of the *Philosophical Records of the Sung and Yüan Dynasties,* made a study of the *Diagram,* and came to the conclusion that it is of Taoist origin. On the basis of this conclusion later editors of the *Records,* proceeding as if the *Diagram* of Chou Tun-i were not a piece of orthodox Confucianist writing, did not assign it the place of the top-ranking document in the Chapter on Chou Tun-i, but instead gave this priority to the *T'ung shu.*

However, Huang Tsung-hsi wrote a lecture in which he seems not to have opposed the term, "ultimate of nothingness," but rather to have defended it. He thought that on the one hand it was wrong to cling to the viewpoint of being, and to know only what is worldly; but, on the other hand, that it was also wrong to believe in the Taoist and Buddhist theory that being came out of nothingness. Huang Tsung-hi's view was that being and nothingness should not be separated. This shows the proclivity of the Chinese mind to remain within this world, and not to go beyond it.

In the Chinese theory of creation there are some points worthy of mention. (1) Creation is based on the idea of change. (2) No kind of matter makes the world, but rather the two forces, *Yang* and *Yin,* positive and negative. (3) The elements which make up plants, animals, and mankind, are both material and immaterial. (4) The physical and the metaphysical are two aspects of the same universe, and should not be separated.

Let us now turn to the other work of Chou Tun-i, the *T'ung-shu.* It seems that the editors of the *Philosophical Records of the Sung And Yüan Dynasties* had some doubts about the authenticity of the *Diagram* attributed to Chou Tun-i, because the expression, "ultimate of nothingness" never appears in the *T'ung-shu.* These editors appreciated the *T'ung-shu* all the more because it appeared to them as strictly orthodox Confucianist. According to my view, both works were written in the same style and the same spirit. In both works Chou Tun-i attached more importance to the *I-ching.* Also he uses the same terminology: *Jen, I, Chung, Cheng* in the two books. He included his theories of the two forces, the five elements, and manifoldness and oneness in the *T'ung-shu* as well as in the *Explanation of the Diagram of the Supreme Ultimate.* The reason why Chou Tun-i did not let the expression, "ultimate of nothingness," appear in the *T'ung-shu* was that the latter work had nothing to do with the process of creation, but rather dealt with the different aspects of human life.

Chou Tun-i's *Comprehensive Understanding* is divided into forty sections. In these we find his philosophy about the unity of the world. Based on the tradition of the *I-ching,* he discusses the fundamental concepts from the viewpoint of the unity of the world, rather than from that of intellectual analysis. Here are some of his pregnant remarks:

"Truth is the foundation of sagehood. Great, indeed, is the generating power of *Ch'ien* (the Creative); all things owe their beginning to it. This is the foundation of truth. The course of

Ch'ien alters and shapes beings, until each attains its proper nature.
Then truth is firmly established. This is the idea of the highest
good. It has been said: That which lets *Yin* work at one time, and
Yang at another, is *Tao*. As continuer it is good. As completer it
is nature. Primordiality and potentiality of success form the forward movement of truth. Furthering and perseverance constitute
the return to truth. Great indeed, is the change which is the
source of nature and the heavenly order."[9]

Chou Tun-i shows here that *Ch'ien* and truth are of the same
character. Truth also contains the four attributes: primordiality,
potentiality of success, furthering, and perseverance. Truth means
nothing other than world-constructing reason.

In the section discussed above, Chou Tun-i applies the concept
of truth to the universe. Then he turns to apply the same concept
to sagehood. This equation between truth and sagehood suggests
Buddhism, according to which the Buddha is the Creator.

"Sagehood is nothing but truth. Truth is the foundation of
the five human relations, and the source of all activities. While at
rest, it signifies nothing; while active, it signifies being. It is right
to the utmost degree, enlightened, and broadminded. If the five
human relations and all activities, are not rooted in the truth, they
are all wrong. They are caprice, darkness, and obstacles. When
there is truth, nothing will be evil. All this is so easy, and yet so
hard to execute. If one is firm and exact, there will be no difficulty. It has been said: On the day when one can control one's
self and return to the rules of decency, the whole world will reach
the stage of goodness."[10]

These quotations from the *T'ung-shu* may be too terse for the
Western public, so let us add a few words of explanation.

Since the intellectual atmosphere in Chou-Tun-i's time was
filled with much interest in cosmological studies, men like himself,
Chao Yung, Chang Tsai, and the Ch'eng brothers, went back to
the *I-ching*, which is the *Book of Genesis* in China.

This work consists of Sixty-four Hexagrams by which all
kinds of phenomena, beginning with the creation of the world, are
explained. These Hexagrams are written in strokes. The first
Hexagram, called "Ch'ien", is a picture of three unbroken strokes,
which stands for the complete *Yang*, the Creative Principle, Heaven,

or the Sun. The second Hexagram, known as "K'un," consists of six broken strokes which represent the *Yin*, the Receptive Principle, the female, the earth. This dyad, *Yang* and *Yin*, is the driving force of the universe, and of all the changes in the universe. The first Hexagram, "Ch'ien," represents, sometimes, not only itself, but also is understood as if the "K'un" diagram was included in it. As the Hexagram, "Ch'ien" represents creation, it possesses four attributes: Primordiality or Supremacy, Potentiality of Success, Furthering, and Perseverance. In life, the first thing which is evident to everybody is the endless going on of life after life. This endless process of life after life comes from the sun, because the work of the sun proceeds endlessly.

Here one is reminded of the words of Plato in the *Republic*: "You would say that the sun is not only the visibility in all visible things, but of generation and nourishment and growth, though not himself a generation?" "Certainly." "In like manner the good may be said to be not only the author of knowledge in all things known, but of their being and essence, and yet the good is not essence, but far exceeds essence in dignity and power."[11] Plato's "sun" and "good" are Chou Tun-i's "Truth" and "Ch'ien."

The nature of the universe is understood as if the author is himself in the place of the Creator, thus putting himself in a position where he could know the main qualities. "Primordiality" is the highest good, to which all beings owe their beginning. "Potentiality of Success" means clouds passing and rain falling, from which all beings take their form. "Furthering" is a process of shaping and altering in the time of development until each being attains its own specific nature. "Perseverance" means conservation and preserving an entity in firmness and stability. These four virtues which constitute the order of the world show an affinity to the thought in Jowett's Introduction to the *Timaeus*: "We may return to the argument: Why did God make the world? Like man, he must have a purpose and his purpose is the diffusion of that goodness or good which he himself is. The term goodness is not to be understood in this passage as meaning benevolence or love, in the Christian sense of the term, but rather law, order, harmony, like the idea of good in the Republic."

I may add that the meaning of the "Ch'ien" hexagram is much nearer to Plato's Theory of Creation than to the *Book of Genesis* in the Old Testament, where creation is entirely by divine fiat. Plato's name for reality in the highest reach, the Highest Good, is the true meaning of "Ch'ien".

Let me quote Jowett's words in his Introduction to the *Republic*: "The question has been asked, In what relation did Plato suppose the idea of good to stand to the nature of God? Or is the idea of good another mode of conceiving God. The latter seems to be the true answer. To the Greek philosopher the perfection and unity of God was a far higher conception than his personality, which he hardly found a word to express, and which to him would have seemed to be borrowed from mythology. To the Christian, or to the modern thinker in general, it is difficult if not impossible to attach reality to what he terms mere abstraction; whereas to Plato this very abstraction is the truest and most real of all things. Hence, from a difference in form of thought, Plato appears to be resting on a creation of his mind only. But if we may be allowed to paraphrase the idea of good by the words 'intelligent principle of law and order in the universe embracing equally man and nature', we find a meeting point between him and ourselves."[13] The Chinese idea of creation is much nearer to the Greek philosopher than to the Hebrew prophet.

Furthermore, Plato calls this world the fairest and most perfect, according to an eternal and unchangeable pattern. Since heaven represents an unchangable pattern, so a day, a month, the four seasons, and the beginning and end of a year, come in regular periods. From the regularity of the periods, the Chinese learned the virtues of truth, enlightenment, honesty, harmony, and the Golden Mean. This is why Chou Tun-i says that sagehood is no other than Truth. This is the reason why Chou Tun-i's *T'ung-shu* deals with these three questions in its first chapter, since their contexts are inter-related.

Now I come to our philosopher's idea of subtlety, an idea which he is fond of emphasizing. He believes that after a matter has become distinct and clear, it no longer affords an opportunity for change. Since the matter has, as it were, come to the surface, it is already too late for revision. And before it is clear and distinct there is a stage when matter can hardly be noticed. To this latter situation he gives the name "Subtlety" which is something preconscious, and which is near to the idea of "petites perceptions" of Liebnitz, or the subconscious of modern phychoanalysis. Chou Tun-i tells us that if one in the state of "subtlety" scrutinizes one's mind carefully one can find a way to control it. He says:

"Truth means actionlessness or doing nothing. Subtlety is the seed of good and evil. Love is *Jen*. What is appropriate is righteousness. What is reason shows us the principles of decency. What gives one understanding is wisdom. What makes one observe or hold fast is faith. Whoever practices these virtues in a natural and easy way is a sage. Whoever abides in, or returns to them is a wise man. Whoever sees the most subtle or the invisible, whoever can fathom the unfathomable, he is a divine character."[14]

Then Chou Tun-i goes on to merge the three ideas: Truth, Divine Character, and Abstruseness.

"What is calm and motionless," he says, "is Truth. What gives response when affected is the Divine Character. What moves, and does not take the shape either of Being or Non-being is the State of Subtlety. When Truth attains the utmost, it is Enlightenment. When the Divine Character can give response, it is delicate. When the State of subtlety is hidden, it is abstruse. One who attains Truth, Divine Character, and Subtlety, is a Sage."[15]

The state which Chou Tun-i is discussing in these last passages is the step which lies between visibility and invisibility, or between cognisability and precognisability. This stage the Chinese mind took much into consideration, because to control a thought or a violition while it is still in formation is far preferable to the attempt to control it after it has been formed.

In concluding this chapter I give an appreciation of Chou Tun-i quoted by Huang Pai-chia, a nephew of Huang Chung-yen who had doubts about the authenticity of the *Diagram of the Supreme Ultimate*. This appreciation was written by Chu Hsi. Huang Pai-chia quoted it because he saw its fairness, and wished to use it to counterbalance the depreciatory comments by his uncle.

"The works of Chou Tun-i are the *T'ung-shu*, and the *Diagram of the Supreme Ultimate*, which through the Ch'eng brothers were transmitted to the public. These works are complementary to each other, as inside is to outside. Chou Tun-i traces the world back to One Reason, two forces, and five elements, in order to give a fundamental outline of the reality of the *Tao*. He also tells the people how to weigh the value of morality, literature, and official position, in order to lift the people out of pettiness and vulgarity. His way of approach to sagehood and government is simple and precise without falling into idle talk. There is no scholar from the Ch'in and Han Dynasties down, who can compete with him. Also his profundity and comprehensiveness have seldom been reached by scholars of this century."[16]

Chou Tun-i no doubt was the founder of the new philosophy in the Sung Dynasty, just as Descartes, Spinoza, and Leibnitz were the founders of modern philosophy in Europe.

References

1. Chou Tun-i, *Collected Works,* Book 8.
2. *Sung shih* (History of the Sung Dynasty), Book 427.
3. Chou Tun-i *Collected Works,* Book 1.
4. Wang Shou-jen, *Collected Works of Wang Yang-ming, Ch'uan-hsi lu* (Record of Instruction and Practice), Book 3.
5. Chu Hsi, *Collected Works,* Book 1, letter to Lu Chiu-shao.
6. All these points of controversy between Lu and Chu in *P.R.S.Y.,* Book 12.
7. *Loc. cit.*
8. *Ibid.,* Book 11.
9. *Loc. cit.*
10. *Loc. cit.*
11. *The Dialogues of Plato,* Vol. 2, p. 337.
12. *Ibid.,* p. 495.
13. *Ibid.,* p. 134.
14. *P.R.S.Y.,* Book 11.
15. *Loc. cit.*
16. *Loc. cit.*

CHAPTER EIGHT

Cosmological Speculations
of Shao Yung and Chang Tsai

Shao Yung was considered by Chu Hsi as one of the five founders of the Sung philosophy. In the *Philosophical Records of the Sung and Yüan Dynasties*, Shao Yung appears as such, but with the note that he was unorthodox. However, in the *Cheng-i-t'ang Collection*, edited by Chang Po-hsing (1651-1725), Shao Yung's name was not included. Chou Tun-i's work tops the list, then follows that of the Ch'eng brothers, but there are no works by Shao Yung. In the *Tao-t'ung-lu* [*Line of Succession of the Tao*], a book in the *Cheng-i-t'ang Collection*, Mencius is followed by Chou Tun-i, the Ch'eng brothers, and Chu Hsi, but Shao Yung's name is missing. This collection is limited so strictly to the productions of the orthodox school of Chu Hsi that even the writings of Lu Chiu-yüan and Wang Shou-jen [Wang Yang-ming] are omitted. The reason for Shao Yung's exclusion, however, is different from that of the other two, who were expelled for their idealistic tendencies. Shao Yung's rejection was because of his relation to the Taoist school. In a part of the *Cheng-i-t'ang Collection* entitled *Lien-lo-feng-ya* [*Anthology of Poems from the Schools of Lien-ch'i and Lo-yang*], some of his works are included, but they are poems, which indicates that Shao Yung's literary attempts were appreciated, although his philosophical efforts were regarded by the editor as not up to the standards of Confucianism. This omission by Chang Po-hsing reveals much about Shao Yung's

159

anamolous position among Sung philosophers. Let us look at his life and work.

I like to call Shao-Yung a Chinese Pythagoras, because his philosophy was of a mathematico-theological nature. Shao-Yung was a number-theorist, who believed that in various cosmical periods the same persons and events are repeated. He evolved a mathematical formula that the earth, when it goes through a life of 129,600 years, comes to the end of its first *Yang*. Shao Yung also agreed with the Greek Pythagoreans in his theory that musical harmony consists of a numerical proportion in the lengths of musical strings. He held that in the pursuit of truth, that is, in religious mathematical study, one finds the calm disinterestedness which frees one from the distractions of the body, and prepares one for the moral process of purification. Thus, between Shao Yung and the Pythagoreans there were several similarities of *Lebensanschauung*.

Shao Yung was born in A.D. 1011. Even as a boy his self-confidence enabled him to accomplish some remarkable feats. He clothed himself in cotton and lived on vegetables, a way of life which, incidentally, again reminds us of the Greek Pythagoreans. Then he said to himself: "If the people of former ages could make friends with their contemporaries, why should not I myself see something of the world?" So he took a trip from his home into the provinces of Shantung, Kiang-su and Hupeh. After his return he met Li Chih-ts'ai, a magistrate of Kung-ch'eng District, and began the mathematico-theological studies for which he is famous. At that time the ministers Fu Pi and Ssu-ma Kuang, the latter was the author of the historical work *Tzu-chih-t'ung-chien*, were retired in Lo-yang. They made the acquaintance of Shao Yung, and bought him a home. It is said that Shao Yung liked to sit in a wheel-barrow drawn by a man, and that when the people heard him coming they cheered. Many times he was recommended for appointment as a high official, but he always refused.

He was to some extent a prophet. Thus before Lu Hui-ch'ing was appointed premier, Shao Yung heard the singing of a bird and said: "When the country is prosperous, the people of the north will be in power; when the country is in disorder, the people of the south will be in power. The singing of the bird tells me that a man of the south will be appointed premier." The appointment of Lu-Hui-ch'ing, a man from Fukien, one of the southern provinces, confirmed the prophecy.

Several stories are told in connection with Shao Yung's death-bed prophecies. On his death bed Ch'eng I, Ssu-ma Kuang, Chang Tsai and others came to pay their last respects. When Ch'eng I begged for a final word, Shao Yung raised his two hands. The younger philosopher, not catching the idea, asked a second time. Then the dying man answered: "You must leave the road ahead of you wide open. Otherwise you will not let other people walk on it." Meanwhile, guests in the outer rooms discussed his burial place. Although he was not within hearing of them, he knew what they were talking about, and he called his son in to explain that he did not wish to be buried nearby, but preferred to lie in the cemetery of his ancestors. It happened that at this time a friend named Ou-yang Fei passed through Lo-yang and took the opportunity to call upon the dying man. During their conversation Shao Yung told all the details of his life — for a reason which nobody could guess; but after his death, when the question of what posthumous title the emperor should bestow upon him came up and when the decision was left to Ou-yang Fei, it became clear that the philosopher had had a vision of what his friend's responsibility was to be. Shao Yung died at sixty-seven.

As a man he can be best pictured in the words of his own poem about himself.

> "Character same as the pine-tree and —
> Literary style as splendid as the poppy;
> Caliber as great as a mountain or river;
> Sentiment as fine as the wind or the moon.
> My face and physical shape are borrowed from
>   you (Heaven).
> After toying with the ball (the world,
>   the Supreme Ultimate).
> I come and go as I please."

One of his essays, *The Man Mr. Nameless*, contains a description of his own character. "The man Mr. Nameless was born in the province of Hopeh and brought up in the same place.

Afterwards he went to the province of Honan and died there. When he was ten years old, he studied in his home village, and exhausted what there was to know about the village. From ten to twenty per cent of his crudeness was removed. When he was twenty years old, he studied in the district and learned everything about the district. From thirty to forty per cent of his crudeness was taken away. From thirty years of age, he studied in his county, and knew all there was to know about his county. Then his crudeness was reduced to fifty per cent. At forty he studied the ancients, and knew all about them. His crudeness was reduced to twenty per cent. When he was fifty years old he became a student of Heaven and Earth, and knew all about Heaven and Earth. Then his crudeness was down to zero.

"At first his village was ill at ease because of his strangeness, and asked the district about his character. The people of the district had discovered his sociability, and so they said that he was not strange. Later the district went to the county, and asked whether he was popular, and his study perhaps superficial. The answer of the people of the county was that he was a poor mixer, so could not be a man of superficiality. The county suspected him of narrow-mindedness, and it asked the people in all directions whether he was narrow. The answer was that he could not be placed in a relation of equality with any ordinary being which is limited in shape and function, and that therefore he could not be narrow-minded. Yet the people from all directions were still suspicious of his character, and they asked people of the present day and of ancient times about him. The answer was that there was no one who could be his equal. Then the people raised the question before Heaven and Earth; but even Heaven and Earth did not know what to answer. The people from all directions were too puzzled to know what to call him. At last the name Mr. Nameless was given. Nameless meant that he was a man who could not be named.

"Anything which has a shape is a finite thing. Each finite thing can be called by a name. The people asked: 'Has this man a physical body?' The answer was that he had a body, but that he left of it no traces. 'Could he work?' The answer was that he could work, but that he worked without doing anything for his own purposes. A man who leaves traces, and who has an individual purpose, can be discovered and is knowable. But as long as a man leaves no traces, and works without individual purpose, he cannot be discovered or named by Spirits. There is much less chance that mankind can know and name him.

"Whatever creates the manifoldness of things is Heaven and Earth. Whatever creates Heaven and Earth is the Supreme Ultimate. How can one give a name to the Supreme Ultimate? How can the Supreme Ultimate be within the scope of human knowledge? The term 'Supreme Ultimate' was coined because of the impossibility of naming it. 'The Supreme Ultimate' means merely 'The Nameless.' "[1]

Because of the boasting which this autobiography confirms, he has been considered by Chinese scholars as relatively unorthodox. Yet it gives an indication of the breadth of Shao Yung's knowledge, and of the adeptness of his cosmological speculations.

His most important work is *Cosmic Periods of the Great Ultimate*. This is an astrological treatise, a calculation of the cosmic days, months, and years, in which the future can be forecast. Another work is The *A Priori Position of the Hexagrams,* in which he adjusts the positions of the sixty-four hexagrams to the arithmetical series 1:2:4:8:64, a theory found in the *I-ching*. He also wrote a treatise *On Objectivity*: questions and answers between a fisherman and a woodcutter.

The first two of these works: *Cosmic Periods* and The *A Priori Positions,* are too remote from our present life, and too abstruse for understanding. Thus, they will not be dealt with here. However, Shao Yung's method of calculating the Cosmic Periods is of sufficient interest to be given as follows:

COSMIC DAYS	COSMIC MONTHS		SOLAR YEARS
30	January, 1 month		10,800
60	January - February,	2 months	21,600
90	Jan. - Feb. - March	3 months	32,400
120	Jan...etc...April	4 months	43,200
150	Jan...etc...May	5 months	54,000
180	Jan...etc...June	6 months	64,800
210	Jan...etc...July	7 months	75,600
240	Jan...etc...August	8 months	86,400

COSMIC DAYS	COSMIC MONTHS			SOLAR YEARS
270	Jan...etc...Sept.	9 months		97,200
300	Jan...etc...Oct.	10 months		108,000
330	Jan...etc...Nov.	11 months		118,000
360	Jan...etc...Dec.	12 months		129,600

NOTES:

The *First Yang,* 10,800 Solar Years, or January (the first month), or 0 hour to 2 *ante meridiem,* is the time of the birth of Heaven.

The *Second Yang,* 21,600 solar years, which consists of the first and second months, includes in its latter half, February, or 2 hour to 4 *ante meridiem,* and is the time of the creation of the Earth.

The *Third Yang,* 32,400 solar years, or the first three months, includes in its last third, March, or 4 hour to 6 *ante meridiem,* and is the time of the birth of mankind.

The first six months, ending with June, or 11 *ante meridiem* to 1 *post* meridiem, 64,800 solar years, reaches the culminating period of mankind corresponding in human history to the reigns of the Sage-Emperors Yao and Shun.

The first seven months, ending with July, when *Yang* begins to decline, and *Yin* to rise, make 75,600 solar years. One has now reached the period of the Emperor Shen-tsung of the Sung Dynasty, under whom Shao Yung, the author of the cosmic-chronology lived.

The period extending through December, when the culmination of *Yin* occurs, is the end of 129,600 solar years. This is the time of the end of the world.

This whole Cosmic year or era or period, with its twelve Cosmic Months, recurs endlessly according to an identical pattern.

This theory of cosmic periods opened to Shao Yung a vision of the Universe in tremendously long and vast terms, which freed him from the life of daily events. Since he was devoted to religio-mathematical studies, he believed in eternal truth, and was, accordingly, above human limitations and untainted by subjectivism. For this reason he advocated objectivity. His meditations on objectivity are sufficiently remarkable to quote:

"What is called an objective view of the natural world," he says, "is not the view of one who looks at the world through one's eyes, but rather the view of one who looks with one's mind. Again it is not the view of one who looks at the world from the standpoint of one's mind, but rather the view of one who looks from the standpoint of the natural laws of things. Why can a sage understand the nature of thousands of things? Because he is capable of reflective thinking. Reflective thinking means the sort of thinking that contemplates the manifoldness of things not from the egoistic point of view. To contemplate the manifoldness of things from the non-egoistic point of view means to look at them from the point of view of things. This view of things from the things themselves destroys the view from the ego."[2]

From his theory of periods and his theory of objectivity Shao Yung deduced his own way of considering past and present.

"What is past and present," he says, "is like day and night in this world. If one looks at the present from the present, this present is called present. If one looks at the present from the future, this so-called present is also the past. If one looks at the past from the present, this past is past. If one looks at the past from the past itself, this past is present. Therefore, we know that the past is not itself the past, and the present is not itself the present. The so-called past and the present originated in a subjective point of view. It is quite possible that before the past of thousands of years ago, or after the future of many thousands of years ahead, mankind did, or will, relinquish the subjective point of view."[3]

Shao Yung warned the people not to have excessive confidence in sense-knowledge, but to respect the mind that is devoted to research in eternal truth. "Man is *homo sapiens*", he says, because his eyes can have the sight of thousands of things, his ears can listen to all kinds of sounds, his nose can smell all sorts of odors, his mouth can distinguish the tastes of all kinds of food. Sights, sound, smells, and tastes originate from the character of the things. Ears, eyes, nose and mouth are the means by which a man responds. The character of the things themselves is not definitely expressed in their functions, but the functions can be adapted to the changes of their environment. Their functions, again, are not fixed by their real character, but by their position in cosmic change. The *Tao* of man and of the physical world is expressed in the mutual stimulation of character and function. But man also belongs to the physical world. A sage is nothing but a man. There is a thing which remains a thing. There is a thing which can surmount 10 things, 100 things, 1,000 things, 10,000 things, 1,000,000 things, 10,000,000 things. That which has risen to the top of 10,000,000 things, is it not a man? A man may remain in one man. He can also surpass 10 men, 100 men, 10,000 men, 100,000 men, or 1,000,000 men. He who has risen to the top of 10,000,000 men, is he not a sage? We know, therefore, that man is the highest among physical objects, and that a sage is the highest among men. The highest of men is he who can observe 10,000 minds by one mind; who can observe 10,000 bodies with one body; who lives in one generation, yet can understand 10,000 generations. It is he who can put himself of the will of Heaven, who can talk with his mouth in the speech of Heaven, who can use his hand in the work of Heaven, who can do what Heaven wishes to do. This means that he is man who knows the rotation of heaven, the geography of earth, the nature of physical objects, and the life of mankind. This is to say, he knows the work of Heaven and Earth, the process of creation, the turning of the clocks of the present and past, and the choice of men who should be at the helm."[4]

When one reads this essay in which Shao Yung emphasizes man's smallness and the unreliability of human sense-knowledge, one cannot help but compare him with Spinoza. The latter, applying the geometrical method to ethics, was interested in eternal truth just as Shao Yung was. Spinoza says:

"There is no individual thing in Nature, than which there is none more powerful or stronger."[5] Uberweg, the historian of Philosophy draws a conclusion that man, who, as an individual being, is a part of the whole complex of Nature, and whose power is a finite part of the infinite power of God or of Nature, is necessarily subject to passions, that is, that he is thrown into conditions of which he is not himself the full cause, and whose power and increase are determined by the relation of the power of the external cause to his own power."

As Shao Yung gives priority to the sage's position in a community, Spinoza pays high respect to the men who are guided by reason, that is, who seek their good according to reason, and who strive to obtain nothing for themselves which they do not also desire for other men, and who are, therefore, just, true, and honorable. Shao Yung's valuation of the sages is like Spinoza's valuation of the man of reason, because the man who is guided by reason is freer in a community where he lives according to laws made for all citizens, than in a condition of isolation where he obeys only himself.

Shao Yung's enthusiasm for his theory of the cosmic periods led him to call himself a student of Heaven and Earth. Does not Shao Yung mean what Spinoza says in the following words? "The highest endeavour of the mind, and its highest virtue, are to know things with that most perfect kind of knowledge which proceeds from the adequate idea of certain divine attributes to the adequate knowledge of the essence of things. The more we comprehend things in this way, the more we do comprehend God."[7] Spinoza means that in so far as the mind apprehends under the form of eternity, it has the knowledge of God. Although Shao Yung was omitted in Chang Po-hsiang's collection of philosophical writings, he was much appreciated by Chu Hsi. Someone asked Chu Hsi: "How could Shao Yung's mental horizon be so broad?" How could he reach it? Chu Hsi's answer was: "In his field of knowledge, the whole Universe, from its beginning to its end, the past and the present, was covered. This is the reason why he possesses such a vast mental horizon. Who, in the present generation, can compete with him?"[8]

There is no doubt that Shao Yung will be more and more appreciated in this age of scientific and philosophical progress.

Chang Tsai, like those who preceded him was one of the founders of Sung philosophy, but his starting point was different from that of Chou Tun-i and Shao Yung. He was as ambitious as they in building a metaphysical system which he constructed on the theory of ch'i. In the beginning of the world, according to Chang Tsai, there existed ch'i, and since one cannot live outside the world one cannot theorize except upon the basis of *ch'i*. One does, indeed, use mind or reason in philosophizing, but even mind or reason is not deducable apart from *ch'i*. *Ch'i* is the ultimate reality and the primary mobile force of the universe.

In Western thought one is familiar with the cleavage which runs down through the history of philosophical speculation. Thus, in ancient Greece, there was Platonism as against Aristotelianism; in the Middle Ages, there was Nominalism as against Realism; and in modern times, there is the conflict between rationalism and empiricism. In China, there was a similar conflict, but the point of contention was whether reason or matter came first. Chu Hsi, who tried to synthesize the two opposing schools, believed that although reason becomes manifest only when one studies the physical world, still in the analysis, reason has a prior existence. This priority Chu Hsi was able to establish by arguing backwards. The later idealists were in basic agreement with Chu Hsi, but philosophers were not looking at who were staunchly realists and who held that matter (*ch'i*) comes first. Chang Tsai was the exponent of the theory that matter is antecedent to reason as far as the creation of the universe is concerned.

Though, as we have seen, there is a similiar conflict among the philosophers in the West, the specific question argued in Europe and China has been different. In the case of Realism *versus* Nominalism in the Middle Ages, the problem centered on whether the class-term or the particular thing is real. In the modern period, rationalism and empiricism present the same controversy in a new dress, the empircists maintaining that human knowledge begins with sensation — with the study of particular things in the external world, while the rationalists emphasize the importance of innate ideas. The rationalist insists that concepts or universals, formed from synthetic judgment *a priori,* or from the forms of understanding, are capable of being considered apart from sensations or experience.

Though this problem has engaged Occidental thinkers for centuries, the opposing camps in China have been concerned with a different question. They have asked the question: "Does the metaphysical *Tao* come first, or is it to be found only in the physical world? In other words, the *Tao* is real, everlasting and unchanging, while the physical world is merely phenomena in a state of flux. If the *Tao* is the essence or origin of the physical world, it must be antecedent to the world. But the opposing school, like the nominalists and empiricists in Europe, took the stand that the *Tao* cannot be found apart from the physical world. According to this school, the metaphysical *Tao* is inseparable from the physical *ch'i*. These two schools argued for close to a thousand years from the Sung Dynasty down to the Ch'ing Dynasty. There was a third school which sought to effect a compromise between them and advanced the theory that while the *Tao* cannot be separated from *ch'i*, we are compelled if we argue backwards [*i.e.*, reduce] to postulate that *Tao* precedes *ch'i*. This advocacy for the priority of the *Tao*, which was the achievement of Chu Hsi, suggests Kant's defense of the synthetic *a priori* judgments, or forms of the understanding.

But enough of these introductory comments! They do provide a background without which it would be impossible to understand the significance of Chang Tsai's thought. Let us now proceed to the basic facts of life.

Chang Tsai was born in the village of Heng-ch'u in the Mei District of Shansi Province. As a boy of eighteen he felt like joining the army because he wished to aid in organizing a volunteer corps to restore the territory of T'ao-hsi. It so happened that he corresponded with Fang Chung-yen who persuaded him that one might find pleasure as a Confucianist scholar pursuing philosophy, and that there was not much point in pursuing a military career. Thus it was that the youthful Chang Tsai turned his attention to the *Chung-yung* and henceforth devoted himself to the study of the *Tao*. His approach was through Buddhism and Taoism, but his objective was the comprehension and elucidation of the *Five Classics*.

In A.D. 1061, Chang Tsai visited the capital and made the acquaintance of the Ch'eng brothers. For a while he lectured on the *I-ching*, but after he became sufficiently familiar with the Ch'eng brothers to appreciate that his own scholarship on this classic was far behind theirs, he discontinued his lectures.

Afterwards he received the *chin-shih* degree and was appointed magistrate of Yün-yen District, where he started his work to improve the moral atmosphere of the community. At the beginning of each month he summoned the elders together to lecture them on their ethical duties. He also tried to inform himself about complaints brought against the district government. He had the elders bring his messages to all the residents so that his instructions would be available at every corner.

In due course, Chang Tsai was recommended by the censor Lu Kung-chu to be given an audience before Emperor Shen-tsung. Asked for his views about governmental policy, our philosopher alluded to the Three Dynasties as an example of what a political regimen should be. Then he had a talk with the powerful statesman-reformer, Wang An-shih, who asked for his co-operation. Chang's reply was: "If you are willing to work for the common interest, everybody will help you. If you want to teach a jade-cutter how to cut jade he will refuse your advice."[9] Wang An-shih gave him the position of provincial commissioner of justice, but later owing to friction between Chang's brother and Wang, the philosopher resigned his post and returned to his native village, Heng-ch'u.

Back home, Chang Tsai remained in his house surrounded by books, sometimes reading, sometimes reflecting. He strove indefatigibly to think out every problem. When at night a new theory emerged on his intellectual horizon he would jump out of bed to write it down. The Ch'eng brothers said of him: "What Chang Tsai attained was more from hard thinking than from natural insight."[10] He paid little attention to his personal appearance and subsisted only on vegetables. It was at this time that he made his immortal statement, now familiar to every Chinese: "To set up a universal mind for heaven and earth, to give new life to man, to continue the philosophy of the former sages which has been interrupted, and at last to give peace to future generations for 100,000 years."[11]

But Chang Tsai did not remain long in this idyllic atmosphere. In 1076, through the recommendation of Lu Chi-kung, he was appointed to a high post in the ministry of ceremonies, which happened also to be his last official position, for when the emperor was about to forget to perform his usual sacrifice to heaven, and when Chang Tsai memorialized him on the matter, His Majesty refused to listen to the philosopher who forthwith resigned. He died on his way home, in his fifty-eighth year.

Chang Tsai's chief work is his *Cheng-mêng* (*Corrections of Youthful Folly*), consisting of 17 chapters. Comparable to Chou Tun-i's *T'ai-chi-t'u* and *T'ung-shu*, it is one of the great theoretical systems of the Sung Period. The titles of the 17 chapters are as follows:

(1) The Great Harmony
(2) The Triad and Dyad
(3) The *Tao* of Heaven
(4) The Divine Character
(5) Animals
(6) Truth and Enlightenment
(7) Largeness of Mind
(8) The Golden Mean and the Right
(9) The Highest Development
(10) Originality
(11) Thirty Years of Age
(12) The Virtuous
(13) Government
(14) *The Book of Changes*
(15) Music
(16) The Sacrificial Ceremony to Heaven
(17) The Principles of Ch'ien

Two sections were separated from the seventeenth or last chapter and given the independent title of *Western Inscription* and *Eastern Inscription* respectively.

Let us now deal with Chang Tsai's philosophical system. His philosophy starts with the one word *ch'i*, which may be interpreted as "matter" or "being". He believed that at the beginning of the universe there was this *ch'i* or Great Ethereal. Here are a few passages dealing with this subject.

"The Great Ethereal cannot exist without ch'i. *Ch'i* cannot help but consolidate itself into physical objects. But physical objects will again dissolve into the Great Ethereal. In consolidation and in dissolution, they obey the law of necessity."

"That the Great Ethereal is shapeless is the essence of *ch'i*. Its consolidation or dissolution is the manifestness of *ch'i*."

"The *ch'i* of Heaven and Earth may consolidate or dissolve itself into a thousand forms. It is Reason which is the action principle behind this principle of change."

"The *ch'i* fills the Great Ethereal. It goes up, it comes down, or it flies high without cessation. This is what the *I-ching* refers to as the real secret of the changes, or what is called by Chuang-tzu the dust flying like a wild horse. *Ch'i,* which sometimes goes up or at other times comes down, is the seed of fullness or emptiness, or the beginning of motion or rest. What goes up is the light, *Yang* part; what comes down is the heavy, *Yin* part. It can consolidate or dissolve in the forms of wind and rain, snow and frost, mountains and rivers, and myriad other things."

"When *ch'i* consolidates itself it has shape and becomes visible to the eyes. When *ch'i* does not consolidate itself and has no shape it will not be visible to the eyes. After its consolidation it manifests itself in the external world. When it dissolves, can one say that becomes nothingness?"[12]

Chang Tsai's meaning is that in the beginning of the universe there was *ch'i* a physical world. Motion and rest are contained in the two modes of *ch'i*: *Yang* and *Yin.* He calls what is manifested in the world and fills it as the "phenomena." This explanation is most obvious in the last chapter of his work. "What can be expressed is Being. What is Being is phenomenon. What is phenomenon is *ch'i*." The meaning is that everything in the world is made of *ch'i.* But this quotation should not be understood as implying that Chang Tsai denied the existence of a supra-sensible world. As a Confucianist scholar he could not have agreed with the materialist standpoint. What he wanted to say was that *Tao,* or moral values, is inherent in matter or *ch'i.*

The reason why Chang Tsai took this standpoint was that with *ch'i* as the starting point of his philosophical system, he could combat the idea of nothingness or emptiness of the Buddhist and Taoist schools. This becomes clearer in the following quotation:

"The fact that *ch'i* consolidates or dissolves itself into the Ethereal is just like ice consolidating or dissolving itself into water. If one knows that the Ethereal consists of *ch'i*, one will find that there is no such thing as nothingness. When the sages discussed the question of human nature and the *Tao* of heaven, they reached the utmost truth with their saying that there is the wonderful change of the Three (Heaven, Earth, and Man), and of the Five (the Five Elements). This is the meaning of the *I-ching*. The other schools of philosophy are superficial in confining their discussion only to the question of a distinction between Being and Nothing. This is not the right way to wisdom."

"The former sages also did the work of contemplation, and of observation. They tried to discover what is the cause of the hidden and the evident, and they never said anything about Being and Non-being."[13]

Chang Tsai brought the Buddhist and Taoist concept of annihilation into relationship with his standpoint in another way. "It is impossible", he says, "that there should be no *ch'i* in the Great Ethereal. Ch'i cannot do otherwise than consolidate itself into different kinds of things. The different kinds of things cannot do otherwise than dissolve into the Great Ethereal. This process, at one time of consolidation, at another time of dissolution, like the comings-in and goings-out of our daily life, is carried on according to the necessity of natural law. As the sages could exhaust the *Tao* to the utmost, so they took all sides into their comprehensive view. Thus they revealed their divine character. Yet those who talked about annihilation and nothingness neglected the side of Being.

"On the other hand, we find also those who preferred the life of this world, and who clung adamantly to the theory of Being, as if changes were impossible. These contrary points of view gave birth to the same result: loss of the right path."[14]

In a long section in the first chapter of the book, *Cheng-mêng*, the elaborate discussion of *ch'i* and the Buddhist and Taoist schools gives the impression that Chang Tsai was determined to be antagonistic to these schools.

"If one knows," he says, "that the Ethereal is filled with *ch'i*, the various aspects of Being and Non-being, the hidden and the evident, divine character, nature, and the heavenly order, can be brought under a unifying idea without splitting into a duality. Consolidation and dissolution, coming-in and going-out, visible and invisible, can be traced back to an identical origin. This is the work of those who understand the significance of the *I-ching*.

"But if, on the other hand, one holds to the view that the Great Ethereal produces *ch'i,* I must say that this is absurd. Since the Great Ethereal is infinite, and *ch'i* is finite, the difference in their character and functions is such that it would be impossible for the one to grow out of the other. This is why one falls into the view of Lao-tzu that Being grows out of Nothingness. One forgets the normal truth that Being and Nothingness are inseparable.

"Further, if one holds to the Buddhist view that the manifoldness of this is only an illusion in the Great Ethereal, one mixes together the two ideas of universal manifoldness and Emptiness. But they are so contradictory that they cannot be mixed. Furthermore, what is called reality (or nature) is one thing, and what is called a physical object is another. This intermingling of the idea of Reality, and physical objects is the reason why many people succumb to the Buddhist notion of the illusory character of the world.

"Ignorance of the nature of *Tao* is derived from the superficiality of people, who, knowing just a little about Emptiness, overlook the actual workings of the *Tao* of Heaven. This narrow subjective view is disguised under the name of illusion. One's own insight, which is not clear enough, is distorted into turning the actuality of the universe into a phantasm. These people, in regard to their knowledge of what is hidden and what is clear, are not in a position to take a comprehensive view, and so they just leap into a false conjecture.

"Such people do not know that at one time *Yin,* at another time *Yang* (in other words, *ch'i*) are the forces which hold the universe under control. This is the way to look at the universe in which Heaven, Earth and Man are maintained in a balance. The neglect of this point is what has caused people to mix Confucianism, Buddhism and Taoism in a chaotic mass. This is why those interested in the *Tao* of Heaven, human nature, and the heavenly order, are carried away by an imaginative and confused picture leading them to believe either in the theory of illusion or in the Taoist notion that Being comes from Non-Being. Such an approach to true virtue is misguided and leads to onesideness and exaggeration."[15]

Since Chang Tsai's starting point was *ch'i*, which, in turn, was driven by the two forces *Yin* and *Yang*, he was much interested in duality, or the phenomena of opposites. He says: "The alternation of sun and moon brings forth light. The alternation of cold and heat produces a year. The principle behind the universe is one of duality.". . .[16] This is reminiscent of Plato, for whom all things have opposites and for whom all things are generated out of opposites.

It is interesting to note that Chang Tsai came to the conclusion that duality is impossible without unity, and that also unity cannot exist without duality. Now what is duality? It is fullness and emptiness, motion and rest, consolidation and dissolution, purity and filth. In the final analysis, they all constitute the One.[17] Chang Tsai explained that in every physical object there are opposites, and that because of the opposites there is counter-action. When there is counter-action, there is hate and discord. But when there is discord there will eventually be reconciliation. This doctrine suggests the teaching of Empedocles, who held that the history of the universe, is an oscillation between the alternates of Love and Hate. If there had been intercourse in the ancient world between Europe and China, one might have suspected that the Chinese had been influenced by the Sicilian.

Though Chang Tsai paid much attention to the idea of duality, it is difficult to classify him as a dualist, or, indeed, as a monist, or as a materialist or idealist. He left his system in a fluid state, lacking consistency, so I shall not attempt to pigeon-hole him. Chang Tsai's first premise was *ch'i*. As far as the creation of the universe is concerned he gave priority to *ch'i*. Yet he undoubtedly was not a materialist. His philosophy begins with *ch'i* or matter, yet he never intends to explain the work of mind or spirit in terms of physics. Much less does he intend to deny the independence of mind or the autonomy of the moral law. Rather, he sees in *ch'i* a kind of miracle-working matter, and he tries to find the *Tao* in *ch'i*. When *ch'i* is pure and light it is Heaven; when it is dirty and heavy, it is earth. He arrives at the theory that what goes up and comes down in *ch'i* is the same as floating and sinking, motion and rest, light and darkness, that occur in the physical world around us. He goes on to assume that what is called Being and Non-Being, visibility and invisibility, divine character, human nature, and heavenly order, constitue a unity and not a duality. Here are Chang Tsai's own words:

"In the Great Harmony [One commentator says that this term means *ch'i*] there is *Tao*. Inherent in this is the nature of floating and sinking, ascending and coming down, rest and motion, challenge and response. Here also lives what is called conquering and overcoming, bending and being straight. Beginnings are easy and simple; endings are vast and firm. An easy beginning is *ch'ien*. What imitates the easy is *k'un*. What is dispersed and yet has a shape is *ch'i*. What is light and intangible is divinity. What does not go like a wild horse may be called the Great Harmony. If one understands all this, one knows the *Tao*."[18]

In the next section Chang Tsai also says: "Though within *ch'i* there are thousands of forms of condensation and dissolution, of defensiveness and offensiveness, yet there is reason which is orderly and true. If one knows that the ethereal and empty is *ch'i*, then what is called Being and Non-Being, visibility and invisibility, divine character, human nature, and heavenly order, constitute a unity and not a duality."[19]

Here we see that Chang Tsai postulates *ch'i*, equating it with the principle of *Tao*. In other words he points out traces of *Tao* in the natural process of *ch'i*. Such a combination of metaphysics with natural science is bound however, to lead to contradiction and confusion. On the one hand *ch'i* is co-ordinated with *Tao*; on the other hand, *Tao* appears as the highest product of *ch'i*. Chang Tsai, it would seem, postulates a common character for *ch'i* and *Tao*, and loses the differences between the two in a theory of abstract identity. This is why he was criticized by the Ch'eng brothers and by Chu Hsi.

"Chang Tsai", say the Ch'eng brothers, "applied the terms 'ethereal' and 'the Great' to the *Tao* of Heaven. The term 'ethereal' can only have meaning when applied to a finite thing which is tangible. *Tao* itself, or the methaphysical world, cannot be expressed in terms of space or shape. *Tao* should be the supreme principle which includes everything, and so it cannot be qualified as things which occupy space."[20]

Chu Hsi says: "Such terms as 'the Great Harmony' and 'ethereal' can only be applied to *ch'i*, and to what can be dissolved and condensed. As far as the *Tao* or *Ri* (Reason) is concerned, the only way to express it is Chou Tun-i's way: 'the Ultimate of Nothingness, or in turn, the Supreme Ultimate.' "[21]

These critical remarks suggest that for these authors there exists apart from *Ch'i* [the physical world] a metaphysical principle which is not mixed up with it. This distinction between the phenomenal and the intelligible, or between matter and form, is so deep-rooted both in Greece and China, that any theory of identity like that advocated by Chang Tsai does not satisfy the desire to search for an ideal pattern.

Though Chang Tsai attached great importance to *ch'i*, out of which, owing to its light and pure nature, the transformations due to dissolution and condensation grow, he did not explain the work of mind in physical terms.

"If your mind is amplified you can put yourself in a position to discover the nature of things in the world. If you cannot put yourself in this position, then your mind has left the things outside. The mind of the ordinary man is limited to sense-perceptions. What the sages sought to attain was to exhaust nature, so they never tied their minds down to the senses only. They looked upon the world as if all things were part of themselves. Thus Mencius said: 'To develop the mind so that you can know nature and Heaven.' Thus the mind assumes the greatness of Heaven with nothing left outside. A mind which leaves things outside cannot be equal to the Universal Mind. Sense-perceptions are the products of the interaction between the senses and external things. It is not so with the moral sense. Knowledge of the moral sense has nothing to do with the senses."[22]

Chang Tsai knows that a man can think, judge, generalize, be kind to others, have convictions, be a martyr. Man's work is basically different from that of *ch'i*, so our philosopher never tries to explain the operations of mind as a natural process. His conclusion, thus, in the paragraph quoted above, is that mind or moral values has nothing to do with the senses or with *ch'i*. It is clear that Chang Tsai's taking *ch'i* as his initial premise in his theory of the creation of the universe has not driven him to explaining mind or spirit in terms of physical elements, as do the modern materialists of the West.

Because Chang Tsai attached so much importance to *ch'i* he was the first philosopher to point out that there are two kinds of human nature: One is the physical nature, the other is the essential nature. The essential nature is good, while the physical nature, whether good or bad, depends upon the *ch'i* which makes it.

"After a man has taken shape he is endowed with physical nature. If a man knows how to come back to himself he can keep his essential nature intact. Physical nature is not considered as nature by a man of noble character."[23]

This distinction between essential nature and physical nature was much appreciated by Chu Hsi, who said:

"The theory of physical nature, originated by Chang Tsai, was a great contrbution to the school of sages, and shows the way to future generations. We had never heard of such a theory previously. Since the establishment of his theory, other doctrines have faded away."[24]

Chang Tsai's theory rendered a great service to the art of personal cultivation. He stressed that to improve one's self is to change one's physical nature. Doing away with one's desires, controlling one's imagination, suppressing the search for fame and money, are the methods of changing one's own physical nature. When one reaches the stage where one's own physical nature can be modified this means that one can control one's self or can return to one's essential nature, which is originally good.

Chang Tsai's prominent position among the Sung philosophers was largely a result of his essay: *The Western Inscription*. This work was so highly appreciated by the Ch'eng brothers that they considered it the masterpiece of exposition on the nature of *Jen* which had never been equaled by anybody since the Ch'in and Han Dynasties. Chu Hsi said of it: "In the school of Ch'eng, *The Western Inscription* was used as a primer for beginners." This is what the inscription says:

"*Ch'ien* is our father; *K'un* is our mother. I, as an individual, am exceedingly small and limited, living in the middle between the two of them. As far as the expanse of Heaven and Earth, there is our body. As the Heaven and Earth command, there is our nature. The people of the world are our brothers; things are our fellows. The great king is the first-born child of our parents. His first minister is the one who is keeper of the household. To respect age means to take old people as old people should be taken. To love lonely and single persons means to take younger people as younger people should be taken. The sages are men who equalled Heaven and Earth in regard to moral excellence. The wise men are the most gifted among men. All those who are overworked, crippled, infirm, paralyzed, lonely, childless, widows, or widowers, are our brothers and sisters, who are in difficulty and cannot help themselves. If one protects them, this is to serve Heaven with reverence. If one does one's work with joy and without grudge, this means that a son waits on his parents with the sense of filial duty. To do the contrary is to violate one's own moral virtue. It is also to work against the principle of *Jen*. He is also an accomplice in evil-doing who works against the endowment of natural gifts. Only he who fulfills his mission is said to belong to the elect few.

"Men who know the changes of the universe are like sons telling past stories of their parents. Men who can understand divine actions thoroughly are like sons following in the footsteps of their parents. One who does not shame one's self before the rain-drops falling from the roof of one's house will not dishonor one's parents. One who keeps one's mind in peace and nourishes one's nature, is like a son serving sick parents at night without failure.

"The Great Yü's abstention from wine shows that in his mind he was considering how to eliminate his desires and how to recompense his parents for their love. The education of the younger generation embraces the idea which inspired Ying K'ao-shu who wished to extend love for parents to include love of mankind. To serve parents without ill-will and until they are satisfied was the work of Shun [one of the ideal Emperors of ancient China]. Shen Sheng's deep obedience to his parents was that after being slandered, he waited for death by burning. The most noteworthy example of a son who returned his body physically and spiritually perfect to his parents was that of Tseng Shen. Then there was the son who exposed himself to extreme danger because of the order of his parents.

"Riches, power, fortune and happiness are the things that make our life beautiful. However, poverty, humbleness, worry and sorrow are the things that cause us to forge ahead towards future success.

"When I live I do as I am ordered. When I die I return to tranquillity."[25]

This essay, *The Western Inscription*, is considered one of the most important documents of Sung philosophy because it expounds the theory of *Jen* the sense of universal love. In so doing it remains true to the Chinese tradition by its emphasis on the son-parent relationship, although the application of this relationship is analogical. The essay goes so far as to say that the borderline of Heaven and Earth is our body, and that the commanding will of Heaven and Earth is our nature. Why does the concept of love here have such cosmic significance? This significance may be attributed to the influence of Buddhism. Confucius and Mencius took *Jen* as the starting point for their philosophy, so that they, like the founders of religion — Sakayamuni and Jesus Christ — understood *Jen* as the fountain of human virtues. But the usual way of discussing *Jen* or the moral virtues in China was to confine them to gradation, beginning with parents and extending to other members of the community. In the words of Chang Tsai: "As far as the expanse of Heaven and earth there is our body; As the Heaven and Earth command, there is our nature", was something seldom heard before. Compare *The Western Inscription* with the following vows of the Bodhisattva:

> "Great Mother Earth
> All creatures
> Provide and nourishes,
> But from none of them
> She seeks a favor special, nor is she to any partial:
> So is the Bodhisattva.
> Silence his awakening of the Heart,
> Until he gains the depths of the Law

And realizes the highest knowledge,
He toils to save all creatures,
Himself no favor seeking, nor to others granting any:
Regardless of friend and enemy,
Embracing all with simple Heart
He fashions one and all for Bodhi."[26]

The ideal of Bodhissattva is more explicitly exemplified by Vimalakirti, whose conversation about the correlation between the illness of sentient beings and his own illness has been well known to the poets and the people at large ever since the T'ang Dynasty.

When Vimalakirti was asked why he did not feel well, he answered: "From ignorance there arises desire and that is the cause of my illness. As all sentient beings are ill, so am I ill. When all sentient beings are healed of their illness, I shall be healed of my illness too. Why? The Bodhisattvas will suffer no more illness. When an only son in a good family is sick, the parents feel sick too. When he is recovered, they are well again. So it is with the Bodhisattva. He loves all sentient beings as his own children. When they are sick he is sick too. When they are recovered he is well again. Do you wish to know whence this sympathetic illness is? The illness of the Bodhisattva comes from the all-embracing love."

Though Confucianists do not have their motive for preaching love in the desire to get rid of the circle of life and death, yet from them there also is a great flow of love towards mankind simply because the illnesses of the people are so innumerable that the situation unavoidably demands it. The revival of Confucianism would have been impossible without the accent on intense love for human beings. This was the motive of Chang Tsai's *Inscription*.

The Western Inscription shows plainly that Chang Tsai's idea of love has nothing to do with his theory of *ch'i*. It may be assumed that his premise that the *Tao* can be found only within *ch'i*, namely, among physical objects, is valid only as far as the creation of the physical world is concerned. But *ch'i* plays an important role. In Chang Tsai's dealing with human values, he begins with the four fundamental virtues: *Jen, I, Li, Chih*. He presupposes innate ideas. They are the source of the moral law and of its autonomy. Nevertheless, we may say that according to Chang Tsai there are two worlds. In the physical world the *Tao* cannot be separated from *ch'i;* yet when he deals with human beings, he returns to the Chinese standpoint that the moral law is independent of the physical world. His distinction between the senses and the moral sense is a proof that the moral sense is independent of the circumstances in which physical objects exist. Here is a gap which Chang Tsai did not explain clearly. In this respect his philosophy suggests the two realms of Kant's world: one, where knowledge begins with the external world; and the other, where the moral law is autonomous.

In conclusion, we can say that Chang Tsai's contributions to the Sung philosophy can be said to come under four points: First, he called the attention of philosophers to the study of the physical world. He himself discussed problems of astronomy, botany, and biology. Second, because he did not try to explain mind or moral values in terms of physical elements, he believed that the moral law stands by itself. It is autonomous. Third, Chang Tsai was the first man to draw a distinction between essential nature and physical nature. The former is purely good. The latter is tied to the physical world so that it is mixed with evil. Fourth, he gave a cosmic significance to the virtue *Jen,* which formerly had been confined to family-life. Thus he aroused the feeling of cosmic love towards humanity and the world as a whole.

References

1. *Sung-wen-chien* (The Mirror of Sung Literature), Book 149.
2. *P.R.S.Y.*, Book 9.
3. *Loc. cit.*
4. *Loc. cit.*
5. Spinoza, *Ethics*, Part 4, Human Servitude, p. 145.
6. Uberweg, *History of Philosophy*, Vol. 2, p. 77.
7. *Ibid.*, Part 5, Power of the Intellect, pp. 214-215.
8. *P.R.S.Y.*, Book 9, Chu Hsi's words quoted by Huang Pai-chia.
9. *Ibid.*, Book 17.
10. *Ibid.*, Book 18.
11. Chang Tsai, *Collected Works*, Book 12.
12. *Ibid.*, Book 2, Section 1.
13. *Loc. cit.*
14. *Loc. cit.*
15. *Loc. cit.*
16. *Loc. cit.*
17. *Loc. cit.*
18. *Loc. cit.*
19. *Loc. cit.*
20. *Erh-ch'eng yü-lu* (Dialogues of the Ch'eng Brothers), Book 8.
21. *Chu-tzu yu-lui* (Dialogues of Chu Hsi), Book 99.
22. Chang Tsai, *Collected Works*, Book 3, Section 7.
23. *Ibid.*, Book 3, Section 6.
24. *Loc. cit.*, Chu Hsi's comment.
25. Chang Tsai, *Collected Works*, Book 1, Hsi-ming (Western Inscription).
26. D. T. Suzuki, *Outline of Mahayana Buddhism*, Luzac and Company London, 1907, p. 391.

CHAPTER NINE

The Rational Basis of
Sung Philosophy: Ch'eng Hao

It often happens that philosophical thought, after a period of speculation on cosmology, returns to the more immediate problems of human life. When the theorizings about the unity of the world have begun to appear too speculative and pretentious, philosophy comes back to an examination of the nature of ideas, of morality and of the limitations of knowledge. In Greek thought there was first the so-called scientific period in which Thales, Anaximander, Pythagorus and Heraclitus propounded their respective theories about water, the boundless, number and fire as the fundamental essence of the cosmos. Then came an age of moralizing when Socrates and the Sophists betook themselves in a different direction, namely, human conduct. They began to be occupied with ethical and epistemological reflections: What is knowledge? What are the criteria of right and wrong? Can virtue be taught?

As with Greek philosophy, so also with Chinese philosophy during the Sung Dynasty. Following upon the cosmological speculations of Chou Tun-i, Shao Yung and Chang Tsai came the Ch'eng brothers, who concerned themselves mainly with moral and epistemological reflections. They tried to put *ri-hsüeh* [philosophy of reason] on a theoretical basis, and argued that *ri* [reason], in contrast to the senses, is the foundation upon which a new philosophy must be built. Also they pondered about the relation between human nature and reason. Is there any distinction between the two? If so, then it becomes impossible to find any sort of rational ground within human nature. But if, on the other hand, there is no distinction between human nature and reason, then it becomes reasonable to seek rational grounds within human nature. This conception of the relation between human nature and reason is the most important of the contributions of the Ch'eng brothers. It stands next to *ri* itself as the foundation of the new philosophy.

The Ch'eng brothers devoted themselves to other questions. What is the correct approach to sagehood? How can one live a life in conformity with the standard of reason? Are knowledge and meditation equally significant as avenues to sagehood? How can the philosophy regain continuation of the Confucian tradition? To all these problems Ch'eng Hao and Ch'eng I attempted to offer solutions. They turned the trend of Chinese thought from cosmology to an examination of the problems having to do with human life.

A sketch of these two philosophical brothers will be presented here and in the next chapter. It is hardly possible to treat them separately because their utterances have been handed down under a common authorship, namely, the "Two Ch'eng Masters". There is indeed no way in which to distinguish the work of one from the other. But all the same attempt must be made, and a careful study of the text shows that there are differences between the two brothers which are interesting and important. We need not show much despair as seems to be explicit in Fung Yu-lan both in the Chinese and English editions of his *History of Chinese Philosophy*.

Ch'eng Hao, the older brother, was born in Honan Province in A.D. 1032. His father, Ch'eng Hsiang, was an iconoclast, as may be seen in his way of asserting his authority as a magistrate. There was once, for instance, a rumor that a criminal who had been executed in his district had become a god. The body had been thrown into the river, but according to gossip it was seen to float upstream. Ch'eng Hsiang gave instructions that the body be thrown into the river again. Needless to say, the corpse sank and the superstition disappeared. Another instance of his critical temper may be seen in the manner in which he handled a rumor about a halo which was said to appear around the head of a stone image of the Buddha. People had flocked to witness the miracle, and had even trampled upon one another. Ch'eng Hsiang merely ordered that he be informed the next time the halo appeared. Of course, the next time never came. The father of the Ch'eng brothers had a fine and critical mind which accepts only what is reasonable. When he made the acquaintance of Chou Tun-i, he asked him to be tutor to his two sons.

When Ch'eng Hao won his *chin-shih* degree, he was appointed justice-of-the-peace in Shang-chih District.

When he carried out a carefully thought-out policy for administration, he tried to do everything possible for the welfare of the people. This humane point of view was reflected in his dissatisfaction with the system of tax-collection which was in force when he first arrived at Shang-chih. The practice was to send the taxes-in-kind (grain) paid by the farmers to the borders of the province. Since the distance was great and since the cost of transportation was heavy, it was difficult to get the grain back again in times of famine. Ch'eng Hao changed the practice by ordering the rich to buy surplus grain and to keep it until there was shortage. In this way he won popular acclaim. His administrative policy is also interestingly shown in his habit of lecturing to people who came to visit him at his office. He delivered sermons about their moral obligations, about how they should serve their parents and brothers, about how they should work in co-operation with the other members of their community, etc. He appeared to be very humane in his visits to the children's schools where he would teach the pupils correct pronunciation. At the expiration of a term of three years the people loved Ch'eng Hao as if he were their father.

Then in 1071 he was appointed censor. During an audience granted him by Emperor Shen-tsung he was asked to come more often. On one of these occasions his conversation lasted until past the noon hour, when the court-chamberlain had to remind him that His Majesty's luncheon was ready. We may assume that the censor's discourses which so fascinated the emperor had as their purport to make him a Philosopher-King in the Platonic sense. It is interesting to note in this connection that Ch'eng Hao, like the Sung thinkers in general, confined his advice to ways of rectifying the mind and controlling desire. He invariably moralized on a high level and seldom if ever betrayed any interest in discussing current policies or events.

This pure philosophical attitude of Ch'eng Hao even in practical life is well illustrated in his behaviour towards the prime minister, Wang An-shih, with whom he was ordered to attend a cabinet meeting. He took exception to the great statesman's continual shouting, and expressed the opinion that in the deliberations of state affairs one should be calm and patient and should not behave as if in a personal quarrel. Wang An-shih felt ashamed and quieted down. Whereupon Ch'eng Hao made it a practice of pointing out to him that a good statesman should deal with policy as the Great Yü dealt with water, which was to direct it to the proper channels and not try to stop it. It is not wise to be stubbornly determined to carry out a policy when there was opposition from many sides. There never was a statesman who was successful when his policy was attacked by many people. Even more unwise for a politician it would be to attempt to carry out a policy by dismissing opponents who were known to be loyal and straightforward. The prime minister did not always agree with the philosopher, but he admired him for his honesty.

Eventually Ch'eng Hao resigned the censorship and accepted the post as a military judge. During his term of office a mob of more than five hundred soldiers, who had been assigned to do conservancy work on the Yellow River, rioted and requested to be allowed to enter the city. Ch'eng Hao advised his colleagues to meet the demand of the soldiers or else they might start a rebellion. But his colleagues were fearful that such compliance might offend the commander. The philosopher promised to take full responsibility upon himself, and the city gates were thrown open. He announced to the soldiers that they could enter the city on what today would be called "a three-day-pass", and that after the expiration of this period they must go back to work. Subsequently the commander heard about Ch'eng Hao's role in this affair and threatened to report it to the emperor. Ch'eng Hao, however, was not disturbed, because he knew that if the commander turned informer he would get into difficulties himself.

Ch'eng Hao showed his ability in different ways during his tenure of the military judgeship. His office was near the Yellow

River. Once he learned of a break in the dyke at Ts'ao-ts-un, and he knew that if it was not mended there would be danger of inundation of the Sung capital. At first he tried to muster the army to make repairs, but a friend remarked that it was useless. He succeeded in persuading some swimmers to plunge into the river and throw a rope across it so that the laborers were ferried from both banks. The work was exceedingly hard but the result was that the break in the dyke was plugged up. In the midst of the work an immense piece of lumber floating down-stream had swung into a cross-wise position between the two banks, and got stuck. Ch'eng Hao took advantage of this accident by utilizing the log to strengthen the dyke.

Another instance of Ch'eng Hao's humane method of administering the law occurred while he was assigned to a magistracy in the Yangtze Valley. The district where he officiated was a lair of pirates. Ch'eng Hao captured one of them, and forced him to give information about the others. Then he invited the entire gang to live along the banks of the river to aid navigation by hauling the boats along the shore with ropes.

When Emperor Che-tsung ascended the Dragon Throne, Ch'eng Hao was appointed an under-secretary in the Ministry of the Imperial Family. But before departing for his new duties he died, in his fifty-fourth year.

There is a eulogy of our philosopher in the *History of the Sung Dynasty*. "Ch'eng Hao", according to this record, "was a talented man who devoted himself to the study of *Tao*. The kindliness and agreeableness of his disposition were apparent in the expression of his face and body. The friends and pupils who followed him for many years never saw him once in indignation. He knew how to handle people, and always remained calm even at times of haste. From the age of fifteen or sixteen, when he and his brother started their studies under Chou Tun-i, he lost interest in a civil career, and turned his attention to *Tao*. At first he read widely, including the books of Lao-tzu and Buddhism. But after a very long period of reading he returned to the Confucian *Classics*, and felt at ease in them. His equal has rarely been found since the Ch'in and Han Dynasties."[1]

The posthumous title which the emperor bestowed on Ch'eng Hao was "Teacher of the Enlightenment of *Tao*."

As a philosopher, Ch'eng Hao laid the foundation of Sung philosophy, sometimes known as *ri-hsüeh* [philosophy of reason], because he stressed the function of *ri* [reason]. He also said that the term *t'ien-ri* (heavenly reason) was the product of his own reflection. Later his brother, Ch'eng I, evolved the idea that human nature is reason. Sung philosophy is sometimes called *hsing-ri-hsüeh* (philosophy of human nature as reason). The credit for coining the expressions *ri-hsüeh* and *hsing-ri-hsüeh* should be given to the two Ch'eng brothers.

Let me now quote some passages from Ch'eng Hao on *ri* (reason). "The reason", he says, "which lies in the manifold things of the world never stands singly, but is one of a pair of opposites. This is nature's way. Whenever I think about this I cannot help but dance with joy." Again: "Everything comes in opposites. *Yin* has *Yang* as its counterpart. Good has evil as the entity opposed to it. When *Yang* grows, *Yin* declines. When good increases, evil decreases. This theory of opposites is applicable to all types of phenomena. We must keep this in mind."[2]

These words remind one of similiar thoughts put into the mouth of Socrates in Plato's *Phaedo*. "Are not all things which have opposites generated out of their opposites? I mean such things as good and evil, just and unjust — and there are innumerable other opposites which are generated out of opposites. And I want to show that this holds universally of all opposites."[3]

Ch'eng Hao proceeds to show that opposition is universal. "It is natural that crudity be opposed by culture. The theory of pairs of opposites is the fundamental principle of life. When one says 'up' there is 'down'. When one says 'this' there is 'that'. Neither side can work by itself. There must be two to initiate any operation. Only those who understand *Tao* will grasp the point of what I am saying."[4]

Ch'eng Hao's assumption is that there is a principle of reason in everything. Thus, he is convinced of a rational basis for the oneness of the world, from its beginning down to its various manifestations. "It is said in the *I-ching*," he writes, "that after the endowment of human kind by heaven, everything in this world had a rule. In other words, each being has its reason. To execute a purpose in conformity with reason is easy. But to violate reason is difficult. To do things in conformity with reason means to waste no energy."[5]

"Oxen are domesticated for the cultivation of fields, horses for riding. Each is trained according to its constitution. It is against reason to ride on oxen or to use horses only for field work."[6]

These quotations from Ch'eng Hao, I believe, are enough to reveal the intellectual climate of his period, when the conviction of a rational basis to explain the phenomena of the world had become deep-seated. This is the driving force of Sung philosophy. But what is this rational basis? Is it reason ordained by heaven? Or is it a product of the human mind? According to the Ch'eng brothers, this reason (or *ri* — to use the Chinese term) is in the nature of things, ordained by heaven and discovered by man. Because *ri* is ordained by heaven, it is natural and unalterable. Man's reason lies in his nature, and this latter consists of four virtues: *jen, i, li,* and *chih.* These four virtues are the essential properties of a man's nature. They also establish his reason. This is why Ch'eng I said that human nature *is* reason. In other words, reason, embodying these virtues, makes a man a rational being.

Ch'eng I even went further. He knew that a thoroughgoing principle underlies the heavenly decree, reason, human nature, and mind. "What is ordained by heaven", he wrote, "is the heavenly decree. What persists in things is reason. What makes a man is his nature. What acts as the determining factor for man is mind. When mind operates, *i.e.,* thinks, the resultant thoughts may be good or bad. After mind has ceased operating, the thoughts that remain are the work of the emotions rather than of mind."[7] In this the Sung philosophers tried to find a rational explanation for all phenomena, including knowledge of the physical world and judgments of human value. Their interest is in the unity of the constitution of man and things rather than in human knowledge of epistemology, or in such questions as Kant raised: "How is knowledge possible?" How ought a man behave?" "What can a man hope?" Metaphysics, ethics, psychology, and some natural science are contained in Sung philosophy; but there is no epistemology in the sense characteristic of Western thought. What common element there is in Sung and Occidental philosophy is confined to the search for a rational basis of human life and the physical world.

Here, as a digression, I should like to say a few words about the alleged difference between the opinions of the Ch'eng brothers concerning the nature of *ri* or *Tao,* and whether there is any resemblance of the Chinese concept of *ri* to the Platonic Idea. These are questions asked by Fung Yu-lan in his *History of Chinese Philosophy.*

According to Fung Yu-lan, there was a difference in opinion between the Ch'eng brothers, in regard to the nature of *ri* or *Tao.* Fung Yu-lan quotes the following from Ch'eng I: "Existence or non-existence, addition or reduction, cannot be postulated about *Ri.* All *Ri* are complete in themselves; in them there can be no deficiency — all the *Ri* are pervasively present. We cannot say that the *Tao* of kingship was more when Yao . . . exemplified it as a king, nor can we say that the *tao* of sonship was more when Shun . . . exemplified it as a son. These remain what they are."[8] [In this quotation I have substituted my romanization *"ri"* for Fung's *"li".* The reader will probably also note that Fung understands *ri* as a plural noun, while I understand it as a singular noun. It is difficult to comprehend how he can interpret it as plural when he construes *Tao,* its equivalent, as a singular. However, whether *ri* is understood as singular or plural it is in either case a metaphysical concept.]

It is clear from Fung Yu-lan's discussion that he equates Ch'eng I's conception of *ri* with the Platonic Idea, and that he regards Ch'eng I's doctrine, in this respect, as different from that of Ch'eng Hao who, he says, held *ri* to be the natural tendency of things. Fung asserts in the Chinese edition of his *History of Chinese Philosophy* that according to Ch'eng Hao, *ri* is inseparable from concrete things, while for Ch'eng I the contrary is the case. If I may say so, Fung's making a Platonist out of Ch'eng I is entirely the work of his imagination. Both Ch'eng brothers emphasized that a demarcation must be drawn between *Tao,* the metaphysical world, and *ch'i,* the world of matter. The quotation which Fung mistakenly attributes to Ch'eng I has to do with the nature of the eternal *Tao* or *ri.* This *Tao* or *ri* cannot be considered as susceptible of addition or reduction. The quotation is irrelevant to whether Tao is dependent upon or independent of *ch'i*. Ch'eng Hao is as strict as Ch'eng I in maintaining a distinction between *Tao* and *ch'i*, because *Tao* being metaphysical is incorporeal, and *ch'i* being physical is corporeal. In regard to the drawing of the line between these two worlds I find no divergence in opinion between the Ch'eng brothers. Both believe that *Tao* is not findable outside of *ch'i*, the physical world, and also that *ch'i* is not findable outside of *Tao*, the metaphysical world: in other words, that outside of *Tao* there is no physical world and that outside of the physical world there is no *Tao*. *Tao* and *ch'i* are inseparable. Such being the case, how can Fung Yu-lan, be correct in asserting that Ch'eng I believed *Tao* to be separable from *ch'i* — believed ultimate metaphysical reality to be something in addition to, and detachable from, the world of matter? What possible justification is there, in short, for Fung's notion that Ch'eng I was a Platonist?

Let us pursue this critique of the Platonization of Ch'eng I still further. Ch'eng I's interest in the physical world was so intense that it would have been impossible for him to conceive of searching for *Tao* except through the study of the physical world. True, he often remarked that *Tao* is complete in itself, but by this comment he meant only that *Tao* and the physical world are distinct, as it were, and should not be confused with one another.

Fung's propensity to exaggerate the doctrinal differences between the Ch'eng brothers leads, in my opinion, to considerable misinterpretation. I suspect that his notion that, for Ch'eng Hao, *Tao* is the natural tendency of things, is based on a distortion of that philosopher's conception of Tao. Fung must have noticed the following words of Ch'eng Hao: "What makes *Yin* appear at one time, and *Yang* at another time, is *Tao*. *Yin* and *Yang* are forces within the physical world, yet *Tao* is implied here." In these sentences a clear line is drawn between what is *above* [*i.e.*, the metaphysical], and what is *below* [*i.e.*, the physical]. But if Ch'eng Hao attaches importance to this distinction, how can one say that for him *Tao* is only the natural tendency of concrete things? Ch'eng Hao fully appreciated that *Tao* is unfindable outside of the physical world. Still this view does not preclude him from holding *Tao* is indivisible and complete in itself.

According to the Ch'eng brothers, the *Tao* (the metaphysical world) cannot be found outside of *ch'i* (the physical world). That is, the metaphysical world is inseparable from the physical world. If this is the position of Ch'eng I, I do not understand how one can identify his *Tao* with the Platonic Idea. If one comprehends the Platonic Idea as an unchangeable form, one may say that although *ri* is also abiding and everlasting, nevertheless it, or the *Tao*, in Chinese philosophy means no more than what is called in the West moral or natural law. Moreover, from the theory of the Platonic Idea there follows the doctrine of "participation" or the doctrine that things imitate the forms. It is inconceivable that in Ch'eng I's mind the relationship of participation between ideas and things should have been envisaged. To suppose that any analogy exists between *ri* and the Platonic Idea is to confuse, rather than to clarify, the meaning of philosophical concept in the East and West.

Lastly, I should like to offer a proof that Fung Yu-lan's assignment of certain quotations to Ch'eng I is the result of his own misunderstanding. The following words, which the *Philosophical Records of the Sung and Yüan Dynasties* attribute to Ch'eng Hao, are, by Fung Yu-lan, put to the credit of Ch'eng I. Ch'eng Hao says: *Ri* is completely there, and it can be neither increased nor decreased. One cannot say that the *Tao* of kingship was realized when Yao exemplified it as king; nor can one say that the *Tao* of Kingship was extinct when Chieh did not rule in accordance with it as a King. *Ri* remains what it is."[9]

This passage from the *Philosophical Records of the Sung and Yüan Dynasties* is proof that Fung Yu-lan's mis-assignment and misinterpretation are quite a distortion! His error possibly comes from his bias for making *ri* the equivalent of the Platonic Idea.

As a further illustration of the problem of the relation between *ch'i* and *Tao*, I shall deal with the question of human nature as Ch'eng Hao understands it. This question was raised a thousand years previously by Confucius and Mencius. Mencius believed that human nature is good. Hsün-tzu said that it is evil. When we come down to the Sung Dynasty, we find that philosophers like Chang Tsai and the Ch'eng brothers have begun to differentiate between the physical nature and the essential nature of man. It was necessary to draw this distinction because the actual cases of evil men were so evident. The Sung philosophers explained that while human nature in its origin is good, after a man's birth he is endowed with a body, and here lies the origin of evil. It comes from the deficiency of the physical elements. This distinction between the physical and the essential nature made it possible to hold to the teaching of Mencius, and at the same time rendered intelligible the fact of evil in human nature. In other words, evil issues from the endowment of the human body.

The Sung philosophers were firmly convinced that evil could be removed by personal cultivation. Says Ch'eng Hao: "Human nature is what comes from life. So it is tied to *ch'i*. When one is born with a nature, *ch'i* is an ingredient. The endowment of human life may be good and bad in human nature. Sometimes a man from his boyhood is good; other times, a man from his boyhood is evil. This is the result of his endowment. One may say that goodness comes from his nature, but one may not say that evil also comes from his nature, because nature is co-ordinated with life. In the *Book of Rites* (*Li-chi*) it is said: 'There is calmness in life.' After the period of calmness follows the period of birth. Nature begins with birth. After birth nature in its pure form cannot be found. What is called nature in ordinary language is not nature in its pure form. What is called nature in ordinary language corresponds to what is "continued" in the sense of the *Book of Changes* [according to which the "continued" means the "no more original"]. We should also understand the theory of the goodness of human nature in this sense. Goodness in the process of "continuation" may be illustrated in the following way: Water is what flows downwards, but in some places it flows into the sea without becoming dirty. This is not the result of human labor. In other places, water becomes dirty after flowing a short distance; sometimes it becomes dirty after flowing a long distance. Also sometimes it is more dirty, sometimes less dirty. But whether dirty or pure, it is water.

"In this metaphor we have a lesson for mankind: men should not forget their work of purification. Much work of purification will purify water in a short time; less work of purification will purify it in a longer time. But when it becomes pure it is the same water as it was before. It is not that a different kind of water — pure water — is substituted for the dirty water; nor is it that the dirty water can be set aside. So the purity of water is like the goodness of human nature. And therefore it is incorrect to say good and evil are opposites in human nature. This fundamental principle is a Heavenly Decree. To be in conformity with this principle is Tao. To cultivate one's self in conformity with the principle and to share what is appropriate to one's self is education. From the commencement with the Heavenly Decree, down to the work of education, human nature remains as it is. It is neither increased nor decreased. This is why the Emperor Shun said that after his ascension to the throne, the possession of the world meant the same to him as if he had not possessed it."[10]

Ch'eng Hao in these paragraphs discusses the problem of human nature at two levels: the physical and the metaphysical. He knows well that human nature cannot be found without the human body. That is, Tao cannot be found outside of the physical world. Yet he gives priority to Tao, because it is on a higher level, and determines what human nature should be. Ch'eng Hao also knows well that Tao cannot be independent of ch'i, but Tao still has greater power than ch'i, and is superior to it. This is Ch'eng Hao's own refutation of Fung Yu-lan's interpretation that the Tao or ri is merely a natural tendency of concrete things.

I should like to mention at this point that Sung Philosophy is not only a logical and metaphysical theory, but also furnishes a way of approach to personal cultivation. If one talks but does not live up to what one says, one will be considered dishonest. So besides the intellectual attitude towards Tao and ch'i, real belief in Tao depends upon how one behaves. One must not only believe, but must also act accordingly. This is the way to sagehood. Thus, in Chinese philosophy, the aspect of personal cultivation is equally important as logical and metaphysical theory.

I come now to Ch'eng Hao's theory of personal cultivation. He wrote two essays: Know Jen, and Tranquillity in Human Nature, both of which are as important in Sung philosophy as Chou Tun-i's Diagram of the Supreme Ultimate, or Chang Tsai's Western Inscription.

Ch'eng Hao's essay, *Know Jen,* is as follows: "The first thing for a scholar to know is what is *Jen.* The meaning of *Jen* is that one should feel oneness with the whole universe. Righteousness, decency, knowledge or wisdom, and honesty, may be considered parts of *Jen.* If one recognizes this fundamental principle, one may preserve it by means of sentiments of truthfulness and attentiveness. This principle requires neither restraint nor searching. But if one's mind is negligent, then restraint is necessary. Otherwise, there is no use in fastening shackles to one's self. When one does not recognize the principle, one must search for it. After one has become familiar with it, why need one search for it? The principle of *Jen* is an idea to which nothing can be equal. Even the word 'great' cannot describe it. The whole work of Heaven and Earth is man's work. Mencius said: 'The manifoldness of things is complete in myself.' Again he said: 'To return to one's self and to find that one is in a state of truth is the supreme happiness.' Not to be in a state of truth means that one's self and truth are separated; and any exertion to compel one's self to become reunited with truth is achieved with extreme difficulty. Under such circumstances, there is no happiness. The essay: *The Western Inscription* imparts to us a thorough understanding of this idea. Just keep your mind in a state of *Jen.* You need add nothing. Mencius also said: 'As if you were devoted to something but that this something requires no correction. The mind should not be negligent, and you should not try to help growth.' The significance of this remark is that no extra exertion from you is needed. Maintaining your mind thus, you will certainly attain to the state of *Jen.* The innate wisdom and the innate ability are born with you, and cannot be lost. As long as you have not discarded your old habits, you will have to exercise vigilance over your mind. But by the proper maintenance you will change habits. This theory is rather simple. The important point is to keep your mind in the state described. Once you feel happy with your mind in this state, then you need not worry about losing what you have achieved."

Perhaps this word *Jen* needs clarification. It means the same as "love" in the moral sense. The British moralist, Joseph Butler has said something approaching *Jen* in his theory of "benevolence." In one of his sermons, Butler said:

"When Benevolence is said to be the sum of virtue, it is not spoken of as a blind propension, but as a principle in reasonable creatures, and so to be directed by their reason: for reason and reflection come to our notion of a moral agent — Reason, considered merely as subservient to Benevolence, as assisting to produce the greatest good, will teach us to have particular regard to these relations and circumstances; because it is plainly for the good of the world that they should be regarded."[12]

If we compare the words of Ch'eng Hao — that virtues such as righteousness, decency, wisdom, and honesty, are the constituent parts of *Jen* — with the words of Butler — that benevolence is the sum of virtue, it is clear that the two philosophers are in basic agreement. Ch'eng Hao's assertion that the meaning of *Jen* is that one feels oneness with the whole universe, is again confirmed by Butler's idea connecting benevolence with the Love of God. "That which we more strictly call piety", says Butler, "or the love of God ... someone may perhaps imagine no way connected with Benevolence, yet surely they must be connected, if there be indeed in being an object infinitely good."[13]

This comparison between Ch'eng Hao and Joseph Butler will, I hope, convince the reader that there is a real kinship between the East and West, which is not generally admitted. The comparison will also throw light on why Ch'eng Hao's essay, *Know Jen,* was effective as proposing a way of approach to *Tao.* The reason was that it considered the people's happiness or unhappiness as one's own pleasure or pain, and this consideration is the only basis upon which one can integrate one's self with mankind.

For further illustration of Ch'eng Hao's theory of *Jen,* let me quote this: "The doctor of medicine", says Ch'eng Hao, "gives the term '*not-Jen*' to the disease of paralysis. This term '*not-Jen*' is an excellent opposite to *Jen.* A man with *Jen* should feel as if he were united with the whole universe. Every part of the world should feel to him as he feels his own body. When a man does not have the sense that all portions of the world are part of himself he is just like the paralytic, who loses feeling of the limbs and the power of voluntary motion because the blood fails to circulate throughout his body. Therefore, a feeling of universal love for all people is a prerequisite for sagehood."[14]

Ch'eng Hao says elsewhere : "When you watch the hen protecting her chicks you behold the nature of *Jen*."[15]

When Chang Tsai raised the question: "Why does human nature, even when it intends to be quiet, always remain affected by external things?" Ch'eng Hao wrote an essay in reply entitled *Tranquillity in Human Nature, Being a Reply to Chang Tsai*. Before we turn to the text let me explain briefly the meaning of this title. J. P. Bruce in his *Chu Hsi and His Masters* translated the title *A Treatise on the Steadfast Nature* [16] as against my rendering "tranquillity in human nature", or "how to tranquillize human nature." The Chinese words are *ting-hsing*. The word *ting* Bruce unfortunately took as an adjective, hence "steadfast". But *ting* is not an adjective, even though in the Chinese language words immediately preceding nouns often are adjectives. *Ting* here is a verb, hence my translation "to tranquillise". Aside from this grammatical detail, there is another flaw in Bruce's translation. The meaning referred to by these words is not "steadfast nature", but is the idea of the Buddhist *Samdhi*, suggested in a Chinese way. In the context of this essay *ting* signifies a state of repose — which is clear in the very first sentence of the essay. Therefore, I prefer to render the title *Tranquillity in Human Nature* because this expression is equivalent to the Buddhist *Samdhi*.

At any rate this is what Ch'eng Hao wrote: "Tranquillity means quietness in time of activity and inactivity. One should not anticipate what is to come. Neither should one take the view that there is something inside, or something outside. When one considers that the external world is something outside, and that one's mind is compelled to follow what transpires on the outside, the result will be that one's own nature will be divided into two: the inside, and the outside. It follows that one's nature will go outside when it is stimulated by external things. If it goes outside, one may ask: 'What remains inside?' As long as one is preoccupied by the idea of cutting off, in one's self, the effects of external stimulus, one will be oblivious of what is inside. It is better to know that in human nature there is no separation of inside and outside. To try to separate the inside from the outside is not the way to attain tranquillity. The normal way of Heaven and Earth is for the mind to pervade the manifoldness of things. Yet they accom-

plish this without the mind's being aware of its own doing. The
normal way of the sage is for his sentiment to go along with the
manifold things. Yet he does so without his sentiment being conscious of itself. Therefore, the way of the man of noble character
is perfect broad-mindedness and complete fairness. When events
come, he knows how to handle them. In the *Book of Changes* it
is said:

> 'Perseverance brings good fortune;
> Remorse disappears.
> If a man is agitated in mind,
> And his thoughts go hither and thither,
> Only those friends
> On whom he fixes his conscious thoughts
> Will follow.'

"As long as one concerns one's self with the elimination of
external stimulus, one will find that when one thing disappears in
the east, something else will come from the west. Such appearing
and disappearing will go on endlessly. One will discover that time
will be not enough to cut off from one's self the stimulus from
outside.

"The mind of man is forever blinded with bias and prejudices, so that it is impossible for him to attain *Tao*. The main
reason for this mentality is that a man has selfish motives, and
is busy with the application of his own cleverness. When a man has
selfish motives, they prevent him from knowing that the only adequate response to the external world is to adapt one's self to what
comes. When a man is confident of his own cleverness, he forgets the
use of his natural gift of light. When he is preoccupied with disgust at the stimulus coming from outside, he can find a place in
his mind where can keep light, and where things from the outside
can be mirrored. The *Book of Changes* has the saying:

> 'Keep still. Keeping his back still
> So that his body can no longer go farther,
> He goes into the courtyard
> And does not see his people.'

Mencius says: 'Why I am disgusted with knowledge is that sometimes it brings sophistry,' Therefore it is preferable to forget both
the inside and the outside, rather than to exclude the outside for
the sake of keeping the inside. When one forgets both the inside
and the outside, one's mind will be clear and distinct, and will be
occupied with nothing. Being occupied with nothing leads to
tranquillity. Tranquillity leads to light. When one is full of light,
why should one worry about the question of giving response to
external stimuli?

"When the sage feels joy, it is because there should be joy
under the cirumstances of things. When the sage feels rage, it is
because the circumstances of things require rage. Thus, the pleasure and the displeasure of the sage depends upon things, not upon
his own mind. This means that the sage responds to what is demanded by external things. Hence, it is a mistake to take the view
that to occupy one's self with the outside is wrong, and that to confine one's self to search on the inside is right.

"If one compares the pleasure and displeasure of an ordinary
man who is selfish, and who concentrates on his own cleverness,
to the pleasure and displeasure of the sage who is on the right path,
one will learn where the difference lies between the two. The
human emotion which is most easily aroused and the most difficult
to control, is indignation. If one can stop one's indignation as soon
as it takes form, and cooly appeal to reason to find out what is
right and what is wrong, one need not worry about external stimuli. This kind of self-control will bring one half-way to the *Tao*."[17]

In this essay, *Tranquillity in Human Nature*, Ch'eng Hao
dealt with the same idea as that expressed by Chou Tun-i, that
calmness can be set up as a standard for mankind. The Sung
philosophers had learned much from the work of meditation in
Ch'an Buddhism (Zen), now they sought to establish their own
way of meditation. The essay, *Tranqillity in Human Nature*,
is the Chinese counterpart to Ch'an Buddhism.

Ch'eng Hao's search for a way to tranquillity of nature is
well illustrated by his own practices. He once passed a large ver-
anda with many columns and tried to guess their exact number.
Having made one he doubted it, so he made a second guess. He
then asked another person to make a third estimate which hap-

pened to agree with his first guess. His conclusion was that when one's mind is excited, it tends to be over-active, and fall into uncertainty. So Ch'eng Hao gave the advice that the mind should remain in a state of non-attachment.

Ch'eng Hao also made clear why a man becomes narrow-minded in his famous metaphor of looking at heaven from the bottom of a well. "When you look at Heaven", he says, "while sitting in a well, you find, of course, that heaven is small. It is not that heaven really is small, but that your sitting in the well makes it appear small. It is the well that is to blame. Once out of the well, you will find that heaven is really large, since your view of heaven is no longer bound by the narrow circle of the well. Out of the well, you feel the vastness of heaven. When you enter the well the next time, you will not believe only in what you see."[18] By this metaphor, Ch'eng Hao has told us again that our mind should be as free as possible from all kinds of restriction.

Ch'eng Hao, after his long practice of sitting quietly and meditating, could acquire the composure of Buddha. He was never rigid in dealing with men. Indeed, his attitude towards them was always kind. He looked dignified, but he showed warmth in his contacts with other persons.

Ch'eng Hao's practice of meditation was a natural concomitant of what has been described in his essay, *Tranquillity of Human Nature*. "It is not", he says, "as if the mind were devoted to something. Yet the mind should neither be negligent nor help to grow. Just make your mind like a mirror, which can reflect anything." "To help to grow" is an expression from Mencius, who meant that the keeping, or cultivation, of the mind should be done in a natural way. "To help to grow" is a sign of artificiality, an indication of hurrying the mind. Even if the intention is good, there is still a bias, and this should be avoided.

Ch'eng Hao repeated again and again that indulgence in things — whether in gambling, collecting curios, or books — causes one to lose one's mind.

As regards Ch'eng Hao's political philosophy, I shall be brief. From the Sung Dynasty on, it was the custom among the philosophers to consider the rulers of the Three Dynasties, and the Emperors Yao and Shun, as philosopher-Kings of the Platonic type.

Advice was seldom given to an emperor on questions of raising money or military expansion. The major premise for good government was rectification of the mind and having a true will. This is similiar to Plato, who said in *The Republic* that he who is to be a really good and noble guardian of the state should require in himself "philosophy and spirit and swiftness and strength." Here, "philosophy and spirit" mean much more than what the terms ordinarily stand for. The Chinese manner of speech is more abstract than that of Plato. Thus Ch'eng Hao said:

"The proper course for an emperor is to be interested in ancient history and in learning, to distinguish between good and evil, and to distinguish between people who are loyal and those who are disloyal. The emperor should aim at what is right. Once he decides upon such a course, the country will be well governed."

"When the Emperor Shen-tsung asked Ch'eng Hao how this decision can be made, the philosopher's reply was to rectify the mind, to have a true will, and to choose the good and to cling to it tenaciously. As long as the right principle has not been discovered, one will listen to many sides, and still fall into error. When the will is not determined, even though the good is discovered, the will will persist in its divergent course. Ch'eng Hao continued his advice to the emperor to observe the instructions of the sages, and to believe in them; to take the former emperors as models and to follow them determinedly; not to be attracted by considerations of utility which aim at momentary achievement; and not to become a prisoner of the populace or of the vulgar crowd. When the emperor exhibits a firm faith in *Tao*, reaches the highest stage of enlightenment, and employs wise men to the exclusion of those who are disloyal, he will no doubt have a good government, as was done during the Three Dynasties."[19]

Such was the fundamental principle of Ch'eng Hao's political philosophy. In regard to his practical policy, I have stated his Ten-Point program in the third chapter.

Ch'eng Hao's attitude towards Buddhism is interesting. His criticism is deeper than Han Yü's. "According to the sages", says Ch'eng, "life and death are an ordinary matter. There is nothing to fear. The vital problem for the Buddhists is life and death, so they harp upon this point. Those who practice the Ch'an may be different, yet even their aim is to gain by their meditation."[20]

"What the Buddhists call 'worldly nets' is the fundamental principle of human relations according to our sages. To get rid of the principle of human relations is the highest point to which the Buddhists aspire. But the fundamental principle of human relations can never be eliminated. The sensations of hearing and seeing; the desires of drinking, eating, and sex; and the sentiments of joy, rage, sorrow, and pleasure, come from human nature. The Buddhists believed that not until these are done away with can a man attain reality. But I believe that such a way is contrary to reality."[21]

The Chinese way is not to close oneself to the outside world, or to cut all contact with it, but rather to make one's mind the master of the situation and the measure or standard of conduct. Then one is in no danger of being misled.

I should like to close this chapter with a few quotations from Ch'eng I in appreciation of his older brother. Ch'eng I says: "He was endowed with a natural gift, and he knew how to cultivate himself. He was as fine as gold, and as smooth as jade. He was magnanimous, and yet he was strict with himself. He sought harmony, yet he was not accommodating or opportunistic. His loyalty was as good as metal and rock. His filial piety and brotherly love could win the sympathy of spirits. When he came into contact with persons, his face revealed kindness like the warmth of the sun in the spring. When one listened to him, his words penetrated as rain water penetrates plants. His mind was broad so that he had deep insight. To one who wished to survey his depths, he appeared like an ocean, which knows no bounds. Thus it is difficult to describe his personality with words. He spot-lighted the falsehoods of the subtle reasonings of the heretical schools, and he clarified the doubts which for ages puzzled the people. No scholars since the Ch'in and Han Dynasties has ever attained the stage which Ch'eng Hao reached."[22]

Other philosophers in appraising Ch'eng Hao have described him as being in the Sung Dynasty what Mencius was in the ancient period. Ch'eng Hao's interest was concentrated on two problems: first, a rational basis for Sung philosophy; second, emphasis on the concept *T'ien-ri* (Heavenly Reason), which was later developed into the tenet: "Human nature is Reason". These two ideas were also advocated by Mencius. Accordingly, Ch'eng Hao was given a permanent position in the history of Sung philosophy, known as the Ch'eng-Chu School, in contrast to Lu-Wang, the School of Lu Hsiang-shang and Wang Shou-jen, whose principal idea was that mind is reason.

References

1. *Sung shih* (History of the Sung Dynasty), Book 427.
2. *Erh Ch'eng i-shu* (Posthumous Works of the Two Ch'engs), Book 11.
3. *The Dialogues of Plato*, Vol. 1, (The Phaedo), p. 397.
4. *P.R.S.Y.*, Book 13.
5. *Erh-Ch'eng i-shu*, Book 11.
6. *Loc. cit.*
7. *P.R.S.Y.*, Book 13.
8. Fung Yu-lan, *A Short History of Chinese Philosophy*, Macmillan Co., New York, 1948, p. 286.
9. *P.R.S.Y.*, Book 13.
10. *Loc. cit.*
11. *Loc. cit.*
12. *British Moralists*, edited by L.A. Selby-Bigge, in two volumes, The Clarendon Press, Oxford, 1897, Vol. 1, p. 241.
13. *Ibid.*, p. 224.
14. *P.R.S.Y.*, Book 13.
15. *Loc. cit.*
16. J. P. Bruce, *Chu Hsi and His Masters*, Probsthain and Co., London, 1923, pp. 47, 259.
17. *P.R.S.Y.*, Book 13.
18. *Loc. cit.*
19. *Erh Ch'eng i-shu*, Book 2 (Ch'eng Hao's Memorial on Kingship).
20. *Ibid.*, Book 1.
21. *Ibid.*, Book 2.
22. *Ibid.*, Book 7, *I-ch'uan wen-chi* (Collected Essays of Ch'eng I).

CHAPTER TEN

The Rational Basis of Sung Philosophy, Continued: Ch'eng I

The first part of this chapter resumes the discussion of whether there was any difference of opinion between Ch'eng Hao and Ch'eng I in an attempt to clarify the implications of the concepts *Tao* or *Ri.*

According to Fung Yu-lan's interpretation, Ch'eng Hao took the *Tao* or *Ri* to be a natural tendency in concrete things, while Ch'eng I regarded it as the Platonic Idea. However, the view that the *Tao* is metaphysical was common to both Ch'eng Hao and Ch'eng I, and in no sense can be confined to Ch'eng I. Quotations which Fung Yu-lan attributes to Ch'eng Hao, describing the nature of the *Tao* and *Ri,* and the other quotations also concerning this question, appear to me to be from the common background of both brothers. For comparison let me cite a remark from each brother:

Ch'eng Hao	Ch'eng I
"The Appendix of the Book of Changes says: 'The metaphysical is *Tao*, the physical is *Ch'i* — Again it says: 'One time *Yin* appears; another time *Yang* appears. This is *Tao*.' *Yin* and *Yang* belong to the physical	"One time *Yin* appears; another time *Yang* appears. *Tao* is not the same as *Yin* and *Yang*. What causes *Yin* to appear at one time, and *Yang* to appear at another time, is *Tao*." "Apart from *Yin* and *Yang*

Ch'eng Hao

world, yet *Tao* is implied. In this sentence a clear line between what is above (metaphysical and what is below (physical) is drawn."[1]

Ch'eng I

there is no *Tao*. What causes *Yin* and *Yang* to appear is *Tao*. *Yin* and *Yang* are *Ch'i*. They are the physical. *Tao* is the metaphysical. The metaphysical is the more comprehensive."[2]

It is evident in this comparison of texts that Ch'eng I never regarded the *Tao* as separable from *Ch'i*. Thence, it follows that between the two brothers there was no difference of opinion. Furthermore, the quotations make it clear that the interpretation of the *Tao* as what is complete in itself, cannot be attributed to Ch'eng I alone, but must be considered as stemming from the common background of both brothers.

Now, following this line of thought, I shall present Ch'eng I's philosophical system. He believed the same as Ch'eng Hao in so far, first, as the *Tao* is inseparable from *Ch'i*: and in so far, second as the *Tao* is to be found only in the *Ch'i*, yet is on a higher level and has greater power. If it should be asked whether Ch'eng I's philosophical view was completely identical with that of Ch'eng Hao, my reply is that the fundamental principles were the same, but that there was a nuance of difference. Ch'eng I was more emphatic in stressing intellect or thinking, while Ch'eng Hao's starting point was *Jen*. If an analogy is required, let me cite an example from Western philosophy, that of Kant and Hegel. Kant considered that God, Freedom, and Immortality are the postulates of the Practical Reason, while Hegel tried to include God in his system of logic. Hegel, in other words, was more of an intellectualist than Kant. If a shade of difference is to be found between Ch'eng Hao and Ch'eng I it is that Ch'eng I was more of an intellectualist than Ch'eng Hao.

Nevertheless, the temperament of the two brothers was different. Chu Hsi said: "Ch'eng Hao was magnanimous, while Ch'eng I was sharp and to-the-point. In the elder brother lay strength of insight and decisiveness; in the younger brother, in his early years, lay strictness of character, and in his later years mellowness."[3]

Each of the three philosophers: Chou Tun-i, Ch'eng I, and Ch'eng Hao had a formula for personal cultivation. For Chou Tun-i the formula was: "Calmness sets up the standard of humanity." Ch'eng Hao substituted for "Calmness" the expression "Tranquillity in human nature". Ch'eng I made yet another substitution: "For spiritual nurture, concentration of mind is needed; for the advancement of learning, realization of knowledge is the way."[4] In this passage, the simultaneous occurence of "concentration of mind" and "realization of knowledge", indicates that for Ch'eng I knowledge or intellect was a factor of equal importance to mental concentration or calmness.

Ch'eng I was younger than his brother Ch'eng Hao by one year. He was reputed to be so talented that even in his boyhood he never acted improperly. When he was fourteen years old, he was tutored by Chou Tun-i along with his elder brother. In his eighteenth year, he sent a memorial to Emperor Jen-tsung saying that he, as Emperor, should keep in mind the right principles of government and the welfare of the people; that he should disregard the opinions of the vulgar; and that he should aspire after the highest achievements. The Emperor refused him an audience.

In the same year, Ch'eng I entered the government academy, and was assigned as a subject for an essay: "To what kind of learning did Yen Hui devote himself?" When the rector, Hu Yüan, received Ch'eng I's essay he was greatly astonished by the student's wealth of knowledge, and immediately appointed him a teacher in the academy. In 1059 he was awarded the degree of *Chin-shih*. Thereafter, he was frequently recommended for employment in high office, but always refused. Eventually, however, he was recommended to the throne by Ssu-ma Kuang as an extraordinary man, and was appointed a secretary to the cabinet. After being received by Emperor Che-tsung, he was transferred to the post of lecturer to the Emperor. It was then that he submitted the following memorial: "One's habit grows out of what one learns, and advancement is made when the mind is improved. Parents who have looked after their children well, have customarily employed men of noble character as tutors. This is the way parents have found most efficacious in forming the character of their sons. Your Majesty is still young. Though you are gifted by birth, yet tutorship should still be a matter to think over. If, every day, more time is devoted to receiving men of good character, and less time to wives and eunuchs, there should ensue a good transformation of character and habit. I propose that more scholars should be invited to give lectures, and also that they should be asked to stay longer so they can give more advice. They should be permitted to remonstrate with Your Majesty when Your Majesty makes a mistake. With time, Your Majesty's virtue will be naturally improved."[5] When Ch'eng I was told that Emperor Che-tsung, while out walking, refrained from even killing an ant, he was so glad and explained that if the Emperor developed this habit it could be the source of great benefit to the people.

Though Ch'eng I served as a lecturer to Emperor Che-tsung from the time of his coronation, and continued to give advice, the philosopher did not remain long in imperial favor. Another literary school, headed by Su Shih or Su Tung-p'o, famous for his literary style, was jealous of Ch'eng I because the latter in his saintly attitude towards *Tao* and in his discussion of the *Tao* antagonized Su Shih. One of Su Shih's followers, therefore, .requested Ch'eng I's dismissal.

When, after eight years of regency by the Empress, Che-tsung ascended the throne, men like Chang Chun and Ts'ai Pien came into power, and they ran the government under the slogan: "Back to the reform policy of Wang An-shih!" These men were much more dangerous to Ch'eng I than was Su Shih. Chang Chun was appointed prime minister, and proceeded to suspend everybody who had been antagonistic to Wang An-shih's policy. Ch'eng I was sent back to his home village, and the order was issued that every book which he published should be burned. But since the expulsion was general for anybody who had opposed Wang An-shih, Su Tung-p'o was banished also. Ch'eng I was exiled to Fou-chou in Szechuan Province.

Four years later these orders were relaxed, and Ch'eng I was permitted to return to his former posts and his property was restored. Government orders from 1094, the first year of the "Back to the reform policy", to 1126 were very confused. One year exiles were called back and reinstated to their former positions the next year the names of all those who had been expelled were engraved on a stone in a so-called *List of Traitors*. When it was dicovered that Ch'eng I had retreated to a mountain to write, he was commanded to destroy all that he had written. In 1104 Emperor Hui-tsung himself composed a blacklist of 309 names, and a monument which the blacklist was engraved was set up in the Wen-te Palace. A similar list, composed by the prime minister, Ts'ai Ching, was sent to all the provinces to be engraved on monuments. In 1106 a meteor destroyed the monument in the Wen-te Palace, and again there was some relaxation of orders for those banished. Among these was Ch'eng I who enjoyed a brief respite. But he died in 1108, at the age of seventy-five; and the Northern Sung Dynasty came to an end in 1127. The charges brought against Ch'eng I during the period of persecution — that he spread perverse theories to corrupt youth — reminds one of the charges brought against Socrates in Athens. Ch'eng I's disciples Yin Shun and Chang I followed him around and worked as his assistants. When the order was issued that his pupils should be dispersed, he instructed them to practice what he had taught them, and to stay with him no longer. Only four pupils attended his funeral service.

The philosophical ideas of Ch'eng will be presented under different headings. As a student of Chou Tun-i and a co-worker with his brother Ch'eng Hao, Ch'eng I's metaphysical opinions show no difference from those of the other two thinkers, at least in so far as his ideas of the Supreme Ultimate and of the line of demarcation between the metaphysical and physical are concerned. He went along with Chou Tun-i and Ch'eng Hao though he was not merely their pupil. He had his own ideas, especially in stressing the function of intellect or thinking.

1. CH'ENG'S BELIEF IN RATIONALITY

"All things in the world", says Ch'eng I, "can be understood in the light of reason. Each entity works according to its principle or the order of nature. In each, therefore, there is reason."[6]

"All transformations in the world are incalculable; but in the elements of *Yin* and *Yang* and in the periodical returns of the sun and moon, of day and night, and of cold and heat, there is a normal course."[7]

"Investigation of reason may be carried out in many ways: by reading books, by discussion, by evaluting the personalities in history and their actions, and by discerning the correct responses to what comes. All these kinds of procedure may be called investigation of reason."[8]

Firmly convinced of rationality in all phenomena, Ch'eng I asked people to believe only in what is conceivable. On one occasion when someone told him a story about seeing a ghost, he asked: "Did you see it with your own eyes? One should believe only in what one sees with one's own eyes. What is told as a story is not worthy of credence. Even what one sees with one's own eyes may be caused by an ocular deficiency."

This characteristic of his thought may be further illustrated by a dialogue. "An inquirer after truth asked Ch'eng I: 'Do ghosts and divinities have features?' The philosopher replied: 'Yes, they do.' The questioner resumed: 'If they have features, then it is certain that ghosts and divinities exist.' Ch'eng I commented: 'The so-called ghosts are transformations of the universe.'

"The same inquirer asked: 'Why do rains and clouds come from high mountains and rivers?' Ch'eng I explained: 'Rains and clouds are the condensation of air or matter.' The question was further asked: 'But since the sacrificial offerings are made, must there not be divinities [to account for the rain]?' Ch'eng I replied: 'It [rain] has a material cause. People overlook this point, so they go to temples to pray. They do not know what rain and dew are — so they pray for rain and dew in the temples. They think it impossible that mountains and rivers should make the rain and clouds, but instead go to statues formed out of mud and wood to pray for rain and clouds. If mountains and rivers cannot make rain and clouds, how can idols of mud and weed be efficacious?'

"The subject was pursued further. The questioner asked: 'Is this possibly a case of a man-made wonder-story?' The philosopher answered: 'There is not even wonder involved here. This is merely a case of a kind of imagination coming from human psychology. When rain and clouds occur after prayer, the connection is purely accidental. Once when I was in Ssu-chou there was a rumor about the appearance of the sage, Confucius. Some said that he looked this way, others said that he looked that way. They never agreed about how he looked. This also was a case of a wonder story arising from human imagination.'

"Formerly Chu Ting, a pupil of Ch'eng I, became magistrate of Ssu-chou. After a great fire in the city the magistrate requested the soldiers parade with an image of the Buddha in the street in order to put a stop to the fire. Ch'eng I inquired of Chu Ting: 'Why did you not let the image of the Buddha walk during the fire? If it had been burned then this would have shown that the Buddha can work no wonders. But if it had extinguished the fire, then the people would have more faith than ever in the Buddha. Why did you not deal with the Buddha in such a way?' Ch'eng I added that Chu Ting's knowledge could reach only so far!' "

In this dialogue we have good evidence of how firm and positive Ch'eng I was in his conviction of the rationality of the universe. His mind was what we to-day call scientific.

So certain was he of the validity of the principle of reason and the oneness of reality that he said: "What is directed by heaven is the heavenly order. What is right in principle is reason. These are one and the same." In this passage he expresses his belief that the world of experience is the embodiment of reason. Both in the physical and moral realm there is an eternal order which reason dictates. Man's duty is to know and obey this order which reason imparts and finds. Ch'eng I's words bring to mind an utterance of Giordano Bruno: "The heavens are a picture, a book, a mirror, wherein man can behold and read the form and the laws of supreme goodness, the plan and total perfection." Elsewhere Bruno said: "From this spirit, which is One, all being flows. There is one truth and one goodness penetrating and governing all things. In nature are the thoughts of God. They are made manifest in figures and vestiges to the eyes of sense; they are reproduced in our thoughts, where alone we can arrive at consciousness of true being. We are surrounded by eternity and by the unity of love."[10] Because of this oneness there is the possibility of rational explanation. These words of Giordano Bruno could be endorsed not only by Ch'eng I, but also by Chou Tun-i, Shao Yung, Chang Ts'ai and Ch'eng Hao.

II. CH'ENG I'S THEORY THAT HUMAN NATURE IS REASON

If Ch'eng I had stopped with his first theorem that a rational basis can be found in all things, this alone would not have made him a great authority in Sung Philosophy, for the Chinese are interested in morality. There was needed a criterion for all ethical valuations. Otherwise morality would be merely subjective and, as Protagoras said, man would be the measure of right and wrong. If such were the case, there would be in the final analysis no measure of right and wrong at all. This is why in Chinese philosophy the search for an ethical standard is the cardinal objective. Mencius contributed the idea that in human nature there are four virtues: benevolence, righteousness, decency and knowledge common to all human beings. There yet remained the question: What is the relation between the four virtues and reason? Are they identical with reason or different from it? After Mencius, this question had to be answered. And Ch'eng I gave the answer in his formula: Human nature is reason. This formula may be attacked on the ground that many persons act contrary to reason. It may also be refuted by the demonstration that in human nature there are emotions, instincts and desires, convictions, enthusiasms, which are not reducible to the one source, reason. Accordingly, many philosophers hesitated to approve the doctrine that human nature is reason. Ch'eng I brought the concept of human nature and reason together because he believed (1) in the theory of the goodness of human nature, and (2) in the theory that this goodness is imbedded in the four virtues which constitute the forms of thoughts in moral judgments by human beings. Let us read in Ch'eng I's own records how he explained the relation between human nature and reason.

"Someone asked: 'If human nature is in essence enlightened, why is it sometimes obscured?' Ch'eng I answered: 'This question should indeed, be pondered. Mencius was right in upholding the thesis that human nature is good. Others, such as Hsün-tzu and Yang Hsiung, did not know what human nature is. Mencius was above all other philosophers in that he knew what human nature is. There is no human nature which is not good. It may be not-good, but this comes from its working-capacity. Human nature is reason, and it is the same in everyone, from Yao and Shun down to the man in the street.' "[11]

In another context Ch'eng I said: "Human nature *is* reason, or, in other words, one may speak of 'human nature *as* reason,' or of *rational* nature. Reason from its very beginning cannot be other than good. The emotions of joy, anger, sorrow, and happiness, when they remain in the state prior to the being expressed, are good in themselves. If their expression fits the requirements of the occasion they are also good. But if their expression does not fit the occasion, they may be evil."[12]

"Again someone asked: 'Do the emotions of joy and anger come from human nature?' Ch'eng I replied: 'They do. When a man is born, he is endowed with human nature. After he has been thus endowed, he also has emotions. When there is no human nature, there will also be no expression of emotions.' Then the question was raised: 'Is the relation of the emotions to human nature the same as that of wave to water?' Ch'eng I said: 'Yes. When water is clear, quiet, and level, as if it were a mirror, then its nature is properly what the nature of water should be. But when water flows against stones or sand, or from a high level, then there will be rapid currents. Also when the wind blows over it, waves are formed. But currents and waves are accidental to the nature of water. Inherent in human nature there are only four virtues: there is nothing evil in it. But as there will be no wave when there is no water, so there will be no emotion where there is no human nature."[13]

The four virtues of Chinese philosophy have the same meaning as the categorical imperative in Kant's Practical Reason. According to Kant, the essence of the moral life consists in obedience to the law as such, where no admixture of natural impulses or particular emotions is allowed. This is called the Categorical Imperative. The German philosopher's point is that if anything is to be one's rational duty, it must be of such character that it can be acted upon by all rational beings under all circumstances without resulting in inner contradiction. The fundamental principle of moral conduct, according to Kant, is: *So act that you can also will that your action should become a universal law.* This formula was later criticized in Germany for being formalistic, in that it over-stressed the aspect of universal law as such. In China, morality or the tendency to do good, was considered to be inborn, since a man is endowed at birth with the innate idea of the four virtues. Because of the innateness of the four virtues a man is disposed to do what is virtuous. Chinese philosophers did not attribute wrong-doing to the essential or original nature, but to the physical nature, which, mixed with *ch'i* contains the seeds of deficiency. Here are two ways of explaining the moral life: the formalistic way of Kant, and the idea of the four virtues according to the Chinese. The Kantian way was to look at the question from the viewpoint of form, while the Chinese observation proceeds from the essential facts of human life. Though the two views may be different, they are the same in that both see man as a rational being. Thus, it may be noted, the Eighteenth Century conception of man as a rational being is much nearer the Chinese view than is the present day Freudian or Bergsonian irrationalism.

The Eighteenth century is a significant period in that the dif-ference between European and Chinese moral ideas then was much less then than it is now. Let me quote a few sentences from Adam Smith's *Theory of Moral Sentiments*.

"That this is the source of our fellow-feeling for the misery of others, that it is by changing places in fancy with the sufferer, that we come either to conceive or to be affected by what he feels, may be demonstrated by many obvious observations, if it should not be thought sufficiently evident of itself. When we see a stroke aimed and just ready to fall upon the leg or our own arm or another person, we naturally shrink and draw back our own leg or our own arm; and when it does fall, we feel it in some measure, and are hurt by it as well as the sufferer."[14]

Mencius says as follows: "The reason I say that all men have a mind which cannot bear to witness the suffering of others is this: Even now-a-days, when men suddenly see a child about to fall into a well, they will all experience a feeling of alarm and distress. They will feel so not that thereby they may gain the favor of the child's parents; nor that thereby they may seek the praise of their neighbors and friends; nor that thereby they will avoid the reputa-tion of being unmoved by such a thing. Generalizing upon the basis of this case we shall see that to be without this feeling of distress is not to be human."[15]

It would be impossible to find any two texts nearer to each other than these two passages from Adam Smith and Mencius. Both Mencius and Adam Smith traced moral conduct back to the same source. The only difference is in the term they use to designate this source: Smith calls it "sympathy", Mencius calls it "jen".

If I may make another comparison, let me quote from Mencius and Joseph Butler. "What a man is capable of doing", says Mencius, "without learning it first, is his innate ability, what a man is capable of knowing without learning it first, is conscience which is innate. Every child loves his parents. When he is older, he respects his elder brother. Out of love to parents grows *jen*. Out of respect to elders grows *i*. These are the same in all men."[16]

Here Mencius calls our attention to the role of conscience. Joseph Butler, in eighteenth century England does likewise. In a sermon, Butler says: "There is a principle of reflection in men, by which they distinguish between, approve and disapprove their own actions. We are plainly constituted such sort of creatures as to reflect upon our own nature. The mind can take a view of what passes within itself, its propensions, aversions, passions, affections, as respecting such objects and in such degrees; and of the several actions consequent thereupon. In this survey it approves of one, disapproves of another, and towards a third is affected in neither of these ways, but is quite indifferent. The principle in man, by which he approves or disapproves his heart, temper, and actions, is *conscience*."[17]

The title of another sermon by Butler: *Upon the Natural Supremacy of Conscience,* confirms the idea that for him the conscience occupies the highest position in the constitution of human nature. And thus again we have an illustration of the unanimity of opinion between eighteenth century Europe and the Chinese philosophers. Such being the case, it seems to me that if we were not prejudiced by present day irrationalism we would feel that Ch'eng I had a perfect right to state his theory in the form: "Human nature is reason."

III. CH'ENG'S DUAL WAY OF SELF-CULTIVATION.

Before proceeding to Ch'eng I's theory of the dual way of self-cultivation I should like to repeat what I said about the role of Chinese philosophy. Its function is different from that of Western philosophy, because its main interest does not lie in epistemology. Chinese philosophy is concerned, first, with knowledge, and second, with giving the right response to what presents itself before the individual.

Chinese philosophy has two objectives: first, investigation of reason, which means study of the principles of things in world; second, rectification of mind, which means the attainment of mental calmness, the elimination of excitement, and behaving correctly in the face of what is required of you. The rectification of mind is effected by keeping the mind calm, and by getting rid of its stirrings. This is accomplished by decreasing or eliminating desire. The first objective is dependent upon knowledge, for just as definition, concept, and categories play an indispensable role in Western philosophy, so also they are the foundation of Chinese philosophy. For example, Mencius said: "The principles of righteousness and reason are what the mind of all mankind approves."[18] This means that the principles of righteousness and reason are the differentiae of the class, man. To this extent, the role of concept is vital to Chinese philosophy. But the second objective, the rectification of mind, is carried out with the sole aim of keeping the mind in peace. This is called by Ch'eng I "spiritual nurturing through concentration of mind." This second objective is not covered by the Western term "evaluation" because, as C. I. Lewis says, "Evaluations are a form of empirical knowledge, not fundamentally different in what determines their truth and falsity from other forms of empirical knowledge."[19] Though the term "evaluation" comes relatively close to the Chinese idea of seeking out the right ethical principles, yet it does not carry the requirement of keeping the mind calm and clear, and of giving the right response to what is required. I hope that these introductory remarks will prepare the ground for understanding Ch'eng I's two ways of personal cultivation.

A new philosophy must have a way of approach. In Europe there was the great debate about induction versus deduction, between the empiricists and the rationalists. In China, Chou Tun-i proposed calmness as the way, because peace of mind is the prime requisite for right thinking and doing. But Ch'eng I shows us a dual road: "For the purpose of spiritual nurturing, concentration of mind is necessary; for the progress of learning, realization of knowledge is the way."[20] The Chinese philosophers were not like the Europeans who were interested in inquiring after the validity of scientic laws. The Chinese thinkers could not forget the subject of moral approval and disapproval. The mind's function of evaluating is as important as its function of knowing. Ch'eng I attaches equal importance to both sides.

Since Ch'eng I was convinced of a rational basis for all phenomena he was interested in knowledge of the physical world. This led him to believe that thinking or knowledge is the key. He was the first of the Sung philosophers to attach importance to the intellectual process as distinct from the valuational. In this respect he was followed later by Chu Hsi. "Knowledge or understanding", said Ch'eng, "must precede action. It is like having light in front of you when you walk along the road."[21] A student asked him: "How can one become awakened?" Ch'eng I replied: "The first thing is the realization of knowledge. Realization of knowledge necessitates more thinking; more thinking leads to awakening."[22] "Without deep thinking, one cannot attain to *Tao*."[23] Yet somebody remarked: "I feel very keenly the limitations of my intellect and my incompetency." Then he asked: "What can I do?" Ch'eng I answered: "You should realize knowledge. With the realization of knowledge you will make progress. When you devote yourself to thinking, you will improve in knowledge, which is a necessary precondition of virtue."[24] If the reader wishes further evidence of Ch'eng I's emphasis on the importance of knowledge, he will find it in the following dialogue: "An inquirer said: 'The advice has been given that a man may improve himself morally by following the example of strenuous exertion; but is not the realization of knowledge much more difficult?' In reply Ch'eng I commented: 'You are mistaken to suppose that it is easy to follow the example of strenuous exertion. First of all, a man must know. He cannot do until after he knows. If he does not know, his doing is just like a puppet's new play. If you should follow what Yao and Shun did, without their knowledge, intelligence and insight, how could your actions be in comformity with all the principles of decency, providing the occasions with the proper movements and gestures? If when you follow examples of strenuous exertion, you first understand the examples internally, that is, within yourself, then you can express them externally. To imitate, unthinkingly, the examples of strenuous exertion means merely to follow observance; but it does not mean possession of knowledge within yourself. According to the *Chung Yung* there are nine principles for the rule of a country: personal cultivation, respect for wise men, love of relatives, etc. In many other formulations love of relatives comes first; but in this formulation it is second to the respect to wise men. There must have been a reason for giving it a relatively subordinate place. Unless you understand first the principles involved in the types of conduct you try to follow, how can your attempts be more than mere imitations of strenuous exertion? Moreover, exertions at best are short-lived. It is only when you understand clearly the principles involved that you can carry on."

"There are several kinds of knowledge: some superficial, some profound. Once I met a man who was hurt by a tiger. This man's story was very vivid, and it inspired an intense feeling of fear, because he had had personal experience of what he described. Those listening to him knew also that a tiger is a terrifying beast, but they were unable to repeat the story with the same reality, because they had not been subject to the same personal experience. True knowledge must be as real as was the experience narrated by this man. The case is the same with the taste of barbecue. An aristocrat and a peasant both know that barbecue is delicious. But the aristocrat can describe it much more realistically than the farmer, because the former has tasted it personally. Knowledge in the true sense of the word, therefore, must come from actual acquaintance, not from a second-hand source. If you know clearly, you will be able to act with ease. I myself at twenty could understand the meaning of the *Classics* quite well, and my knowledge then was not much different from what it is today. But now I comprehend the deeper meaning of the *Classics,* because of years of consistent thinking about them."25

Ch'eng I gave another example to illustrate the various ways of knowing. "If one knows the real truth", he said, "Then one knows what to do and what not to do. If a learned man is told to steal, he will refuse, because he knows that stealing is wrong. Other acts he may do as he likes. Those in high position can converse in such a way that they give the impression that power and riches mean nothing to them. But when they come to the critical juncture of losing or gaining, they invariably prefer what they gain to what is morally right. This is because their knowledge is not genuine. But when they come to the critical juncture of falling into water or of being burned by fire, they know clearly what not to do. In this case their knowledge is genuine. When one sees evil-doing with the same real knowledge as when one looks to falling into boiling water, one will no longer commit evil, because one will distinguish clearly between good and bad. In the old days many men preferred death because they knew that martyrdom was the only right course left to them. This is the meaning of true knowledge."26

With Ch'eng I true knowledge had the same signification as it did for Socrates in Plato's *Apology.* "A man who is good for anything", said Socrates in this Dialogue, "ought not to calculate the chance of living or dying; he ought only to consider whether in doing anything he is doing right or wrong."27

In connection with Ch'eng I's theory of knowledge I should like to add a few words about his method of attaining correct knowledge. When he discussed the question of method, he encountered the many difficulties attendant upon confining one's self to the study of a sample in one's own mind, or of making an exhaustive study of external things — that is, the problem of deduction *versus* induction in European philosophy and science. Ch'eng I wrote: "There are many ways of inquiring after the reason of things: by reading books, discussion, evaluating the personalities of the past and present, and by handling correctly the things which come to you. All these procedures fall under the heading: "Investigation of Reason."28

Someone asked about the meaning of the expression "Invest-igation of Reason". Should one study everything, or should one just pick up one or two specimens in order to find reason in them? Ch'eng I explained: "It is impossible to have a comprehensive knowledge of all things. If you study one or two things it is impos-sible for you to possess a knowledge in which all things are compre-hended. Even Yen Hui, who was known as one who could infer about ten things from knowing one thing, could not have done this. But you can study one thing today, and another thing tomorrow, and after a process of accumulation and becoming accustomed to the items you have learned you will one day be awakened to compre-hensive understanding."[29] This answer of Ch'eng I is suggestive of the method of induction and deduction in modern science. But the aim of Chinese philosophy was different from that of mod-ern science. Chinese philosophy sought to find truth in order to acquire the correct response in moral action. Thus, Ch'eng I advocated the study of samples. Whether Ch'eng I's method was epistemologically sound is a question, but it was the method which the Sung philosophers used, and is today still one of the most commonly used scientific techniques.

For Neo-Confucianists the fundamental concern was the state of mind. So their interest was to keep the mind in peace. This state was not attained through the mere art of knowing but through adequate discipline. Or in the words of Ch'eng himself:

"The first thing for a scholar to do is to concentrate or con-solidate his mind or will. One proposal has it that the way to avoid the disturbances of hearing, seeing, knowing and deliberat-ing, is to forsake sagehood and to throw away knowledge (Lao-tzu). Another proposal has it that the way to stop the stirrings of think-ing and weighing is to practice meditation and Samdhi (Buddhism). But the function of the mind is like that of a mirror. This being the case, how can you put a stop to the reflection of the mind? The mind cannot be stopped. To avoid stirrings, the mind must ex-ecute the function of being its own master. To execute the function of being its own master the mind must be in a state of concentra-tion, or, *chu-ching*, the state of devotion at the time of offering sacrifices to heaven or the ancestors. When the mind is in this state its conduct is that of a master or host. It is like a bottle filled with water, which, even if it is thrown into the ocean, will not permit the sea water to enter it. If the bottle were not filled, it would naturally not be able to prevent the outside water from flowing into it. A mind cannot be occupied with two things. If it is occupied with one thing, then it has no time for the other thing, because the first thing occupies the whole of the mind. Thus, even the presence of a subject in the mind can put a stop to stirrings and agitations. If the state of concentration is substituted for the preoccupation with a subject, the effect will be the same. *Ching* means the 'singleness' or the 'being devoted to one thing' of the mind, and 'singleness' means the 'not seeking other things.' When 'singleness' is present in the mind, a man does not bother himself about seeking the chain of things that follow each other. The state of *ching* is described in the *I-ching*: '*Ching* keeps straightforwardness inside; righteousness keeps square-dealing outside.' 'Straightforwardness' means singleness. No lie, no negligence, no shame before the raindrops from the roof — all belong to the work of mental concentration."[30]

How to concentrate the mind in order to preserve it in peace, and how to train it so that it will give correct responses to whatever approaches it, are for Ch'eng I matters of vital importance. He insisted that one must make a master of one's mind. His disciple Lu Yu-shu said: "I am suffering from the stirring of thoughts which come to me, one after the other." Then he asked: "What am I to do to stop this?" Ch'eng I gave the same answer as before. "Your situation resembles fighting robbers in a house with crumbling walls on different sides. Before you have finished with the robbers from the east, others come from the West. They come into your house from all sides, so that they are too many for you to resist. Your house has many openings, which enables them to enter easily. This means that your house is not strong enough to look after itself. Or again, your situation resembles the empty bottle. When it is thrown into the river, water flows into it. If the bottle were already full when it was cast into the river, none of the outside water could have entered. In other words, the bottle already filled represents the presence of a master. When there is a master, no external enemy can harm you: you are safe."[31]

Not only should the mind be kept to itself, but since the mind is stirred by what stimulates the senses, the functioning of the senses also should be controlled. Ch'eng I prescribed four warnings; for sight, hearing, speaking, and action.

I. WARNING FOR SIGHT.

Mind is empty. Its response to the external world is traceless. The key to the achievement of this state is: Be on guard against sight, first of all. When obscurity hangs before you like a curtain, what is within will slip away. If what is without is under control, then what is within will enjoy peace. Self-control is for the purpose of enabling you to return to the rule of decency, and to become true to yourself.

II. WARNING FOR HEARING.

A man's endowment comes from the nature of heaven. When he is stimulated he is bewildered and loses the sense of rectitude. Great indeed is the first-awakened! He knows where to stop and he gains tranquillity; he knows how to prevent what is wrong and he preserves what is true. Therefore, the rule is: Do not hear what is contrary to decency.

III. WARNING FOR SPEAKING.

The work of the human mind is expressed by speech. When you keep away from hurrying and untruth, you will enjoy peace and concentration within. This is the key by which you can determine quarelling and friendship; by which you can determine whether happiness or misfortune, glory or dishonor, will come to you. A too easy talk will lead to falseness; too long a talk to confusion. Boastful talk will make others angry. It will bring on the same effect as your misdeeds. The best advice is: Say nothing wrong.

IV. WARNING FOR ACTION

A philosopher knows what is subtle, so he tries to be true, even in his thought. A man of will is watchful of his character, so he is careful about his actions. If your action conforms to reason, you will be happy. If it follows desire, you will be unhappy.

In times of bustle you should be watchful of yourself. In ordinary times you should control yourself with a sense of awe and dread. Eventually, this caution in action will become part of your nature, because you will have become inured to it as a habit, and you will achieve the same goal as Sages and Wise Men.[32]

Ch'eng I's philosophy found its clearest expression in his essay. *To What Kind of Learning Did Yen Hui Devote Himself?* This word is important for the Sung School, because ever since the time of Han Yü, Yen Hui was the perfect example of the man who found *Tao*. Yen Hui's way to sagehood was to the Sung philosophers what the Bodhisattva was to Buddhahood. Because of the importance of this essay of Ch'eng I, it is worth quoting *in extenso*:

"It is reported that the number of pupils who studied under Confucius was 3000. Yen Hui is regarded as having been the most devoted to learning. All 3000 of the pupils knew the *Shu-ching* and the *Shih-ching* and the liberal arts. What was the difference between Yen Hui and the rest of the 3000 pupils? What was the learning to which Yen Hui devoted himself? The answer is that Yen Hui devoted himself to the attainment of sagehood. The question will naturally be asked: Is sagehood attainable through study and learning? The answer is Yes. How, then, can it be done?

"In heaven and earth there is a wonderful store of natural gifts. Man is endowed with the best of the five elements. In origin he is true and calm. Prior to the operations of his mind, he has the five characteristics: *jen, i, li, chih, hsin* (honesty). With his body, he comes in contact with the external world, and thus becomes stimulated within. With this stimulation seven kinds of emotions are expressed: joy, anger, sorrow, fear, love, dislike, and greed. When the emotions are agitated and become violent, a man's nature suffers from a lack of equilibrium. Those who are 'awakened' try to hold their emotions in check in order to adjust their expression to the principle of the Golden Mean. Such people are on the right track and their nature will take a proper course of development. The emotions can thus play no more than their natural part. But those who are ignorant do not know how to control their emotions. Rather, they indulge themselves in violent expressions, and this leads them astray. Thus they injure their nature by putting an axe to it, as it were. The emotions get the upper hand of man's nature, and he is no longer master of himself. The proper way of learning is to rectify the mind by a rigid discipline over nature. He who can observe the Golden Mean will also realize truth, and thus attain sagehood.

"The man of noble character learns how to enlighten his mind and by knowing how to nourish it, he leads an exemplary life in his daily work. From enlightenment his way leads to truth. In thus exerting his mind to the utmost, he succeeds in the realization of his nature. Once his nature is realized he can return to himself and be true to himself. Then he is almost a sage.

"*The Grand Standard*, a chapter in the *Shu-ching*, has the following passage: 'Thinking gives insight; insight leads to sagehood.' The way to truthfulness towards yourself begins with the firm belief in *Tao*. When belief in *Tao* is firm, life in one's daily work becomes earnest. This exemplary life involves the idea of rigid discipline. Then the mind does not for a single moment leave the virtues of *jen, i, chung* (loyalty) and *hsin* (honesty) or play them false. In times of stress or of emergency, he remains firm and unwavering. Whether going out or staying home, whether speaking or remaining silent, he is the same unchanging person. When he thus becomes accustomed to the exemplary life, his movements and behavior will conform to the principles of decency, and licentiousness and lewdness will completely disappear.

"The efforts of Yen Hui were directed to the following principles: Do not see what is indecent; do not hear what is indecent; do not speak what is indecent; do not act indecently. Confucius paid him the compliment of saying that he was one who, when he discovered something good and worthy, embraced it carefully and did not let it go. Confucius also praised him for not transferring his indignation from one person to another, and for not repeating mistakes. He knew how to find out what was wrong, and once he did, he never committed the same misdeed again. Such was Yen Hui's way of devoting himself to what pleased him, and such was his devotion to learning. Even so, with seeing, hearing, speaking and acting brought into conformity with the principles of decency, Yen Hui still lacked something to complete his achievement of sagehood. If he was a true sage he could have discovered what he sought without the effort of thinking; he could have trodden on the right path without exertion; he could have proceeded along the road of the Golden Mean without effort. But Yen Hui could not find what he looked for, except by thinking; and he could not pursue the right tract, except by exertion. However, this difference between Yen Hui and the true sage so small as to be almost negligible.

"Mencius said: 'He who is substantial and has light is great; he who has light and can transform himself in various ways is a sage; a sage is mystical and divine.' Although Yen Hui was substantial and had light, he fell short in that he could adhere only to what was good and could not transform himself in different ways. But he devoted himself to learning, and with his maturity he could no doubt in time have reached the stage of transforming himself. It was for this reason that his early death distressed Confucius. It was to Confucius' regret that Yen Hui did not attain sagehood.

" 'To transform yourself' means to be able to perceive without thinking, and to follow the right path without exertion, which is to be divine. Confucius, speaking to himself, said that after his seventieth year he could do what he wished without being contrary to the laws of the universe. This was the stage of transformation.

"Someone asked: 'Is it correct to say that sages are born, and that no one can become a sage by study?' The answer is this: Mencius said: 'Yao and Shun were Yao and Shun by nature; King T'ang and King Wu came back to themselves.' 'By nature' is 'by birth': Yao and Shun were endowed with wisdom 'by birth'. 'Came back to themselves' means that King T'ang and King Wu acquired their wisdom 'by learning'. The same distinction holds good between Confucius and Mencius: the former was born wise; the latter learned his wisdom.

"Subsequent generations misunderstood the significance of this passage and thought that sagehood was not attainable by learning. Thus the way to sagehood was lost. People did not try to 'come back to themselves' but sought satisfaction only from externals. They applied their efforts to wide reading, memorializing, and writing beautiful literary styles. In this way they forgot *Tao*. This is why the interests of the present generation differ from the kind of learning to which Yen Hui devoted himself."[32]

It should be borne in mind that this essay, from which we have so copiously quoted, was written when Ch'eng I was only eighteen years old and that it laid the foundation of all of his later ideas.

Before concluding this chapter I should like to say a word about Ch'eng I's work as a commentator on the Confucian *Classics*. It is common knowledge that in China a tradition is carefully preserved. But to say this is not to say that the tradition does not undergo any change. Since the death of Confucius, many new ideas or schools of thought have arisen, even though they are confined within the Confucian tradition. The *Classics* remained the same, but many new commentaries have been written which interpret the *Classics* from fresh points of view. New terms were coined, and old terms acquired new meanings. Especially was this so with the commentaries written by the Sung philosophers.

This re-interpretation of the Confucian *Classics* by new commentaries will become more understandable if we apply the analogy to European thinking. Suppose that the rationalists and empiricists, wishing to attach themselves to Plato, deliberately wrote commentaries on *The Republic, the Symposium, The Apology,* and the other dialogues, then the language of Plato would have remained as before, but its sense or meaning would be something as understood only by the rationalists and empiricists. In this way, tradition would have been preserved, and yet there would be a complete change of meaning. Just such work of re-interpretation of the Confucian *Classics* was performed by Ch'eng I, who composed commentaries on the *I-ching,* the *Shu-ching, Ch'un-ch'iu* and the *Li-chi.* And why did he do it? The answer is to be found in his own words: "The farmers, under burning sun and driving rain, work in the fields and produce grain in order that I may have food. The craftsmen, exerting themselves laboriously, make all kinds of implements, utensils and furniture, for my use. Officers and soldiers burden themselves with weapons in order to protect my country, so that I may feel secure. If I do nothing to benefit the people, but merely waste my life, I shall be like a worm or an insect.

Therefore, I resolve to write commentaries on the *Classics* of the former Sages. This is my way of serving the people."[33]

When Ch'eng I died, his writings were still banned, but Hu An-kuo sent a memorial to the emperor, giving Ch'eng I and Ch'eng Hao credit for the revival of the doctrines of Confucius and Mencius. The works by the Ch'eng brothers have since become an indispensable auxiliary to the study of the Confucian *Classics*. This was the Chinese way of putting new wine in old bottles. New thoughts were presented in the language of the old sages. Thus, tradition and novelty were blended together. By such blending, original thoughts were expressed without having to bear the label of originality, and the continuity of tradition was unbroken. I am willing to admit that there is also disadvantage in this process. When so many interpretations were given to the same book, much confusion was created among the scholars, so much so that the question "Which is true Confucianism?" became inevitable. And in recent times there has been the cry: to do away with Confucianism altogether! "Down with Confucianism" is a slogan which has often been heard. It is natural desire to be free from the shackles of tradition and a plea to express one's ideas without having to admit the authority of the sages. The habit therefore of having to hang on the band-wagon of Confucianism which was started in the Han Dynasty may be gone!

References

1. *Erh Ch'eng i-shu*, Book 11.
2. *P.R.S.Y.*, Book 15, Ch'eng I.
3. *Ibid.*, Book 16, Chu Hsi's words quoted by Huang Tsung-hsi.
4. *Ibid.*, Book 15.
5. *Ibid.*, Book 15, Ch'eng I's biography.
6. *Ibid.*, Book 15.
7. *Loc. cit.*
8. *Loc. cit.*
9. *Erh-Ch'eng i-shu*, Book 22.
10. I. Frith, *Life of Bruno*, Paul, Trench, Trubner and Co., London, 1887, p. 278.
11. *P.R.S.Y.*, Book 15.
12. *Loc. cit.*
13. *Loc. cit.*
14. *British Moralists*, Vol. 1, p. 258, Adam Smith.
15. *Meng-tzu*, Book 2, Part 1, Chapter 6.
16. *Ibid.*, Book 7, Part 1, Chapter 15.
17. *British Moralists, op. cit.*, Vol. 1, p. 201.
18. *Meng-tzu*, Book 6, Part 1, Chapter.
19. C. I. Lewis, *An Analysis of Knowledge and Valuation*, The Open Court Publishing Co., LaSalle, Ill., (1946), p. 365.
20 *P.R.S.Y.*, Book 15.
21. *Loc. cit.*
22. *Loc. cit.*
23. *Loc. cit.*
24. *Loc. cit.*
25. *Loc. cit.*
26. *Loc. cit.*
27. *Dialogues of Plato*, Vol. I, Apology, p. 326.

CHAPTER ELEVEN

The Period of Transition between Ch'eng I, A. D. 1033-1107, and Chu Hsi, A. D. 1129-1200

The period between the later part of Ch'eng I's life and the birth of Chu Hsi marks the decline of the Northern Sung Dynasty and the rise of the Southern Sung. The government was confused about foreign and domestic policy and about the various schools of philosophy which had arisen. The reason for this perplexity was two-fold: (1) under an absolute monarchy separation between scholarship and state was impossible. In China, the emperor was not only head of the state but also the leader of its spiritual life. He could confer not only his blessing, but also his disapprobation, on Buddhism, Taoism, or Confucianism. Moreover, he could reject the commentaries on the Confucian *Classics* done by one school on one day, and approve the commentaries done by an opposing school the next. This unlimited power gave rise to political difficulties at a time when scholars were divided into parties and were busy creating new ideas and thought.

The second reason for the perplexity of the government was that since no separation of scholarship and state existed, no freedom of conscience or thought for the scholars was possible. Those in power could use political weapons to persecute thinkers with whom they disagreed. Thus, during the Northern Sung Dynasty

Ch'eng I suffered and during the Southern Sung Dynasty Chu Hsi had his difficulties.

A discussion of the political situation in the period between these two philosophers is perhaps not entirely out of place. The Sung period was an era of intellectual speculation, scholarship and art. Militarily it was far behind the Han and T'ang Dynasties. From its beginning it was threatened by two enemies: the Liao in the northwest, and the Hsia in the west — i.e., present day Ningsia Province. The first Sung Emperors were most anxious to dispose of their enemy, the Liao. The second Emperor, T'ai-tsung, even went to the battle-field as commander-in-chief three times (979, 980, 986 A.D.), but failed on each occasion. His successor, Chen-tsung, in 1004, signed a peace treaty with the Liao, stipulating that they should be recognized as a brother-country, and that the Sung should pay an annual tribute of 300,000 taels.

With the army of Kansu Province in western China, a ruler of the Tanguts, Chao Yüan-hao, conquered present day Ningsia and became powerful. The Sung Emperor, at first considering him merely a bandit leader, put a price on his head. But a war lasting from 1038 until 1048 exhausted both sides. Although a peace agreement was signed in 1044, many "incidents" along the border caused war and peace to alternate for five years.

The Sung government, because of its struggle with these two enemies, lost heavily in human life, and was burdened with military expenses, so that the demand for finding sources of revenue, and for strengthening the defenses, was great. This explains why Wang An-shih's reform policy was adopted and put into practice.

For philosophy, the Sung period was an age of thinkers. I have already dealt with the five founders of Neo-Confucianism. It was an age of literary men like Ou-yang Hsiu and Su Shih (Su Tung-p'o), who were either poets or greater creative artists. Also it was an era of painters, among whom Li Ch'eng, Fan K'uan and Emperor Hui-tsung were well known. The period also produced a man on the political stage who was destined to launch a new political experiment. This was Wang An-shih. He turned back to the remote past of Yao and Shun for inspiration and justification, as the Sung philosophers did in the realm of philosophy. Wang was one of the leading literary lights of the age, of whom it was reported in the *History of the Sung Dynasty* that he could write with such speed that it seemed as if his brush flew. He did not use much effort, and yet his essays were great literary masterpieces. Ou-yang Hsiu, reading some of them, recommended him to the government for a position. But Wang An-shih's ambition was to start a great political and social movement, and he declined every subordinate position offered him. One of his famous essays, a memorial of 100,000 words to Emperor Jen-tsung, reminded His Majesty that if he determined to take the former sage-emperors as his models, he should make use of their ideas and of his men of talent in order to govern the country well. When Emperor Shen-tsung ascended the throne, Wang An-shih won the imperial confidence and was appointed the first adviser. He proposed a program of reform in which the following items were included: (1) Law of Green Shoots, namely, Credit to the farmers. (2) Law of Equalization of Transportation, namely, sale of commodities paid by the people as taxes, without bringing the commodities to the capital. (3) *Pao-chia*, namely, a militia system based upon tithing. (4) Breeding of Horses. (5) Remission of Forced Labor. (6) Land-survey.

These measures of Wang An-shih cannot be described in detail in a book about Chinese philosophy. Suffice to say that what he had in mind was to make China militarily strong and financially adequate in order to fight against the two external enemies of Liao and Hsia. Since census-taking, regimentation and economic transaction were involved in the program of reform, and since the Chinese people had become accustomed to living under a *laissez-faire* policy, Wang An-shih's ideas aroused great opposition on all sides, especially among the conservative statesmen like Ssu-ma Kuang, Su Shih and the Ch'eng brothers. But Wang An-shih was obstinate and strongly opinionated as his famous utterances testify: (1) *Natural calamities* need not be taken as signs of warning from heaven; (2) *Ancestors* need not be taken as examples; (3) Public Opinion may be disregarded. When conservative statesmen with noble intentions opposed him, he dismissed them and replaced them by his own henchmen, who often were men of dubious character. At first he seemed powerful enough to put his program into practice, but as the opposition grew stronger, he grew weaker;

so that after eight years of his economic experiments he had to resign in 1076 A.D. Nevertheless, his policy remained in force for twenty years, until finally it was abrogated in 1086 under the regency which ruled in the name of Che-tsung, the young son of Emperor Shen-tsung.

In 1086 the Empress-regent recalled Ssu-ma Kuang, an opponent of Wang An-shih, and all of Wang's reform-policies were wiped out. But the feud between reform and the conservative parties did not stop here. After the death of Ssu-ma Kuang which occurred in the same year, and after the decease of the Empress-regent in 1093, young Emperor Che-tsung took the reins of government in his own hands, and reinstated the reform party. Chang Chun, a follower of Wang An-shih, was made prime minister and restored the policy of Emperor Shen-tsung. After 1101, when Hui-tsung ascended the throne, a brief period ensued in which the so-called restoration of the reform policy was discontinued. But in 1103 Ts'ai Ching came to power, and he issued a blacklist of 309 traitors among whom almost all ex-premiers and ex-ministers were marked for degradation or banishment. Men like Ssu-ma Kuang, Wen Yen-po, Su Shih and Huang T'ing-chien were all involved, and it was so ordered that they were not allowed to memorialize the emperor, and their descendants were deprived of the right to work as civil servants.

While these political factions were battling, the Chin (Kin) or Nuchen tribe rose to power in northern China. The Sung government jumped at the opportunity of allying itself with these barbarians in order to destroy the Liao. The Chin thus had a free hand to occupy Peking, and the Liao were annihilated. Later, however, the Chin relinquished the policy of alliance with the Sung, and in place of the Liao, became the enemy which threatened the security of the Sung Dynasty. In 1127, the Emperor Hui-tsung and his son Ch'in-tsung were captured and sent as prisoners of war to a place outside the Great Wall. The Sung capital, K'ai-feng-fu, also fell to the Chin. The Sung Dynasty had to retreat south of the Yangtze Valley.

The reform policy of Wang An-shih was initiated in 1068. He himself died at Nanking in 1086, but the faction which fought for the program in his name continued to play a role in Sung pol-

itics until the withdrawal of the Dynasty from north of the Yangtze
Valley. Since Wang's movement had a bearing on the development
of Sung philosophy, I should like to say a few words in reply to
two questions which are often asked: What was the relation between the party of Wang An-shih and the other schools of thought?
Why was there a political feud among the various schools? In
this connection, the first point to be mentioned is that Wang An-
shih wrote commentaries on the Classics: on the *Shih-ching*, the
Shu-ching and the *Chou-li*. He also took a stand on the *Ch'un
Ch'iu* asserting it to be a kind of "Government Gazette" in the
form of unrelated sentences. Wang's manner of interpreting the
Classics was not altogether acceptable to the Ch'eng brothers who
paid the highest respect to these venerable works. Though the
political reformer and the philosophical brothers did not actually quarrel about the matter, Yang Shih, protector of the orthodox tradition in south China under the Southern Sung, demanded
the repeal of the three commentaries of Wang An-shih. The
Ch'eng brothers, moreover, had their own ideas about government.
They aspired after the political ideas of Yao and Shun, and
were less interested in the immediate achievement of measures
which would make the Sung Dynasty militarily and financially
powerful. The fact that Wang An-shih's commentaries were, despite all scholarly opposition, actually pronounced the authoritative
text for candidates for the state examinations was possible only
because the government was, as has already been mentioned, an
absolute monarchy. Scholars had no guarantee whatever of their
right to freedom of conscience or freedom of expression. Their
discussions of *Tao* and *Ri* could at any moment be banned as false
or heterodox theory.

There was at the time a literary school in Szechwan, headed
by Su Shih (Su Tung-p'o), which did not champion any special
movement such as the reform policy of Wang An-shih or the philosophical studies of the Ch'eng brothers. The father of the Su family,
Su Hsün, and his sons, the brothers Su Che and Su Shih, were
literary people who wrote so beautifully that their works are invariably included in Chinese anthologies. Not only were their
writings original, but they also had their own explanation of the
origin of the Classics. They were moreover masters of satire. The

father, Su Hsün, wrote an essay criticizing Wang An-shih for his untidiness and came to the conclusion that Wang must be a repellent personality, or a man whose conduct was out of keeping with normal behavior or common sense. The Ch'eng brothers were repugnant to the Su family because of their pretensions to saintliness. The narrowness of their viewpoint, and their lack of the spirit of accomodation, were in any case unpleasant. The Su family went in more for literary refinement than for the ascetic morality of the Neo-Confucianists. Herein lay the cause of friction between the Su family and the Ch'eng brothers. But in spite of their mutual hostility, they were both banished by the party of Wang An-shih. Straightforward men as they were, the Su's and the Ch'engs knew not how to gain the favor of emperors, or grab power after the expert manner of Chang Chun and Ts'ai Ching. They were even exiled as criminals. The Northern Sung Dynasty collapsed soon after their banishment.

Ch'eng I, who long out-lived his brother Ch'eng Hao, died in 1107, during the reign of Emperor Hui-tsung. He was thus able to educate many pupils who handed his doctrines down to later generations. Among these pupils were Yang Shih, Hsieh Liang-tso, Yu Tso and Lu Ta-lin. Following is a kind of "genealogical" listing of the generations between Ch'eng I and Chu Hsi:

> Ch'eng I
> Yang Shih
> Lo Tsung-yen
> Li T'ung
> Chu Hsi

A short discussion of these philosophers who filled the transition between Ch'eng I and Chu Hsi is perhaps not out of place. None of them had anything new to contribute to philosophical thought. They were largely followers who carried on the spirit of their masters. The only exception was Hsieh Liang-tso who wrote a preface and a commentary to the *Lun-yü,* which is refreshing reading because of its simplicity and utter lack of pedantry.

"The language of the sage", writes Hsieh Liang-tso, "is plain, but its meaning is deep. Language is a form of expression and as such it has its limitations. The actual meaning however is often so deep as to be unfathomable. What is limited may be studied by means of philology and etymology, but what is unfathomable must be read with understanding and intelligence. Take the instance of making a new acquaintance. On the first day we meet a stranger, we notice mostly his external features. But on the next day, after a long talk with him and when he opens his heart, we know him more intimately. The difficulties involved in learning to know a person may be applied to the appreciation of Lun-yü.

"My pupils, let me tell you how to read the Lun-yü! (I) Do not relax too completely if its language is plain. (II) Do not become frightened if its language is subtle. (III) Do not get angry if it gives a stern warning. (IV) Do not regard its assertions as exaggeration and lose faith in them. There is no use in studying a book of Confucius through philology. Otherwise there is no use in my writing a commentary on it...

"This book [i.e., the Lun-yü] exists in the world not because it is easily practicable, or because it can immediately produce results. If it is compared with the teaching of the Taoists in regard to concentration of mind, or with the doctrine of the Buddhists regarding the search for reality, I doubt that it could compete with them. Nor is it comparable to the books of Chuang-tzu and Lieh-tzu in their discussion of heaven, nature, and fate, or in the beauty of their literary style. In respect to the elegance and wealth of material as in a garden where all kinds of flowers grow, the Lun-yü is not equal to the books of Ssu-ma Ch'ien or Pan Ku or Yang Hsiung. If we compare it with medical books we shall find that it gives us no prescription for curing disease or for maintaining health. Nor does it provide information about how to enforce laws as the writings of the Legalist School do. It has nothing in common with books of poetry which inspire us with a sense of beauty. It is not useful after the manner of books about fortune-telling and gambling. Rather the Lun-yü belongs to a class quite apart from all the types cited above. It is not attractive. But it is like old music — simple and dignified. It is like rice wine which never intoxicates. Who can be fond of such a book? Perhaps most people would wish to throw it into a dust heap."

Hsieh Liang-tso goes on to explain why the *Lun-yü* is difficult to read. "It tells us the virtue of like-mindedness, but the people are more interested in conspiring and playing tricks. It warns us about the man who puts on a smiling face and speaks cleverly, but who lacks integrity. In spite of this warning we know the world still prefers flattery. The world is interested in making profit by all sorts of dubious methods, but in the *Lun-yü* Confucius says that ill-gotten gains and high position remind him of fleeting clouds. He finds happiness in eating simple food and lying on plain bedding."[1]

This preface and the commentary to which it is affixed are an excellent example of how the generation after Ch'eng I were intent upon going back to the Confucian *Classics*. It is worth emphasizing that among all the pupils of Ch'eng I, Hsieh Liang-tso was the least pedantic. But the enthusiasm for such writing nonetheless, marks a change in the course of development of the Sung philosophy.

Yu Tso left expositions of the *I-ching,* of two chapters of the *Shih-ching,* of the *Chung-yung*, of the *Lun-yü,* and the *Meng-tzu.* Yin Shun, on his death-bed, when he was asked to inscribe a last memorial to the emperor, said: "My commentary on Mencius is my posthumous writing to the emperor."[2] This change in the course of Chinese thought is a sign that after a period of searching for new ideas and systems the Chinese mind relapsed into its favorite occupation of interpreting the *Classics*.

This will be as appropriate a place as any to sketch briefly the life of Yang Shih who introduced the school of Ch'eng I to South China. When Yang Shih completed his studies under Ch'eng Hao, and was seen off, Ch'eng Hao remarked: "There goes our *Tao* to the south!"[3] Yang Shih was so deeply devoted to the Ch'eng school that in his fortieth year he returned to study and serve with even greater respect under Ch'eng I. He was given the *Western Inscription* of Chang Tsai to read, and at first suspected that Chang Tsai's theory was affiliated with Mo-tzu's doctrine of universal love. Afterwards he learned from Ch'eng I the theory of the unity of reason and the manifoldness of phenomena, and he began to become convinced of the correctness of Chang Tsai's position. Yang Shih was appointed magistrate in many districts. His way of governing was to adopt simple measures which the people could follow, and thus he was popular. When Ts'ai Ching, at the time the most powerful minister in the government, took advice from a fortune-teller to dig a lake for the purpose of acquiring auspicious omens around the tomb of his mother, Yang Shih wrote a letter to the emperor censuring him for the waste of labor. In 1122, when the Northern Sung Dynasty was approaching its end, Ts'ai Ching was advised that it would be wise at that critical moment to invite men of experience to join the government and thus win the confidence of the people. It so happened that at the time the King of Korea made an inquiry of a Chinese emissary about the whereabouts of Yang Shih. When word of this inquiry came to the attention of the Sung Emperor, it brought back his memory to the importance of Yang Shih's work, and he recalled the philosopher to government service. This service of Yang Shih in the 4th year of Hsün-ho (1132 A.D.) was however much criticized by Chu Hsi and others. They did so because he participated in the government when Ts'ai Ching, who was considered unworthy of his co-operation, was in power. Yang Shih made many daring proposals among which was the suggestion that Wang An-shih's three commentaries on the Confucian Classics should be abandoned. Also the controversy about whether the policy towards the Ch'in should be one of war or peace had reached the boiling point, and thousands of students at the government academy made demonstrations in favor of war. Yang Shih was appointed president of the academy to appease the students. He constantly advised Emperor Kao-tsung on many important items of the day. He resigned in 1132 and died two years later, in his eighty-third year. Because of his long life he was able to establish the Ch'eng school firmly in the south. Also he was able to prepare the way for the achievements of Chu Hsi. Yang Shih's writings, as was the case with his colleagues, consisted largely of commentaries on the Confucian Classics.

The man who succeeded Yang Shih was Lo Ts'ung-yen, born in Fukien Province. When he was forty years old he paid a visit to Yang Shih, who had recently returned from northern China. Lo remarked that if he had not met Yang Shih his life would have been wasted. He was considered the best of all the one thousand pupils of the elder philosopher from whom he heard about Ch'eng I, and then he decided to sell his property in order to raise enough money to defray traveling expenses for a visit to Ch'eng I. Upon his return to Fukien Province to resume his studies under Yang Shih, he was appointed in 1130 as justice of the peace in the district of Po-lo. At the expiration of his term, he withdrew to the mountain of Lo-fou, and settled there as a hermit. He died at the age of sixty-four years.

Lo Ts'ung-yen lived during the period of transition from the Northern Sung Dynasty to the Southern Sung, and thus was much worried about the political situation. His main work is entitled *Following the Steps of Yao,* a record of the good deeds of the former emperors of the Sung Dynasty. The term "Yao" is used as a common noun meaning an "ideal Emperor". The remainder of his writings are commentaries on the *Ch'un-ch'iu,* the *Shih-ching,* the *Lun-yü,* the *Meng-tzu,* etc.

The successor to Lo Tsung-yen was Li T'ung, under whom Chu Hsi studied. When Li T'ung was twenty four years old he became a pupil of Lo Ts'ung-yen, who instructed him to practice meditation as he himself did. Once, while in the midst of meditation, Lo Ts'ung-yen told his pupils to investigate the state of the mind before the emotions of joy, anger, sorrow or happiness came into play. In this pre-emotion state of mind a person knows best what the Golden Mean is. After acquiring this knowledge from Lo Ts'ung-yen, Li T'ung returned to his home and led a retired life. In his sixty-first year he received Chu Hsi as his student. Chu Hsi had been sent by his father, Chu Sung, who had been a schoolmate of Li T'ung, and who paid many compliments to the latter, calling him "a teapot made of ice", "the moon in autumn", and "as spotless and transparent" as those two objects. Li T'ung taught his pupils that there is no use in spending a disproportionate amount of time in reading and writing. What is important is to practice the knowledge gained from books. Every written word presents a task. The purpose of tasks is to exemplify in one's daily life what has been written. This advice of Li T'ung exercised a profound influence upon Chu Hsi and later generations, because in China knowledge and moral life are one and inseparable. Chinese philosophy has invariably required that a man's philosophy be lived in accordance with his philosophical convictions. The questions and answers between Li T'ung and his great pupil were recorded by the latter, and have come down to us. After Chu Hsi left his master, he continued to correspond with him, and visited him often, until Li Tsung died in his seventy-first year.

This line of descent from Yang Shih to Li T'ung has been studied by Chinese scholars with extreme care because of its climax when it deals with Chu Hsi. An example of such study is the *Tao Nan Yuan Wei* (*Record of the Promulgation of Tao Southward*)[4] written in the Ming Dynasty.

But the important thing is to turn now to an examination of Chu Hsi's thought. He was the most prominent of the Sung philosophers. Without him Neo-Confucianism would not have exercised the profound influence on Chinese thought that it did for the next eight centuries.

References

1. *P.R.S.Y.*, Book 24.
2. *Ibid.*, Book 27.
3. *Ibid.*, Book 25.
4. *Cheng-i t'ang ch'uan-shu* (Cheng-i t'ang Collectanea), *Tao-nan yuan-wei* (Record of the origin of Tao southward)

CHAPTER TWELVE

Chu Hsi, The Great Synthesizer

The name Chu Fu-tzu was familiar to me from early boyhood when I was at school. It comes next only to K'ung Fu-tzu. "Fu-tzu" means a teacher or master, and is seldom used except when attached to the name of K'ung, Meng or Chu. K'ung Fu-tzu has been Latinized into "Confucius"and Meng-tzu into "Mencius"; but there is no Latin equivalent for Chu Hsi.

The fact that "Fu-tzu" has been appended to Chu Hsi's name is an indication of his authoritative place in the orthodox Confucianist tradition from his own time to the close of the Ch'ing Dynasty. To what does he owe so elevated a position? Officially, the reason is that his commentaries on the *Four Books* and other *Classics* were declared, in the Ming Dynasty, to be the texts upon which papers by candidates at the state examinations were to be based. This imperial sanctioning of his commentaries made them as important as the Confucian *Classics* themselves. They alone were studied at the government academy, while all other philosophical writings were banned.

Why then were Chu Hsi's texts favored by the authorities? The answer is that his careful interpretation re-inforced the Confucian orthodoxy. Successful in the gigantic task of synthesizing philosophy and literature, he achieved three goals: (1) He not only evolved his own theoretical system, but also adopted the writings of the founders of Sung philosophy into this system as its constituent parts. (2) On the basis of his own system he wrote commentaries on the *Four Books* in order to identify himself with the Confucianist tradition — or in other words, to bring Confucius, Mencius, and the other sages into the orbit of his integration. (3) Like Confucius, he also edited works which were not philosophical, but important as part of the Chinese heritage.

The following list of Chu Hsi's original contributions, commentaries and recensions gives an idea of the breadth of his interests, the vastness of his knowledge, and the immensity of his capacity for hard work.

A.

(a) *Chou i pen i* [*Original Meaning of the "Book of Changes"*]

(b) *I hsüeh ch'i meng* [*Rudiments of the "Book of Changes"*]

(c) *Shih-chi chuan* [*A Collection of Comments on the "Book of Poetry"*]

(d) *Hsiao ching k'an wu* [*Corrections of Misprints in the "Book of Filial Piety"*]

B.

(a) *Ta hsüeh chang chü* [*Punctuation and Re-division of the Text of the "Great Learning"*]

(b) *Chung yung chang chü* [*Punctuation and Re-division of the Text of the "Doctrine of the Golden Mean"*]

(c) *Lun meng chi chu huo wen* [*Commentary on the "Analects" and the "Meng-tzu" in the form of Questions and Answers*]

C.

(a) *T'ai chi t'u shuo chieh* [*Comments on the "Explanation of the Diagram of the Supreme Ultimate"*]

(b) *T'ung shu chieh* [*Explanation of the "Comprehensive Understanding"*]

(c) *Hsi ming chieh i* [*Explanation of the "Western Inscription"*]

D.

(a) *Ch'u tz'u chi chu* [*Investigation of the Comments on "Ch'u Yüan's Elegies*]

(b) *Han wen k'ao i* [*Investigation of the Essays of Han Yü*]

E.

(a) *Lun meng ching i* [*Essential Meaning of the "Analects" and the "Meng-tzu"*]

(b) *Meng tzu yao lüeh* [*Essentials of the Meng-tzu*]

F.

(a) *Tzu chih t'ung chien kang mu* [*Outlines and Details of Chinese History*]
(b) *Pa ch'ao ming ch'en yen hsing lu* [*Records of the Illustrious Ministers of the Sung Dynasty*]
(c) *Ku chin chia chi li* [*Rites of Sacrificial Offering in the Family*]

G.

(a) *Chin ssu lu* [*Records of Reflective Thought*]
(b) *Ch'eng shih i shu* [*Posthumous Works of the Ch'eng Brothers*]
(c) *I lo yüan yüan* [*Origin of the School of Chou Tun-i and of the Ch'eng Brothers*]

Under classes C and G are the writings of the founders of the Sung philosophy, collected and expounded by Chu Hsi. Under A, B and E are re-interpretations by Chu Hsi of the writings of Confucius, Mencius and others, in order to bring himself into the Confucianist tradition. There was no deliberate intention of a-dapting Confucius to himself, but the fact remains that Chu Hsi did re-interpret the books of the Confucian School in his own sense, and that his re-interpretations have prevailed to this day. Under D and F are titles which indicate that Chu Hsi's interests extended beyond philosophy. Ch'ü Yüan's *Elegies* and Han Yü's *Essays* are purely literary, and Chu Hsi's editing them is comparable to Confucius' editing the *Book of Poetry*. His writing the *Tzu-chih-t'ung-chien-kang-mu* corresponds to Confucius's editing the *Spring and Autumn Annals* or to Aristotle's compilation of the Greek constitutions, or writing *Politics*. The *Family Rites* is in the same class as chapters from the Confucian *Book of Rites*.

Beneath all these writings of Chu Hsi lies one dominating aim: to review and prepare for publication every work which has contributed to China's intellectual heritage. High aspiration, vast learning, and tremendous labor enabled him to complete a gigantic task. But the breadth of his knowledge alone does not account for his being a second Confucius. Rather it is his ability to create a synthesis of his own philosophical system with the Confucian writings. From his success in this task has come his position as supreme authority in Chinese literature and philosophy: after Chu Hsi the Classics entered a new era.

CHU HSI'S BOYHOOD AND MATURITY (1130-1154)

Chu Hsi was born in the 4th year of Kao-tsung of the Southern Sung Dynasty (A.D. 1130), twenty-seven years after the death of Ch'eng I. It was a period of migration to the south, the Sung capital having been moved from north to south of the Yangtze. When he was four years old his father pointed to heaven and taught the little boy the word "t'ien" (heaven), whereas, much to the astonishment of the elder Chu, the child asked: "What is above heaven?"[1] On another occasion, while the future philosopher was playing with other boys, he drew in the sand the *pa-kua* (Eight Trigrams). He first made up his mind to become a sage after reading in Mencius the words: "Yao and Shun were just the same as any other man."[2] His father, in his last will and testament, expressed the wish that the boy should have three teachers: Liu P'ing-shan, Liu Ts'ao-t'ang and Hu Hsi-ch'i. The will said, in part; "These three men, whom I respect, possess profound knowledge, and you, Chu Hsi, should go and learn under them."[3] Subsequently, he married the daughter of Liu Pai-sui. When he took his M.A. degree, an examiner remarked: "His essays are full of proposals for the improvement of government policy. He may become a great man in the future." He won the *chin-shih* or doctorate when he was nineteen years old. He said of himself at the time: "In spite of advice from many people that I follow a civil service career, I am determined to become a sage."[4] His interests were from the beginning many-sided: Buddhism, Taoism, literature, poetry and military science were all eagerly studied, though he became convinced later in life that it was impossible to pay attention to such a variety of subjects. When he was twenty-four years old he was appointed assistant to the magistrate of T'ung-an, and his service was marked by solicitude for the welfare of the people, particularly in respect to their cultural welfare. He provided a library and gathered the people to offer sacrifices to Confucius. After four years of this work, he thought he had enough and resigned, accepting a sinecure as supervisor of a Taoist temple where he could have time for philosophical contemplation and writing. Subsequently he was recommended to Emperor Kao-tsung who declined to interview him.

FORMATION OF SYSTEM OF THOUGHT AND PROLIFIC WRITING (1154-1178)

In 1160 Chu Hsi traveled by foot to visit Li T'ung, and this marked the turning-point in his thought. His vacillation between Buddhism and Confucianism ceased, and his devotion to the latter became established. His apprenticeship under Li T'ung lasted for ten years until the master's death in 1163, and the influence of the older man can still be traced in Chu Hsi's *Record of Questions and Answers*. Li T'ung himself had been a pupil of Yang Shih, and thus had been taught to practise what he learned from the classics, and not to pay undue attention to purely speculative matters. Chu Hsi's *Questions and Answers* deals chiefly with the interpretation of the *Lun-yü*. He seems to have been profoundly influenced by his master in one basic idea, and that is, the principle of the Unity of Reason and the Manifoldness of Phenomena. He was, from very early days convinced of the Unity of Reason, but it was from Li T'ung that he learned that knowledge of the infinite variety of things is equally important though extremely difficult. From then on his mind was absorbed in both facets of the principle.

In 1162 Kao-tsung died. Upon the ascension of his son Hsiao-tsung, Chu Hsi addressed the throne with a memorial in which he stressed two points: (1) The Emperor should investigate things and realize knowledge in order to find the highest principles; only then can he make his will true, and rectify his mind. (2) War against the Chin people is imperative: there should be no peace with them. Later (1163) Chu Hsi went personally to the capital to have an audience with the new Emperor, and on this occasion he repeated the two points he had made in his memorial and added a third point; that the Emperor should guard himself against allowing petty men to block the way of good men. Hsiao-tsung appeared uninterested in his remarks, whereupon Chu Hsi went home.

From 1163 to 1178 was the most prolific period in the philosopher's life. In these fifteen years he produced the following works:

(1) *Hsieh shang ts'ai hsien sheng yü lu*   [*Conversations of Hsieh Liang-tso*]   (1159)

(2) *Lun yü yao i*   [*Essential Meaning of the "Analects"*]   (1163)

(3) *Lun yü hsün meng k'ou i*   [*Oral Lessons on the "Analects" as a Text-book for Boys*]   (1163)

(4) *K'un hsüeh k'ung wen*   [*Records of Hard Work and Fearful Listening*]   (1164)

(5) *Ch'eng shih i shu*   [*Posthumous Works of the Ch'eng Brothers*]   (1168)

(6) *Lun meng ching i*   [*Essential Meaning of the "Analects" and "Meng-tzu"*]   (1172)

(7) *Tzu chih t'ung chien kang mu*   [*Outlines and Details of Chinese History*]   (1172)

(8) *Pa ch'ao ming ch'en yen hsing lu*   [*Records of the Illustrious Ministers of the Sung Dynasty*]   (1172)

(9) *Hsi ming chieh i*   [*Explanation of the "Western Inscription"*]   (1172)

(10) *T'ai chi t'u shuo chieh*   [*Comments on the "Explanation of the Diagram of the Supreme Ultimate*]   (1173)

(11) *T'ung shu chieh*   [*Explanation of the "Comprehensive Understanding"*]   (1173)

(12) *Ch'eng shih wai shu*   [*Additional Works of the Ch'eng Brothers*]   (1173)

(13) *I lo yüan yüan*   [*Origin of the School of Chou Tun-i and of the Ch'eng Brothers*]   (1173)

(14) *Ku chin chia chi li*   [*Rites of Sacrificial offering in the Family*]   (1174)

(15) *Chin ssu lu*   [*Records of Reflective Thought*]   (1175)

(16) *Lun meng chi huo wen*   [*Commentary on the "Analects" and "Meng-tzu" in the Form of Questions and Answers*]   (1177)

(17) *Shih chi chuan*   [*A Collection of Comments on the "Book of Poetry"*]   (1177)

(18) *Chou i pen i*   [*Original Meaning of the "Book of Changes"*]   (1177)

ADMINISTRATIVE AND POLITICAL WORK (1179-1196)

During the preceding fifteen years (1163-1178) Chu Hsi was offered many positions in the government, but refused all of them. After 1178, however, a period of administrative activity in his life started. He was appointed prefect of Nan-K'ang and his friends advised him to accept it for at least one term. Although he preferred to retain his sinecure at the Taoist temple, his reticence was not respected and he was compelled to assume the official duties of the prefecture. In Nan-K'ang he built a temple to the memory of Chou Tun-i, instituted the White Deer Grotto Academy, and reduced taxes. During a famine he did much relief work, and encouraged the repairing of the dykes along the Yangtze. In 1181 he was transferred to Chekiang Province as tea and salt commissioner, but not until after he refused an offer to be an adviser to the Emperor. Although he rejected this latter honor, he took advantage of an audience, when he submitted seven memorials. He fulfilled his duties as Tea and Salt Commissioner for two years, and was then appointed High Commissioner of Justice in Kiangsi Province. But his labors were interrupted when Cheng Ping, with the aim of putting Chu Hsi in an unfavorable light, impeached the school of the Ch'eng brothers. Chu Hsi accordingly requested permission to return to his sinecure at the Taoist temple, and there he remained for five years. In 1188, however, he was granted an audience by the Emperor, who offered him a Vice-Ministership of the Army, which, in his customary manner, he refused. Shortly afterwards, he also rejected the Presidency of the Advisory Board. Meanwhile he submitted memorials to the Emperor which were noted for the straightforwardness of their language. In 1189 Emperor Hsiao-tsung died. His son Kuang-tsung succeeded to the throne, and Chu Hsi declined appointment as Commissioner of Transportation in Kiangnan Province. However, he accepted another prefectship, in Chang-chou, where he did the same kind of work as he had done in Nan-K'ang. He effected tax relief, opened educational institutions for the people, and made land surveys. In 1194, when Kuang-tsung died and Ning-tsung became emperor, Chu Hsi was offered the post as an imperial lecturer. But his lectureship lasted only forty days, because a powerful man in the palace, Han T'o-chou, disagreed with him. He was dismissed and sent home.

It is worth emphasizing, though at the risk of repetition, that Chu Hsi throughout his whole life devoted only nine years to public service. This includes his short term as assistant to the magistrate of T'ung-an. This meant, of course, that China suffered a lamentable loss in not taking advantage of his talents, especially during the Southern Sung Dynasty when his great abilities could have been of much assistance in saving the country.

It is interesting to inquire why Chu Hsi was often dismissed from office. The Sung School had its own philosophical views and its members firmly upheld them. Accordingly, the members found it difficult to see eye to eye with other people on the questions of the day. If they had been mere philosophers in the Western sense, giving lectures and publishing articles, they could have talked or written as much as they pleased. But being Chinese they felt an obligation to put their philosophical tenets into practice in government policy. In so doing, they were connected with the political arena, and not infrequently they found themselves in difficulties. Now, as it happened, when Kuang-tsung died in 1194, Han T'o-chou married the niece of the Empress, and persuaded the latter to put Hing-tsung on the throne. He then became the man behind the throne, and Chu Hsi, knowing that he would be hard to deal with, proposed to the prime minister, Chao Ju-yü, to bestow on him some reward but let him go. Chao, however, seemed to take the philosopher's advice lightly. Chu Hsi was in the habit also of lecturing the young emperor daily and of warning him not to yield to his surroundings. But instead of doing any good, the emperor prepared a note for him saying that he regretted that Chu Hsi's great age made it difficult for him to stand while lecturing, and that it would be better for him to take a position in a temple. Chao Ju-yü saw this note, and returned it to the emperor. But a eunuch gave it to Chu Hsi.

Even after the philosopher's dismissal, Han T'o-chou continued to hound him. At first Chu Hsi's school was labelled the school of "Tao-scholarship", which was not intended in any complimentary sense. Later, since this term was found to be not sufficiently insulting, the school was called one of "false theory." His opponents went even further by saying that it consisted of traitors. It was alleged to be a clique which entertained the purpose of usurping the government. One of Han's friends, Kao Wen-hu, even addressed a memorial to the emperor asking that Chu Hsi be put to death. From these experiences of the philosopher one sees clearly that it was exceedingly difficut for the Neo-Confucianists to carry on under the repeated persecutions of the Northern and Southern Sung Dynasties.

CLOSING YEARS (1196-1200)

After dismissal from the imperial court, Chu Hsi began writing a book about the history of the rites. In the meantime, his pupil Ts'ai Yüan-ting was declared a criminal by the government and exiled to Tao-chou. At the farewell party which the old master gave in his honor, many eyes were filled with tears. The remainder of Chu Hsi's life was devoted to writing. Following is a list of the works he produced in this last period.

(1) *Han wen k'ao i* [*Investigation of the Essays of Han Yü*] (1197)
(2) *Shih chi chuan* [*A Collection of Comments on the "Book of History"*] (1198)
(3) *Ch'u tz'u chi chu* [*Investigation of the Comments on "Ch'ü Yüan's Elegies*] (1199)

From 1199 Chu Hsi became completely a private citizen. In 1200 he added a section (*Making the will true*) to the *Ta-hsüeh*. In his view this section was originally a part of the Classic but had been lost. It was his duty to replace it by a supplementary chapter which was supposed to be a reconstruction of the original. This chapter was challenged by Wang Shou-jen in the Ming Dynasty, and became one of the great subjects of controversy in the history of Chinese philosophy. On the fifth day of the third month of the sixth year of Ch'ing yüan (A.D. 1200) Chu Hsi died.

The best biography of the philosopher and appreciation of his character was written by his pupil Huang Kan, who mentioned three principles underlying the master's system of thought and his daily life. "His way of approach to philosophy," said Huang Kan, "consisted (1) in investigation of reason to improve knowl-

edge; (2) in putting into personal practice the knowledge he acquired, and (3) in concentration of mind, which is essential to
any approach to philosophy, and implicit in the other two principles. If concentration of mind is not exercised during the improvement of knowledge, only confusion and stirrings of the mind will
issue, and the understanding will not be sufficiently clear to
grasp the principles of righteousness. If concentration of mind
is not exercised during personal practice, the results will be relaxation and negligence, and personal exemplification will be impossible. The way to attain concentration of mind is to be devoted to
singleness of purpose. About this last point Chu Hsi wrote a
warning for himself. He considered it the basis of education for
the young and for those aspiring to advanced study."

Huang Kan's account of his teacher's philosophical system
will be discussed later, but here I shall quote his account of the
master's daily life. "As regards his personal appearance, his facial
features were dignified, his language was to the point, his movements were steady and respectful, and his thinking was straight.
He rose before dawn, and wearing a robe, a hat and square shoes,
every day he worshipped his ancestors in the family temple, and
paid respect to the sages of old. Then he went into his study
where his books, tables and things he needed were arranged in a
very orderly fashion. At the dining table the dishes and chop-sticks
had to be laid out according to a prescribed plan. When he felt
tired, he would take a rest by closing his eyes sitting bolt upright.
After resting, he took a short walk. He retired at midnight. When
awakened during the night, he sat up, well covered, and waited
until dawn. His features and movements were in conformity with
habits which never changed, whether in youth or in his old age,
whether in midsummer or in midwinter, whether at leisure or in
haste. In his private life, he showed the utmost filial piety towards his parents, and love towards the younger generation. Since
he showed such respect and affection, there was harmony in his
family. When offering sacrifices, he carefully observed form, even
to the minutest detail, and if anything went wrong he worried the
rest of the day, but if all went well he was happy. At funerals he
expressed sorrow, wore correct mourning clothes, and partook of
the foods that were properly served. He was polite to all visitors

who called on him. To relatives, however distant, he showed love. To neighbors, however humble, he showed respect. He never overlooked any detail of what should be done on the occasion of others' birthdays, weddings, periods of mourning, distress, etc. In regard to his personal comforts, he wore just enough clothing to keep himself warm, ate just enough to prevent starvation, and lived in a house just well enough constructed to protect him from the wind and the rain. Surroundings which other people might have found unbearable Chu Hsi accepted with complete satisfaction. In matters of public service, his district program and his proposals to the emperor were based on a policy which was properly orientated and dignified. Though he was unfortunate in his political career and was unable to carry out publicly his *Tao*, he was able, in retirement, to illuminate his *Tao* so brilliantly that it will enlighten coming generations for a thousand years."

CHU HSI'S SYSTEM OF PHILOSOPHY

Chu Hsi was a great thinker. His mind was thorough and comprehensive. It envisaged the universe as a unity, and its different aspects as coherent parts of that unity. The list of his writings shows how wide were his interests. Like Aristotle, who first broke knowledge down into its various branches or sciences, Chu Hsi strove to bring all Chinese learning under his scrutiny. Yet he had his own principle of organization: the unity of reason and the manifoldness of the phenomenal world. By means of this principle he brought the *Diagram of the Supreme Ultimate* of Chou Tun-i, the *Western Inscription* of Chang Tsai, and the ideas of the Ch'eng brothers into his system and assimilated them. He accomplished this not by mere appropriation, but by applying to them his own principle, so that they seem to be woven into a masterpiece of art. The thoroughness of his mind prevents him from omitting anything that was necessary for the completeness of his system. The acuteness of his mind gave him the power to see clearly any flaw in an argument, a problem, or a book. Thus, for example, in regard to the two versions of the *Book of History*, the modern script version and the ancient script version — Chu Hsi raised the following question: Why should the modern version, which was complicated in its content, have been remembered by the scholar Fu Sheng, while the ancient version, which was easy to understand, should have been forgotten by the scholars who studied the Confucian Classics? Chu Hsi did not try to solve the problem, but the keenness of his intellect enabled him to see that there was a problem of the two versions — a problem which, at the end of the Ming and beginning of the Ch'ing Dynasties, was revived as a question of textual criticism.

Another example of his acuteness occurred while he was editing the *Collected Dialogues of Hsieh Liang-tso.* He found some passages which did not seem to fit in with the whole text, and so he deleted them. Afterwards he came into possession of another edition of Hsieh's works in which these passages were already omitted. He was pleased about this corroboration of his judgment. His brilliance was also evident in all his controversies — with Lu Hsiang-shan, about the *Diagram of the Supreme Ultimate,* and with many other contemporaries.

Chu Hsi's method was constructed on a firm foundation. This may have been in part the result of his dislike of exaggeration, whether in the field of the transcendental world or of practical life. He preferred a method which was sure, practical and empirical. Also perhaps his natural interest in the manifoldness of phenomena was an incentive to keep this thought at the factual level. Not only Chu Hsi's principle of organization, but also his system of philosophy itself may be expressed in the form: Unity of Reason and Manifoldness of the phenomenal world. He attached equal importance to both aspects. He was fascinated by the immense variety in the realm of nature, and yet he did not overlook the unity of the source from which they emanated. In other words, he emphasized both the One and the Many. He can neither be classified as a monist nor as a dualist. Both terms are inapplicable to his thought.

There is an occidental dictum according to which every philospher must be labeled either as a Platonist or as an Artistotelian. Where then does Chu Hsi belong? I have no hestitation in saying that as a student of the phenomenal world he was an Aristotelian; but yet he was also a Platonist in his idealism.

First, let me point out where Chu Hsi agrees with Aristotle:
(1) Both agree in their opposition to the Platonic view that Ideas
exist for themselves apart from concrete objects which are merely
their copies. (2) Both also agree that the Idea as the One apart
from and beside the Many does not exist. Nonetheless, a principle
which Chu Hsi calls *ri* must be assumed as present in the Many.
(3) The Chinese philosopher and the Stagirite further agree that
the universal has no independent existence apart from the individual, though the former is the proper object of knowledge. The
universal notions combine in one whole all the essential attributes
of objects. They represent what Aristotle calls "Form" and what
Chu Hsi calls "*ri*" (4) While Aristotle considers matter, in which
Form or *ri* inheres, to be not absolutely non-existent, he nevertheless regards it as existing in the sense of possibility or capacity.
Chu Hsi does not concern himself with the question of whether
matter is existent, but he would gladly agree that matter is capacity. Both arrive at the same conclusion, though I cannot give
a detailed examination of their arguments here. (5) The Stagirite says that matter does not exist deprived altogether of form.
The Chinese philosopher asserts that no *ch'i* exists without *ri*.
Rather, only the individual thing exists, and it is a whole resulting
from the union of matter and form. (6) Aristotle holds that an
immaterial form-principle exists, while Chu Hsi says that *ri* is
prior to *ch'i* and eternally is. (7) Chu Hsi would be ready to
agree that *ri* or form, which subsists in the organic whole of creation, is at once form, end, and moving cause. (8) What is remarkably common to Aristotle and Chu Hsi is that matter is the
ultimate source of imperfection in things and that it is the principle of individuation and plurality. (9) The Greek and the Chinese
both assert that an entity exists which imparts motion but is itself
unmoved. This is God according to the former, and Heaven according to the latter. Chu Hsi says that Heaven is Reason. So
Aristotle says that God is the immaterial and eternal form, self-
thinking reason, absolute spirit. (10) God or heaven as the prime
mover must be one whose essence is pure energy. It must be eternal,
unalloyed and immaterial form. It is the good *per se,* towards
which all things tend. It is the eternal *prius* of all development.

Since there are so many points of agreement between Chu Hsi and Aristotle, I believe that my designation of Chu Hsi as, in certain respects, an Aristotelian is not far-fetched. However, it would be incorrect to think of him as an Aristotelian *only*, because his preoccupation with *ri* is so strong that he may also be considered a Platonist. In the field of philosophy of nature, Chu Hsi is clearly an Aristotelian. But in the field of moral values, which is the main interest of Chinese philosophers, he is just as firmly convinced that there exists an eternal, unchanging truth, which is complete in itself. Whether this truth is in the shape of an archetype may be laid aside. In the philosophy of moral values there is no question of Plato's three beds: the ideal bed of God, the bed made by a carpenter, and the bed designed by a painter. The sole question is why an ideal type of life, in a family or in a state, cannot be realized. Chu Hsi held that the non-realization of the ideals is the effect of obstacles offered by matter. If he had been a thoroughgoing realist, he would have admitted simply that the realization of Platonic ideas in this world is sometimes impossible. But as a moral and political thinker, he believed that *ri* eternally is, and that the cause of its non-realization, or the cause of the non-realization of the *Tao,* lies in mankind as a physical vehicle. Chu Hsi was aware that men cannot be constituted without *ch'i.* Therefore, the hinderances attendant upon *ch'i* are unavoidable. In other words, to express the situation mildly, Platonic ideas face difficulties in trying to get realized in this world. To go one step further: perfect ideals are, as a matter-of-fact, dreams, from the point of view of the realist, but from the point of view of Chu Hsi, ideals or *ri* exist eternally. There is no doubt, therefore, that he was a Platonist in the realm of moral values.

The interpretation may be advanced that for Chu Hsi *ri* is a unity prevailing in both the physical and moral worlds. This is true. Nevertheless, in the physical world different kinds of physical objects exist: for instance, plants and animals. Chu Hsi never defies this heterogeneity, because the facts compel acceptance. But this term *ri*, although he applies it in natural as well as moral philosophy, in reality has a very different connotation in the latter from what it has in the former. *Ri* as the principle of organization in the natural world must face facts. In the moral realm it is a synonym for ideals. Indeed, the usage of this word *ri* in Chinese philosophical terminology would seem to be ambiguous.

Now I come to Chu Hsi's doctrine concerning the unity of reason, heaven and the Supreme Ultimate. This last subject has already been dealt with in the chapter about Chou Tun-i, which included Chu Hsi's comment. The problem to be considered next is: How closely is the Supreme Ultimate related to the unity of reason?

THE UNITY OF REASON

Chu Hsi said: "From the beginning to the end, *ri,* the only reality is one, but millions of things share it in order to acquire essence. Each particular thing forms a Supreme Ultimate in itself. Is then the Supreme Ultimate divided? The answer is: The Supreme Ultimate is one, but each thing shares it so that each thing forms a Supreme Ultimate. It is just like the moon which is one, but which is reflected in many rivers and lakes and is seen everywhere. One cannot say that the moon is split up."[5]

A pupil once asked Chu Hsi: "Last year I heard that *ri* is one, but that its manifestations are many. What is the meaning of these manifestations? Probably *ri* is one, but its operations are carried out in various ways." The philosopher replied: "In this world there are many kings, ministers, fathers and sons, and each has his own functions. There are also different kinds of trees and different kinds of houses, and these also differ in their nature. Mr. Chang cannot be at the same time Mr. Li, just as *yin* cannot simultaneously be *yang.* Therefore, *ri* is one, but its manifestations are demonstrated in thousands of ways. From the point of view of manifestation, one sees variety; from the point of view of *ri,* one sees self-identity and the pervading power of *ri.*"[6]

Another pupil asked Chu Hsi: "If *ri* is one why are there five human relationships among mankind?" The master answered: "You may say that there is only one *ri,* or that there are five kinds of *ri,* but the underlying principle is one."[7]

Chu Hsi was asked about priority in the relationship of *ri* to *ch'i.* Is *ri* prior to *ch'i?* Or is *ch'i* prior to *ri?* The reply was: "*Ri* cannot exist without *ch'i.* But *ri* is metaphysical; *ch'i* is physical. From the difference in their nature, metaphysical and physical, an order in their priority may be inferred. *Ri* is incorporal, but ch'i is corporal, and has dregs."[8]

Someone asked: "What is the meaning of the assertion that *ri* must exist before *ch'i*?" Chu Hsi replied: "It is difficult to assert definitely that an order of priority exists between *ri* and *ch'i*. But if one traces back to the origin, one must admit that *ri* is prior. Nevertheless, *ri* is not independent of *ch'i*; rather *ri* inheres in *ch'i*. If there were no *ch'i*, there would be no place for *ri* to stay."[9]

Then someone inquired: "How do you find *ri* which inheres in *ch'i*?" The philosopher said: "When *yin* and *yang* and the five elements, despite their complications, follow always a definite course without falling into disorder, this course is *ri*. If *Ch'i* is not consolidated, *ri* will have no place in which to inhere."[11]

Thus far the quotations I have given have to do with Chu Hsi's doctrine of the unity and priority of reason. But how closely did he suppose the unity of reason to be related to the Supreme Ultimate? In his conception *ri* is identical with heaven and the Supreme Ultimate. Thus, he says repeatedly that heaven is *ri* and that the Supreme Ultimate is *ri*. A few more quotations from Chu Hsi will throw light on these conceptions of heaven and the Supreme Ultimate.

A seeker after truth inquired: "Is the Supreme Ultimate before the creation of the world, something unformed which is the universal essence or *ri*?" The philosopher answered: "The Supreme Ultimate is the *ri* of heaven, earth and all things. In regard to heaven and earth, there is in each of these a Supreme Ultimate; but, in fact, there is in every particular thing a Supreme Ultimate. Before the creation of the world, *ri* exists."[12]

Someone inquired: "What is the meaning of the statement: 'Before creation *ri* exists?'" Chu Hsi answered: "Reason, *ri*, exists. There is the world. If there were no *ri* there would be no world, no mankind, no things. Since *ri* exists there is *ch'i* in circulation, which produces a variety of things." Then: "Is *ri* the motive power which produces the variety of things?" The answer: "When there is *ri*, so also is there *ch'i* in circulation, which produces."[13] Following Ch'eng Hao and Ch'eng I, Chu Hsi identified heaven with reason.

Somebody asked the meaning of the expression "the mind of heaven and earth", the "reason" or "law of heaven and earth". Does the reason or law of heaven mean the way or order? Does the expression "mind of heaven" imply something which rules? Chu Hsi answered: It is correct to say that mind is what rules. What rules is reason."[14] He also said: "The Empyrean is what is called heaven. It is what rotates endlessly. It is incorrect to say that a person sits in heaven who judges the sins of men. It is also incorrect to say that there is no ruler at all."[15]

Someone asked: "We find the following sentences in the classics: 'The Lord of Heaven imparts a mind to the people. Heaven assigns a great mission to men. In order to help the people heaven established kingship. Heaven makes creatures and lifts them up according to their capacities. When they do good, heaven blesses them. When they do evil, heaven punishes them.' Does all this signify explicitly or implicitly that in the Empyrean there is a ruler?" Chu Hsi answered: "All this signifies simply that there is reason."[16]

In conclusion I should like to add a few words of commentary on the meaning of the three terms *ri*, the Supreme Ultimate and heaven. Chu Hsi explained repeatedly that the Supreme Ultimate is *ri* and that heaven is *ri*. As he uses the terms, their meaning is identical. But it is well to remember that this word *ri* in Chinese is much wider than the Western counterpart, reason in the ordinary sense, but similar to the idea of Universal Reason of the Stoics. The Chinese term denotes (1) the lines in a piece of stone or wood. By extension it gradually reaches to the meaning of the principles of existence, or the constitution of all things. It refers (2) to the supreme law of the physical and moral world. It means (3) the highest good, which heaven exhibits in the process of creation. Thus it is that Chu Hsi can say that the Supreme Ultimate is *ri* or that heaven is *ri*. In the theoretical sense, *ri* is moral or natural law. In the sublime sense, *ri* is the Prime Mover of Aristotle, because Chu Hsi identified *ri* with heaven and the Supreme Ultimate. If Aristotle's idea of the Prime Mover is, in Europe, the first attempt to found a theistic theory on a philosophical basis, so Chu Hsi's identification of *ri* with the Supreme Ultimate is, in China, the first attempt to establish a philosophical basis for the concept of a first cause.

MANIFOLDNESS OF MANIFESTATIONS (or RELATION OF *CH'I* TO *RI*)

Just as Aristotle held that the concept or universal cannot be isolated from the particular, and that it is not in a transcendent sphere but is immanent in the particular, so Chu Hsi believed that *ri* inheres in *ch'i*, and that *ri* cannot exist without *ch'i*. The notable difference between the Greek and the Chinese philosopher, is that for the former concepts or universals are understood in the Western sense as logical ideas, while, for the latter, *ri*, besides expressing the common characteristics of a class, is understood to possessses a life-content which controls the physical and the moral world. It is identified with the four cardinal virtues of human nature and with the underlying principle of the creation of the phenomenal world.

Chu Hsi has been styled a dualist because he called attention to the variety of phenomenal manifestations. Without thorough study of the Many, he insisted, it is impossible to understand the One. He stressed the importance of investigating phenomenal manifestation, but he never forgot the unity of reason. Indeed, Chu Hsi would more aptly be regarded as occupying a peculiar position between Monism and Dualism than as being a dualist. This question may be left undecided for the moment, until we finish our study of his theory of the relation of *ri* to *ch'i*.

"Before creation", he said, "there is *ri*. When there is *ri* there is the world. If there were no *ri* there would be no world."[17] This remark apparently implies that the philosopher believed in the priority of *ri*; but, on the other hand, he also said: "When there is no consolidation of *ch'i*, *ri* will have no place to inhere." When all is said and done, therefore, Chu Hsi reminds his pupils not to hold a definite view about the priority of *ri*, but rather to look at the problem from both sides: If there were no *ri* there would be no world; if there were no *ch'i*, *ri* would have no place to stay. From this attitude one would be led to believe that Chu Hsi assumed *ri* and *ch'i* to be two equally fundamental factors.

Theoretically, *ri* is prior to *ch'i;* actually the interrelationship is suggested in his simile: "*Ri* hangs on *yin* and *yang* like a man riding a horse."[18]

Let us examine further the difference in the nature of *ri* and *ch'i.* "I assume", Chu Hsi says, "that *ri* goes in the company of *ch'i.* When *ch'i* is consolidating, *ri* is there too. *Ch'i* is the sort of thing that can coagulate into a mass, and form a shape. *Ri,* on the contrary, is without will, emotion, deliberation or knowledge or design. While *ch'i* is coagulating, *ri* is inside of it. For example, any living being, whether a man, an animal, or a plant, must have, while it is growing, a seed. Without a seed nothing can grow. This seed is *ch'i,* matter. As for *ri,* it belongs to a sphere of immateriality, pure essence and possibility. It leaves no trace and knows no design, while *ch'i* is capable of consolidation and production. When *ch'i* is present, *ri* dwells inside."[19]

The *ri* described in this paragraph suggests Aristotle's end, form, or final cause; and the *ch'i* reminds one of the Greek philosopher's matter, which can move and change. In the natural world different kinds of things exist, — men, animals, plants, inanimate bodies. For Chu Hsi, these dissimilarities are the result of the endowment of *ch'i.* In some cases, the combination of elements of *ch'i* is perfect; in other cases, it is imperfect, or subject to deficiency or privation. Thus, there are gradations of perfection among the various kinds of things. Does this not remind one of Aristotle's view that nature cannot always attain her end, because of the obstacles which matter interposes?

Someone once asked Chu Hsi: "Animals have knowledge of the senses, but plants do not. Why?" The master replied: "Animals have blood. So they have knowledge of the senses. We cannot, to be sure, assert that plants have knowledge. Nevertheless, in instances of excessive cutting they wither, and thus appear to have some feeling. We all have noticed that flowers and trees in the sunshine bloom, and are vigorous and full of vitality. Even the bark on trees cannot prevent their blossoming. Old and withered trees decay and shrink because they have lost this vital strength."[20] Elsewhere Chu Hsi quotes Shao Yung: "What is rooted in the earth is heavy and dirty. What looks upward is light, signifying intelligence. Apes can stand like men, so they have some intelligence. The heads of birds and animals are on a horizontal plane, so they are half-ignorant, half-intelligent."[21] Does this discussion of Chu Hsi not remind one of the words of the Stagirite? "Even in the lowest animals, there is something admirable, full of purpose, beautiful and divine. The plants are less perfect than the animals; among the latter those which have blood are more perfect than the bloodless."[22]

Chu Hsi traces back the dissimilarities in the different kinds of things to the role played by *yin* and *yang*, the two types of *ch'i*. Aristotle teaches that in the act of generation the form-giving principle proceeds from the male, and the form-receiving principle from the female.

Regarding inanimate bodies, Chu Hsi also believed that there are reasons for their existence. For example, a boat can only sail on water, and a cart can only be driven on land.[23]

An inquirer once asked: "Does something which is dried and withered have a principle of its constitution or a reason?" Chu Hsi replied: "The herb-medicines, rhubarb and wolfbane [*aconitum variegatum*] are dried plants, yet they are so different in nature that the one cannot be substituted for the other."[24]

The philosopher illustrated the relation between *ri* and *ch'i* by the following simile: "*Ri* is to *ch'i* as a pearl is to water. When *ri* is in pure *ch'i*, it is like a pearl in clean water, so that the pearl is transparent. When *ri* is in soiled *ch'i*, it is like a pearl in dirty water, so that the pearl cannot show its brightness. A thing that is foul or obscure is like a pearl fallen in the mud."[25]

Chu Hsi also said: "When *ri* is present, so also is *ch'i* present. As long as *ch'i* is there, you will find *ri* too. By being endowed with a pure *ch'i* a man may become wise or a sage, just like a pearl in clean water. But by being endowed with a soiled *ch'i* a man may become ignorant and wicked, just like a pearl in dirty water."[26]

As Aristotle finds that all organic creations, even in the lowest animals, there is something admirable, beautiful and divine, the Chinese philosopher says the same thing in different words: "Tigers and wolves know the relation of parents and children. Bees and ants know the relation of queen and subordinates. Ospreys know the separate functions of male and female. This shows that even the animals are endowed with some qualities of intelligence."

Chu Hsi and Aristotle reached the same conclusion that gradations of perfection are the effects of obstacles interposed by matter. A doubter once commented to the Chinese philosopher: "A man and a thing are each endowed with *ri*, so they have its nature. A man and a thing are also endowed with *ch'i*, so they have their physical body. A man's quality: whether he is clever or dull, kind or cruel, varies in accordance with his endowment of *ch'i*. But as far as diversities among things are concerned, I wonder whether these differences are attributable to a *ri* which is less perfect or to a *ch'i* which obscures." The master explained: "The amount of *ri* with which a thing is endowed is proportional to its amount of *ch'i*."[27] In this is contained Chu Hsi's explanation of the differences between the various kinds of things: inanimate objects, plants, animals and mankind. It is the Chinese philosopher's philosophy of nature, and in it one finds much similarity to the natural philosophy of Aristotle, as in the striking resemblances between the two thinkers in their metaphysical speculations.

Before bringing this section to a close I should like to present Chu Hsi's conclusions as to the relation between *ri* and *ch'i*. An inquirer remarked to the philosopher: "I saw in your letter to Huang Shang-po that you hold the following view: In regard to the origin of different kinds of things, you believe that *ri* is self-identical, but that *ch'i* varies. In regard to the individuals constituting the different kinds of things, however, you hold that in their equipment of *ch'i* they are alike, while in their endowment of *ri* they are dissimilar. How can I understand these two statements? In the first case, referring to the origin of things, the endowment from heaven is self-identical, so that there is unity of *ri*. But because the combinations of the two forces *yin* and *yang* and of the five elements are in varying proportions, there is heterogeneity of *ch'i*. On the other hand, referring to things as individuals, they are made of the same elements. Hence, from the point of view of nature their *ch'i* is one. Nevertheless, among the different kinds of individuals some are ignorant and some are intelligent, so that their endowment of *ri* is heterogeneous. Such is my understanding." Then the inquirer proceeded to ask: "Is my understanding correct?" Chu Hsi answered: "By the term 'identity' or similarity of *ch'i* one refers, for instance, to the commonness of such feelings as coldness and warmth, hunger and satiety, instinct of self-preservation and fear of death, inclination to escape danger and love of safety. These kinds of feeling in general prevail among men and animals. By the term 'heterogeneity of *ri*' I may cite the following examples: Bees and ants know the relation of queen and subordinates. So they have a modicum of intelligence about the sense of duty. Even tigers and wolves are acquainted with the relation of parents and children. Thus, they have an inkling of the feeling of love. They are like a mirror which is bright in one or two parts, but otherwise dark."[28]

Chu Hsi placed man in the highest rank of the hierarchy of creatures, because man possesses reason. In this respect again Chu Hsi resembled Aristotle, for the Greek philosopher also regarded reason as the distinguishing feature between man and animals, plants and other physical objects.

HUMAN NATURE: ESSENTIAL AND PHYSICAL

The discussion of the relation between *ch'i* and *ri* leads to the question of human nature, because the *ch'i* with which man is endowed constitutes his body, and the *ri* with which he is equipped makes up his intelligence and moral character. Let us look at how Chu Hsi understood the combination of *ch'i* and *ri* in human beings. He applied his same theory of matter as obstacle to man's perfection. Somebody asked: "If *ch'i*, or matter, makes things different in their degree of foulness and ignorance, does human nature, as a gift from heaven, also vary in its grade of perfection or imperfection?" Chu Hsi replied: "Human nature can neither be perfect nor imperfect. It is like the light of the sun or moon. If one is in an open field, this light is visible; but if one is under a shelter or in a house, it is cut off, partly seen and partly unseen. *Ch'i* befouls, as the shelter obscures the sun. When there is dirt, brilliancy is diminished. In regard to man, however, the situation is different, because human understanding, after the obscurity or ignorance has been removed, returns to its original perfection. Even animals, though they are limited in their sensibility because of their shapes and bodies, have a bit of intelligence. For example, tigers and wolves know how to love, otters and beavers understand a little about how to offer sacrifices, and bees and ants recognize a queen."[29]

Elsewhere Chu Hsi remarked: "Nature is like a sun-beam, but the endowment men receive from nature varies, as a sunbeam through a crack varies. Men and things are wrapped up in their physical elements, so that they are not open to the light. Ants are so insignificant that they know only to serve as subordinates under a queen."[30]

A seeker after knowledge asked: "Is nature among men and things the same or different?" The philosopher answered: "Nature among men and things is the same, but their equipment of *ch'i* differs. This will be more intelligible if we speak metaphorically of water. It gives off one color when it is in a white bowl, and another when it is in a blue bowl." The philosopher commented again: "Nature is a difficult subject to discuss. You may also describe it as many and various. It is like a sun-beam in a crack: sometimes long, sometimes short; sometimes big, sometimes small. But it is always the same sunbeam."[31]

Speaking again of the union of *ri* and *ch'i* in man, and of the reason for the differences in intelligence among humans, Chu Hsi said: "Man is born by the combination of *ri* and *ch'i*. The *ri* of heaven is vast and limitless, but if *ch'i* did not exist, *ri* would have nothing to hang to. Therefore, after operations by *yin* and *yang*, and through their consolidation, accumulation and reproduction, *ri* found a place to adhere. Man's power of speaking, moving, thinking and designing is the effect of *ch'i*, but *ri* is there too. Man's sense of filial duty, brotherhood, loyalty, honesty, benevolence, righteousness, decency and wisdom comes from his endowment of *ri*. But the various ways of combining the two forces of *yin* and *yang* and the five elements result in remarkable differences in the degree of perfection in the nature of men and things. From the point of view of *ch'i*, all *ch'i*, whether in human beings or inanimate objects, is the same; but from the point of view of perfection or imperfection, the portion of *ch'i* which man receives is the best, while the part which things acquire is partial and vague. Since human beings get the nobler portion, their *ri* is like light, unobscured. For example, human heads which are oval resemble heaven; human feet being rectangular suggest earth, which is flat and straight. since man has the best part of *ch'i,* he possesses the knowledge of reason and is intelligent. Things, on the other hand, acquire only what is fragmentary in *ch'i.* Thus, animals and birds live on a horizontal plane, and plants stick their heads down into the earth and protrude their branches upward. Animals possess a small amount of intelligence. For instance, a crow knows enough to feed its parents, an otter understands how to offer sacrifices, a dog can watch, an ox can plough. But man's intelligence is much wider and is capable of a vastly greater variety of deeds. Intelligence is what distinguishes man from the brutes and from inanimate objects. Nevertheless, even among men there are degrees of difference in intelligence and stupidity, purity and filth. Some are born geniuses, because their *ch'i* is undefiled, bright and homogeneous, and without the obstructions of ignorance and foulness. Others can learn and improve themselves. Some are fools, whose minds are so beclouded that they must labor indefatigably in order to improve themselves."[32]

In this paragraph we have met the remarkable similarity between Chu Hsi and Aristotle. Both philosophers considered man's reason to be divine and immortal, and to be the faculty which distinguished his highest soul from the vegetative soul of plants and the sensitive, appetitive and locomotive souls of animals.

Hitherto we have been studying Chu Hsi's explanations in the form of questions and answers: conversations in which an inquirer or seeker after knowledge poses a problem, and the master provides a solution. Chu Hsi's expositions also sometimes take the form of papers about certain questions addressed to him with the purpose of eliciting his approbation or disapprobation. Following is such a paper, concerning human nature, which was submitted to the philosopher, and won his assent.

"The nature of man and things is the same in some respects, and unlike in other respects. One must know both the similarity and dissimilarity, then one is qualified to discuss the question of human nature. When the Supreme Ultimate moves with the two forces, and creatures are produced by the operations of the two forces, this is the origin of man and things. This is the common source. But out of the challenges, responses and combinations of the two forces and five elements come an immense number of varieties, which multiply. This is dissimilarity. The common element is *ri*. The differences are *ch'i*. Man by his natural constitution is endowed with *ri*, which is shared by all, and from which none can deviate. Man in his physical constitution is shaped by *ch'i*, which is different in each and which cannot be made uniform. Therefore, you, my teacher, in your book *Questions on the 'Ta-hsüeh'* said: 'From the standpoint of *ri* many things come from the same origin, so that there is no diversity of rank. From the standpoint of *ch'i*, man gets the best part, so that he comprehends and is full of a sense of rectitude. But things receive only what is partial and obscure. Hence a difference of perfection obtains among them. Though *ch'i* varies, the endowment of *ri*, which lays the foundation of human nature, distinguishes man from other things. Man's senses and movements are the effect of *ch'i*. His moral sentiments of benevolence, righteousness, decency, and wisdom come from *ri*. Sensations and movements are common to man and animals. Moral sense is also partially possible to the brutes, but they do not know it in its entirety.' "[33]

This paper, which Chu Hsi approved, is merely a confirmation of Ch'eng I's formula: "*Hsing* (human nature) is *ri* (reason)."

Now, as we approach the end of this section, I shall discuss the stand which Chu Hsi took in the controversy about human nature. Since in China philosophers were primarily interested in moral values, they concentrated most of their efforts on the problems connected with human nature, which was their central theme, just as the idea of "concepts" or "universals" was the central theme of the European philosophers. Views about human nature were many and confused in China. Confucius said: "In nature people are near one another, but habits separate them." Mencius, not following in the footsteps of Confucius, formulated the theory that human nature is good. Opposing Mencius, Hsün-tzu, basing his views upon observation of the practical life of man, believed that human nature is evil. Han Yü, attempting a reconciliation between Mencius and Hsün-tzu, held that there are three kinds of human nature: it may be good, bad, or a mixture of both. This is the history of the controversy prior to the Sung Dynasty.

The theory that human nature is good is the foundation of Neo-Confucianism. If the Sung philosophers had not been able to keep this hypothesis intact, their house would have fallen. Why? Because unless the doctrine of the goodness of human nature is maintained the formula *"hsing* is *ri"* collapses. The Sung philosophers had a standpoint from which to fight Hsün-tzu and other schools, and the Buddhists. Their theory of the goodness of human nature was their base. If they lost, they could not fight at all, much less gain victory. They knew no other way to attack Hsün-tzu for the sake of Mencius. They knew no other way to clarify Han Yü's doctrine of the three kinds of human nature. The theory of the goodness of nature, moreover, was for them of vital importance because it furnished the best proof of the Buddhist's ignorance of *ri* in human nature, which ignorance led the Buddhists to their fallacious conclusion that this world is an illusion.

Since the theory of the goodness of human nature was important, the Neo-Confucianists were constrained to abide by the formula of Mencius. But it also was incumbent upon them to fight against Hsün-tzu's perception of the evilness of human nature. Fortunately, one of the founders of the Sung School, Chang Tsai, propounded the doctrine of two kinds of nature: the essential and the physical. By the former, the Neo-Confucianists were able to defend the theory of the goodness of human nature, and by the latter to explain the reason for the evilness of human nature. This bifurcation is the key to Sung philosophy's success in defending Mencius and at the same time in explaining Hsün-tzu. Also it furnished a base from which to attack Buddhism.

Someone asked: "What is physical nature?" Chu Hsi answered: "When you talk about your nature, in the sense of a gift from heaven, it is no longer nature in this sense, because of the *you*, who was born; and human nature is bound to be mixed with *ch'i*, the physical elements. Indeed, except for these physical elements, where would your nature stay?"[34] Again Chu Hsi commented: "When there is no physical element, even *ri* has no home. When the physical element is light and pure, there will be less obscurity and privation. When there is less obscurity, the heavenly *ri* will win. But if the obscurity is more, desire will win. This shows that human nature is essentially good, and this is the reason why Mencius believed in the goodness of human nature. It is also the reason why the Ch'eng brothers asked the people to return to their original nature. From these thoughts, also, it follows that the physical nature should be differentiated from the essential."[35]

The Ch'eng brothers enunciated a formula in their discussion of nature which reminds one of Kant's dictum: "Intuitions without concepts are blind; concepts without intuitions are empty." The Chinese philosophers said: "The study of human nature without the study of ch'i can never be complete. The study of ch'i without the study of human nature can never attain clarity and distinctness." Chu Hsi appreciated this dictum so deeply that he considered it extraordinary, and an original contribution by the Ch'eng brothers never anticipated by the sages of antiquity.

How much importance Chu Hsi attached to the theory of the bifurcation of nature can be seen from the following conversation with a student, Tao Fu, who asked: "Who started the theory of physical nature?" Chu Hsi answered: "It was begun by Chang Tsai and the Ch'eng brothers. It was a great contribution to the school of the sages, and will be a guide to future generations. This theory was not known previously. For example, Han Yü's division of nature into three kinds: good, bad, and a mixture, is evidence that he missed the point of the physical aspect of nature. Moreover, it is impossible to suppose that nature exists in three kinds. Even the theory of the goodness of human nature as enunciated by Mencius touches only the essential, and ignores the physical. It was precisely for the reason of neglecting this physical element that such a controversy as that in which Hsün-tzu participated, about the evilness of human nature, arose. If the discovery of Chang Tsai and the Ch'eng brothers had been made long ago, there would have been no controversy. Once the theory of Chang and the Ch'engs has been established, other notions will fade away very quickly."[36]

After this appreciation, Chu Hsi proceeded to quote from Chang Tsai: "Being born, one acquires physical nature. If one can return to one's self, one will find one's original or essential nature." Then Chu Hsi repeated the dictum of the Ch'eng's: "Discussion of nature without taking ch'i into consideration is bound to be incomplete. Discussion of ch'i without taking nature into consideration cannot attain clarity and distinctness."[37]

The pupil, Tao Fu, continued to make inquiries. "If man", he asked, "is endowed with the four virtues, why are there wicked men after birth?" The master answered: "This is because of *ch'i*. Without study of *ch'i*, knowledge of *ri* cannot be complete. If one is limited in one's investigation of the various aspects of *ch'i*, without inquiring into what is good and evil, one can never clearly know the essence of *ri*. Thorough understanding has not occurred since Confucius, Tseng-tzu, Tzu Ssu and Mencius."[38]

MIND AND PERSONAL CULTIVATION

After we have become acqainted with Chu Hsi's metaphysics and philosophy of nature, let us study his theory of human psychology. Aristotle says in his *Nichomachean Ethics* that we become good by doing good deeds. That is to say, a man is virtuous or acts virtuously when he performs the act (1) knowing what he does, (2) choosing the act for its own sake, and (3) as the result of a permanent disposition. Aristotle means that virtue must be a disposition developed out of a capacity by the proper exercise of that capacity. In Chinese philosophy, the central concern is to keep the mind intent on good and on doing good. Or to express the same idea in negative terms, it is to eliminate desire for profit and power, to take control of the passions of joy and anger, and to get rid of excitements and stirrings of the mind, in order that the mind' may dwell in calmness and be qualified to make correct judgments about what should be done. Naturally, love of mankind and sense of duty towards one's parents and sovereign give the positive content to one's actions. Thus, the cultivation of a disposition for good is the prime concern for both the Chinese philosophers and Aristotle.

Chu Hsi, in the preface to his *Commentary on the "Chung-yung" (Doctrine of the Golden Mean" according to Chapters)*, said: "In the Chinese classics are the words of Yao: 'Keep to the proper mean.' These words were later the message of Shun, who said to Yü: 'The mind of man is full of danger. The mind of *tao* is subtle and delicate. In proficiency and unity keep to the proper mean.' What Yao had said in one sentence, Shun expanded into three sentences, because elaboration was neccessary. According to my view, the work of mind is to feel and know and to be intelligent.

But why should there have been a difference between the mind of man and the mind of *tao*?. The reason is that the mind works on two planes: it may be motivated (1) by the desire of the physical world, or (2) by correct principles of heaven and nature. Thus it is not surprising that the operations of the mind should vary radically. At the former level, it will go wild and become wanton. At the latter level it will become subtle, and go forth to search for what is right. All men, however, are alike in that they have a physical body. Accordingly, even the wise man has desires: that is to say, he has the mind of the common man. On the other hand, since all men have the same spiritual endowment, even the fool has the mind of *tao*. Whether a man has the mind of *tao*, or desires, depends upon how he controls his mind. If he is ignorant of how to control it, what was already dangerous will become more dangerous; what was already subtle will become more subtle. Indeed, the *ri* of heaven is not in a position to overcome selfish desires. By the word 'proficiency' Shun meant the spirit of distinguishing clearly between these two minds; and by 'unity' he intended that the spirit hold to the right principle of the mind in its original state. If one abides by self-cultivation of this sort, one can make the mind of *tao* one's master, and mind of desire one's slave. What was formerly full of danger will now become secure; what was invisible will be clear. Thoughts and movements will be neither defective nor excessive. Instead, they will maintain the proper mean."[39]

In an essay entitled *Inspection of the Mind*, a refutation of the Buddhist way of contemplating the mind, Chu Hsi said that an inquirer once asked whether it was true that Buddhists had a method of contemplating their own minds. The master replied, "Yes, they do. But according to my view, the mind is the master of the body and it is unique without a duplicate. It is the host, and not a guest. It is the commander, and not a receiver of commands. And therefore it is the mind which observes things. Moreover, it takes notice of the principles of things. Now the Buddhists hold that there is another point of view from which the mind may be observed. Besides my mind, there is another mind which can observe my mind. But the question arises: Is mind one or two? Is mind host or guest? Is mind the commander or the receiver of commands? Shall we not busy ourselves with these questions in order to find the correct answer?"[40]

Again, continued Chu Hsi, a searcher after the truth asked: "What is the meaning of the words of our sages: 'proficiency', 'When you keep it, it stays', 'realize the mind', and 'know the nature'?" The master replied: "The words of our sages and the way of Buddhists seem as much alike as the red and purple violet. But this needs clarification. The so-called mind of man is the motive of desire. The subtle mind of *tao* is the interior of the heavenly reason. The mind, to be sure, is one; but it has two names, according to whether it is on the right or the wrong track. When it possessess 'proficiency' and 'unity' it is on the right track, and it pays no heed to deviation. Such a mind can obliterate distinctions and go back to the primal unity. Such a mind achieves the proper mean, without deficiency and without excess. However (Chu Hsi continued), this is not to say that the mind of *tao* is one, that the mind of man is a second one, and that a third mind exists which unifies the other two in a condition of 'proficiency' and 'unity.'

"The words 'when you keep it, it stays' do not mean that what you keep will stay. Nor do the other words, 'When you lose it, it is gone' mean that what you lost is gone. Rather, the meaning is that all depends on the mind. When the mind keeps *itself*, what was lost will be there. But when the mind loses itself, what stayed there will be gone. The word 'keep' implies that the conscience, which knows righteousness, is part and parcel of yourself. Thus, the signification of knowing the mind is utterly different from that of the Buddhists, who meant by "Knowing the mind" conciousness of the light of feeling, and awareness of the innermost consciousness. The Buddhists sought an isolated light in the recesses of the mind, which was not at all the same as what Confucius wished to 'keep' and to have 'stay.' " [41]

In this controversy two different conceptions of mind come to view. What the Buddhists called mind was the innermost consciousness only, which has nothing to do with the external world. The assumption of the Neo-Confucianists, on the other hand, was that man on the transcendental level is endowed with principles called *ri*, which enable him instinctively to know love, sense of duty, decency and wisdom. On the natural level, thus, mind can feel, understand, and discriminate between right and wrong. The Buddhists' innermost consciousness, of course, exists as part of the natural mind. But this natural mind is under the control of human nature, namely, *ri.* The Sung philosophers' theory of essential nature is very much like the Indian concept of *Citta*-purity. Yet the Sung philosophers transformed the "mind-only" theory by placing mind on the high level of *ri,* so that mind is considered to be bound by *ri,* and is not regarded as pure consciousness, which would be free of the necessity of discriminating.

From these two conceptions of mind issued the doctrine of nature *qua* reason, which Chinese philosophers used as a shield to defend themselves against the Indian spear, to which, according to the Buddhist boast, nothing was impervious. Let me summarize, at this point, an essay on "Stimulation and Tranquillity according to the Chapter on Music by Chu Hsi where the terms "nature", "emotion" and "mind" are explained. "According to the chapter on music", said Chu Hsi, "in the *Li Chi (Book of Rites),* 'Man is born in a state of calmness. This is his nature from heaven. When man is stimulated and moved by external things, this is desire arising from nature'. In these lines is a discussion of the subtle quality of nature and emotion, which have the same origin as life itself. When man is born with the proper means conferred on him by heaven, he is perfect, equipped with all kinds of *ri.* But this is prior to the stage when he becomes subject to stimulation, and is part of the state of nature. Besides his nature, a man has a physical body. Since he has a body and a mind, he cannot help but receive sensations from the external world. Having sensations he is moved, and his desires begin to work. Then he faces the problem of choosing between good and evil. Out of these desires comes emotion. When an object is presented he knows what it is, and he reacts by liking or disliking it. Sensation belongs to the operations of the mind; liking and disliking, to the emotions. When liking and disliking are under control, the reins are in the hands of nature. When liking and disliking are not under control, the emotions will burst forth like a flood." [42]

The quotations from Chu Hsi which I have summarized should make it plain that the point of view from which the Neo-Confucianists studied mind was that of moral values and of the transcendental. Sensation, feeling, willing and knowing on the natural level were taken as of secondary importance only. But now, since we have studied mind in the light of this transcendental meaning, I should like to direct our attention for a few moments to a consideration of the logical functions of mind.

Among the writings of Chu Hsi, though there were none exclusively devoted to logic as a special study in the sense of Aristotle's *Organon* there was throughout, a strict and lively sense of the values of definition. Chu Hsi attached great importance to definition. It is known that he weighed every word before he wrote it down, and that he made strenuous efforts to determine the precise meaning of every word in a text. Following is a list of several of his definitions:

1. *Tao* is a way or a course which all things follow. Also, it is what is approved by all men.

2. *Tao* is *ri*. What is followed by everyone is called the way *(tao)*. As a principle exhibited in each individual thing, it is called *ri*.

3. *Ming* is the decree of heaven.

4. *Hsing* (Nature) is *ri* (reason).

5. What is decreed by heaven is called *ming*. What a man receives from heaven is nature. Both are identical with *ri*.

6. Human nature is that with which a man is endowed by heaven. It is perfect, containing no evil. Human nature is *ri* of mind.

7. Mind is the master or determining factor of the body. Mind is the intelligence of man, and in mind are contained the principles of form and the responses to what comes from without.

8. Conscience is essentially tne mind of goodness.

9. Mind is the consciousness of man. It is his master and provides his responses.

10. Emotion is the eruption of the mind.

11. Purpose is the direction of the mind.

12. Will is the decision of the mind.

13. Knowledge is what one knows about the principles of events and things.

14. Truth is what is real. In relation to *tao* it is the actual *ri*. In relation to man it is the real mind.

15. Proper mean signifies no inclination to either side.

16. Harmony is the blending of what one does with the occasion.

Many other terms, such as substance, reality, essence, function and application appeared in Chu Hsi's writings, but he gave no definitions of them. The great difference between Chu Hsi and Aristotle is that the former wrote no *Organon*. The reason is that after Mo-tzu, who was the only Chinese philosopher to write about logic, no Chinese ever had any more interest in the subject. Yet in the controversies which Chu Hsi carried on with Lu Chiu-yüan, Ch'en Liang and many others, hardly a sentence occurs in which there is not reference to one logical principle or another, such as definition, law of contradiction, universals or particulars, inductive or deductive method, or line of demarcation between the metaphysical and physical spheres. Otherwise, of course, there could have been no such thing as a theoretical debate. Though Chu Hsi wrote nothing explicit about logic, there can be no doubt that he was a logical thinker. His philosophy, based on the unity of reason and the plurality of manifestations, was a logically thought-out system.

In concluding this section, a few words concerning Chu Hsi's method of personal cultivation are in order. He applied Ch'eng I's dual way, realization of knowledge and spiritual nurturing, to himself. His wide interest in various fields of knowledge was proof of his application of the first of these two ways. His daily life, as described in his biography by Huang Kan, where many allusions to his ability to concentrate are given, is a proof of his application of the second of Ch'eng I's courses. Chu Hsi knew how to combine the two ways into a unity. Realization of knowledge, he pointed out, depends upon concentration of mind. In concentration of mind the two fields, knowledge and spiritual nurturing, become one.

CRITICISM OF BUDDHISM, AND WORK
ON THE CONFUCIAN CLASSICS

Between the national character of the Indians and that of the Chinese there is a world of difference. One expresses itself in preoccupation with religion or a future world; the other, in an interest in this world or ethics. One is speculative, the other practical. The Indian negates human life, the Chinese affirms it. Though the two are thus temperamentally opposite, Indian Buddhism was well received in China when first introduced, because the Chinese found in it a new experience to which they had hitherto been strangers. This part of Buddhism the Chinese have retained to the present day; but the other part, which dealt with human life, suffered a heavy assault under Han Yü of the T'ang Dynasty. In the Sung Dynasty, the dominant form of Buddhism was that of the Ch'an school. The philosophers of the period realized that merely to attack it was not the best way to curb the spread of that religion. Instead they tried to evolve a better system, one which would appeal to the people and which could be substituted for Buddhism. Both Ch'eng I and Chu Hsi concentrated their efforts on this, in the hope that the people might be won back from Buddhism to Confucianism. There were those who doubted that it was possible to detach the Chinese from a religion which had dominated them for many centuries. Nevertheless, during and after the Sung Dynasty, the decline of Buddhism became a reality.

Chu Hsi's observations of the course of the spread of Buddhism are found in the following words: "Buddhism was introduced in the reign of Ming-ti of the Han Dynasty. Prince Ying of Ch'u devoted himself to it, but understanding was deficient. In the time of the Chin and Southern Sung Dynasties, (one of the dynasties in the period when China was divided into North and South) the doctrines of Buddhism spread far and wide. Those who were interested in the new religion first made use of the terms familiar to Lao-tzu and Chuang-tzu. The best example is Hui Yüan's expression of Buddhist ideas in the language of these philosophers. When Bodhidharma came to China between 516 and 534, the other schools seemed to have waned. His new method of teaching Buddhism was to concentrate on the mind without using a text-book. During these periods Confucianism was never studied and was forgotten. The superficiality of the school of Lao-tzu gave Bodhidharma a great opportunity to spread his teaching. He talked in such a clever way that nobody could compete with him. The intelligentsia were fascinated by him. I have seen many portraits of the patriarchs of the Ch'an school and they seem to be truly extraordinary personalities."[43]

This description of the spread of Buddhism is quite accurate. But it does not mean that Chu Hsi was willing to endorse it. In fact, he did all he could to show to the people that these foreign ideas were hollow and that the important thing was to return to their own spiritual heritage.

What Chu Hsi and the Sung philosophers used as their weapon to fight Buddhism was the theory of *ri* (reason). The Buddhists called attention to pure consciousness, which they maintained was the only vital thing. The Confucianists, on the contrary, said that besides mind with its capacities of feeling and knowing, there is a level of transcendence, in which are to be found the cardinal virtues, of love, righteousness, decency and wisdom. These virtues are forms of mind which operate for the realization of *ri*. This Confucianist conception of mind, which was at variance with the Buddhist insistence on maintaining purity of consciousness, was based on the existence of *ri*. Chu Hsi's reply was: "*Ri* is a reality of which the Buddhists are ignorant." [44]

When asked: "Why is Buddhism wrong from the beginning?" Chu Hsi replied: "What is decreed by heaven is nature. This is the belief of the Confucianists. But the Buddhists say: 'Essence or reality is emptiness.' What we call reality is regarded by them as emptiness. This is the great difference between the Confucianists and the Buddhists. What we Confucianists regard as real, they deny." [45]

Another difference between the Confucianists and the Buddhists was that the latter confused mind with nature. This clash of ideas is expressed in the following dialogue between Chu Hsi and Hsü Tzu-jung. Hsü inquired: "Has a dried herb nature, or has it no nature?" Chu Hsi commented: "As long as a thing exists, the principle of its existence, or *ri*, exists. What is wrong with you is that you confuse the conscious mind with nature. This is a mistake of the Buddhists. They have tried to clean the mind and make it as bright as possible. Their effort is like peeling skins, one after another, from bamboo shoots until nothing more is left to peel off. They conceive of mind as a bright mirror. This brilliant tiny spot they call nature or reality. But it is mere consciousness, mere mind, and has nothing to do with nature." [46]

Such was the weapon which the Sung philosophers used to pull down the thousand-year-old mansion of the Buddhists. As we consider these debates today, it will seem to us that the Chinese philosophers then confused Buddhism as a religion with Confucianism as a system of moral ideas. This confusion may have been unavoidable, because Buddhism was a religion based upon a thorough-going theoretical system. But from our modern point of view we find no difficulty in separating the two universes of religion and ethics. There is after all a boundary line between them. There is no reason why Buddhism as a religion and Confucianism as an ethical system cannot co-exist side by side each other, without being opposed to each other.

Apart from his attacks on Buddhism, the major work of Chu Hsi expressed itself in his attempt to give new vitality to the Confucian tradition. Of his conversations consisting of 140 books, 72 were concerned with this discussion of the Confucian classics. Again, of these 72 books 50 dealt with the *Four Books*. These figures show that his time and effort were largely devoted to an elucidation of the Confucian classics. It was also the most effective way to present his own philosophy. By analogy we might imagine that Kant, with the desire of creating a tradition of his own, had commented on the works of Plato and Aristotle, giving to them an original sense of his own. This is exactly what Chu Hsi did with the writings of the Confucianists.

In his preface to *A Collection of Comments* on the Book of Poetry we read: "Someone asked me: 'Why was the Book of Poetry written?' My answer was: A man is born in calmness. This is his nature, conferred on him by heaven. When a man, attracted by the external world, has sensations, this is what is known as the operation of nature. When he is affected, he begins to think and to express himself in language. What cannot be exhausted in plain language goes into songs of joy and expressions of sorrow, with rhyme and rhythm. This is why the *Book of Poetry* was written.

"Then a second question was raised: 'What is the lesson conveyed by the *Book of Poetry?*' My explanation was that poetry is the expression of the emotions in rhythmical language. The emotions sometimes may be morally right and sometimes morally wrong, so that what is expressed may be either right or wrong. According to the sage-emperors, the emotions were rightly expressed if their language could be used for purposes of teaching. Even if the emotions became violent, their expression might be pedagogically useful as a warning; rulers could apply them to reflection; and measures might thereby be suggested.

"In the period of prosperity under the Chou Dynasty the songs that were sung at the sacrifices in the Temple of Heaven and at the ceremonies in court, all the way down to the ditties that were sung at village gatherings, were written in rhythmical language expressing moral sentiments, and were circulated among the people in many lands. This was part of the work of popular cultivation. Poems recited among the feudal kingdoms were also collected by the emperor on hunting trips or trips of inspection, for purposes of exhibition, and he gave prizes to the authors to show his approval. After the reign of King Chao and King Mu, the Chou Dynasty deteriorated, and the capital was removed to the east. These awards to the poets were then stopped. This was the age when Confucius lived. Although he could not exercise the power of reward or punishment, he could at least collect all these poems, edit and rearrange them, eliminating all repetition and retaining what was worth preserving. This was the work of simplification which has made the *Book of Poetry* immortal. Thus, scholars can now study the poems using them as models, and improve themselves on the basis of what is taught in them in matters of good and evil. Though Confucius could do nothing that an emperor can, yet his teaching has been handed down from generation to generation for thousands of years. This is the lesson conveyed by the *Book of Poetry*."[47]

In this preface Chu Hsi discussed his own philosophy and thus gave to the *Book of Poetry* a moral twist.

Since the Ming Dynasty, Chu Hsi's commentaries on the *Four Books* have been texts for all boys to read, in much the same sense as the Bible is read by Christian children. The *Four Books* was fertile ground for the elaboration of Sung Philosophy, and it was so used. The *Ta-hsüeh,* one of the *Four Books,* contained a scheme of eight items for instance which were in substantial agreement with the system of the Neo-Confucianists. Its "investigation of things" and "realization of knowledge" were necessary steps in the search for moral and natural law in the phenomenal world. Its "rectification of mind" and "making will true" bore an affinity to the Sung idea of keeping the mind calm and on the right track. The remaining items, from "personal cultivation" down to "peace in the world," all fell within the sphere of Sung philosophical inquiry. Man as an individual, as a member of a family and as a citizen of a state, should develop moral qualities in order to achieve his greatest happiness. Because of this agreement between the *Ta-hsüeh* and the teaching of the Neo-Confucianists, Chu Hsi considered it as perhaps the most important of the *Four Books.*

In the *Chung-yung,* another of the *Four Books,* the Sung philosophers found the Confucian concepts of heavenly order, human nature, *Tao,* teaching, truth and enlightenment. Indeed, the term "proper" or "golden mean", common to Aristotle and the Chinese Confucianists, came from this treatise. If the *Ta-hsüeh* listed the definite steps for moral development, the *Chung-yung* contained the loftiest principles of metaphysics of the ancient period.

Still another of the *Four Books,* the *Lun-yu,* was acknowledged by Chu Hsi to be a discussion of the moral life by concrete examples by way of aphorisms. It consists of answers to questions raised by the pupils of Confucius, and hence was not intended as a systematic study of ethics or philosophy.

The fourth of the *Four Books,* the *Meng-tzu,* was the work of a man who lived in the period of the Contending States when power-politics dominated. In this book Mencius fought against the advocates of war and diplomacy and stressed moral values as their counter-proposals. His theory of the goodness of human nature and his principle of taking Yao and Shun as the archetypes of the philosopher-king marked him out as being on a higher level of existence than the diplomats and strategists competing for power. Mencius in fact fought for what Jesus wanted when he said: "For what is a man profited, if he shall gain the whole world and lose his own soul?"

In conclusion, what is Chu Hsi's position as a philosopher? If we consider the thinkers of the world, whether of the East or of the West, I have no hesitation in saying that Chu Hsi belongs to the greatest: His position is that of Plato and Aristotle in the Greek period, or of Descartes, Leibnitz and Kant in the modern age. He evolved a mighty system, his mind was remarkably acute, his analytical powers were exceedingly keen, his thirst for knowledge was insatiable, and his understanding was comprehensive. His system was built upon a firm grasp of empirical details which, however difficult or elusive, never escaped him. Yet his thought was never scattered. Rather it operated with a focal point bringing all departments of knowledge into an impressive unity. For this reason it is difficult to classify him. Chu Hsi is neither a monist nor a dualist; neither a Platonist, nor an Aristotelian.

He cannot be called a monist if for no other reason than his repeated use of the formula: "What is metaphysical is *Tao,* what is physical is *ch'i,*" is suggestive of a strong dualistic position. The phenomenal world he believed to be a combination of *Tao* and *Ch'i.* This as well as many other evidences show that he is not monistic. Yet Chu Hsi maintains that if we trace back far enough we must come to the conclusion that *ri* is prior to *Ch'i.* Thus he believes in the unity of spirit or soul.

Should I then say that Chu Hsi is a Platonist because of his belief in the priority of *ri?* No, for the reason that for him this belief is no more than mere supposition. He never applied it in his discussions of the noumenal or intelligible world. If Chu Hsi cannot be considered a dualist nor a Platonist in the monistic sense, what then is his most appropriate label? The term by which to designate him is perhaps the Indian philosophical name: advaitist. Since he neither inclines unambiguously towards monism nor stops short at dualism, he seems to be for a nuance between monism and dualism, which corresponds to advaitism, in the Chinese sense rather than in that of the school of Sankaya.

The result of all this is that it becomes difficult to call Chu Hsi a Platonist, or to identify his *ri* with the Platonic ideas. No doubt he believed in the existence of *ri,* which is complete in itself, unchangeable and everlasting; but we cannot attribute to him the doctrine that Ideas are archetypes. The parable of the three beds — the bed of God, the bed of the carpenter and the bed of a painter — is beyond the comprehension of Chu Hsi. He would have agreed that there is a principle or reason for the bed, which would have been the law of its constitution. But this principle or reason would have borne more kinship to the laws of nature in physics and chemistry than to the Platonic ideas. This is why I object to Fung Yu-lan's identification of *ri* with these Platonic ideas.

If Chu Hsi does not suggest the basic position of Plato, he is certainly no neo-realist either, another serious mistake made by Fung Yu-lan. If Chu Hsi recalls realism, it is certainly realism of the Aristotelian kind. Chu Hsi studied the phenomenal world as it is, that is from the point of view of *ch'i,* yet he never forgot the important existence of a final cause, which he named the Supreme Ultimate, and which Aristotle called God. For Chu Hsi "each particular thing possesses a *ri,* and the many kinds of *ri* coalesce into the unity of *ri.*"[49] This is the basis of Chu Hsi's interpretation of the one and the many. There were two aspects to his system: the oneness of reason, and the manifoldness of phenomenal manifestation. Both of these aspects were firmly based on common sense — not on mysticism. The equal importance which he attached to these two phases is the reason why he is not merely a Platonist or an Aristotelian, but a combination of both. He is an exception to the Western dictum that every philosopher must be either a Platonist or an Aristotelian.

References

1. Sung-shih (History of the Sung Dynasty), Chapter 429, Chu Hsi.
2. Legge, Vol. 2, *The Works of Mencius,* Book 4, Part 2, Chapter 32.
3. *Sung-shih,* Chapter 429, Chu Hsi.
4. Wang Mou-hung, *Chu-tzu nien-p'u* (Chu Hsi's Chronology).
5. *Chu-tzu yu-lui,* Book 94, about Chou Tun-i.
6. *Ibid.,* Book 6, Section on Hsing (Human nature) and Ri.
7. *Loc. cit.*
8. *Loc. cit.* Book 1, Section on Ri and Ch'i.
9. *Loc. cit.*
10. *Loc. cit.*

11. *Loc. cit.*
12. *Ibid.*, Book 1, the first question and answer.
13. *Loc. cit.*
14. *Loc. cit.*
15. *Ibid.*, Book 1.
16. *Ibid.*, Book 1.
17. *Ibid.*, Book 1, the first question and answer.
18. *Ibid.*, Book 94.
19. *Ibid.*, Book 1.
20. *Ibid.*, Book 4, Section on Hsing (Human nature) and Ri.
21. *Loc. cit.*
22. Aristotle, *De Partibus Animalium*, I, 5.
23. *Chu-tzu yu-lui* (Dialogues of Chu Hsi), Book 4, Section on Hsing (Human nature) and Ri.
24. *Ibid.*, Book 4.
25. *Loc. cit.*
26. *Loc. cit.*
27. *Loc. cit.*
28. *Loc. cit.*
29. *Loc. cit.*
30. *Loc. cit.*
31. *Loc. cit.*
32. *Loc. cit.*
33. *Loc. cit.*
34. *Loc. cit.*
35. *Loc. cit.*
36. *Loc. cit.*
37. *Loc. cit.*
38. *Loc. cit.*
39. *Chu-tzu wen-chi* (Collected Essays of Chu Hsi), Book 11, in Cheng-i t'ang ch'uan-shu.
40. *Ibid.*, Book 13.
41. *Loc. cit.*
42. *Loc. cit.*
43. *Chu-tzu yu-lui* (Dialogues of Chu Hsi), Book 126, about Buddhism.
44. *Loc. cit.*
45. *Loc. cit.*
46. *Loc. cit.*
47. *Chu-tzu wen-chi* (Collected Essays of Chu Hsi), Book 7.
48. *Chu-tzu yu-lui* (Dialogues of Chu Hsi), Book 94.
49. *Loc. cit.*

CHAPTER THIRTEEN

The Debate Between
Chu Hsi and Lu Chiu-yüan

Having discussed if Chu Hsi can be considered a Platonist or an Aristotelian, the conclusion was he is both at the same time. In the present chapter we shall confine ourselves to another issue, that of rationalism *versus* empiricism, or in Chinese phraseology, whether mind is complete in itself and innate or whether it comes from without. This question was discussed by Chu Hsi and Lu Chiu-yüan, leaders of two schools of thought known respectively as the Ch'eng-Chu and the Lu-Wang schools (Wang refers to Wang Shou-jen). The diversity of opinion, on the matter, from the time of its inscription with Chu Hsi and Lu Chiu-yüan, was so wide, especially when Wang Shou-jen joined the discussion, that it became a full-fledged controversy at the end of the Ming and in the early days of the Ch'ing Dynasty.

The issue may be likened to the conflict between rationalism and empiricism in European thought. As in the West the empiricists believed that mankind is a *tabula rasa* and that knowledge is formed by sensations and impressions, so the followers of the Ch'eng-Chu school emphasized the importance of the acquisition of knowledge. Similarly, as with the rationalists in the West, who held that man is born with innate ideas upon which all judgments of science and ethics are based, the Lu-Wang school argued for the innateness of human understanding.

Let me begin then by sketching the life and character of Lu Chiu-yüan. He was born in the ninth year of Shao-hsing during the reign of Kao-tsung of the Southern Sung Dynasty, that is in 1132 A.D. He was thus a contemporary of Chu Hsi, but nine years his junior. As a child he was very serious and took no part in play. It is said that one day to the surprise of his father he asked: "Where is the limit of heaven and earth?"[1] When he was eight, reading the *Lun-yü*, he asked another question: "Why are the words of Yu-tzu (a disciple of Confucius) so complicated, as compared with the simple and direct language of Confucius?"[2]

When Lu Chiu-yüan was thirteen years old, it is said he came across two characters *Yü* and *Chou*, which his teacher explained meant respectively the four directions together with "up" and "down" and the past and the present. The boy commented that the two characters were really an exact definition of the universe, and that man, whose nature is infinite, lives in an infinite universe. He then took up his brush and wrote the following words:

"What concerns the universe concerns me: it is my duty.
What concerns me concerns the universe.
The universe is my mind; my mind is the universe.
A sage born in the eastern sea has the same mind and the same reason;
A sage born in the western sea has the same mind and the same reason;
A sage born in the northern or southern sea has the same mind and the same reason;
Going back to the sages who were born thousands of generations ago, and forward to the sages who will be born thousands of generations hence, one finds the same reason."[3]

At sixteen Lu Chiu-yüan practiced archery and horsemanship, because he wanted to fight the barbarians who had conquered northern China. At twenty-four he obtained what was equivalent to the M. A. degree, and in the following year his father died. He was married at twenty-nine. In the eighth year of Ch'ien-tao (A.D. 1172) he attended the state examination for the *Chin-shih* degree.

Among the examiners was Lü Tsu-ch'ien or Lü Po-kung, a friend of Chu Hsi, who when he read the papers recognized at once the unquestioned talent of the candidate who turned out to be Lu Chiu-yüan. All the names were under seal.

With this success, Lu Chiu-yüan became so well-known in the capital that many young men came to study under him. One of his disciples, Yang Chien, asked him the question: "What is the original mind?" Lu answered by quoting from the *Meng-tzu.* "Commiseration is the beginning of *Jen;* the sense of shame is the beginning of righteousness; modesty is the beginning of the sense of decency; approval and disapproval are the beginning of wisdom and knowledge. All these point to the original mind; they are your mind." But Yang Chien was still puzzled and said: "I have known these words since boyhood, but still I do not understand the nature of mind."

Yang Chien was then serving as the assistant to a magistrate and had occasion to give judgment on the sale of a fan. On issuing the verdict, he approached Lu Chiu-yüan once more with the same question. The master then replied: "When you gave your verdict, you made the distinction between right and wrong, because your mind knew it. This knowing mind is your original mind."[5] From then on Yang Chien was convinced that the mind is omniscient.

In 1175, Lü Tsu-ch'ien made arrangements that his brother Lu Chiu-yüan meet Chu Hsi at Goose Lake in Kiangsi Province, in order to effect a reconciliation of their philosophic views. (This meeting will be discussed later.) In 1181, Lu called upon Chu Hsi, who was at the time prefect in Nan-k'ang, and was invited to give a lecture at the White Deer Grotto Academy.

Lu was appointed professor at the government academy when he was 46 and became concurrently reviser in the Bureau of Government Orders. Five years later he was, like Chu Hsi, transferred to the position as supervisor of a temple. Such a position meant retirement from the government service, and opportunity to carry on his private studies. It was then that the correspondence began between him and Chu Hsi about the *Diagram of the Supreme Ultimate.*

During his retirement, Lu Chiu-yüan had ample time to devote to his disciples. He was also asked to write and make his views better known.

It was then that he said: "The *Six Classics* are my footnotes; and I am the footnote to the *Six Classics*."[7] This was a very bold remark. When asked to explain himself, he said that knowledge of *Tao* meant the amplification of *Tao* inherent in one's nature. There is thus no reason why the *Six Classics* should be considered as supreme authorities or as anything more than footnotes to one's self. It is on this point that Lu differs so widely from Chu Hsi, for Chu Hsi thought so highly of the Classics that he spent all his life writing commentaries about them. But Lu gave priority to *Tao* and the self and assigned the classics to a subordinate position.

After Kuang-tsung ascended the throne Lu Chiu-yüan was appointed Commissioner of Military Affairs in Ching-men. When he assumed office he made the announcement that all military or civilian personnel could bring any case to him any time they wished. There were to be no office hours. In cases involving family relations he asked both sides to destroy their papers; such matters should be solved through reconciliation, and not by strictly legal means. He meted out punishment only to those who refused to accept his reasonable recommendations. Lu had remarkable insight into the character of people and of the civil servants under him — whom he knew to be either good or corrupt. A case involving theft was brought before him. No one could be sure of the culprit. Lu Chiu-yüan gave two names to the police and had the persons named arrested. When they were brought into his presence they confessed they were the thieves and returned the articles they had stolen. He let them go free on condition they would reform themselves. Indeed, Lu Chiu-yüan's knowledge of human character was so profound that the people considered him uncanny. He enforced the tithing militia system everywhere, and that was a very effective way to clear the land of thefts and robberies. Ching-men being on the border of Hupeh Province, he decided that a city wall should be built in the interests of safety. He enlisted the services of a few thousand workmen, and completed the wall in twenty days. He went personally to inspect the work and impressed upon the people that they should be thankful of the labor. With the construction of the city wall trade and business increased, and Ching-men became a prosperous town. Within two years of his duties as commissioner he was able to write to a friend and say that law suits had been reduced in the district to only two or three a month, and that robbers, who previously had abounded, were now no more. He died in 1192 in his fifty-fourth year.

In turning to Lu Chiu-yüan's philosophical ideas two Chinese philosophical concepts are indispensable in any study of this thinker. In the book *Chung-yung* is a remark which points the approach to philosophy: "Supremacy of virtue and search for knowledge." When this book was written, these two "ways" were probably understood to be combined, and as combined they were the road of approach to philosophy. But during the controversy between Lu Chiu-yüan and Chu Hsi the remark was cut in two: the first half was tagged on to Lu Chiu-yüan who held that human nature possesses innate ideas for doing good, and the second half was applied to Chu Hsi who considered seeking knowledge as the chief approach to *Tao*. On this matter Lu Chiu-yüan had this to say in a letter to Tseng Chai-chih:

"Reason is a natural gift from heaven; it is not imparted from outside. Reason is the master. As long as the master is there, nothing can seduce you, and no false theory can bring you to a state of uncertainty. On the other hand, if reason is not so bright, there will be no master. The result is that one is likely to become extravagant in his theories, and will depend more on such external sources as books than on one's own mind which should be the master. The natural gift from heaven will then become a guest. Thus, the host is turned into a guest, and the guest into a host: the positions of host and guest will be reversed. Those who trust such external sources as books lead themselves into confusion. So simple and obvious a truth, which is clear to any woman or boy, is not understood by scholars. They entangled themselves in all kinds of elaborate systems. What a pity that they bury themselves in vain theorizing — The true *Tao* has disappeared, and false theories have taken over, so that scholars have fallen into a pit...

"Later commentators on the *I-ching* regarded this book as so subtle and profound that very few dared discuss it. But the sages have already made these observations:

'The creative knows through the easy;
The receptive does things through the simple.
What is easy, is easy to know;
What is simple, is simple to follow.
He who is easy to know, wins allegiance
He who is easy to follow, attains results
He who has allegiance can endure for long.
He who accomplishes results can become great.
To endure is the disposition of the sage.
Greatness is the field of action of the sage.
By means of the easy and simple we grasp the laws of the
    whole world. When the laws of the whole world are
    grasped, then there is perfection.' "

Here a Chinese philosopher pleads for simplicity. He believed that the least complicated and the simplest method is the true method. If one goes about in a round-about way, that is if one seeks more and more knowledge rather than directly applies one's mind, one goes off in the wrong direction. This attitude of Lu Chiu-yüan's is basically different from that of Chu Hsi.

Another statement of Lu is worth quoting: "Mencius said: '*Tao* is like a highway. How can it be difficult to understand?' Confucius said: 'Is *Jen* so far from us? If I devote myself to *Jen, Jen* is there.' Again Confucius said: 'When one day you can control yourself and go back to the principles of decency, the whole world will follow the course of *Jen*.' Mencius said: '*Tao* is near, but the people seek it in a distant place; the matter is easy, but the people make it difficult.' Mencius said: 'If a man can give full development to the feeling which makes him shrink from injuring others, his sense of *Jen* will be more than can be put into practice. If he can give full development to the feeling which refuses to steal, his sense of righteousness will be more than can be put into practice.' Mencius said: 'Men have these four principles just as they have their four limbs. When men, having these four principles, say that they cannot develop them, they play the thief with themselves, and he who says of his prince that he cannot develop them plays the thief with his prince.' Mencius said: 'To say that I am unable to dwell in *Jen* and pursue the path of *I*, is what we mean by throwing one's self away.' "

Lu Chiu-yüan's comment on this passage of Mencius was: "All these words of the former sages agree with each other. As there is the same mind or the same reason, so also there is but one essence or way of mind or reason." Then he proceeded again to try to confirm his theory by reference to Confucius and Mencius. "Confucius said", he remarked, " 'My *Tao* is a pervading unity.' Mencius said: '*Tao* is one and only one.' '*Tao* consists of two courses: one is *Jen* and the other is its opposite, *Non-Jen*.'

"What is called love of parents comes from reason; what is called respect for the elder brother comes from the same source. The sense of commiseration aroused at the time of seeing a child fall into a well comes from reason. The sense of shame aroused at the sight of something disgraceful comes from the same reason. The sense of disapproval aroused by seeing things which cannot be endured comes from the same reason. The right and our knowledge of the right; the wrong and our knowledge of the wrong; and the sense of distinguishing between what is right and what is wrong, all come from the same reason."

When Lu Chiu-yüan arrived at the ultimate stronghold of rationalism, namely, conscience or innate knowledge, he again resorted to Mencius: "The ability possessed by men", he commented, "without having been acquired by learning, is innate ability, and the knowledge possessed by them without the exercise of thought is their innate knowledge." Innate ability and innate knowledge, in other words, are a gift from heaven, so that they are already in one without ever having been acquired from without. "This was why," Lu continued, "Mencius said: 'All things are already complete in us. There is no greater happiness than to be conscious of one's self in a state of truth, when one indulges in self-examination.' "

In the course of his letter to Tseng Chai-chih, Lu referred to a message he had sent to Chu Hsi. "In my letter to Chu Hsi", he said, "I told him that the people in ancient times were more sub-

stantial and less clever. Before words came deeds. What was
knowable they said was knowable; what was unknowable they said
was unknowable — Words meant deeds; deeds meant words. Words
were coordinated by deeds; deeds were coordinated by words.
With the decline of the Chou Dynasty, literary discussion dominated. The facts were buried beneath words and opinions. Discussions became diffused. The world of scholarship was full of
artificiality, plagiarism, bias and prejudice. This is why even
Tzu-kung, as a disciple of Confucius, believed that his master
attained *Tao* by reading widely and by memorizing."[8]

The allusion to Tzu-kung's words is highly significant, because
Lu Chiu-yüan expressed his disapproval of Chu Hsi's way of approach to *Tao,* the way *via* knowledge-seeking. Lu Chiu-yüan's
own philosophy is based upon three principles:

(1) *To establish what is fundamental or great, which principle he learned from Mencius.* This principle consists in the
recognition of the supremacy of mind and in the elimination of the
desires of the senses. Lu Chiu-yüan agreed with Mencius that if
one submitted one's self to the authority of the mind one would
be able to find the right way for one's self, because one would be
complete in one's self.

(2) *To eliminate desire.* Though a man is complete in himself, yet he is often obscured or beclouded. Why? Because he is
excited by sensation, desire and passion, or because he becomes
one-sided as a result of his likes, prejudices and personal opinions.
In substantiation of this second principle, the following quotation
from Mencius appealed to Lu: The master said "To nourish
the mind there is nothing better than to reduce your desire to as
little as possible. Here is a man whose desires are reduced: the cases
in which the absence of mind occurs will be very limited. Here
is a man whose desires are many: the cases in which the presence
of mind can be kept will be greatly limited."[10] Lu also followed
closely the idea of nourishing the mind, expressed in Mencius'
famous story of the Niu Mountain. The trees of Niu Mountain
were once very plentiful. Being situated on the borders of a large
state, they were cut down with axes and hatchets; could they then
retain their beauty? Still through the activity of the life force day

and night, and the nourishing influence of the rain and dew, they were not without buds and sproutings which continued to spring forth, but then came the cattle and the goats which grazed upon them. It was because of these things that one noted the bare and stripped appearance of the mountain. When people now see it, they think it was never thickly wooded. But is this the nature of the mountain? So also with regard to what properly belongs to man; shall it be said that the mind of any man was without *Jen* and *I*? The way in which a man loses his proper goodness of mind, is like the way in which the trees are denuded by axes and hatchets. Hewn day after day, can it (the mind) retain its beauty? But there is a development of its life day and night, and in the calm air of the morning, just between night and day, the mind feels in a degree those desires and aversions which are proper to humanity, but the feeling is not strong, and it is fettered and destroyed by what takes place during the day. The fettering taking place again and again, the restorative influence of the night is not sufficient to preserve the proper goodness of the mind; and when this proves insufficient for that purpose, the nature becomes not much different from that of the irrational animals, and when the people now see it, they think it never had those endowments. But does this condition represent the feelings proper to humanity? Therefore, if it receive its proper nourishment, there is nothing which will not grow; if it lose its proper nourishment, there is nothing which will not decay."[11]

(3) *Not to consider knowledge-seeking as fundamentally important.* Lu Chiu-yüan was convinced of the supremacy of mind, and basing his belief on this conviction, he deprecated the view that mind should increase its power by seeking more knowledge.

He believed that one could approach *Tao* by restoring the purity and brightness of the mind, and not by seeking more knowledge. In a letter to Hu Chi-sui, Lu wrote: "There is a way of attainment of truth in one's self: — if a man does not know what is good, he will not attain truth in himself. Now-a-days nobody makes efforts to be clear about what is good and to know what is right. Yet by reading and learning one tries to accumulate nonessentials. One's entire life is then buried in literary work. It is just as if one, intending to climb to the top of a mountain, falls into a valley; the farther one goes, the more remote one is from the mountain summit. Or it is just as if one, desiring to go to Kwangtung, betakes one's self instead to north China. The farther one travels, the more distance one is from one's destination. Such a man makes a mistake with his very first step. He may inquire, during his journey, about the way, and he may calculate distances, but he is lost in the valley, or bound for north China."[12]

Lu was strong in his belief that a man is complete in himself, and is under no necessity to seek knowledge from the outside; thus his oft quoted words: "What kind of books did Yao and Shun study?" The meaning is that the former Sages, who lived in a primitive period, perfected themselves without having books to read. This is a way of saying that true knowledge is created by the human mind itself.

These three points which we have discussed are the framework of Lu's philosophy, and it is in these that Lu differed from Chu Hsi. Further, Chu Hsi explained the nature of mind by positing two levels, while Lu Chiu-yüan expounded the nature of mind on the basis of one level only.

It will be recalled that in the chapters on the Ch'eng brothers and on Chu Hsi, the one level of mind was explained by the formula: "*Hsing* is *ri*", that is, "Human nature is reason", and that at this level the four virtues were inborn: *Jen, I, Li* and *Chih*. Then there was the other level the work of which was merely to be conscious. A man knows what is right and what is wrong because he operates at the upper level; whereas his knowledge of what is white and what is black, or of this and that, is the work of mind *qua* consciousness. As a result of this theory of two levels, the Ch'eng and Chu schools drew a line between the metaphysical and physical worlds, and between the mind of *Tao* and the mind of man.

Lu Chiu-yüan, on the contrary, drew no such distinction between the two worlds or between the mind of *Tao* and the mind of man, because for him such a demarcation would have been superfluous, since the mind was one and indivisible. Against the formula of Chu Hsi, Lu Chiu-yüan said: "Mind is *ri* (reason)". When he was asked: "What is the difference between *Hsing* (nature) *hsin* (mind), and *Ch'ing* (emotions)?" Lu answered: "This naming will only lead to unnecessary differentiation. It comes, to be sure, from general opinion, and you are not to be blamed. People now-a-days are exceedingly careful about the meanings of terms, but they forget what is most vital namely, that *Hsing, Hsin* and *Ch'ing* stand for the same thing, and differ only verbally. If you insist upon a differentiation between them, you may express yourself in the following way: When heaven is concerned, it is called nature (*Hsing*); when man is concerned, it is called mind (*Hsin*). I merely follow your way of naming. There is no necessity of expressing yourself in this manner."[14]

Thus, from the point of view of Lu Chiu-yüan this problem of the distinction between nature, mind, *etc.*, was a problem merely of nomenclature. But as a matter of fact something far more fundamental was involved. Chu Hsi did not deny that mind brings the four cardinal virtues to expression, but he thought that these virtues exist at a high level of mind, that is, at the level of human nature, whereas mind as an organ of consciousness exists at a lower, namely, natural level.

Lu Chiu-yüan went farther to deny the difference between the mind of *Tao* and the mind of man. His argument ran as follows: "The distinction between heavenly reason and human desire is not, in principle, quite correct. If heaven is reason and man is desire, then heaven and man will be fundamentally different in nature. The *Book of History* says: 'The mind of man is dangerous; the mind of *Tao* is subtle.' 'Mind of man' has been interpreted by many people as human desire, and 'mind of *Tao*' as heavenly reason. With this interpretation I do not agree, because mind is one only, and cannot be divided into two."[15]

We may go a step farther by saying that Lu Chiu-yüan denied the line drawn between the metaphysical and the physical. He said: "What is metaphysical is called *Tao* (infinite), what is physical is call *Chi,* utensils (finite). Even heaven and earth are utensils, that is, physical. But the growth, protection, shaping and sustaining of things must have reason."[16]

Lu Chiu-yüan's insistence upon reducing the two worlds to one explains his opposition to Chu Hsi's explanation of the *Di-*

agram of the Supreme Ultimate, because while Chu's cosmology began with Nothingness, Lu's cosmology began with Being.

Characteristic of Lu Chiu-yüan was that, as an idealist, he attached much importance to mind, but denied the existence of a higher level of *Tao,* forms or ideas.

Two European terms distinguish the doctrines of Lu and Chu: Lu recognized that the mind operates at one level only, namely, the "natural" level; Chu appreciated that besides the natural level there is also a "transcendental" level where reason operates. Ch'eng-Chu's theory of two levels reminds one of Kant's doctrine of sense material and form of sensibility, according to which the matter of phenomena is given to us by the empirical world, while its form must be *a priori* in the mind, and must be capable of being considered by itself apart from sensations.

One level was sufficient for Lu Chiu-yüan because he thought that mind knew well enough what is right and what is wrong, and there was no use in introducing an upper level. This reduction of the two levels to one, however, did not bring Lu near the position of the European empiricists who also work at one level, but rather it drew him towards the Fichte-like idealists for whose *Ego* Lu Chiu-yüan's *mind* was substitute.

Because of Lu Chiu-yüan's rejection of the two-level theory and his attachment of greatest importance to mind, he was criticized by Ch'en Shun, a disciple of Chu Hsi, who said: "Lu Chiu-yüan teaches his pupils to devote themselves to meditation in order to keep the mind to themselves. There is no work to be done in the line of reading, debating, or research. Lu's way is rather simple and direct, so the younger generation is attracted by him. It is not wrong for one to keep one's mind to one's self. However, mind according to Lu consists of sensitivity, responsiveness and consciousness, and this is the best part of man. If mind in its nature consists merely in sensitivity, responsiveness and consciousness, then its function is indistinguishable from what can be done by the animals, because they also know the way of self-preservation by seeking safety and avoiding danger. This is what is called by Shun 'the mind of man', but not 'the mind of *Tao*'. Lu mixes the two, thus committing the same error as Kao-tzu [a philosopher who argued with Mencius] who maintained that nature is born in man [*i.e.*, nature at a natural, not a transcendental level]. The error is also similar to that of the Buddhists who hold that any sentient being partakes of Buddhahood; or to that of the Ch'an followers, who believe that water-carrying and woodcutting are a part of meditation. This same confusion, in the thought of Yang Chien, results in a mixture of mind with human nature, and of the physical with the metaphysical. Yang Chien supposes that *T'ien, Tao,* or *Te,* though differing in name, are the same thing. This mixing or confusing indicates that the school of Lu neglects the step of investigation of things, or of knowledge-seeking. In other words, it keeps a weighing machine without marks on it, or a measuring-stick without division of inches."[17]

It was in 1175, when Chu Hsi was in his forty-sixth year and Lu Chiu-yüan in his thirty-seventh that their meeting took place. Besides the two philosophers and Lü Tsu-ch'ien, there were Lu Chiu-ling (also a brother of philosopher Lu), Ch'en Liang, and three others who were interested in philosophy. The purpose of the meeting was to find a basis for reconciliation between the opinions of the two schools. Chu Hsi's way of approaching *Tao* was to read widely, and then to go back to the essential. The Lu brothers believed that a student of philosophy should concern himself with the original mind first, and then later branch out to wide reading. Chu thought that Lu's approach was over-simplified, while Lu criticized Chu for being too scattered and distracted. However, they were willing to meet to settle their differences. On the first day of the assembly, Lu Chiu-ling who was on the side of his philosophical brother, argued with Chu Hsi, and immediately afterwards Chu was allowed to defend himself. The next morning Lu Chiu-ling brought the following verses:

"A child knows how to love and also to respect others as it
    grows
The mind is handed down by the sages.
When there is such a foundation, one can build a house
    on it.
One never hears that many-storied house
Can be put up without a foundation.

Too much interest in commentaries leads one to a thorny
    path.
Too much attention to questions of detail and to subtleties,
Causes one to lose oneself in the sea.
The friends assembled here are enjoying great pleasure at
    the present moment."

After reading these lines Chu Hsi commented: "It is beautifully written, but I find that the second line (referring to mind)
is not quite right." Then he and his companions started to walk
towards Goose Lake. Whereupon, Lu Chiu-yüan produced a few
more verses in the same rhyme as the preceding one by his brother:

"Passing graveyards, one shows sorrow,
Passing an ancestral temple, one shows respect.
This is the mind of mankind, which is unchangeable.
One drop after another of water will grow into a mighty
    ocean,
One handful after another of stones will pile up into a
    high mountain.
What is simple can end in greatness.
What is scattered can only float on the surface.
In order to find the way from the low to the high
One should distinguish between the true and the false
    at this moment."

With these lines Chu Hsi was again displeased. But the conference lasted for another two days. Then the philosophers dispersed. Lü Tsu-ch'ien, who promoted the meeting, only listened
without saying much. It was not for three years that Chu Hsi wrote
something in reply to the verses of the Lu brothers.

"I appreciate your devotion to the work of virtue very
    much,
Even more so after three years of separation.
Helping myself along with a cane I walked out of the
    Valley,
And found that you had come by sedan chair from another
    mountain.

We exchanged views about the study with which we were
  occupied,
And went to the depths to discover how new knowledge
  could be improved.
What worries me is the question of silence [meditation].
I doubt that there is a difference of opinion between
  ancient and modern days."[18]

These three compositions show how deep-rooted was the divergence of belief between the two sides. This does not mean,
however, that the philosophers were unfriendly towards each other.
The differences of opinion were exaggerated by the pupils of the
two schools, so that eventually an erroneous impression was created
that the philosophers themselves were enemies. Actually, Chu
Hsi's letters sometimes express great appreciation of Lu's method
of appealing directly to the mind, and he was even willing to
admit that sometimes he stressed the literary side too much.

In 1181 Lu Chiu-yüan called on Chu Hsi, who was at the time
prefect of Nan-k'ang. During a trip on a nearby lake, the latter
philosopher said: "Since the beginning of the world there have
been water and mountains; but where could the coming together
of two such friends as we have been found?"

Then Chu made a request to deliver a lecture to the students
of White Deer Grotto Academy on the text:

"Confucius said: 'What a man of noble character knows is
  righteousness.
What a mean fellow knows is profit.' "

Lu Chiu-yüan commented as follows: "In this chapter the
distinguishing marks of a man of noble character and a mean
fellow are righteousness and profit respectively. The meaning is
very clear, but readers who cannot reflect upon themselves when
they apply the standard, will not be benefitted. When I read the
chapter myself I was much moved. The key to its understanding
lies in how one makes up one's mind. A man's understanding is
a product of what he has become accustomed to, and what he has
become accustomed to is a product of how he had made his mind
up, or in what direction his mind works. If one's mind is directed

to righteousness, one's thoughts and actions will necessarily be righteousness. Familiarity with righteousness will lead to an understanding of righteousness. But if, on the other hand, one makes up one's mind to gain profit, one's thoughts and actions will be in the direction of profit. Naturally therefore one will understand only profit. This shows the importance of how one makes up one's mind.

"The state examination as an institution for selecting people has existed for a long time. Most well-known scholars and statesmen have been successful candidates at this examination. A student who wants to find a career must submit himself to it. Whether one is successful or fails depends largely upon one's skill and on the likes and dislikes of the examiners. Whether a man is a noble character or a petty fellow has nothing to do with the examination.

"Yet students look at the state examination as something to which they aspire. Very few can regard it with contempt. What they read is superficially the books of the sages; but what they aspire to is entirely different from what the sages said. Furthermore, once they have succeeded in their careers, what they talk about is whether their grades were high, medium or low, and the amount of their salaries. The policy of the government and the welfare of the people they do not take seriously to their hearts. After joining the administration they will acquire much experience, and become experts. They will, of course, have a kind of understanding, but it will be irrelevant to righteousness.

"Students who perceive that this is not the right attitude for a man, and who make efforts to avoid falling in with mean fellows, must repent and exert themselves strenuously in behalf of righteousness. They must read widely, inquire carefully, think thoroughly, analyse clearly, and practice seriously. If they really have a comprehension of righteousness when they enter the examination hall, they will be able to write on their papers what they have learned and what they have determined to do, and they will not deviate from the ways of the sages. Even as they move along in their civil service career, they will discharge their duties and do their appointed tasks well. In their hearts they will cherish and remember that their obligation is to their country and to the

people, and not for personal advancement. Conducting themselves thus, they will naturally be considered men of noble
character."[19]

After Lu Chiu-yüan had delivered this lecture, Chu Hsi expressed his thanks by saying that it touched the hearts of all the
people, and that he Chu himself could not go to such depths.
Then he asked Lu to write it down so that it could be inscribed on
stone.

From this lecture one can draw the conclusion that Chu and
Lu were most friendly. In 1187 there began the correspondence
between them concerning the Supreme Ultimate, which lasted for
several years. The main points of this controversy have already
been dealt with in my chapter on Chou Tun-i, and will not be
repeated here. The fundamental difference between them was that
Lu Chiu-yüan was not interested in the problem of the absolute,
in the process of creation, and in metaphysical speculation in general. In spite of all Chu's efforts to convert him, he was never
convinced. Nevertheless, the disagreement at first had only to do
with the specific problem of the *Diagram of the Supreme Ultimate,*
and Chu Hsi did his best to remain on friendly terms with Lu Chiu-
yüan as a philosopher. But from 1185 Chu began to attack Lu
in letters, openly and continuously for ten years. The trouble
started with an epitaph which Chu had been asked to write for the
tombstone of Ts'ao Li-chih, and in which he had said: "Knowledge of *Tao* cannot be attained by sudden conversion. It proceeds
step by step from the rudimentary to the profound, and from the
near to the remote."[20] The significance of this passage is that it
implies that knowledge-seeking is a necessary condition for the
attainment of *Tao.* And then in his private letters, Chu often
calls Lu a believer in Ch'an Buddhism insinuating that the latter
philosopher had learned the way of sudden conversion from that
sect. Lu Chiu-yüan did, indeed, learn much from the Ch'an Buddhists in his early years, including perhaps the idea that sudden
enlightenment can lead one to perfection. Yang Chien's conversion to Lu's doctrine of the original mind is evidence of this.

And yet basically Lu Chiu-yüan was a Confucianist in his
views and had nothing to do with Buddhism. In a letter to Wang
Shun-po Lu very severely castigates Buddhism. He says:

"Using the motives of selfishness and public spiritedness as criteria, I tried to distinguish between Confucianism and Buddhism. According to Confucianism, a man born into this world is a *Homo sapiens,* and is the noblest among all things and animals. He is co-ordinated with heaven and earth, constituting a trio. In heaven there is the *Tao* of heaven; on earth, the *Tao* of earth; and a man lives the *Tao* of man. As long as a man fails to perform his proper functions, he is not equal to heaven and earth. A man has his five senses, and each sense has its own function. Humanity is gifted with its own sense of right and wrong, of gain and loss. The so-called work of education and culture is based upon man's proper nature. The motive of Confucianism, therefore, is for the common good, and Confucianism is public spirited. But Buddhism thinks the other way. It holds that humanity is tied up with the chain of life and death, with soul-transmigration, and with all sorts of suffering. These are painful things, and mankind should try to be free of them. Those who are relatively enlightened grasp the point that there is no question of life and death, of soul-transmigration, or of suffering. The vows of the Bodhisattvas inform us that these divine beings labor ceaselessly for perfection. But though this is the starting point of Buddhism, the aim is to be freed from the trammels of pain, so that the motive is one's own benefit, and hence the motive is selfish. Since Confucianism is public-spirited it affirms life while Buddhism is selfish and negates life. Even Confucionists reach a stage which is incorporeal, spaceless, inaudible and ineffable, yet their attitude towards life is always affirmative. The Buddhists, on the other hand, aim at endless work of deliverance. Because Buddhists are also men, they cannot throw away the moral values which Confucianists hold as being so important. Though they relinquish family life, they try in their prayers to return the four kinds of benefits that they received. They cannot give up completely the values of life, so they have to pay attention to life, too. But they consider the values of life to be of secondary importance, and thus do not take them as the basis of their reasoning. Confucianists, on the contrary, consider moral worth to be what distinguishes man from the animals. Men of noble character, therefore, do their utmost to keep it despite the fact that there are mean individuals who forget it. Buddhists deplore being tied up with the chains of life and death. One who is not free of these fetters is considered by them as being one who floats in the ocean of life and death. But, I do not see that the sages of the Confucianist school ever floated on the ocean of life and death. What the Buddhists deplore has no relevance to our sages. The Buddhists do not grieve for the mistakes of the Confucianists, but the Confucianists sorrow over the errors of the Buddhists. Therefore, the characterization of one as selfish and of the other as public-spirited provides the distinction between Confucianism and Buddhism."[21]

This letter, of course, is clear enough evidence that Lu Chiu-yüan was no Buddhist in the general sense.

But the question arises: Was Lu a Ch'an believer in thought? Even though the charge that he was a Buddhist has been refuted, the fact remains that Lu was attracted to the concept of the original mind. In my opinion Lu may be called a believer in Ch'an thought only in the methodological sense. He lived at a time while the Ch'an school flourished, and this school did regard book-reading, intellectual pursuits and erudition, as being unessential, concentrating on inner realization and sudden awakening for the attainment of truth. Lu could not help but be attracted and influenced by these ideas. He forsook the negative attitude towards life of the Ch'an school but kept their method of seeking the original mind. Methodologically he applied their technique by calling the mind directly to attention in the interests of moral perfection, and also for the sake of the cause of Confucianism. In this sense I am inclined to agree with Chu Hsi's verdict that Lu Chiu-yüan was a Ch'an follower. But I must enter the proviso that the application of this method of mental hygiene has nothing to do with Buddhism in general, nor with Ch'an thought as such.

The collected works of Lu Chiu-yüan were published in the Ming Dynasty in 1561, by Wang Toung-mu, High Commissioner of the Treasury in Kiangsi Province. His foreword to the collected works is a defense of Lu, asserting that the philosopher was not a Ch'an believer, in spite of his attachment to mind and his depreciation of knowledge-seeking.

There are I think, three ways to judge Lu's work: (1) to attack him because he was wrong; (2) to reconcile him with Chu

Hsi by denying that there was any real contradiction between them (3) to praise him as the pioneer of the School of Mind.

(1) As we have seen, the first to attack Lu openly was Chu Hsi himself, whose position was that the sages never asked the people to meditate, and that it was better for them to read widely, inquire carefully, think deliberately, analyse clearly and practice earnestly. A man is endowed with reason, but that reason is easily beclouded by physical nature and selfish desires; and the only sure path to salvation lies through knowledge-seeking. A man who relies completely on the energy of his own mind falls into the error of the schools of Lao-tzu and the Buddha, who held that emptiness is the goal, and moral values not worth cultivating.

(2) Those who have judged Lu by trying to reconcile him with Chu are well represented by Hsü Chieh[22] (1503-1583) of the Ming Dynasty. His position was that supremacy of virtue and knowledge-seeking should form a unity. The supremacy of virtue is the goal to the attainment of which knowledge-seeking should be applied. Knowledge seeking is the way of attaining the supremacy of virtue. For apart from the supremacy of virtue, to what else can knowledge be applied? These two aspects, therefore, should be knit together into an indissoluble union. Hsü Chieh's conclusion was that both ways lead to sagehood. Though Lu Chiu-yüan emphasized the supremacy of virtue, he never forgot knowledge-seeking, and though Chu Hsi stressed knowledge-seeking his ultimate goal was, after all, the supremacy of virtue. There should, thus, be no basic contradiction between these two philosophers.

(3) The representative of the third school of judging Lu was Wang Shou-jen, who considered himself as Lu's legitimate successor. His appreciation of the older philosopher may be found in his preface to Lu's collected works:

"The science of sagehood is the science of mind. What was tranmitted from Yao and Shun to Yü lay in the words: 'The mind of man is full of danger: the mind of *Tao* is subtle. Be proficient and unitive. Hold the mean firmly.' This was the source of the science of mind. What was called 'the mean' was the mind of *Tao*. When the mind of *Tao* exists, in its proficiency and unity, it is *Jen*, which is also the mean. The work of Confucius and Mencius was to devote the self to *Jen*, which in turn was derived from the transmitted message about proficiency and unity. In later ages there grew up the belief that the object of one's seeking should be on the outside rather than the inside. Therefore, even a disciple of Confucius, Tzu-kung, thought that the work of his master consisted of wide reading and memorizing, and that *Jen* became a matter of giving more alms to more people. Tzu-kung's mistake was corrected by Confucius in his remark that what he sought was a pervading unity, and that the exercise of *Jen* should begin with one's self. The meaning of this remark was simply that endeavor should begin with one's own mind. In Mencius' days, Mo-tzu understood *Jen* to consist, as it were, in rubbing the entire body smooth, from the crown to the heel, in an effort to confer benefits on the whole kingdom. At this same time, Kao-tzu supposed that *Jen* was on the inside, while *I* (righteousness) was on the outside. The science of mind became completely deteriorated. It was Mencius who refuted the theory of the externality of *I*. Mencius insisted that the work of the philosopher should be to seek the mind which has gone astray. Again he said that *Jen, I, Li,* and *Chih* were not derived from the outside, but were innate. With the decline of the 'royal way', power-politics prevailed. The utilitarians disguised their objectives under the name of heavenly reason, but what they actually sought was their self-interest. The so-called reason was just a name to deceive the people. As long as they did not consider mind as the source, where could reason find a place to stay? Since then, mind and reason have become separated, so that the effort toward proficiency and unity was lost. Many philosophers went off along devious ways, and became interested in the various aspects of life such as knowledge, terms, numbers, and institutions. That was how the so-called 'investigation of things' originated. What such philosophers did not know was that mind *is* reason, and that neither mind nor reason can be found in the external world.

"Subsequently, when the doctrines of Buddha and Lao-tzu gained the upper hand, devotees of these schools espoused the theory of emptiness. They overlooked human relationships and the principles of the phenomenal world. Yet their aim was the enlightenment of the mind. But mind is correlated with knowledge of the world. When knowledge of the world is overlooked, how can one find one's mind?

"In the Sung Dynasty Chou Tun-i and the Ch'eng brothers traced their thought back to its source in Confucius and Mencius. Chou drafted the *Diagram of the Supreme Ultimate*, and established the human standard in *Jen, I, Chung* and *Cheng* (rectitude). He also formulated the doctrine of calmness. Ch'eng Hao advocated the theory of tranquillity. Since then, the tradition of proficiency and unity was restored. Then Lu Chiu-yüan was born in the Southern Sung Dynasty. Though Lu's character with respect to peaceful-mindedness was not the equal of that of Chou Tun-i or of either of the Ch'eng brothers, yet the simplicity and directness of his method made him a successor to Mencius. His daring arguments were the result of his temperament, but his belief in the supremacy of mind was identical with that of Mencius. Therefore, I say that the philosophy of Lu Chiu-yüan is the philosophy of Mencius.

"Many people disliked Lu Chiu-yüan because of his difference of opinion with Chu Hsi. The former philosopher was condemned as a follower of Ch'an, as a Buddhist who disregarded human relationships and the principles of the phenomenal world, and whose attitude towards life, therefore, was negative. If the doctrine of Lu Chiu-yüan had really been negative, then it would have been justly condemned as of the Ch'an school. But the works of the Ch'an school and of Lu Chiu-yüan are still in existence, and it is easy to compare the one with the other. Similarity and difference between them may be readily seen by anyone who looks, without having to spend much effort in research.

"Nevertheless, the label of being a Ch'an, having once been started, was believed by many people. The situation resembled that in which a dwarf, lost in a crowd around a stage, is unable to understand all the laughing and crying. The unfortunate dwarf represents the critic who believes what he hears without seeing with his own eyes, or one who knows the meaning of the letter without understanding the significance of the spirit.

"In this world much approval and disapproval, similarity and difference, derive themselves from subjective and habitual ways of thinking, which even the learned cannot avoid.

"The prefect, Li Mao-yüan, has asked me to write a preface for the collected works of Lu Chiu-yüan. What can I add to the words of Lu? If those who read these collected works can reflect in their own minds and abandon their habitual ways of thinking, they will find out whether rice is good or bad according to whether it is finely or coarsely ground."[23]

The affinity of Wang Shou-jen to Lu Chiu-yüan is clearly revealed in this preface. That is why these two thinkers have been combined to form one school, called the Lu-Wang school, or the School of Mind. It created a great stir in the Chinese philosophical world after Chu Hsi.

To me it appears that there was a natural tendency for the doctrine of the two levels of mind (*i.e.*, Transcendental Reason and mere consciousness) to dissolve into the conception of a synthesis of the mind. This natural tendency explains why the Lu-Wang school gained ascendancy over the Ch'eng-Chu school.

References

1. Lu chiu-yuan, *Collected Works*, Book 36.
2. *Loc. cit.*
3. *Loc. cit.*
4. *Loc. cit.*
5. *Loc. cit.*
6. *Loc. cit.*
7. *Ibid.*, Book 34.
8. *Ibid.*, Book 1.
9. *Meng-tzu*, Book 6, Part 1, Chapter 15.
10. *Ibid.*, Book 7, Part 2, Chapter 35.
11. *Ibid.*, Book 6, Part 1, Chapter 8.
12. Lu Chiu-yuan, *Collected Works*, Book 1.
13. *Ibid.*, Book 1, First letter.
14. *Ibid.*, Book 35.
15. *Ibid.*, Book 34.
16. *Ibid.*, Book 35.
17. *P.R.S.Y.*, Book 58.
18. *Ibid.*, Book 57.
19. *Ibid.*, Book 58.
20. *Chu-tzu wen-chi* (Collected Essays of Chu Hsi), Book 18, (in *Cheng-i-t'ang Collectanea*),
21. Lu Chiu-yuan, *Collected Works*, Book 2.
22. *Ibid.*, Book 1, beginning (Hsu Chieh's preface to the *Collected Works*).
23. Wang Shou-jen, *Collected Works of Wang Yang-ming*, Book 7.

CHAPTER FOURTEEN

The Debate Between
Chu Hsi and Ch'en Liang

In this chapter we shall pursue further the subject of Chu Hsi's relation to another controversy, and see how much of an ethical rigorist he was. Though Lu Chiu-yüan and he were both Confucianists, Chu Hsi was against Lu because Lu was opposed to the idea that the correct approach to *Tao* lies in knowledge-seeking. Like Mencius, who attacked Mo Ti and Yang Chu in his day, Chu Hsi took a militant attitude towards all those whose views differed from his own. When he fought Lu he used as his pretext that Lu was a follower of the Ch'an sect; and when he fought Ch'en Liang the charge was utilitarianism.

Utilitarianism as understood here is an ethical and political theory. It takes the view that thought must begin with the given data of human nature in general, including desires, tendencies to avoid pain, preferences for pleasure, ambition to strive for achievement, etc. It maintains also that this realistic attitude towards life is the only rational view and that we should be reconciled to the idea that realization of what is morally right, of what is idealistic, is too much to expect of a human being. This utilitarian attitude was espoused by Ch'en Liang in his ethical and political thinking, and it was this which Chu Hsi took strong exception to. There was a long and bitter debate between the two philosophers.

Before I go into the subject I should like to explain the two terms "rational" and "real", as understood by Hegel in his *Rechts-*

philisophie: "Whatever is rational is real, and whatever is real is rational." Or, as he says elsewhere: "The insight to which .... philosophy is to lead us is that the real world is as it ought to be."

Out of the juxtaposition of these two terms a number of philosophical schools have emerged in the West. Those who are inclined towards the rational, the metaphysical, or the Platonic, believe that an ideal pattern is realizable on this earth. Those who do not believe in the existence of metaphysical ideas, and who are inclined towards what is, or what is actual, are satisfied to confine themselves to what is possible within the limits of human nature. Between these two major views there is a considerable gap which has never been bridged except by Hegel. He tried to show that the real unfolding of human history is the development of spirit or reason, and elaborated a gigantic system of logical idealism which has exercised vast influence in Europe. When he came to the subject of the state, he called it an expression of "real will" or "objective mind". He idealized the Prussian state, which was the embodiment of militarism and his exaltation of the state as having a personality of its own, over and above the personality of the individuals which compose it, made him the target of a severe attack by Hobhouse in England and by John Dewey in the United States.

Is the state an expression of the spiritual life of a community, or is it an instrument for the satisfaction of individual desire? This has always been a question. It puzzled the Greeks in the ancient world, it perplexes modern Europe, and it has been a problem of Chinese political philosophy.

The first school to emphasize the "rational" expected that moral rightness would prevail. Plato himself was the creator of an ideal state, but he knew that the actual falls short of the ideal. For the practical life of mankind is motivated by selfish interest, which is always a great distance from the ideal. Plato said: "Until philosophers are kings, or the kings and princes of this world have the spirit and power of philosophers, and political greatness and wisdom meet in one, and the commoner natures who pursue either to the exclusion of the other are compelled to stand aside, cities will never have rest from their evils — no, nor the human race, I believe — and then only will this our state have a possibility of life and behold the light of day."[1]

This Greek version of the philosopher-king has its counterpart in the Chinese story of the legendary emperors Yao and Shun who were known in China as those who possessed all qualities of courage, wisdom and temperance. In their time the state was supposed to be perfectly governed. The ideal state, in other words, was once actually realized. The later period, under Yü, T'ang, Wen and Wu, was also considered an age when the state was well governed. More so perhaps than Plato, the Chinese did not believe that an ideal pattern of life was something impossible of realization. And they proceeded to explain how, at least in the legendary period, the real and the ideal were in perfect harmony. When Yao and Shun ruled the great *Tao* prevailed. But in the post-Chou dynasties, it was human desire which prevailed, and there followed an interregnum when the great *Tao* ceased to function. Such was, in China, the traditional way of looking at the development of human history. But this view was contested by Ch'en Liang in the Southern Sung Dynasty, when the Chinese mind began again to become active and skeptical. Ch'en Liang asked: "If human history operates with a rational mind, the ideal pattern of life should proceed continuously. Why was the period of Yao and Shun considered the only perfectly governed era, and the post-Chou age regarded as much inferior to the time of Yao and Shun?" There was another question he raised: "If the development of human history is rational, why did the rational mind suddenly disappear in the post-Chou period?" These speculations remind one of Hegel's theory of the "bad state",[2] which according to him, was not a real state, or which was, a very poor example of rational life in politics. What Hegel called a "bad" or unreal state was named by Chu Hsi a period of the "vacancy of *Tao*."

Ch'en Liang was not a Confucianist in the usual sense of Sung philosophy. He was an ambitious man who aspired to restore the Sung Dynasty to its former glory. He is not an important thinker, though he is mentioned in the *Philosophical Records of the Sung and Yüan Dynasties,* and his position in Chinese thought has come largely because of his debate with Chu Hsi.

Ch'en Liang was born in A.D. 1143 and died in 1194. He was interested in literature, and his prose and verse are truly beautiful. His song in memory of Li T'ai-pai can even today lift one's soul to lofty heights in an appreciation of the great poet. He believed himself, in regard to practical statesmanship, to be the peer of Chu-Ko Liang, the prime minister under Liu Pei, founder of the Shu-Han Dynasty, and it was for this reason that he called himself Liang.

At nineteen he wrote an essay entitled *Evaluation of the Ancients,* in which he reviewed the historical past. In 1169 he sent five essays on revitalizing the government to the emperor. But they were shelved without being taken seriously. A few years later he began to teach a group of students who came to study under him. Then in 1175 he attended the conference at Goose Lake discussed in the previous chapter. When, three years later, he again attempted to present a memorial to the emperor about revitalizing the government there seemed to be promise of success. Emperor Hsiao-tsung was so moved by the document that he proposed that it be hung on the walls of the Court as a reminder to ministers. He also proposed that the author be appointed to a responsible position. The ministers, however, disapproved of Ch'en Liang's frank talk, and did everything to prevent the emperor from meeting him. Eventually he received an invitation to an examination. But he did not have the fortune to be taken into government service. When offered a relatively minor position, he remarked: "What I want to do is to carry out a policy!" The opportunity was denied him.

Though on intimate terms with each other, Ch'en Liang and Chu Hsi did not hold the same views. Their friendship can be seen on the inscription which Ch'en made on Chu Hsi's portrait:

"In physical expression you have the pure air of Yang — you show courage.
In emotions you show your joy and anger in the right way.
The ecstasies which you betray in your facial expressions and bodily movements I do not understand;
In your quiet and contemplative life your sorrows I do not know.

You are one who cannot be kept in a fishing boat
   (that is, in a hermitage);
Also you are one who cannot be put into court.
You will wait for the decree of heaven in a world which
   was created a thousand years ago."[3]

This poem shows Ch'en Liang's appreciation of Chu Hsi. But between 1184 and 1186 the philosophical debate began to be violent, and in 1190 Ch'en wrote the following polemic against the scholars of Sung philosophy.

"In recent years there has arisen a philosophy which has as its subject for discussion such topics as *Tao*, virtue, human nature, heavenly decree. Only those who are good-for-nothing belong to this school. They appear earnest, silent and profound; they walk slowly and their speech is careful. They behave as if they were subtle and mysterious, but that is only to disguise their being good-for-nothing. They do not consider knowledge and skill as a worthy part of the *Tao* of the sages. Thus all the scholars have lost what they should know. Since they delight in discussing mind and human nature, they are ashamed to be expert in literature. Since those who are officials prefer to talk about devotion to *Tao*, they forget the nature of government service and clerical work. They deceive themselves with their talk, and are unmindful of the real and the practical."[4]

Ch'en Liang won his *chin-shih* degree when he was fifty-one, and died the following year.

There was one odd circumstance in the life of this philosopher which I have not yet mentioned. This was that he (and his father) had the misfortune to be jailed frequently. It seemed as if they were the victims of ill-luck. The philosopher himself was incarcerated three times. The first time was on the occasion of a murder-case involving his father (1171). The second time was when he, himself, was suspected of murder after a banquet given in his honor by the village alderman, at which pepper was served as a speciality, but where one of the guests died. Ch'en Liang was jailed, but subsequently released by imperial pardon. The third arrest was in 1191, when the philosopher was forty-nine years old.

The reason is not clearly specified in his biography, but it probably had to do with a quarrel with some of his fellow villagers.

The best characterization of Ch'en Liang may be found in his own words: "Philosophers can be familiar with subtle questions of principle and moral value, and can analyze the identity and difference of thoughts in ancient and modern times. They can introspect and disentangle fundamental causes in a minute way. They accumulate a vast amount of what they learn, and they can express their spirituality in their facial features and bodily movements. In these matters I must confess that I am no match for them. But when there is a discussion about political or military emergencies — whether the weather promises wind, rain, clouds, or lightening in a great storm; or when there is a situation where dragons, snakes, tigers and leopards jump and howl before you at once; at such times, if a man is wanted who can make all giants look like dwarfs, or whose bosom is full of the materials of the past thousands of years, then my humble self may be able to render a bit of service."[5]

The meaning of this passage is that in Ch'en Liang's own opinion the scholarly or contemplative life was not for him. What he aimed at was to be a general or statesman.

Before we go into the debate between Ch'en Liang and Chu Hsi there is one more point which needs to be cleared up. This concerns the line drawn between the physical and the metaphysical world. According to Chu Hsi and the Ch'eng brothers, a line of demarcation exists between the metaphysical (what is above form) and the physical realms. The physical is what is manifested in the phenomenal world, and what is above the phenomenal world is the realm of the metaphysical. The Neo-Confucianists, though they were rationalists, did not study the phenomenal world through human institutions as "objective spirit", in the manner of Hegel. There is an interesting similarity between Ch'en Liang and Hegel in the fact that both held reality to exist at one level. Nevertheless, this similarity does not run deep, for what each meant by the "one level" was different. For Hegel, the "one level" at which reality exists was the level of rationality. Human institutions are mere reflections of this objective mind. Hegel was metaphysically an idealist. But for Ch'en Liang and his colleagues, on the other hand, who were partisans of the utilitarian school of east Chekiang province, the "one level" at which reality exists was the level of the physical, and whatever there is of the metaphysical exists within this physical. Ch'en Liang and his co-workers were realists. In Chinese terminology, *Tao* cannot be separated from *Ch'i* (implements or utensils), and *ch'i* is inseparable from *Tao*. The arguments of these Chinese utilitarians was that *Tao* can only be found within *Ch'i*. You can know neither *Tao* nor *ch'i* if you separate them.

As a result of this standpoint, Ch'en Liang and his colleagues were interested in the study of institutions, history and the various kinds of custom. While, in Hegelian terminology, these are all called "objective mind," Chinese philosophers confined themselves to what is visible and tangible. Such was the background of the debate between Ch'en Liang and Chu Hsi — a debate which centered around the questions of political philosophy and the development of Chinese history. On this latter subject, Ch'en wrote ten essays, five of which he sent to Chu Hsi.

Ch'en, in his interpretation of Chinese history, regarded the period of Yao and Shun as a rock founded upon the principles of righteousness and justice. Because of this wisdom the rule which these ideal emperors exercised over the world was very popular. Emperor Yu, fearing that elections, for reason of competition among the candidates, might cause disturbances in the country, sponsored hereditary rule. The overthrow of Emperor Chieh of the Yin Dynasty by T'ang, and of Emperor Chou by King Wu of the Chou Dynasty, were acts in accordance with the will of heaven and the will of the people. Ch'en condemned Ch'in Shih-huang's policy of violence and force which caused the downfall of a dynasty in a few years. On the other hand, he complimented the two important regimes of Han and T'ang. He considered Liu Pang, the founder of the Han dynasty, as being a person of outstanding worth and his opinion of the imperial Li family of the T'ang Dynasty was equally favorable. This family, with the intention of rescuing the people from their suffering, started the revolution against the Sui which resulted in the establishment of the T'ang. Li Shih-min's work for good government was admirable. Ch'en

Liang objected to condemnations of the Han and T'ang Dynasties by the later Confucianists in the following words:

"If the Han and T'ang Dynasties were unable to continue the rule of justice of the Three Dynasties of Hsia, Shang and Chou, how is it that they were able to keep the country in peace and order for three or four centuries? The criticism by the later Confucianists that Han and T'ang subjugated the land with a policy of cleverness and force is unfair. If this kind of critical view be not abandoned, the *Tao* of the sages will never shine, and the troubles in this world will never cease."[6]

When Chu Hsi read Ch'en Liang's five essays, he replied to them by saying that from his (Ch'en's) standpoint righteousness and utility go together, and that *wang* (government by benevolence) and *pa* (government by force) can co-exist. This critical remark was based upon Chu Hsi's philosophical distinction between purity and goodness in the metaphysical world and evil and imperfection in the physical realm.

Ch'en's first rebuttal was as follows: "After the discussion by Mencius and Hsün-tzu of righteousness and utility, *wang* and *pa*, these ideas were never understood by the scholars of the Han and T'ang Dynasties. In our present dynasty (the Sung) philosophers have made a fine distinction between heavenly reason and human desires and accordingly the concepts of *wang, pa,* righteousness and utility, have become clear and distinct. But the view of these (Sung) philosophers that Three Dynasties were governed by *Tao* while the the Han and T'ang were ruled by cleverness and force has never convinced anybody. The philosophers of our present dynasty have even gone further by saying that the Three Dynasties were under the rule of heavenly reason, and that the Han-T'ang dynasties were under the sway of human desires — even though certain measures in these latter two periods, because of chance coincidence with heavenly reason, happened to have kept the empire in peace and order. If this view be correct, the world for fifteen centuries has lived in a vacancy of *Tao,* and the popular mind has pursued its course in a house built of patchwork. But how can beings in such a world prosper, and how can the *Tao* be everlasting? The founders of the Han and T'ang Dynasties were able to carry on their work on a gigantic scale and broadminded basis, so that their government formed a sort of trinity with heaven and earth, and human affairs accordingly were peaceful. Naturally there were deficiencies. Ts'ao Ts'ao (usurper of the Han and founder of the Wei) was not equal to Han and T'ang, and his work was not brought to a successful conclusion. Here was a typical example of rule by human desires. But even Ts'ao Ts'ao achieved something, because there was à little bit of heavenly reason in what he did. Still the label of ruling by human desire may be justly applied to him and to other men of his class. If, however, the same label is attached to Han and T'ang, I believe that this is quite unfair.

"The ideal pattern of the Confucianist is righteousness and *wang*. The achievement of Han and T'ang is called utility and *pa*. The philosophers may discuss according to their own method but the founders of the Han and T'ang Dynasties performed and acted accordingly to their method. What was discussed may be good but what was *done* was also not bad. This interpretation may be considered as an assertion that righteousness and utility may after all go together, and that *wang* and *pa* can exist side by side.

"As far as my own view is concerned, the whole world exists at one level, and comes from one source. T'ang T'ai-tsung (Li Shih-min) did his work from the great heart of a hero. He even corrected his minor faults though they were as tiny as the seconds in a minute. The motive of his achievements was not *pa*. Rather, what he did, I believe, was the product of his correct attitude towards human relations. But in your letter, (Chu Hsi), you condemn his work as not having come from a noble source. Maybe you lay too much stress on his personality and not weigh his words with sufficient care."[7]

I want to call the reader's attention to the statement: "The whole world exists at one level, and comes from one source." This sentence makes plain that Ch'en Liang recognized only the real, and that he had no sympathy for the two-level theory (physical and metaphysical) of Chu Hsi.

Chu Hsi's reply to Ch'en's letter of rebuttal was as follows: "What is heavenly reason? What is human desire? It is not necessary to trace back to instances of *wang* and *pa* in history. You need only reflect on righteousness and utility, rectitude and deviation in yourself. If you engage in more careful self-examination, you will enlighten yourself. If you exemplify the virtues more commonly in your daily practice, you will improve your own determination. Mencius' discussion about the spirit of supremacy, *Hao jan chih ch'i* made him very mindful of the principles of moral value, and his aspiration to shoulder the responsibility of ameliorating the whole world was so determined that it could not have been merely the expression of his sentimentalism or emotion.

"You are highly appreciative of the work of Han Kao-tsu and T'ai-tsung. But you should examine their motives to find out whether their main interest was moral right or their own benefit, the principle of rectitude or something less respectable. In the case of Han Kao-tsu, to be sure, the selfish motive may not be so manifest; but still you cannot deny that it was there. As far as T'ang T'ai-tsung is concerned, his deeds were most certainly motivated by desire. His work, though done in the name of love and righteousness, was actually accomplished for his personal benefit. His rivals were inferior to him, being incapable even of dissembling love and righteousness, and hence T'ang was the fittest and able to achieve his aspirations. If his righteousness is justified merely on the grounds that he left the country in a long period of peace and order, this is to define righteousness in terms of success, which is the same as to pay compliments to a hunter for many kills, but to overlook his disregard for the rules of fair play. During those fifteen centuries there was really a vacancy of *Tao*. An era of small tranquility existed, but the *Tao* that was handed down by Yao and Shun to the emperors of the Hsia, Shang and Chou Dynasties, did not prevail in the world in that later age. The *Tao*, which is everlasting, has nothing to do with human intervention since it remains forever the same. Man may spoil it, but he cannot destroy it. The wisest kings of the Han and T'ang Dynasties never did the least bit to promote it. ... What I expect of you is that you should use your enthusiasm in appreciating the work of men who lived up to the standards of the Three Dynasties, and that you should not waste your time in defending the Han and T'ang Dynasties."[8]

Here is Ch'en Liang's second rebuttal to Chu Hsi. "During the period of the Three Emperors and the Five Kings the whole country lived peacefully. In the time of Yao the fundamental institutions were set up. After Yü and his son Ch'i, the hereditary principle of the imperial family was established. . . . King T'ang overthrew the tyrant Chieh and and the dynasty of Shang followed. After the overthrow of the tyrant Chou, the Chou dynasty took the place of Shang. Although the institutions of the Three Dynasties, Hsia, Shang and Chou, followed one another, they differed in their details. For the same reason the five *pa* differed among themselves. Lao-tzu and Chuang-tzu, deploring the endless fighting taking place, placed the responsibility on the kings of the Three Dynasties. Yao and Shun were lucky to have escaped their condemnation. If the periods of the Three Emperors and the Five Kings had succeeded one another in a peaceful way, the public would not have had so many opinions about the value of government. It was because of Confucius' lack of agreement with Lao-tzu and Chuang-tzu that he defended Yao and Shun and the rites of the Three Dynasties. The work of Confucius immortalized the Three Dynasties. If there had been no defense of the Three Dynasties by Confucius, the people might still believe in the sayings of Lao-tzu and Chuang-tzu. This condemnation by the Confucianists may be useful as long as the mentality of the founders of the Han and the T'ang is not sufficiently clear to all of us.

"The operations of the mind of mankind may be imperfect, but one cannot possibly say that the mind of mankind has permanently disappeared. The institutions which were created for the people may be incomplete, but one cannot assert that in the sense of Yao and Shun they are lost forever. Man, heaven and earth constitute a trinity, but one cannot possibly say that while heaven and earth rotate endlessly the work of man has ceased. If man cannot establish himself, how can heaven and earth proceed alone? Where may *Tao* be found, if heaven and earth are put aside? The statement that *Tao* does not exist because of Yao, and that *Tao* is not extinct because of Chieh (the tyrant of the Shang Dynasty) means that *Tao* can go on working even without the cooperation of man. If your remark that human intervention has nothing to do with whether *Tao* is present or lost has this sort of meaning, then the Buddhist way of abstention from activity is the right course to follow. If every man could be a Yao, the world a few ages hence would be full of Yaos, and *Tao* would be bright everywhere. Or otherwise, if everyone of us could be a Chieh, all mankind would be licentious, the world would be in confusion, and Tao would no longer exist. If the universe could proceed in the vacancy of *Tao*, or could live, as it were, in a house of patchwork, then mankind would have to be a lump of dead clay. If the mind of mankind could persist in a patched-up house, its existence then would resemble that of a half-living, half dead insect. Where might we find that *Tao* works ceaselessly?

"A sage is one who can fulfill all the duties within the realm of human relations, while other persons are not equal to fulfilling all the duties to which they are assigned. Nevertheless, what these latter persons succeed in accomplishing cannot be completely deceptive or disguised. The *wang* form of government may set up all institutions for the welfare of the people, whereas the *pa* form cannot set up all institutions for the welfare of the people, but yet what it *does* set up cannot be a complete infringement. Those who deceive the people, will also be deceived by others. Those who infringe upon the people will also be the objects of infringement. How can those who deceive and infringe upon the people preserve a country in peace and order for a long period? It is said in the *Book of Poetry*: 'There is no failure in managing the horses; the arrows are discharged surely like the blows of an ax!' Of course, a hunter should not disregard the rules in order to fill his bags; yet no one dislikes anybody for having a full bag. For the charioteer in his driving to keep to the rules, and for the arrow to reach its goal — this is the way the man of noble character hunts. Yet nobody has ever heard it said that one so careful with one's arrows prefers to bag no game at all. When the charioteer keeps to the rules and the archer knows very little about shooting, such hunting will net no bag even after a day's expedition. But if — when the archer does not shoot well — the charioteer manages by cleverness of driving to meet the game, even a mediocre hunter may accomplish ten kills in a day. In the former case, the driver kept to his rules and the archer bagged nothing because he did not know how to shoot. In the latter case, the archer did not shoot well, but the driver knew how to go after the game, and consequently several kills were made.

"The section in Book III, Part II, Chapter I of the *Book of Mencius*, dealing with this subject of hunting and abiding by the rules, has not been clearly understood for many years. It has been interpreted in too strict a sense, as if no bag should be made if making the bag involves violating the rules. I must say that my reason for appreciating the Han and the T'ang is not that Han and T'ang captured much game. But I wish to point out that the blame should be put on the charioteers in these two dynasties. Han Kao-tsu and T'ang T'ai-tsung belonged to the class of archers of noble character, but their charioteers were not men of complete integrity. Thus, what these two emperors could accomplish was limited to the suppression of disturbances and the lessening of cruelties. Yet their achievements were immense, issuing, as they did, from the great personalities of the emperors, and from the fact that the emperors dealt on a gigantic scale and broadminded basis. Their accomplishments came from their merciful hearts, after the manner described by Mencius in his parable of the child who fell into the well. The successes of Han and T'ang depended upon the broad basis of their dealings, so that their work could become a rallying point for all people in the empire; their successes could not have been merely the product of small hearts. ... Han Kao-tsu, T'ang T'ai-tsung, and the founder of the Sung Dynasty, were men upon whom the endless rotation of heaven and earth, and the continuation of human tradition depended. Thus, your view that existence and extinction of *Tao* has nothing to do with human intervention is quite mistaken."[8]

From the letter of rebuttal quoted above, Ch'en Liang did not admit any line of demarcation between the physical and the metaphysical, nor any distinction between the philosopher-kings and the ordinary monarchs of later periods. Indeed, he did not acknowledge even the difference betweeen the morally right and the expedient. He believed, in short, in a one-level theory, or in one kind of a world which was natural and real.

Chu Hsi continued to correspond with Ch'en Liang, and thus there was a third letter from him, in reply to his utilitarian antagonist. "Your main theme", Chu Hsi wrote, "is to appreciate Han and T'ang, in the sense of showing that these two dynasties are not different from the Three Dynasties; and to deprecate the Three Dynasties, in the sense of showing that they were not superior to Han and T'ang. The principle behind your formulation is that as times change, the work of the sages should not be taken as an unalterable pattern. The achievements of Han and T'ang, which lay in the suppression of disturbances and the lessening of cruelties, were heroic deeds even though they did not reach the standard of righteousness and reason. But you were hesitant in saying that their way of doing things was contrary to the principles of righteousness and reason. You assert that because heaven, earth and man form a trinity it is unthinkable that the rotation of heaven and earth should go on endlessly, while human activities cease. As long as the rotation of heaven and earth continues, human activities must be considered as remaining at their proper standard. In some respects I agree with you, but in other respects I differ radically from you. . . .

"The section where you expressed the idea that mind cannot have disappeared for all times, and that institutions cannot have been permanently lost, is the most important of your letter. The points in which we agree lie in this section; but so also do the points in which we differ. As long as there is man there is mind; as long as there is mind there are institutions. Men, mind, and institutions can never completely disappear or be lost. From your words 'It cannot have disappeared for all time,' one draws the inference that it may have disappeared for some time. Similarly, from your words 'It cannot have been permanently lost,' there is the inference that it may have been temporarily lost. This is because heavenly reason and human desires go side by side so that continuation and interruption is possible. It cannot be otherwise. But according to origins (or, in Kantian terminology, according to the nature of the Noumenal World) heavenly reason alone should exist, and no human desires. For this reason the educational method of the sages involved doing away with desires and going back to heavenly reason. In regard to the operations of mind, it is expected that mind shall never be lost. Being lost even once would make it inadequate. Also it is hoped that institutions for the good of the people shall never become extinct. For them to become extinct for even one period would render them insufficient.

"Therefore, in the *Book of Poetry* it is said: 'Human mind is dangerous; the mind of *Tao* is subtle. Be proficient and be unitive in purpose and hold fairly to the proper mean.' This was the message given by Yao, Shun and Yü in their respective generations.

"A man after his birth is tied up with a body, so that he is bound to have a human mind. On the other hand, he is endowed with the ideas of the moral sense, so that he is also bound to have the mind of *Tao*. These two minds go side by side throughout his whole life, and the one or the other gets the upper hand. Rightness or wrongness in mind, and peace or disturbance in the world, all depend upon the directions which the mind takes. The categorical imperative is that one should choose carefully without letting the mind of *Tao* become mixed with the human mind. A further requirement is that one should be single in the purpose of maintaining the supremacy of heavenly reason over desire. A man's conduct should always be on the right track, and a country's policy should never run askew. One should leave neither to the dangerous human mind, for after a time the disappearance of the human mind may be taken for granted. Nor should one leave either to the subtle nature of the mind of *Tao* and be comforted that the mind of *Tao* can never permanently dissappear. . . ."

Chu Hsi went on to say that the realization of *Tao* in the world ceased after the work of Yao, Shun, Yü, T'ang, Wen and Wu, and he explained the reason as follows: "After Mencius' death, this philosophy was no longer practiced. Occasionally a hero arose who because of cleverness or scheming performed deeds which by chance coincided with *Tao*. But the foundation of his deeds was laid in motives of selfish interest and desire. Scholars arose who were very able but not humble enough to devote themselves to the work of the sages or Confucianists. These scholars committed themselves to theories which were not morally right but which were conductive of success in their careers. They knew well enough that ethical principles should not be discarded *in toto,* so they exerted their wits in devising excuses in self-defense. This is the reason why they hit upon the theory that *Tao* cannot disappear forever, and that the realization of *Tao* may occur by accident, or blindly. On these narrow grounds they tried to justify the notion that Han and T'ang occupied the same level as Yao, Shun, and the Three Dynasties. What they forgot was that the fundamental principle of the rule of Han and T'ang was completely wrong.

"Though the trinity of heaven, earth, and man persists through the ages and is unchangeable, a differentiation is occasioned by the fact that while the first two members operate without a mind, the last member has desires. The rotation of heaven and earth proceeds eternally, but man's actions are sometimes contrary to *Tao.* And with the moment that marked the first absence of mind from the morally right, *Tao* among mankind stopped. During the period of the cessation of *Tao,* what was in the mind of each of us failed to live up to the proper standard, in spite of the endless rotation of heaven and earth. This latter phenomenon should not be taken as evidence that *Tao* can be eternal. My idea that the existence or extinction of *Tao* depends upon man and that Tao is inseparable from man means that while *Tao* is everlasting its realization hangs upon humanity's understanding it and putting it into practice. The existence of *Tao* has nothing to do with the physical existence of man; nor is the point that *Tao* becomes extinct only when man physically perishes. For everyone of us to become a Yao is never possible. Nevertheless, the human standard can be set up only under the condition that the *Tao* of Yao prevails. Also it is never possible for everyone of us to become a *Chieh,* yet the human standard may be upset when only a few men become *Chieh.* Those of us who firmly believe in *Tao* know that when for one moment a man permits his mind to run counter to Yao and to coincide with *Chieh* that is a situation called the vacancy of *Tao,* or living in a patch-work house. Even the mind which has not permanently ceased, but which has disappeared for only a moment, you call in your terminology an insect half-living and half-dead. *Tao* cannot cease, yet man can put a stop to it. ...

"Man persisted to be identical with himself, and *Tao* remained the same *Tao,* in spite of the time lapse between the Three Dynasties and Han and T'ang. Because of the loss of the Confucian tradition and the loss of the mind-message of Yao, Shun, Yu, T'ang, Wen and Wu, whatever the emperors of the Han and T'ang Dynasties accomplished in conformity with the old tradition was the effect of blind coincidence. For the fact is that the work of the rulers in those later dynasties was wholly based upon human desire. This is why Yao, Shun and the Three Dynasties, on the one hand, and Han Kao-tsu and T'ang T'ai-tsung, on the other hand, should be dealt with separately. If somebody should propose that this dividing-wall should be torn down, then it is advisable to review the mind-message of Yao and Shun, and to re-examine the motives of Kao-stu and T'ai-tsung. This inquiry, moreover, should be carried out under the condition that what is found to be coincident should be retained and what is found to be contrary should be rejected. Only in this manner can *Tao,* which though everlasting is nonetheless the reflection of man's mind, be realized in the world. Yet this inquiry should not be a mere study of historical events in order to *rationalize* coincides which are too often overvalued, as proofs of agreement with the *Tao* of the former Sages."

Chu Hsi next proceeded to explain why Kao-tsu and T'ai-tsung could not be put on the same level as the Three Dynasties. "Kao-tsu," he wrote, "was considered a good emperor because of his issuance of the so-called Three Articles of law. Yet during the Han Dynasties the stipulation of killing family-members up to the third generation was never abrogated, and ministers who had rendered distinguished service were often killed. T'ai-tsung was regarded as worthy because of his suppression of disturbances in the country. Yet he took one of his women from the imperial harem and offered her to his father. All things contrary to the principles of human relations were committed by him. The actions of Kao-tsu and T'ai-tsung were often contrary to reason, seldom in agreement with reason. Moreover, the many actions contrary to reason were important cases, while the few actions in agreement with reason were cases of no importance. Students of history, lacking philosophical wisdom, were unable to find the points wherein Kao-tsu and T'ai-tsung had done wrong, or, if they found the points, they defended the emperors for their success in 'bagging game.' Your proposal of mixing gold, silver, copper and iron in order to make one utensil is evidence that you know only the expedient and practical. Your mind is undoubtedly utilitarian."[9]

Following is a summary of Ch'en Liang's rebuttal to the arguments of Chu Hsi. As usual, he raised exceedingly acute problems.

" (1) You (Chu Hsi) say that mind may have disappeared for a moment. How is it possible that mind has disappeared for fifteen centuries? Good institutions for the welfare of the people may have been stopped for a short time. How is it possible that their cessation has lasted for fifteen centuries?

" (2) Is it not unfair to allege that the work of Kao-tsu and T'ai-tsung was based on selfish motives?

" (3) If what was accomplished by Han and T'ang was a deception and disguise, I must ask: Where was the true mind during those fifteen centuries?

" (4) Is it not much ado about nothing to insist that philosophers who devoted themselves solely to the mind-message of Yao and Shun should have been unable to turn iron into gold? What they actually achieved was only the satisfaction of mistaking silver for iron, and this was the reason for the vacancy of *Tao* for fifteen centuries."[10]

And so Ch'en Liang in this third letter of rebuttal made it clear that he was not in the least convinced by Chu Hsi's arguments. We see here a strict adherence to the standpoint of accepting hard facts only, as if Ch'en were a British utilitarian or empiricist.

After Chu Hsi received this third rebuttal he addressed a fourth letter to Ch'en Liang in which he emphasized the view that the principle or reason which prevails throughout all time is self-identical. The sages, of course, made *Tao* triumph in the world, but this performance was not confined to them alone. The meritorious achievements of the heroes of later ages must also have not been contrary to reason.

"The former sages," Chu Hsi went on to write, "understood the work of being proficient and unitive in purpose, and of holding to the proper mean. Thus everything done by them was perfect. The heroes of later ages, without the advantage of having purity of mind, came in contact with the world and were soon overcome by human desire and selfish motives. Only among those who were gifted was there occasionally a coincidence between their deeds and the principles of the former sages. Of these coincidences, some were good and some were bad. On the whole, the deeds even of these gifted ones were never so pure and complete as they would have been if they had been done by the former sages. The meaning

here is the same as your meaning, (Ch'en Liang), when you referred in your letter to what is complete and what is incomplete. If
one perceives the distinction between these two states, one should
go further in the endeavor to discover the underlying reason for
the distinction. But if, instead, one puts what is complete and
what is incomplete on the same level, and makes a comparative
study of them, one has committed the error of diverging, at first,
by a hair's breadth, and thence being led to a divergence of a thousand miles."[11]

After this correspondence between Chu Hsi and Ch'en Liang,
the latter philosopher referred all the letters to Ch'en Fu-lang to
act as arbiter. Ch'en Fu-liang replied in the following way: "Your
position, (Ch'en Liang), is this: When an achievement is made,
there is virtue inside it; when a success is made, there is reason
inside it.

"Chu Hsi's position is this: If your standpoint, (Ch'en Liang),
is right, then the attempt for a pure mind by the former sages was
a waste of time, because if an achievement can be made accidentally, why should it be necessary to engage in the drudgery of
attaining virtue? Or again, if a success can be made accidentally,
why must one hold to reason?"[12]

Ch'en Fu-liang seems to have been satisfied by neither of the
contestants. He remarked, however, that while Chu Hsi stood on
solid ground, Ch'en Liang was like one who rushed into the imperial court with sword in hand — that is, he was too blunt.

The debate between Chu Hsi and Ch'en Liang was finally concluded by two letters from the latter written respectively in 1185
and 1186. In the earlier of these two letters, Ch'en said: "Everything in the world is a manifestation of *Tao*. The sun shines so
brightly that when one opens one's eyes one can see what *Tao* is.
How can it possibly be said that because all men in the world are
blind nobody can see the light? When a man is blind and succeeds
in grasping a thing, one says that he grasps it blindly or by accident.
But now we are confronted by the question of fifteen centuries.
How is it possible for us to use the term 'by accident' in this connection, implying, as the term would, that all men are blind?

"Among the later heroes, some did things blindly, and thus
their actions were opposed to the teachings of the sages. But when

these later heroes opened their eyes, their deeds shone just as brilliantly as the sun, and there was peace under heaven, and on earth, and a good life among men. The deeds of those who kept their eyes closed are called 'wrong,' and the deeds of those who opened their eyes are called 'by accident.' Now I believe that these later heroes have been accused unjustly. ...

"You (Chu Hsi) are interested only in the sort of metaphysical theory that you consider as eternal truth. You discuss it with only a few of your friends. Your intimates you treat as sworn-brothers, but those who differ from you you exclude. Can anyone possibly maintain that for fifteen centuries all men were blind, and that the life of the world proceeded at the level of human desire and selfishness?

"According to your letter, you make the assumption that prior to and during the Three Dynasties there were no selfish motives and nobody was greedy for power or money. Though the *Book of Poetry* and the *Book of History* tell us the story that all men are pure and full of integrity, as far as I can see, wherever there is a man there are a number of irregularities and corruptions. These books in their entirety were under revision by Confucius and hence their story gives the impression that life at that time was perfect. How can you bear to see the world of the last twenty centuries looking so dark — with the exception of a few Confucianists who alone of all mankind were able to find some shining pearls, and who alone were able for a while to behave themselves in conformity with the sages?"[13]

This letter, written in 1186 was rather apologetic. Ch'en Liang said that he had no intention of differing from Chu Hsi, but that his hope was that what he had written would be complementary to the great philosopher.

Now we are in the position to make a balance sheet of the various opinions of the two combatants in this philosophic battle.

Chu Hsi	*Ch'en Liang*
(1) Chu Hsi is a moral rigorist.	(1) Ch'en Liang is a utilitarian.
(2) Chu Hsi discusses at two levels: physical and metaphysical.	(2) Ch'en Liang talks at one level: The physical, which contains the metaphysical.
(3) Chu Hsi in accordance with	

Chu Hsi

his two-level theory makes two classes of rulers: the philosopher-kings Yao, Shun, et al. and the emperors of later periods.

(4) According to Chu Hsi, in the later periods there were no philospher-kings; hence the vacancy of *Tao* for fifteen centuries.

(5) Chu Hsi says that though *Tao* is everlastingly existent, its realization in this world depends upon man's understanding and practice.

(6) Chu Hsi takes the texts of the Classics as authoritative, though he says nothing against Ch'en Liang on this point.

Ch'en Liang

(3) Ch'en Liang believes, in accordance with his one-level theory, that the emperors of later periods, though their work was imperfect, cannot be regarded as merely selfish.

(4) Ch'en Liang thinks it impossible to believe that there was a vacancy of *Tao* for fifteen centuries.

(5) Ch'en Liang says: Man and mind have persisted to be self-identical from the beginning. How can man have been blind for fifteen centuries without realizing it?

(6) Ch'en Liang does not believe that during and before the Three Dynasties the people were as perfect as the Classics say. Human Beings were the same then as they are now.

Ch'en Liang's correspondence with Chu Hsi may be described as a polemic against the great philosopher's metaphysical theory of the state. It would be an exaggeration to say that Chu Hsi would have agreed with Hegel's dictum: "Whatever is rational is real; whatever is real is rational." Nevertheless, he believed that the state exists only for the common good of the people, and that the function of the state and the ruler is so definite that only Yao and Shun and men of their type ever lived up to the standard. In this conviction Chu Hsi would not budge an inch for Ch'en Liang.

However, Chu Hsi was not consistent in his thinking. Since man lives in two worlds: one physical and the other metaphysical, two sides must be taken into consideration. Man has his wants and desires, so it is natural for him to be unable to avoid mistakes. As a ruler he has his duty to perform, but he cannot be expected to be trained in the same way as Platonic guardians. Thus, Chu Hsi's grouping of the emperors into two classes: philosopher-kings like Yao, Shun, *et al.* and emperors of later ages, is too rigid.

The question of the state, or of government, is part of the general question of life in this world. The life of the people is the background. If Chu Hsi wishes to study human nature at the two levels of the essential and the physical, he must observe and evaluate human nature at both levels, or in both aspects, and accordingly he must consider the state also, or government, on both sides: that is, on the side of ideal purity, and on the side of imperfection. But Chu Hsi did not, in fact, apply this same method to his analysis of the state and government as he did to human nature. If he had, he might have found a theory of the state which would have disposed satisfactorily of Ch'en Liang, just as would Chang Tsai's conclusions about human nature.

Ch'en Liang's severe objection to the view that *Tao* vacated human history for fifteen centuries resembles a similar objection raised by the English philosopher L.T. Hobhouse against Hegel and Bosanquet. "Hegel", writes Hobhouse, "recognizes bad states, but he deals with them very summarily. The state is actual (*wirklich*) and its actuality consists in this, that the interest of the whole realizes itself in the particular aims ... In so far as this unity is absent, a thing is not actual, even if its existence might be assumed. A bad state is such a one as merely exists. A sick body also exists, but it is no true reality. Thus in place of asking to what extent it is really true that individual and universal interests coincide and what we are to do when they are palpably in conflict, how we are to cure the sick state and what is the duty of the individual when he finds himself unable to do so, we find the whole question waved aside by a radically unsound distinction between reality and existence. A sick body, as the sufferer has too much reason to know, is as hard a reality as a sound body, and if Hegel's criterion of reality were to be accepted, no state that is or has ever been, is real."

This criticism by L.T. Hobhouse may also be applied to Chu Hsi's attitude toward China during the fifteen centuries of so-called vacancy of *Tao* because he considered China as, in that period, unreal. This is the conclusion to which a metaphysical theory of the state is bound to lead. If somebody should ask me: "Do you agree with Ch'en Liang's theory of the state?" I should answer that this is another question, and cannot be dealt with here. But I may assert here that the state does, after all, have two sides: physical life and moral value. Study of these two sides may some day give us a better way of government, but until now this better way is still a mystery, as yet undisclosed to mankind. Ch'en Liang's objections contain some good points, but there is over-concentration on the personality of Emperors Han Kao-tsu and T'ang T'ai-tsung. The problems of freedom, of the individual, and of check and balance by the different organs within a government and by the citizens, — these were beyond Ch'en Liang's comprehension.

This controversy between the philosophers Ch'en Liang and Chu Hsi shows how a metaphysical theory of the state can lead to a *reductio ad absurdum*. The political theory that a state can be well-governed only by the personality of a Yao or a Shun, is a Chinese version of the metaphysical theory of the state, and a version which has existed since Confucius and Mencius. It was exposed a little by Ch'en Liang, but it has not yet been criticized scientifically. A genuinely critical study and discussion will certainly be needed.

References

1. *The Dialogues of Plato,* Vol. 2, The Republic, p. 301.
2. L. T. Hobhouse, *The Metaphysical Theory of the State,* George Allen and Unwin, London, 1918, p. 97.
3. Ch'en Liang, *Lung-ch'uan wen-chi* (Collected Essays of Ch'en Liang), Book 10.
4. *Ibid.,* Book 15.
5. *Ibid.,* Book 20.
6. *Ibid.,* Book 3, letter to Chu Hsi.
7. *Ibid.,* Book 20.
8. *Chu-tzu wen-chi* (Collected Essays of Chu Hsi), Book 1.
9. *Lung-ch'uan wen-chi* (Collected Essays of Ch'en Liang), Book 20.
10. *Chu-tzu wen-chi* (Collected Essays of Chu Hsi), Book 1.
11. *Lung-ch'uan wen-chi* (Collected Essays of Ch'en Liang), Book 1.
12. *Chu-tzu wen-chi* (Collected Essays of Chu Hsi), Book 1.
13. *P.R.S.Y.,* Books 53, 56.
14. *Lung-ch'uan wen-chi* (Collected Essays of Ch'en Liang), Book 20.

CHAPTER FIFTEEN

Sung Philosophy at the Close of the Sung Dynasty and the Beginning of the Yüan Dynasty

The last three chapters were intended to clarify the inter-relations between the various schools of Sung philosophy. The two major schools are those of Chu and Lu, and the former, in its advocacy of knowledge-seeking, did much research and writing of commentaries. The *Philosophical Records of the Sung and Yüan Dynasties* however, made the criticism that after Jao Lu and Ch'en Shun there was nothing inspiring beyond philological re-search. The school of Lu, on the other hand, when Yang Chien succeeded to its leadership had in him a strong thinker. This school, even in the time of Lu Chiu-yüan, was known to be related to Ch'an thought. As late as in the Ch'ing Dynasty, when the catalogue of the Imperial Library was compiled, his collected works were given the same label. For this reason, Yang Chien has been seldom read in China. But, he is too great a philosophical thinker to be ignored.

Before proceeding to Yang Chien, a general idea of what hap-pened to these two schools after the death of their founders, Chu Hsi and Lu Chiu-yüan, is in order. At the end of the Sung Dynasty a blending of the thought on the two schools became noticeable, although in this blending the school of Lu was dominant. Pre-cisely because the school of Chu had degenerated into a philological sect, any philosopher who stressed the function of thinking very naturally was inclined towards the rival school.

(A) SCHOOL OF CHU

After the death of Chu Hsi, his followers upheld the cause of knowledge-seeking and commentary writing, and were eager to restate their master's principles. There were three who had been intimate with him. Of these, Ts'ai Yüan-ting was not considered a disciple so much as a friend. His expertness in mathematics and music was such that Chu always referred questions on these subjects to him. About him the master once said: "Other students found the books which are easy to understand difficult, while Ts'ai Yüan-ting found the books which are difficult to understand easy."[1] When Han T'o-chou banned the school of *Tao*, he cited Ts'ai Yüan-ting as one of Chu Hsi's important assistants, and Ts'ai was exiled to Tao-chou. Many of his followers accompanied him, for which reason someone advised the philosopher, saying: "It would be wise to have them disperse." Ts'ai Yüan-ting replied: "How can I send them away when they came to me for the cause of *Tao*?"[2] Ts'ai's works were on the calendar, music, mathematics, the *Hung-fan* (*The Grand Model*, a chapter in the *Book of History*) and strategy. His writings were purely in search of knowledge.

Another of the close followers of Chu Hsi was Huang Kan, who wrote his master's biography after the great philosopher's death and who married his daughter. One may thus infer that he was Chu Hsi's favorite pupil. When the master made a study of rites in the different dynasties, he assigned two chapters on mourning and sacrificial rites to Huang Kan, and asked him to do editorial work. On his death-bed, he requested Huang Kan to complete other chapters about rites which he himself had begun. Huang Kan became prefect of An-ching in Anhwei Province, and was a capable administrator, observing with care what Chu Hsi had taught him. His literary legacy to us consists of commentaries on the Classics.

The third of Chu Hsi's closest followers was Ch'en Shun, who, as a youth, was anxious to get a degree at the state examinations. However, when a friend advised him to devote himself to the study of sagehood, he went to Chu Hsi and became one of his disciples. More than ten years later, it is said, he paid a second visit to his master, finding him stretched out on his death-bed, but he learned much anyhow though the old man lived only a few days. It is interesting to note that Ch'en Shun compiled a useful vocabulary of the concepts of Chu Hsi's philosophy. In this book one may find definitions of the philosophical terms listed in the chapter on Chu Hsi. The same book also contains four lectures, delivered at Yen-ling, which idolize Chu Hsi as the only man to succeed in maintaining the tradition of *Tao* from Confucius down to the time of the founders of Neo-Confucianism.

Among these brief characterizations of the followers of Chu Hsi, there should be a note about a son of Ts'ai Yüan-ting, Ts'ai Shen. When Chu Hsi was intending to write a commentary on the *Book of History,* he found that he was too busy, and so he assigned the task to Ts'ai Yüan-ting. But Ts'ai Yüan-ting also found that he was too busy, and he ordered his son to do it — just one year before the master's death. Ts'ai Shen finished the work nine years later. In his preface to his commentary he wrote: "The government of the Two Emperors [Yao and Shun] and the Three Kings [Yü, T'ang and Wu] was based upon *Tao.* The *Tao* of the Two Emperors and the Three Kings was based upon mind. When we approach their mind we discover their conception of *Tao* and government. Proficiency, unity, and holding to the proper mean was the message of mind handed down by Yao and Shun. To establish the mean and to set up the standard was the message of mind transmitted by T'ang of the Shang Dynasty and Wu of the Chou Dynasty. Other terms — *te* (virtue), *jen, ching* (mental concentration), and *ch'eng* (truth) — though differing verbally, denote the same reason and express the operations of the mind. If one refers to heaven, one may interpret it as the source from whence mind comes. If one refers to the people, one learns that is where the mind manifests itself. Rites, music, education, and culture are institutions derived from mind. Laws, codes, and literary productions are manifestations of mind. The order of the family, the rule of the country, the peace of the world, are extentions of mind. Mighty indeed is the work of mind! Chou of the Hsia Dynasty and Chieh of the Shang Dynasty forsook the mind. As long as mind is preserved, order and peace prevail; but as soon as mind is lost chaos sets in. Order and disorder are de-

termined by the presence or absence of mind. Later rulers, interested in the government of the Two Emperors and Three Kings,
should inquire after their *Tao*. Later rulers who are interested in
their *Tao* should also study their mind. And seekers after their
mind have no other recourse than the *Book of History*."[3]

It is worth noting that in this preface to his commentary on the
Book of History, Ts'ai Shen repeatedly used the word "mind," as
if he attached great importance to it. He wrote this preface nine
years after the death of Chu Hsi, seventeen years after the death
of Lu Chiu-yüan, and when Lu's well-known disciple, Yang Chien,
was sixty-nine years old. The *Book of History* does, of course,
actually contain the message of mind, so that Ts'ai Shen was justified in emphasizing it. Nevertheless, I doubt that Chu Hsi, if
he had lived to see the preface, would have approved of this undue
emphasis. Probably, after Chu Hsi's death, the influence of Lu
Chiu-yüan grew so strong that Ts'ai Shen could not avoid making
some concession to Lu's school. In this preface we behold the first of
Chu Hsi's followers to yield to the school of Lu.

(B)   THE SCHOOL OF LU

The school of Lu was especially powerful in Chekiang province. Among its advocates were Yang Chien, Shu Lin, Shu Huan
and Yüan Hsieh, and among these four, Yang Chien exercised the
widest influence and was the most prolific writer.

Born in 1141, he acquired his *chin-shih* degree at twenty-
nine. Immediately he was appointed an assistant to the magistrate of Fu-yang District. Three years later, when Lu Chiu-yüan
passed through Fu-yang, he called upon Lu, and asked him: "What
is the original mind?" Lu attempted to enlighten him by reminding him of his verdict in a lawsuit involving a fan, referred to in
a previous chapter.

Four years later Yang Chien was transferred as a judge to
the prefecture of Shao-hsing, and when he was forty-two Chu Hsi
recommended him to the imperial court, saying that he knew how
to cultivate himself and was able to govern. In 1188 he was magistrate of Ch'eng District, but he resigned his office until 1190 in
order to conform to the Chinese custom of mourning the death
of a parent for three years. Subsequently he was sent as magis-

trate to Lo-p'ing in Kwangsi province, where he occupied himself with improving the cultural conditions of the people. In 1194 he traveled to Kiangsi province to attend the funeral of his teacher, Lu Chiu-yüan. Finally, he left his post at Lo-p'ing to become a professor at the government academy.

In 1195, the prime minister, Chao Ju-yü, who was a friend of Chu Hsi, was dismissed. Yang Chien joined others in sending a protest to the emperor, whereupon he was assigned to a position in a temple, which was a kind of sinecure and meant retirement. In 1208, he was recalled to government service by Emperor Ning-tsung, and was appointed secretary to the cabinet. In this same year a Japanese monk named Shun-sho, who had come to China to learn the Buddhism of the T'ien-t'ai Sect, visited Yang Chien and asked him for a piece of writing as a souvenir. The philosopher presented him with a few words about his theory of mind.

It was in 1208 that Yang Chien had an audience with Emperor Ning-tsung which lasted an hour and a half, much longer than usual. He was appointed a historian of the Bureau of Historical Recording. In due course he found his suggestions to the emperor were never put into practice. Later he was appointed prefect of Wen-chou, but was recalled after three years and given a high position in the Ministry of Public Works. In 1214 there was a great famine in the kingdom of Chin, and many fled to Sung. The refugees, however, were forbidden to enter Sung territory, whereupon Yang Chien memorialized the emperor asking that the people of Chin be permitted to enter. His proposal was rejected, and Yang requested to be allowed to resign. He was re-instated in his temple position in his seventy-fourth year, and this time his retirement was permanent. He died when he was eighty-six. Yang Chien is known in China as the Teacher of the Lake of Mercy, where he lived for many years.

As a philosopher, Yang Chien was condemned by Chu Hsi for his Ch'an leanings. The following characterization of his doctrine is to be found in the *Catalogue of the Imperial Library* of the Ch'ing Dynasty: "The philosophy of Lu Chiu-yüan was near to Ch'an thinking, but he was not a Ch'an believer. The one who was completely a Ch'an believer was Yang Chien." Because of this condemnation and others of the same kind, the works of Yang Chien were seldom read by Chinese scholars, and some of his books have unfortunately been lost.

Putting aside the question of Ch'an influence, I must say that Yang Chien was by far the ablest and most powerful thinker in the Southern Sung Dynasty. His inspiration and boldness were even greater than those qualities in his celebrated predecessors, Chu Hsi and Lu Chiu-yüan.

His philosophy is summarized in his essay: *The Self and Change.* The title of this tract may be understood better if one recalls the similarity between Yang's doctrine and the German philosopher Schelling's theory of identity. There is, of course, a great difference between the systems of the two thinkers conditioned by the enormous differences of their background, yet their belief in the Absolute Reason of the Universe is the same. Schelling in his *Exposition of My System* bases his coordination of natural and transcendental philosophy upon the theorem that nothing is outside of Absolute Reason, and that everything is within it. Then, he adds, Absolute Reason must be conceived as the total indifference of subjective and objective. His point is that reason is true *per se*. To know things as they are in themselves is to know them as they are in reason. One may say that Yang Chien's essay is another version of Schelling's *Exposition,* because both the Chinese and German philosopher equate the "all" with the *ego*: "All = Ego". This is what Yang Chien wrote:

"Change is the self. It is nothing else. To consider change as only a book and not the self is to err. Nor is it correct to regard change as transformations of heaven and earth, and not of the self. Heaven and earth are the self's heaven and the self's earth. Thus change of heaven and earth are the Self's heaven and the self's earth. Thus change of heaven and earth is change of the self, and nothing else. Selfish people split them. This is to belittle the self."

These words at the beginning of Yang Chien's essay make it clear that for him there was an identity between the self and changes in or of the universe. He went on to write:

"As long as one fails to consider the universe, its changes, and its laws as the self; but takes, instead, one's ears, eyes, nose, mouth and four limbs as the self, one cuts the great whole and underestimates the self. Such a one is blinded by flesh and belittles the self. The self is not limited to the physical body of five or six feet in height. Thus to limit it is to take the same attitude as the man who sits in a well and finds heaven to be small. If one looks at the self within the boundary of the physical body one will naturally not perceive the vastness of the self.

"Let us study the physical body. The eyes are the organ that can see. But what is it that makes the eyes see? The ears are the organ that can hear. But what is it that makes the ears hear? The mouth is the organ that can eat. But what is it that makes the mouth eat? The nose is the organ that can smell. But what is it that makes the nose smell? The hand is the organ that can grasp, bend and stretch. But what is it that makes the hand grasp, bend and stretch? The feet are that part of the body that can walk. But what is it that makes the feet walk? Blood is something that circulates. But what is it that makes it circulate? Mind is the organ that can think and deliberate. But what is it that makes the mind think and deliberate? The eye is visible, but seeing is invisible. The ear is visible, but hearing is invisible. The mouth is visible, but tasting is invisible. The nose is visible, but smelling is invisible. The hand and foot are visible, but grasping and walking leave no trace to be seen. Blood is visible, but the cause of the circulation of blood is invisible. Mind as a nerve center is visible, but what causes mind to think and deliberate is invisible. What is visible may be big or small, this or that, long or wide, high or low. These differences are not reducible to unity. What is invisible is neither big nor small, neither this nor that, neither long nor wide, neither high nor low. It is not divisible into plurality. Seeing and hearing are two, but in their invisibility they are the same. Seeing and hearing, on the one hand, and tasting and smelling, on the other hand, are different, but in their invisibility they are the same. Grasping, walking, circulation, thinking and deliberation are different functions, but in their invisibility they are the same. Of this invisibility it may be said that as far as the eyes are concerned it belongs to seeing and yet it does not belong to hearing. As far as the mouth is concerned, it belongs to tasting and yet it does not belong to tasting. Again, as far as the nose is concerned, it belongs to smelling and yet it does not belong to smelling. This description may also be extended to the grasping of the hand, the walking of the feet, the circulation of blood, and the thinking of mind.

"Thus it is with seeing, hearing, tasting, smelling, grasping, walking, circulation and thinking. But this invisibility is also the self-same invisibility when there is no seeing, hearing, tasting, smelling, grasping, walking, circulation or thinking.

"This invisibility is the self-same invisibility whether in day or night, in sleep or in waking hours, in life or in death. This invisibility is the same when it has to do with heaven, earth, the sun or the moon, the four seasons, the spirits. It is the same in activity or in inactivity: the same in the past or the present, the before or the after, the "this" or the "that", the "one" or the "many", the sage or the common man. This invisibility belongs to everybody, but is overlooked by everybody. It is *Tao*, which all men follow, but the nature of which no man knows. In the sage this invisibility is not more, and in the ordinary man it is not less. It is, in itself, enlightened; but it may also be, in itself, obscured. Also one may say that it is neither obscured nor enlightened. Selfish people in their blindness mistake the obscurity for illumination. When one's self is split, one is in darkness. When one's purpose is single, one is enlightened. Obscurity is relative to enlightenment. If there were no obscurity, there would be no enlightenment. Darkness and enlightenment depend upon man, or are *named* by man. They are irrelevant to heaven."[5]

In this last sentence the term "heaven" refers to the Intelligible World. Yang Chien meant that self is, at the same time, the universe. This unity can only be tacitly understood, and cannot be explicitly described. Elsewhere in this essay Yang Chien remarked: "This unity is the unity of the self; disunity is the disunity of the self." He regretted that his meaning had never been recognized by mankind.

Now that we have delved into Yang Chien's ideas about the identity of the self and the universe, I believe it important that we consider some of his views about mind. Let me translate a few of his poems on this subject;

"What is *Tao*, is mind;
The people try to find Tao elsewhere,
But to seek elsewhere is to seek outside.
Why not seek it where it is, in your own mind?"

"You ask: 'What is mind?'
Mind can think and seek.
It is your mind; why should you ask someone else to
    explain it?
Your mind is the same as what you have."

"The action of mind leaves no traces.
When you try to ponder it you worry.
If you know how to love your parents and to respect your
    elder brothers,
You are on the right track."

"Since mind is as empty and bright as the sky,
It includes heaven, earth, the sun and the moon.
Alas! Here is a piece of uncultivated land,
Where one does not know the directions: neither east
    nor west, neither south nor north."[6]

"Do not decorate your natural gifts of love and respect,
But preserve intact their pristine naturalness and purity,
When you try, by searching, to describe your own mind,
It is as if you sowed thorns in fertile soil."

Only the essence of Yang Chien's philosophy has been presented. His sense of the unity of the self and the universe was as strong as the conviction some other philosophers had of the duality of the moral and physical worlds. Exposition of other phases of his doctrine would have been desirable but unfortunately our space is limited.

(C) BLENDING OF THE SCHOOLS OF CHU AND LU

Although the way of thinking prescribed by Lu Chiu-yüan and Yang Chien was condemned by the great philosopher Chu Hsi, he nonetheless recognized as commendable their exemplary lives as well as the exemplary lives of their disciples. Indeed, if one follows carefully the development of the Lu school, one will find that by the end of the Sung Dynasty it exercised more influence than the Chu school. This is exemplified in the fact that finally the latter school was persuaded to relinquish some of its emphasis on knowledge-seeking. Evidence of the dominating influence of the followers of Lu Chiu-yüan and Yang Chien over the intellectual heirs of Chu Hsi may also be seen in the writings of Wu Ch'eng, the outstanding philosopher of the Yüan Dynasty.

Wu Ch'eng, who lived from 1249 to 1333, was twenty-eight when the Sung empire fell and the Yüan Dynasty was established, so that for more than half a century his life was passed under the Mongols. He was invited to serve the government, but he was never engaged in other than academic work, and after a few years he retired altogether. He wrote voluminously on the Classics. His *modus operandi* was to keep a balance between Chu and Lu. Falling, as he did, under the direct influence of both schools, his remarks about their comprehensive positions, their strength and their weaknesses, are of great value to the historian of ideas.

In one of his essays Wu Ch'eng said: "Four generations after the Ch'eng brothers, Chu Hsi occupied the line of succession. His philological inquiries into the detailed meaning of words reached such an extent that Mencius could not have done better. His disciples were so devoted to this kind of work that they forgot the functions of mind. Since reading and memorizing literature were condemned as vulgar by the school of Chu, why did the scholars bother about philology? Some knew only one Classic, without the least interest in any of the others, so that they were as specialized as the most vulgar. While the Chu school, beginning with 1208, was in this condition, it reached its lowest point from which it was never able to recover."[7]

The year 1208, eight years after Chu Hsi's death, was the fourteenth year of the reign of Emperor Ning-tsung, and seventy-two years before the downfall of the Sung Dynasty. It was also just forty years before the birth of Wu Ch'eng, who thus lived at the time when most could be heard and learned about the weaknesses of the school of Chu Hsi, which had degenerated from true philosophy into mere knowledge-seeking.

But to return to Wu Ch'eng's own words. "The best part of the science of sagehood", he wrote, "is to bring the endowments of heaven to perfection. What heaven endows is virtue, that is, the roots of *Jen, I, Li* and *Chih*. These also are the master of the physical body. Besides the perfection of virtue, nothing is worthy of being called wisdom. Even great statesmen like Ssu-ma Kuang of the Sung Dynasty and Chu-Ko Liang of the Shu-Han Dynasty, although they possessed the best qualities of manhood, cannot be considered as having been familiar with the science of sagehood. Much less may mere philologists, like Ch'en Shun (1153-1217) or Yao Lu (a disciple of Huang Kan), be regarded as members of the school of sagehood. They may be classified as only an inch higher than the devotees of literature and memorizing. The scholars of the Han and T'ang Dynasties were not to be blamed for these deficiencies because they lived in an age when the science of sagehood was not known. It is a great pity that the later growth of the school of Chu Hsi degenerated to such a low point, especially when the Sung Dynasty had its own valuable philosophy."[8]

Elsewhere Wu Ch'eng gave the following warning to someone who had asked his advice: "To this kind of work I devoted myself, and considered that Ch'en Shun and Yao Lu were not yet perfect in their learning. Yet after forty years' devotion I repented that my time had been wasted. I hope that you will busy yourself with the sort of work that takes the supremacy of virtue as being of primary importance."[9]

Another interesting facet of Wu Ch'eng's thought was his criticism of the later followers of the schools of Chu and Lu for fighting each other. "According to Chu Hsi", he wrote, "the first thing to be taught disciples was to read and discuss. According to Lu Chiu-yüan, the first thing to be taught disciples was to know truth and to practice what one knows. The aim of reading and discussing was to attain true knowledge, and then to practice it. True knowledge can be acquired only through wide reading and ample discussion. I believe that the doctrines of both teachers were towards this same goal. But the lesser followers only boasted of their own school and slandered the other. This disputatiousness threw the minds of the two schools into confusion. How difficult it is to transmit philosophical wisdom from one generation to another!"[10]

In another passage Wu said: "If one seeks only in the Five Classics, and does not reflect on one's own mind, it is just as if one bought a pearl in a beautiful box, keeping the box, but returning the pearl. This mistake I am careful to avoid.

"When a student comes to me I always advise him to be single in purpose and to concentrate his mind in order to gain the goal, namely, supremacy of virtue. My next step is to tell him how to seek knowledge. Thus, first my advice is to reflect upon the mind; second to read widely."[11]

When Wu was appointed professor at the government academy, he made a custom of lecturing the students: "While Chu Hsi," he would say, "devoted most of his time to knowledge-seeking, Lu Chiu-yüan championed the supremacy of virtue. If one limits one's efforts to knowledge-seeking, without taking the supremacy of virtue as a goal, one is certain to fall into the pit of philology. So the supremacy of virtue should be the groundwork."[12]

In another essay he pointed out the priority that should be given mind, and again furnished evidence that he was under influence of Lu Chiu-yüan and Yang Chien. "After birth," he said, "a man is endowed with a body — a process which takes place through the concentration of matter. He also is endowed with reason; and thus he has human nature. Mind is master of the body, and the agent of human nature. This same mind was handed down from Yao, Shun, Yu, T'ang, Wen and Wu, the Duke of Chou and Confucius. The tradition of *Tao* also remained the same among these sages. *Tao* is within the mind, and cannot be found outside it. Confucius never pointed out what the mind in itself is, but daily life, which he discussed, was for him, the expression of mind. When daily life was carried on properly the function of mind was fulfilled. Hold fast, said Confucius, to *it*. Let *it* remain ever with you. If you let *it* go, *it* will be lost. This *it*, which was never recorded in the *Lun-yü*, but was alluded to by Mencius, was mind. This shows that Confucius was interested in the work of mind, and the absence of discussion of mind in the *Lun-yü* may have been because such a discussion would have been too speculative for the disciples. Mencius, who was the successor to Confucius, notices that most scholars in his lifetime had forgotten mind. Thus, he pointed out to us some features of mind in itself.

"Here are the words of Mencius concerning mind: '*Jen* is human mind. How lamentable it is to lose the mind and not know how to recover it! The great end of learning is nothing other than to seek for the lost mind. The senses of the ears and eyes have nothing to do with the work of thinking, and may be obscured by external things. To the mind belongs the office of thinking. Let a man establish himself firmly upon the nobler part of his constitution and the inferior part will not be able to take it from him.'

"These words of Mencius were the source from which Lu Chiu-yüan's philosophy was derived. When Mencius discussed the mind he used the term 'original mind' because it is the origin of reason, just as the root of a tree is the origin from which the branches and leaves come. Now-a-days people regard Lu Chiu-yüan as the representative of the school of mind, but they do not know how profoundly he buried himself in this kind of wisdom. For such people 'original mind' is a term only, not a living reality. The wisdom of Lu Chiu-yüan is ineffable — much less may it be expressed by terms. Mind is common to all. Everyone who reflects in himself will find it. Thus, Lu Chiu-yüan was not the only one to carry on the work of mind. There was also each of the sages, from Yao and Shun down to the Sung philosophers. To characterize Lu Chiu-yüan, therefore, as the sole representative of the school of mind, is incorrect, and is done only by those who are not familiar with the labors of the sages."[13]

Was Wu Ch'eng a member of the Chu or Lu school? In the *Philosophical Records of the Sung and Yüan Dynasties* it is said: "Since Wu Ch'eng was a disciple of Yao Lu, he belonged to the Chu school. But he also followed the school of Lu, because his teacher, Ch'eng Shao-k'ai, founded the Tao-i Academy the objective of which was to synthesize the two schools."[14] Thus, it can be assumed Wu Ch'eng held the balance between the two schools. He was confident that between the school of Chu Hsi, which stood for knowledge-seeking, and the school of Lu Chiu-yüan, which championed the supremacy of virtue, there was no real conflict. He believed that knowledge is sought through the senses, but that right and wrong can be judged only by the mind. Nevertheless, this was only a round-about way of saying that knowledge of the senses and knowledge of the moral sense are, after all, two aspects of one and the same mind. This synthesis is clear indication that, as far as Wu Ch'eng was concerned, the school of Chu Hsi had lost the upper hand.

The priority given to mind at the end of the Sung Dynasty was a premonition that the school of mind would flourish in, and dominate, the coming Ming Dynasty. The school of Wang Shou-jen, the leading philosophical spokesman in the Ming Dynasty, was inspired by Lu Chiu-yüan and Yang Chien. Just as the personality of Chu Hsi dominated the school of knowledge, so the school of the supremacy of virtue culminated in the thought of Wang Shou-jen.

In concluding this chapter something should be said about Wen T'ien-hsiang, because he is mentioned at length in the *Philosophical Records of the Sung and Yüan Dynasties*. He was the last prime minister of the Sung Dynasty, and a disciple in the third generation of Chu Hsi. He did not, like Yang Chien, leave us much of his philosophical ideas; yet his testament, written while he was a prisoner under the Mongols, suggests Plato's *Apology*, which describes Socrates' death. This testament still is read widely by Chinese of all classes as a classic example of his unswerving loyalty to his ideals.

Wen T'ien-Hsiang was born in the province of Kiangsi in 1236 and died in 1282. He was at the top of the list of candidates at the state examination when he received his *chin-shih* degree. His examiner, Wang Ying-lin, a follower of the school of Chu Hsi, reported to the emperor that the first candidate showed himself in his paper to be a man of boundless loyalty, and he, Wang Ying-lin, therefore congratulated the emperor on the availability for service to the country of so honorable a man. In 1273, Emperor Tu-tsung appointed Wen T'ien-hsiang Commissioner of Justice in Hunan province. When the Mongols crossed the Yangtze Valley, an imperial decree was issued requesting the people to rise in defense of their sovereign. It is said that upon receiving this document, Wen T'ien-hsiang burst into tears, then organized a militia of ten thousand men. Later he was transferred to be High Commissioner of Justice and concurrently Commander of the Militia in Kiangsi province. When an adviser tried to dissuade him from undertaking such heavy responsibilities, he replied: "I know that this is a most difficult assignment. But the Sung Dynasty has given protection to the people for three hundred years, and now the country needs our service. If the government requests the people to rise during an emergency, and if here a man and there a horse fails to answer the call, the result will be disaster. I fully realize that I am unequal to the task; but I resolve nonetheless to sacrifice myself, even to the extent of becoming a martyr. Then loyal people may rise and do likewise. When righteousness has the upper hand, the determination of the people may be strengthened and then they may follow. When the populace answers the call, there may be a chance of success. In this way, our country may be saved."

In 1275, Wen T'ien-hsiang became prime minister, but that same year the Mongol hordes arrived in Kiangsi and made him a prisoner. He managed to escape and went by sea to Wen-chou in the province of Chekiang, but shortly afterwards, in renewed fighting in Kiangsi, he was defeated and again taken prisoner. This time he was sent to Peking, and because he persisted in his refusal to surrender he was put to death at the age of forty-seven.

In the dress-band of Wen T'ien-hsiang was found his testament, which ran as follows: "According to Confucius, a resolute and virtuous man will not seek to live at the expense of injuring *jen*. He will prefer to sacrifice his life to keep this *jen* intact. Mencius said: 'One should let life go and choose righteousness.' If righteousness is chosen, *jen* will be achieved. Having read the book of the sages, a man should know how to behave himself. Henceforth I shall see to it that nothing disgraceful occurs in my life."[16]

Wen was a disciple of Ou-yang Shou-tao, who in turn was a second generation disciple of Chu Hsi. Wen's doctrine was a kind of activism which merged the self with the universe. This blending of the self with the changing cosmos compels me to the belief that Wen, though a member of the Chu school, was influenced by Lu Chiu-yüan and Yang Chien.

Wen once wrote: "Heaven remains forever because of its rotation. Earth remains long also because of its rotation. Water can remain clean because it flows. The sun, the moon, the planets and the stars can change because of their alterations. What is unceasingly active is capable of long endurance.

"The 'unceasing' in the *Chung-yung* is the same as 'change' in the *I-ching*. The 'change' is imbedded in the 'unceasing.' The 'unceasing' is the spirit, the 'change' is the trace. The rotation of heaven and earth come from the spirit of being 'unceasing.' The sages learned from heaven in order themselves to become 'unceasing.' No permanence is possible without unceasingness."[16]

Applying this concept of being "unceasing" to human life, Wen expounded diligence, hard work, no self-indulgence, sense of awe, as forms of "unceasing." These different kinds of effort were, for Wen, identical with the spirit of activism.

Wen's immortal work is his song, *The Spirit of Moral Supremacy,* which has all the grandeur and strength of Plato's Socratic *Apology.*

"In the universe there is the spirit of moral supremacy,
From which the manifoldness of phenomena takes its shape.
Below are the rivers and mountains,
Above are the sun and stars,
With man is the *Hao-jan-chih-ch'i*[1]
So intense that it fills the universe.
When the world is at peace, harmony reigns at court;
When the world is in disorder, men of backbone appear.
Many men of backbone are immortal in history.
"They may be enumerated:
In the Kingdom of Ch'i lived the historian Chien,[2]
In the Kingdom of Ch'in was the pen of the historian
    Tung Hu,[3]
In the Ch'in Dynasty was the hammer of Chang Liang,[4]
In the Han Dynasty there lived the man Su Wu who kept
    his credentials,[5]
In the period of the Three Kingdoms [c.200 A.D.] was
    the head of Yen Yen,[6]
In the Chin Dynasty was the blood of Chi Shao,[7]

In the T'ang Dynasty were the teeth of Chang Hsün[8] and the tongue of Yen.[9]

"But backbone may also be expressed in other forms:

First in the form of the cape of Liao-tung,[10]

Second, in the form of the memorial[11] begging for an expeditionary army, a memorial so fraught with loyalty and courage that it could bring tears even to the eyes of spirits,

Third, in the form of a long oar[12] driving a boat across the Yangtze, by which resolution to fight the barbarians was shown,

Fourth, in the form of an ivory tablet[13] which struck a rebel.

"This spirit remains good forever, thus enduring for thousands of years.

It is as bright as the sun and moon.

One will embrace it without caring whether one goes to death or life.

Thereby the order of heaven is established and the column of heaven stands.

The major human relations hang closely upon it.

Its foundations is *Tao* and righteousness.

Alas! I lived at the time of the overthrow of my emperor And my humble self could do nothing to save him.

I was taken prisoner and sent to the north in a carriage.

Being put under any kind of ordeal, such as by fire, could only be experienced by me as sweet and such as could not have been found by myself.

The room where I live is full of ghost-fire,

It is pitch dark even in the spring,

I am a mate of cows and horses,

And am fed like the fowls of the air.

One day, shivering with cold, I thought I was dying like a starved man in a ditch.

Yet, though I have dwelt here for two years, no disease has visited me.

Alas! this marshy place is like a paradise to me.

Whence comes my power of resistance that the external

forces of *Yin* and *Yang* cannot infringe upon me?
What I have is my burning heart.
It is as clean as the blue sky which I see above
I am overwhelmed with grief.
Cannot heaven come to my rescue?
The old sages are far from me,
But their pattern has remained before me for ages.
When I read books near the window, the old tradition
    shines upon me like a picture."[18]

This song gave consolation at a time when the Chinese people were suffering from calamities and needed it. During the Second World War (1937-1945), Wen T'ien-hsiangs's life was dramatized, and put on the stage in China, and this song was a favorite among all people. It is the incarnation and the essence of the philosophical genius of the Sung Dynasty and has strengthened the conviction and courage of the people in the subsequent history of the Chinese people.

The Sung Dynasty was crushed under the heel of the alien Mongols. Yet its learned men were courageous in facing disaster. Their martyrdom may be traced back to their moral sense of right and wrong, which taught them to prefer death to an ignoble life.

Other than having touched upon Wu Ch'eng I have passed over the Yüan Dynasty, because nothing of importance for the development of the Neo-Confucianist philosophy happened in that period. The school of mind, started by Lu Chiu-yüan and Yang Chien reached its culmination in the Ming Dynasty, which shall be dealt with in volume two.

NOTES TO WEN T'IEN-HSIANG'S *SONG OF THE SPIRIT OF MORAL SUPREMACY*

(1) *Hao-jan-chih-ch'i*. Mencius' term. Legge translates it "Passion-Nature"; Fung Yu-lan translates it "Great Morale".[19] Neither of these renderings unfortunately convey the meaning of the original. What Mencius meant was some primordial force so cultivated by the individual that it elevated him to a level where his personal soul has the capacity to be in harmony with the universal soul.

(2) The historian Chien, born in the Kingdom of Ch'i. When Ts'ui Shu murdered the king of Ch'i, this historian recorded the name of the murderer, and was accordingly put to death by Ts'ui Shu. The historian's second brother, having heard about the same murder, made the same entry in the record, and he also was executed. When the historian's third brother heard about the murder, he entered the record a third time, and was put to death.[20]

(3) Tung Hu. Also a historian. Ling King, Duke of Ch'in, a fool and a tyrant, was fond of shooting, and enjoyed watching how the people could evade his sling-shots. When he tried to kill his prime minister, Chao Tun, the latter was fortunate enough to escape. Then Chao's brother assassinated the duke as an act of vengeance. Tung Hu, the historian, recorded that Chao Tun, the prime minister, was the assassin. Whereupon Chao pointed out that it was his brother who had killed the duke. Tung Hu replied: "You are the prime minister. At the time of your escape you did not cross the border. And upon your return you did nothing to denounce the assassin. So it is *you* who are responsible for the duke's murder." When Confucius learned of this he exclaimed that Tung Hu was the best historian of antiquity, since he put on record what was right without being prejudiced in favor of the one in power.[21]

(4) The hammer of Chang Liang. An allusion to the hammer by which Chang Liang struck Ch'in Shih-huang for conquering Chang's native country, Han.[22]

(5) The credentials of Su Wu. An allusion to the credentials given Su Wu by the emperor, which he kept with him for nineteen years while he was a prisoner of the Hsiung-nu.[23]

(6) The head of Yen Yen. Yen Yen was a general who served under Liu Chang as prefect of the district of Pa. When this district was conquered by Liu Pei, king of Shu (one of the Three Kingdoms), the commander, Kuan Yu, ordered General Yen to surrender. Yen replied: "In this district there is only a general who prefers death to surrender!"[24]

(7)　The blood of Chi Shao. During the fraternal wars between the eight princes of the Chin [Tsin] Dynasty, when
the battle of Tang-yin was fought, the Chin emperor was
defeated and his ministers fled. Only Chi Shao remained,
who tried to protect his sovereign covering him in court
robes. In short order the loyal Chi was put to death, and
his blood splattered the imperial dress. Afterwards, when
the valets tried to wash away the blood, the emperor said
"It is the blood of Chi Shao. Better keep it!"[25]

(8)　The teeth of Chang Hsün. Chang Hsün (709-757), a general under Hsüan-tsung, fought to no avail for the imperial
government against the rebel, Yin Tzu-ch'i. Subsequently
somebody remarked to Chang: "General, I noticed that
when you ordered the soldiers to battle, your face was
spotted with blood from your teeth, and your eyes were
so filled with passion that it was a wonder they did not
burst. Please tell me the reason." Chang Hsün answered:
"My ambition was to swallow the rebel. Only because of
my weak force was I overcome." It happened that Yin
Tzu-ch'i heard this speech and became very angry. Determining to pull out the general's teeth, he opened his mouth
with a knife but found that only three or four teeth were
left. Still obstinate, Chang Hsün remarked: "I can die only
for the emperor. To surrender to a rebel would be
ignominious."[26]

(9)　The tongue of Yen. Yen Kao-ch'ing (672-756), prefect of
Ch'ang-shan, was taken prisoner by a rebel, An Lo-shan.
An placed a sword upon the neck of Yen's son and said:
"If Yen surrenders, his son will live!" Yen, however, retorted
by calling An a "slave of shepherds" and a traitor to the
emperor. Whereupon the rebel, in a rage, had Yen tied
to a bridge-column and slashed him. Then because Yen
continued to berate him, he had his tongue held with tongs
and cut off.[27]

(10)　The cape of Liao-tung. At the end of the Former Han
Dynasty the whole country was in disorder. Kuan Ning

left the mainland and went to the Liao-tung Peninsula, carrying with him the Chinese tradition of the Five Classics and ancestor worship. Later, many people joined him and built up a new community. Kuan Ning donned a black cape, and other cloth robes. "Cape of Liao-tung" is an allusion to this cape, and is a symbol of the man who is aloof and "above the battle," as it were, and of pure character.[28]

(11) Chu-Ko Liang. He was prime minister of Liu Pei, emperor of the Shu-Han Dynasty. He did not consent to serve Liu until the latter had called upon him in his hut three times. Chu-Ko Liang worked for the unification of the empire. When Liu Pei was succeeded by his son, Chu-Ko memorialized the new emperor, requesting that the army be sent forth to unite the whole of China. This was a typical expression of Chu-Ko's loyalty.[29]

(12) Long oar. When the Ch'in Dynasty was threatened by the Five Barbarians, there was a vast migration from northern to southern China. Tsu T'i led many thousands of people across the river. He pounded on his boat with his long oar, and cried: "I swear to this river, and you are my witness, that I will re-cross, return to the mainland and clean away the enemy!" "Long oar" for the Chinese is the symbol of eliminating barbarians and regaining one's country.[30]

(13) Ivory tablet. During the reign of T'ang Tai-tsung, Chu Tz'u tried to usurp the throne, and attempted to persuade Tuan Hsiu-shih to plot and force the emperor to abdicate. Tuan, however, seized an ivory tablet, the symbol of statesmanship, and struck Chu Tz'u in the face with it, with such force that Chu's face bled. Then Tuan said: "I am sorry that I am not able to cut you to pieces. How can you expect me to be a conspirator?"[31]

References

1. *P.R.S.Y.*, Book 62.
2. *Loc. cit.*
3. *Ibid.*, Book 67.
4. *Ibid.*, Book 74.
5. *Loc. cit.*
6. Yang Ch'ien, *Posthumous Works of Yang Ch'ien*, Book 6.
7. Wu Ch'eng, *Collected Works of Wu Ch'eng*, Book 22, (An essay in memory of a studio.)
8. *Loc. cit.*
9. *Loc. cit.*
10. *Ibid.*, Book 15, (A farewell essay to Ch'en Hung-fan).
11. *P.R.S.Y.*, Book 92.
12. *Loc. cit.*
13. *Loc. cit.*
14. *Loc. cit.*, (Wu Ch'eng's Biography)
15. *Ibid.*, Book 88.
16. *Loc. cit.*
17. *Loc. cit.*
18. *Loc. cit.*
19. *Meng-tzu*, Book 2, Part 1, Chapter 2.
20. *Shih chi*, Book 32. (Feudal history of the Kingdom of Ch'i).
21. *Ibid.*, Book 39, (Feudal history of the Kingdom of Chin).
22. *Ibid.*, Book 55, (Biography of Chang Liang).
23. *Han shu*, Book 54, (Biography of Su Wu).
24. *San kuo chih*, Book 6, (Biography of Chang Fei).
25. *Chin shu* (History of the Chin Dynasty), Book 89, (Biography 59).
26. *Chiu T'ang shu* (Old T'ang History), Book 187, (Biography 137).
27. *Ibid.*, Book 187, (Biography 139).
28. *San kuo chih*, Book 11, (The Kingdom of Wei).
29. *Ibid.*, Book 5, (The Kingdom of Shu, Chu-ko Liang).
30. *Chin shu*, Book 62, (Biography 32).
31. *Chiu T'ang shu* (Old T'ang History), Book 128, (Biography 78).

Appendices

I. *List of Works by Chu Hsi in Chinese*

Ch'eng shih i shu	程氏遺書
Ch'eng shih wai shu	程氏外書
Chin-ssu-lu	近思錄
Chou-i-pen-i	周易本義
Ch'u tzu chi chu	楚辭集註
Chung-yung Chang-chü	中庸章句
Han wen k'ao i	韓文考異
Hsi-ming chieh-i	西銘解義
Hsiao-ching k'an wu	孝經刊誤
Hsieh shang ts'ai hsien sheng yü lu	謝上蔡先生語錄
I-hsüeh ch'i-meng	易學啓蒙
I lo yüan yüan	伊洛淵源
Ku-chin chia chi-li	古今家祭禮
K'un hsüeh k'ung wen	困學恐聞
Lun Meng Chi chu huo wen	論孟集句或問
Lun Meng Ching i	論孟精義
Lun-yü hsün meng	論語訓蒙
Lun-yü yao i	論語要義
Meng-tzu yao lüeh	孟子要略
Pa ch'ao ming ch'en yen hsing lu	八朝名臣言行錄
Shih chi chuan	詩集傳
Ta hsüeh chang chü	大學章句
T'ai-chi-t'u Shuo Chieh	太極圖說解
T'ung-shu Chieh	通書解
Tzu-chih-t'ung-chien Kang Mu	資治通鑑綱目

II. *List of Chinese Terms and Names**

Ch'an	禪	Ch'in Ching-hsien	秦景憲
Chang Ch'ieh	張籍	Ch'in Shih Huang-ti	秦始皇帝
Chang Ch'ien	張騫	chin-ssu	近思
Chang Chio	張角	ching	敬
Chang Chun	章惇	Ching-men	荊門
Chang Hsün	張巡	ch'iu	丘
Chang I	張儀	chou	宙
Chang Liang	張良	Chou Lien-hsi	周濂溪
Chang Po-hsing	張伯行	Chou Tun-i	周敦頤
Chang Tsai	張載	chu-ching	主敬
Chao Ju-yü	趙汝愚	Chu Hsi	朱熹
Chao Tun	趙盾	Chu-ko Liang	諸葛亮
Chao Yüan-hao	趙元昊	Chu Sung	朱松
Ch'en Fu-liang	陳傅良	Chu Tz'u	朱泚
Ch'en Liang	陳良	chung	中
Ch'en Shun	陳淳	Dragon Tiger	
cheng (fairness)	正	Mountain	龍虎山
Ch'eng Hao	程灝	Fang Chung-yen	范仲淹
Ch'eng Hsiang	程珦	fu-tzu	夫子
Ch'eng I	程頤	Fung Yu-lan	馮友蘭
Cheng K'ang-ch'eng	鄭康成	Han Fei	韓非
Ch'eng Shao-k'ai	程紹開	Han Kao-tsu	漢高祖
Cheng Tsai	徵在	Han Ming-ti	漢明帝
chi	極	Han T'o-chou	韓侂胄
ch'i	氣	Han Wu-ti	漢武帝
Chi Shao	嵇紹	Han Yü	韓愈
Chieh	桀	Hao-jan-chih-ch'i	浩然之氣
Chien [Histor-		Hsieh Liang-tso	謝良佐
iographer]	簡，太史	hsin	心
Ch'ien	乾	hsing	性
Chih	知	Hsing-ri-hsüeh	性理學
Chin	金	Hsu Chieh	徐階

---

*Names of articles also included

Sung Chen-tsung	宋眞宗	Tung Ho	董狐
Sung Shen-tsung	宋神宗	Tzu Kung	子貢
T'ai-chi-t'u	太極圖	wang	王
T'ang Hsien-tsung	唐憲宗	Wang An-shih	王安石
T'ang T'ai-tsung	唐太宗	Wang Shou-jen	王守仁
Tao	道	Wang Ying-lin	王應麟
Tao Fu	道夫（黃）	Wen T'ien-hsiang	文天祥
Tao Hsüan	道宣	"Western In-	
Tao-t'ung	道統	scription"	西銘
T'ao Yüan-ming	陶淵明	Wu Ch'eng	吳澄
te	德	wu-chi	無極
t'ien-ri	天理	wu-tzu-hsing	無自性
T'ien-t'ai	天台	Yang Chien	楊簡
ting-hsing	定性	Yang Hsiung	楊雄
"Tranquillity in		Yang Shih	楊時
Human Nature"	定性	Yao	堯
Ts'ai Ching	蔡京	Yao Lu	饒魯
Ts'ai Shen	蔡沈	Yellow River	黃河
Ts'ai Yüan-ting	蔡元定	Yen Hui	顏囘
Tsang Kuo-fan	曾國藩	Yen Kao-ch'ing	顏杲卿
Ts'ao Li-chih	曹立之	Yen Yen	嚴顏
Ts'ao Ts'ao	曹操	Yen Yüan	閻元
Tsu T'i	祖逖	yin and yang	陰陽
Tu Ku-chi	獨孤及	Yin Shun	尹焞
Tuan-chou	端州	Yü	禹
Tuan Hsiu-shih	段秀實	Yu Chi	于吉
Tung Chung-shu	董仲舒	Yu Tso	游酢

III.   *List of Buddhist Schools, Terms, Names of Monks and Books in Chinese*

1.   *Schools*

1. The School of the Satyasiddhi-sastra   成實宗
2. The School of the Three Sastri   三論宗

3. The School of the Nirvana-sutra 　涅槃宗

4. The School of the Dasabhumika-
    sutra-sastra 　地論宗

5. The School of Pure Land 　淨土宗

6. The School of Ch'an 　禪宗

7. The School of the Mahayanasam-
    parigraha-sastri-vyakhya 　摄大乘論宗

8. The School of Abhidharma 　毗曇宗

9. The School of T'ien-t'ai 　天台宗

10. The School of Avatamsaka, also
    called Hua-yen or Hsien-shou
    School 　華嚴宗

11. The School of Vinaya 　律宗

12. The School of Yogacarya 　法相宗

13. The Tantaric Schol 　密宗，眞言宗

2. Terms

Abhidharma	阿毗曇磨	Karuna	慈悲
Agmas, Four	四阿含	Koan	公案
Alayavijnana	阿賴耶識	Maha-Vyutpatti	大莊嚴
Anataman	無我	Mahayana	大乘
Asuras	阿俢羅	Manovijnana	藏識
Atman	我	Nidana, Twelve	十二因緣
Bhajana Loka	器世間	Nissvabhavah	無自性
Bhutatathata	眞如	Non-Atman	無我
Bodhi	正覺	Panna	智慧
Bodhicitta	菩提心	Paramitas, Six	六波羅蜜多
Bodhisattvas	菩薩	Prajna	般若
Dharma	法	Prajnaparamita	般若波羅蜜多
Dhatu	界	Pratyekabuddhas	辟支佛
Dyana	禪	Samadhi	三昧
Gatha	偈	Sila	戒
Hinayana	小乘	Skandas, Five	五蘊
Indra	因陀羅	Sramnas	僧，沙門

Sravakas	聲聞	Tathagatha-garbha	如來藏
Sudhana	須達拏	Tripitaka	三藏
Sunyata	空	Upasaks	優婆塞
Sutra	經	Vimalakirti	維摩詰
Svabhavasunyata	自性空	Vinaya	律
Tathagatha	如來佛	Wheel of the Law	法輪

3. *Names of Monks*

Indian and Central Asian: (see Page 80-82)

Matanga	攝摩騰	Dharmaruki	曇摩流支
Dharmaratna	竺法蘭	Gunabhadra	求那跋陀羅
An-shih-ko or		Dharmagatayasas	曇摩伽陀耶舍
Lokottama	安世高	Sanghabhadra	僧伽跋陀羅
Dharmakala	曇摩迦羅	Sanghapala	僧伽婆羅
Dharmasatya	曇無諦	Ratnamati	勒那婆提
Kalaruci	疆梁婁至	Bodhirucci	菩提流支
Dharmaraksha	曇摩羅刹	Buddhasanti	佛陀扇多
Moksala	無叉羅	Gautma Dharmajina	瞿曇達磨闍那
Dharmaratna	曇無蘭	Paramartha	波羅末陀，眞諦
Sanghadeva	僧伽提婆	Narendrayasas	那黎提拏耶舍
Dharmanandi	曇摩難提	Jainagupta	闍那崛多
Buddhabhadra	佛陀跋多羅	Dharmagupta	曇摩崛多
Punyatara	弗若多羅	Prabhakaramitra	婆羅頗伽羅蜜多羅
Kumarajiva	鳩摩羅什	Atigupta	阿地瞿多
Vimalakshas	毗摩羅义	Buddhapala	佛陀波利
Dharmayasas	曇摩耶舍	Divakara	地婆訶羅
Buddhayasas	佛陀耶舍	Bodhirucci	菩提流支
Dharmaraksha	曇摩羅讖	Devaprajna	提雲般若
Nandi	難提	Sikshananda	施乞叉難陀
Buddhajiva	佛陀什	Subhakarasimha	戌婆揭羅僧訶
Dharmamitra	曇摩蜜多	Vajrabodhi	金剛智
Kalayasas	畺良耶舍	Amoghavajra	不空金剛
Buddhavarman	佛陀跋摩	Dharmadeva	法天
Sanghavarman	僧伽跋摩	Danapala	施護

Bodhidharma	菩提達磨	Nagarjuna	龍樹
Mahakasyapa	摩訶迦葉		

Chinese:

Chih-i	智顗	Hung-jen	宏忍
Chih-yen	智儼	Kuei-shan	圭山
Ch'ing-liang	清涼	Seng-tsan	僧璨
Fa-hsien	法顯	Sung-yün	宋雲
Fa-tsang	法藏	Ta-tien	大顚
Hsien-shou	賢首	Tao-an	道安
Hsüan-tsang	玄奘	Tao-hsin	道信
Hui-ko	慧可	Tu-fa-shun	杜法順
Hui-neng	慧能	Yao-shan-wei-yen	樂山惟儼

4. *Books*

Sukhavatyamritavyuha-sutra	佛說阿彌陀經
Viseshakmita-Brahma-paripricca	思益梵天所問經
Sata-sastra	百論
Sarvastivada-pratimoksha	十誦律比丘戒本
Mahaprajnaparamita Sastra	大智度論
Madhyamika-sastra	中論
Dasabhumi-vibhasha-sastra	十住毗婆沙論
Dvadasanikaya-sastra	十二門論
Satyasiddhi-sastra	成實論
Samyuktavadana-sutra	衆經撰雜譬喩經
Vajracchedika-Prajnaparamita-sutra	金剛般若波羅蜜經
Dasabhumika-sutra	十住經
Sutralankara-sastra	大莊嚴經論
Saddharmapundarika-sutra	妙法蓮花經
Bodhi-hridaya-vyuha-sutra*	莊嚴菩提心經
*End of list on P.114-5	
Buddhavatamsakamahavai-pulya-sutra	大廣方佛華嚴經
Lankavatara-sutra	入楞伽經
Nirvana-sutra	涅槃經

Pratyutpanna-Buddhasammukha-vastit-
    samadhi-sutra
Suvarnaprabhasa-sutra   大方等陀羅尼經
Vidyamatrasiddhi-sastra   金光明經
Vimalakirti-nirdesa-sutra   大乘唯識論
                                         維摩詰經

Bibliography

Aristotle, *De Partibus Animalium.*

......, *Nichomachean Ethics.*

British Moralists, ed. by L. A. Selby-
Bigge, 2 vols. Oxford, The Claredon
Press, 1897.

Bruce, J. P., *Chu Hsi and His Masters.*
London, Probsthain and Co., 1923.

Chang Tsai, *Cheng-meng...*   張載，正蒙

......, *Collected Works.*   張載，張橫渠集

Ch'en Liang, *Lung-ch'uan wen-chi.*   陳亮，龍川文集

Chi Sung, *Ch'uan-fa cheng-tsung-chi*   契嵩，傳法正宗記

Ching-te ch'uan-teng lu.   景德傳燈錄

Chiu T'ang Shu.   舊唐書

Chou Tun-i, *Collected Works.*   用敦頤，周濂溪集

......, *T'ai-chi-t'u.*   太極圖

......, *T'ung-Shu.*   通書

Chu Hsi (ed.), *Chin-ssu-lu.*   朱熹，近思錄

Chu Hsi, *Collected Works.*   朱子全書

Chu-tzu wen-chi in *Cheng-i-t'ang ch'uan-
shu.*   朱子文集正誼堂全書

Chu-tzu yu-lei.   朱子語類

Chüang-tzu.   莊子

Ch'un-ch'iu.   春秋

Ch'un-ch'iu-wei-han-han-tzu.   春秋緯漢含孳

Ch'un-ch'iu-wei-yen-kung-t'u.   春秋緯演孔圖

Chung-yung.   中庸

Erh Ch'eng i-shu.   二程遺書

Erh-Ch'eng yu-lu in *Cheng-i t'ang ch'-uan-shu.*   二程語錄, 正誼堂全書

Fo-fa-chin-t'ang-pien.   佛法金湯編

Frith, I., *Life of Bruno.* London, Paul, Trench, Trubner and Co., 1887.

Fung Yu-lan, *A Short History of Chinese Philosophy.* New York, Macmillan Co., 1948.

Han Shu.   漢書

Han Yü, *Collected Works.*   韓愈, 韓昌黎集

History of the Wei Dynasty.   魏書

Hobhouse, L. T., *The Metaphysical Theory of the State.* London, George Allen and Unwin, 1918.

Hou Han-Shu.   後漢書

Hsin T'ang Shu.   新唐書

Hung-ming-chi.   弘明集

I-ching.   易經

I-ch'uan wen-chi in *Erh Ch'eng i-shu.*   伊川文集, 二程遺書

Legge, J., *The Religions of China.* New York, Charles Scribner's Sons, 1881.

Lewis, C. J., *An Analysis of Knowledge and Valuation.* La Salle, Ill., The Open Court Publishing Co., 1946.

Li-chi.   禮記

Lien-lu-feng-ya.   濂洛風雅

Liu Tsung-yuan, *Collected Works.*   柳宗元文集

Lo Ts'ung-yen, *Following the Steps of Yao.*   羅從彥, 遵堯錄

Lu Chiu-yuan, *Collected Works.*   陸九淵, 象山先生集

Lu-i.   六藝

Lun-yü.   論語

Mencius, *The Works of Mencius,* trans. by Legge.

Meng-tzu.   孟子

Plato, *The Dialogues of Plato,* trans. by B. Jowett in 4 vols. New York, Charles Scribner's Sons, 1890.

San-kuo Chih. 三國志

Shang-tzu. 商子

Shao Yung, *A Priori Position of the Hexagrams.* 邵雍，先天卦位

......, *Cosmic Periods of the Great Ultimate.* 邵雍，皇極經世編

Shih-ching. 詩經

Shu-ching. 書經

Soothill, *The Three Religions of China.* London, Oxford University Press, 1923.

Spinoza, *Ethics.*

Sung Shih. 宋史

Sung-wen-chien. 宋文鑑

Sung-Yüan hsüeh-an. 宋元學案

Suzuki, D. T., *Outlines of Mahayana Buddhism.* London, Luzac & Co., 1907.

......, *Essays in Zen Buddhism.* London, Luzac and Co., First Series, 1927; Third Series, 1934.

Ta-hsüeh. 大學

T'ai-p'ing ching. 太平經

Taisho Tripitaka, No. 1913. Tokyo.

Tao Hsuan, *Kao-seng Chuan.* 道宣，高僧傳

Tao-nan yuan-wei in *Cheng-i-t'ang chuan-shu.* 道南源委，正誼堂全書

Tao-te-ching. 道德經

Tao-t'ung-lu in *Cheng-i-t'ang ch'uan-shu.* 道統錄，正誼堂全書

Tso-chuan. 左傳

Tzu-chih-t'ung-chien. 資治通鑑

Uberweg, *History of Philosophy.*

Wang Mou-hung, *Chu-tzu nien-p'u.* 王懋竑，朱子年譜

Wang Shou-jen, *Collected Works* (*Chu-an-hsi-lu.*)   王守仁，陽明先生集

Winternitz, M., *A History of Indian Lit-erature,* trans. by Mrs. S. Ketkar and Miss H. Kohn, University of Calcutta, 1933.

Wu Ch'eng, *Collected Works.*   吳澄，吳氏文集

Yang Ch'ien, *Posthumous Works of Yang Ch'ien.*   楊簡，楊氏遺書

Yin Shun, *Collected Essays in Cheng-i-t'ang Ch'uan-shu.*   尹焞，尹和請文集

Index

Record of Questions and Answers, 247

Rectification of Names, 30f., of mind, 218

Reflective Thoughts, 50; see also Chin-ssu-lu

Religion, whether Confucianism is, 16f.

Republic, The, 155, 156, 203

Resources, natural, Ch'eng Hao, 71

"Return to Human Nature" 105f., 108-11

Revival, of Confucianism by Li Ao, 76; 105-11

Ri, defined, 44, 45, 259; as meaning Tao, 51; Ch'eng Hao, 190-91; Chu Hsi and Aristotle, 255, 259, 260; relation to Ch'i, 257-58, 260-64; Supreme Ultimate, 258-59

Ri-hsüeh, 190, also see Neo-Confucianism

Righteousness, 299-300; also see I

Rules, of Chu Hsi's Academy, 66-68

Rural Contract, Lu Ta-chün, 73; Wang Shou-jen, 73-75

Sagehood, science of, 60-62; Chang Chieh on, 102; Li Ao, 105f.; relation to rites and music, 108; Chou Tun-i, 60f., 142f., 154, 157; Shao Yung's idea, 166f.; Yen Hui as example, 225-28; Wang Shou-jen, 304f.

Sages, Han Yü on contributions of, 94; Chang Chieh on, 102; Chu Hsi, 326

Samadhi (meditation), 111, 131, 199

Schelling, 338

Scholar-diplomats, 19

Script, 22, problem of modern and ancient, 253f.

Scriptures, Buddhist, see table on 82; translated into Chinese classified, see table on 83

"Self and Change, The" 338-40

Self-essence, 131-32

Senses, Ch'eng I means of controlling, 224f. see also elimination

Shang-chih, 187

Shang Yang, 19

Shao Yung, 159-67; life, work and character, 160-63; theory of Cosmic Periods, 163f.; theory of objectivity, 164f.; idea of the sage, 166f.

Shen Pu-hai, 19

Shih-ching, 20, 96, 278-79

Shu-ching, 20, 69, 226

Sila (conduct), 111

Sin, Ch'an idea, 119

Skandhas (aggregates), 141

Smith, Adam, 216-17

Socrates, compared with Confucius, 30-32; compared with Mencius, 32f.; Ch'eng Hao, 35; compared with Ch'eng I, 221

Soothill, W. E., 16; critique of, 17

Spinoza, 141, 145, 166-67

"Spirit of Moral Supremacy, The", 348-50

Spirituality, Wang Shou-jen, 36f.

Spring and Autumn Annals, see Ch'un chiu

Sramnas (monk), 26

Ssu-ma Kuang, 160, 234

Ssu-ma T'an, 21

State, 310f.; Chu Hsi, 329f.; Hobhouse's criticism of Hegel, 330

Statesmanship, Ch'eng Hao, 188

Su Ch'in, 19

Su Hsün, 236

Su Shih, 210, 235

Subtlety, Chou Tun-i, 156f.

Succession, line of, see Tao-t'ung

Sudhana, 124

Sung Chen-tsung, Emperor, 232

Sung philosophers, compared with Descartes, Spinoza, etc. 140; Ch'en Liang's criticism, 313, 314, 316f.; see also Neo-Confucianists

Sung, Northern, political situation, A.D. 1107-1129, 231-34

Sung Shen-tsung, Emperor, 187, 203

Supreme Ultimate, Chu Hsi, 51; Chou Tun-i, 142, 145, 151f.; controversy betwen Chu and Lu, 146-51; Shao Yung, 163; and Ri, 258f.

Sutras, translation of Buddhist, 27, 79, 114f.; Avatamsaka, 123-24; Five categories, 125; see Appendix for Chinese names